ANGLO-SAXON ART

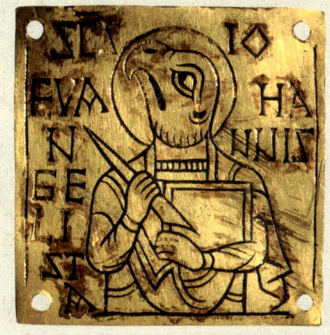

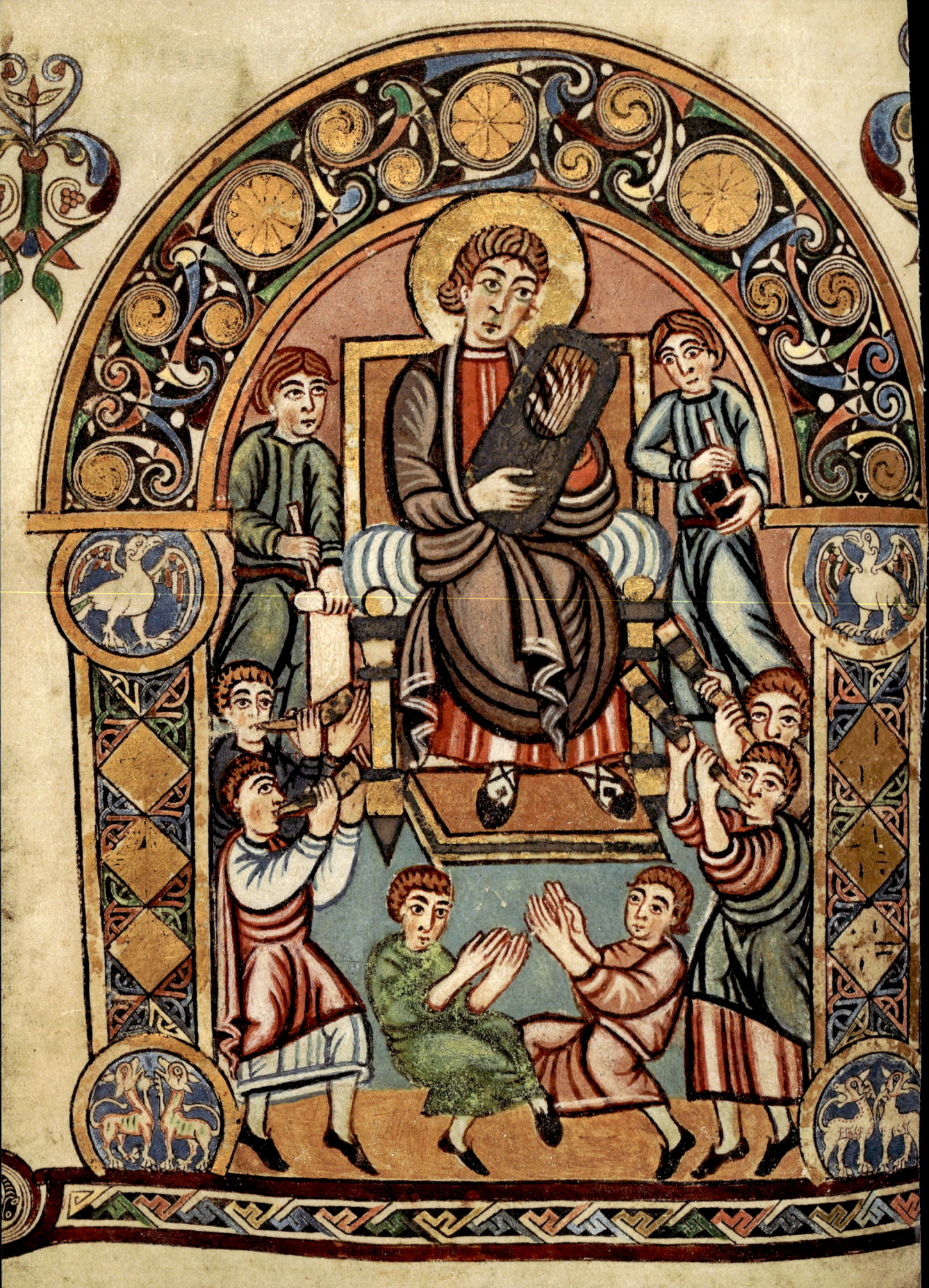

ANGLO-SAXON ART

A NEW HISTORY

LESLIE WEBSTER

Cornell University Press
Ithaca, New York

Generous support for this publication was provided by
The Paul Mellon Centre for Studies in British Art

First published in the United Kingdom in 2012 by
The British Museum Press
A division of The British Museum Company Ltd
38 Russell Square, London WC1B 3QQ

First published in the United States of America in 2012 by
Cornell University Press

First printing, Cornell Paperbacks, 2012

A catalog record for this book is available from the
Library of Congress
ISBN: 978-0-8014-7766-9

Designed by Andrew Shoolbred
Printed in Hong Kong by Printing Express Ltd

The papers used in this book are recyclable products and
the manufacturing processes are expected to conform to
the environmental regulations of the country of origin.

Paperback printing   10 9 8 7 6 5 4 3 2 1

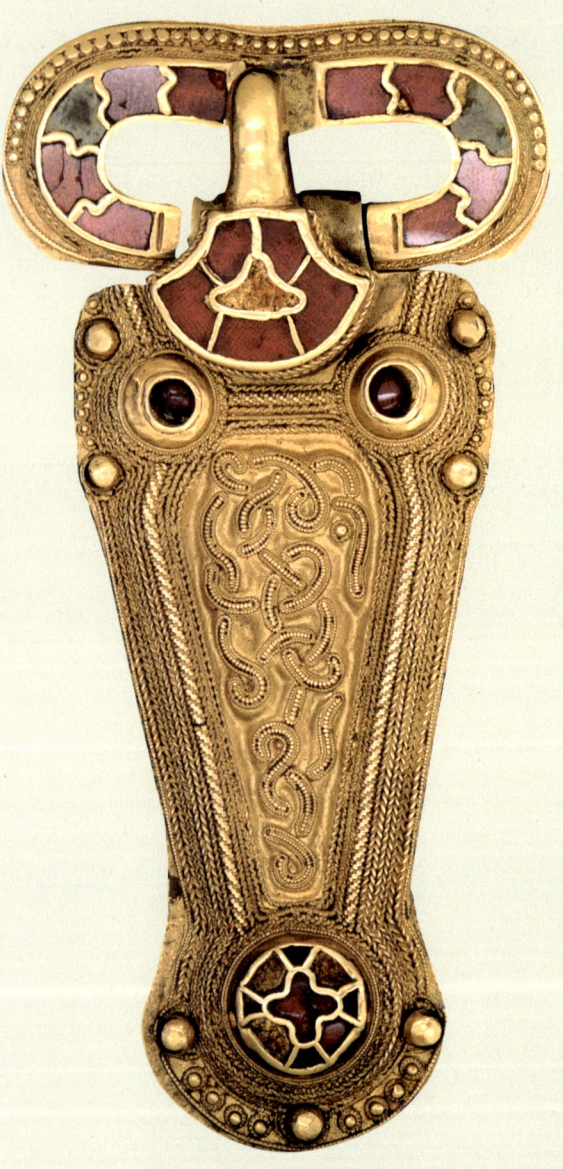

Half-title: Gold plaque from a cross or book cover, inlaid in
niello with the symbol of St John. Brandon, Suffolk. Early
9th century. H. 3.4 cm (British Museum; see p. 136)
Frontispiece: The Vespasian Psalter, fol. 30v: David the
Psalmist with musicians. Canterbury, Kent. Early 8th
century (British Library; see p. 86)
Right: Gold buckle with animal ornament and garnet
and glass inlays. From the princely burial at Taplow,
Buckinghamshire. Later 6th century, H. 9.8 cm
(British Museum; see p. 65)

CONTENTS

Fingers folded me, and the bird's delight repeatedly
made tracks across me with lucky droppings. Across
the burnished rim it swallowed tree's dye, a helping
of fluid, and stepped again onto me travelling a black
trail. Then a man clad me in protective boards, covered
me with hide and girded me with gold. Afterwards the
splendid work of the goldsmith adorned me, encased
in filigree. Now this decoration, and the red dye and
the magnificent settings make known far and wide the
Protector of multitudes, and the punishment of folly,
no less.

The Exeter Book, *Riddle 26*:
the solution is a gospel-book[1]

INTRODUCTION

Anglo-Saxon art is a unique high point of early medieval art; from the jewellery
found in the great ship burial at Sutton Hoo, by way of the Lindisfarne
Gospels, to the Bayeux Tapestry, it is familiar to all of us, dazzling in its
virtuosity, inventiveness and exuberant profusion. It exudes a remote but
intriguing glamour: the glittering restlessness of the early jewellery, the
whirling spirals and endlessly interlacing birds and beasts of Northumbrian
manuscripts, the enigmatic images which decorate the great stone sculptures
– all attract and baffle in the same moment. The eye is immediately and
instinctively drawn to the exquisite beauty and craftsmanship of this art. Yet
its very distinctive aesthetic, so different from the post-Renaissance traditions
of naturalistic portrayal to which we are accustomed, can seem opaque or
enigmatic, sometimes even meaningless. Without the keys to unlock a deeper
understanding of the art of this period, we can miss its whole point. Drawing on
the uniquely rich collections of the British Museum and the British Library, as
well as on other major material in Britain and abroad, this book is an attempt to
present the long history of Anglo-Saxon art in its wider cultural context, showing
how it was shaped, transformed and given meaning by ideas, concerns, traditions
and influences that reverberated throughout this early medieval society.

It is not an easy task to enter into the mindset of any past age, let alone one as distant as the Anglo-Saxon period. The challenge of entering into the Anglo-Saxon mentality is made more complex because the artistic journey is a long one. It begins with the arrival of the earliest Anglo-Saxon settlers from north Germany, southern Scandinavia and the Frisian coast in the early years of the fifth century, and concludes, at least in a political sense, with the Norman Conquest of 1066. These seven hundred years saw extraordinary transformations across Europe: in the aftermath of the Roman Empire, successor states assumed a Roman-style authority, and new agents of change drove in from the north and east. In Anglo-Saxon England, as elsewhere in Europe, the changes were profound, affecting almost every aspect of life. These fundamental cultural shifts were to transform the fifth-century tribal groupings of pagan and essentially illiterate warriors and farmers into a recognizable medieval Christian polity. By the middle of the eleventh century England had developed from these chaotic beginnings into a single kingdom, with all the institutions of a medieval state: a developed urban network and a complex economy, a sophisticated legal system, a carefully regulated coinage, flourishing centres of religion and learning, a vigorous literary tradition, and a remarkable and highly influential artistic heritage which had impact far beyond England itself. It was a diverse society which incorporated, sometimes uncasily, both native British and Scandinavian incomers, but was at the same time conscious of an over-arching Anglo-Saxon identity. Of course, Anglo-Saxon art underwent many transformations over this long period, but there are also underlying continuities, enduring characteristics which thread through the centuries and contribute to its distinctive DNA.

There is a persistent perception of the period after the end of Roman rule in Britain as the 'Dark Ages' – primitive, violent, unlearned, isolated – but the inventiveness and dynamism of Anglo-Saxon art shows how far from the truth that is. Rather than being isolated, Anglo-Saxon connections extended across Europe, through trade and gift exchange, diplomatic envoys, marriages and alliances, through political exile, and later, ecclesiastical missions and pilgrimage. Even the remoter Celtic kingdoms and monasteries of the far west of Britain and Ireland had contacts with the eastern Mediterranean, France and Italy, as the substantial archaeological evidence for two-way traffic shows. Long-distance travel, though slow and often hazardous, was a key agent of change, and its impact on the art of the period is everywhere to be seen. Thus, from the fifth to the eleventh centuries, England's story is one of absorption of many cultural influences – from Ireland on the western extremity of Europe to Byzantium and beyond, and from the Arctic Circle to northern Africa. This is certainly also true of some other parts of Europe; but the transforming effects of these contacts are arguably more visible on the periphery of Europe than in cultures nearer to its centre. The influence of Byzantine art, for instance, extends in sometimes remarkable ways to the farthest parts of north-western Europe, to England, Ireland, and even to Norway and Iceland.

In addition to the many artefacts that have survived, we are blessed with a particularly rich body of Anglo-Saxon literary and documentary sources. These help us to understand not only the cultural porosity of Anglo-Saxon art, but also the wider context that gives insight into the mentality which underpinned it. For example, the imagery of the heroic poem *Beowulf*, with its densely textured, allusive verse, often playing on images of darkness and brilliance, echoes the visual aesthetic of early Anglo-Saxon jewellery, with its dense ornament and busy surfaces which play on contrasts of glitter and plainness. At a different level *Beowulf* and much other Anglo-Saxon heroic and wisdom poetry reveals a keen sense of the past as an active shaper of the present, something we shall also encounter in the iconography of Anglo-Saxon visual art. It is also evident that art and literature share a keen sense of the natural world, its dangers and its beauty, and its hidden, divinely ordained order. In poetry and art alike, evocative animal and plant images recur. These sometimes appear as vehicles for religious ideas, such as the living tree that is Christ's Cross, which addresses the narrator of the poem known as the *Dream of the Rood*, and the biblical creatures of earth, air and water that decorate a chrismatory known as the Gandersheim Casket (see fig. 100). Sometimes they are simply images of the harshness and joys of nature, such as the scavenging wolf and raven – the companions of the battlefield in poetry – and the exuberant birds and beasts which embellish everyday equipment of the later Anglo-Saxon period, such as strap-ends, clasps and stirrup mounts.

Another important feature, shared by Anglo-Saxon art and literature, is a delight in paradox of every kind: verbal and visual riddles abound, and indeed some objects, such as the Franks Casket (see pp. 91–7), are riddles in themselves. Literary riddles, *enigmata*, were used from antiquity in the classroom as an entertaining way to focus concentration, exercise the mind and encourage reflection. In the Anglo-Saxon tradition they invited close and careful study, whether of text or image, to tease out the hidden meaning, as the extract from the riddle quoted at the beginning of this Introduction nicely illustrates. This patient interrogation of text and image was a key element in learning and understanding, from the animal ornament of the earliest Anglo-Saxon jewellery to the later great stone crosses and apocalyptic ivories of the early eleventh century. Although this remains a prominent feature of the art of the Christian period, its underlying visual grammar had its roots in a much earlier, pagan past, in which complex and playful decoration was clearly meant to be understood as well as simply admired.

Semi-naturalistic representations of the human (or divine) image are extremely rare in the earliest Anglo-Saxon art, although highly schematized depictions of masks, profiles, hands and limbs do occur in early metalwork.

Only a very few examples of the human image survive, probably associated with special ceremonies and cults, to show that such a tradition existed in the fifth and sixth centuries. But we should be cautious about making assumptions; the vivid depictions of Germanic legend on the eighth-century Franks Casket hint at a lost body of earlier portrayals of human figures in bone or wood carving, perhaps even in textiles. The arrival of Christianity, however, brought a dramatic change: the imported icons, books and ivory carvings that were essential to the practice of the new religion gave access to classically based models of figural representation. In telling the Christian story, and honouring God through accompanying prayer and worship, the manuscripts, stone sculpture and ivory carvings generated by the Anglo-Saxon Church presented the human figure in new contexts and new ways, quite different from what we know of the earlier tradition of human representation. Yet figures drawn from the secular world remain rare, compared with those found in the art of neighbouring Carolingian or Ottonian Europe. No manuscript image of the celebrated king Alfred the Great (reigned 871–99) exists to compare with those of his contemporary, the king of the Franks and later emperor Charles the Bald (r. 840–77), and indeed, the first surviving manuscript depiction of an Anglo-Saxon king, that of Æthelstan (r. 924/5–39), dates to around 934.

It is not until the end of the Anglo-Saxon period that depictions of everyday life such as the labours of the month that illustrate church calendars – and images of secular women appear, and these are rare enough. Although it has been argued that aristocratic women in Middle and Later Anglo-Saxon England had a greater degree of autonomy than their Norman counterparts, the appearances of secular women in the literature of the period (apart from the feisty female warrior, Judith, and the peace-keeping queens in *Beowulf*) are shadowy, and the depictions of women in visual art are also limited (see p. 182). This is, in part, a cultural tradition shared with other early medieval societies, where women, even powerful queens or abbesses, were generally perceived as taking an ancillary role. But another reason for this, and for the lack of secular high art in general, may be the very obvious fact that what survives today represents but a tiny fraction of the rich art treasures that once filled the halls and courts, churches and monasteries of England, before successive Viking invasions, civil wars, and the accidents and depredations of the ensuing centuries destroyed or consumed so much. Even stone sculpture was vulnerable to destruction or reuse in other contexts, as the dramatic fate of the Ruthwell Cross shows, broken up and buried by Calvinist iconoclasts in the seventeenth century; and decorated textiles, wall-paintings and wood carvings are rare survivals indeed. Of decorated wooden halls, such as Heorot, imagined in *Beowulf*, with its gold-adorned roof and its lavish hangings, not a plank survives, yet such descriptions assume the audience's familiarity with such things.[2] And without the happy survival of the Bayeux Tapestry, made to celebrate the Norman victory of 1066 but embroidered by Anglo-Saxon women, we should only have a brief reference in the *Liber Eliensis* (the Book of Ely) to hint at a tradition of celebrating heroic secular deeds in large hanging embroideries (see Chapter 5, p. 127).

Such losses should rightly make us wary of making judgements. However, working with what survives, a consistent picture emerges of a dynamic and receptive culture, in which classical and Eastern modes of representation mix and mingle with the zoomorphic and curvilinear art of the north and far west to produce a distinctive and influential art, quite different from that of its neighbours. It is a rich and fascinating subject, which has attracted a number of authoritative studies (see the Bibliography, pp. 248–51). These are central to any discussion of the subject, but the aim of this book is to give an accessible overview that covers the entire Anglo-Saxon period, placing it within a broader cultural and historical context, and incorporating the new discoveries and new thinking of recent years.

The book is structured thematically, each of its seven chapters focusing on a key element. At the same time they build a broadly chronological progression that charts the development of Anglo-Saxon art from its first stirrings in fifth-century metalwork to the manuscripts, ivories and sculpture of the mid-eleventh century. The opening chapter, 'Reading the Image, Seeing the Text', explores some of the enduring characteristics of the Anglo-Saxon artistic tradition that can be traced throughout the seven centuries in which it flourished. It includes discussions on visual vocabularies, metaphors and grammars, and their successive adaptations and transformations in the rapidly changing early medieval world. The second and third chapters, 'Rome Reinvented: the early inheritance' and 'Rome Reinvented: the impact of Christianity', deal with the assimilation of Roman art and ideas to an Anglo-Saxon context in successive waves from the fifth to the ninth centuries. The first reviews the influence of provincial Roman art on the earliest settlers and Anglo-Saxon art in the sixth and seventh centuries, and the second the major impact of Roman Christianity and its classicizing traditions on the art of the seventh to ninth centuries. The fourth chapter, 'Celtic connections, Eastern influences', discusses the impact of Celtic and Byzantine art on the Anglo-Saxon repertory, from the later sixth to the early ninth centuries. The potent integration of the Celtic curvilinear tradition with Anglo-Saxon animal ornament, combined with Italian and Byzantine ways of representing the human figure, new techniques of pictorial narration, and a new Eastern menagerie of symbolic creatures, created a hugely influential manuscript style, and had an equally significant effect on metalwork and sculpture. Chapter Five, 'Art and Power', focuses on the ceremonial, political and social dimensions of art during the seventh to ninth centuries, and on its role as a signifier of wealth, power and status, in a rapidly changing world in which competing kingdoms and the church both used art in the service of their authority. Expressions of royal and other forms of power and status are explored through such iconic manifestations as the Sutton Hoo and Staffordshire assemblages, the ambitious manuscripts, sculpture and metalwork of the Mercian supremacy, and the intellectual iconography of products of Alfred's vigorously promoted programme of religious renewal. The sixth chapter, 'Mission and Reform', takes the story up to the eleventh century, examining the impact on Anglo-Saxon art of the work of Anglo-Saxon missionaries and other ecclesiastics abroad in the later seventh and eighth centuries, and of the transforming effects of the Continentally inspired Benedictine reforms of the tenth centuries, which gave rise to a series of magnificent manuscripts and ivory carvings in the tenth and eleventh centuries. Its equivalent impact on secular art of the ninth to tenth centuries leads into the seventh chapter, 'The North Ascendant: the Viking impact', where the focus is on the influence of Viking art styles, first in the Danelaw, and then under the Danish king Cnut (r. 1016–35) and his successors, and on the emergence of a vigorous Anglo-Scandinavian artistic culture in the later tenth and eleventh centuries. Finally, an 'Afterword' discusses the legacy of Anglo-Saxon art after the Norman Conquest, and up to the present day.

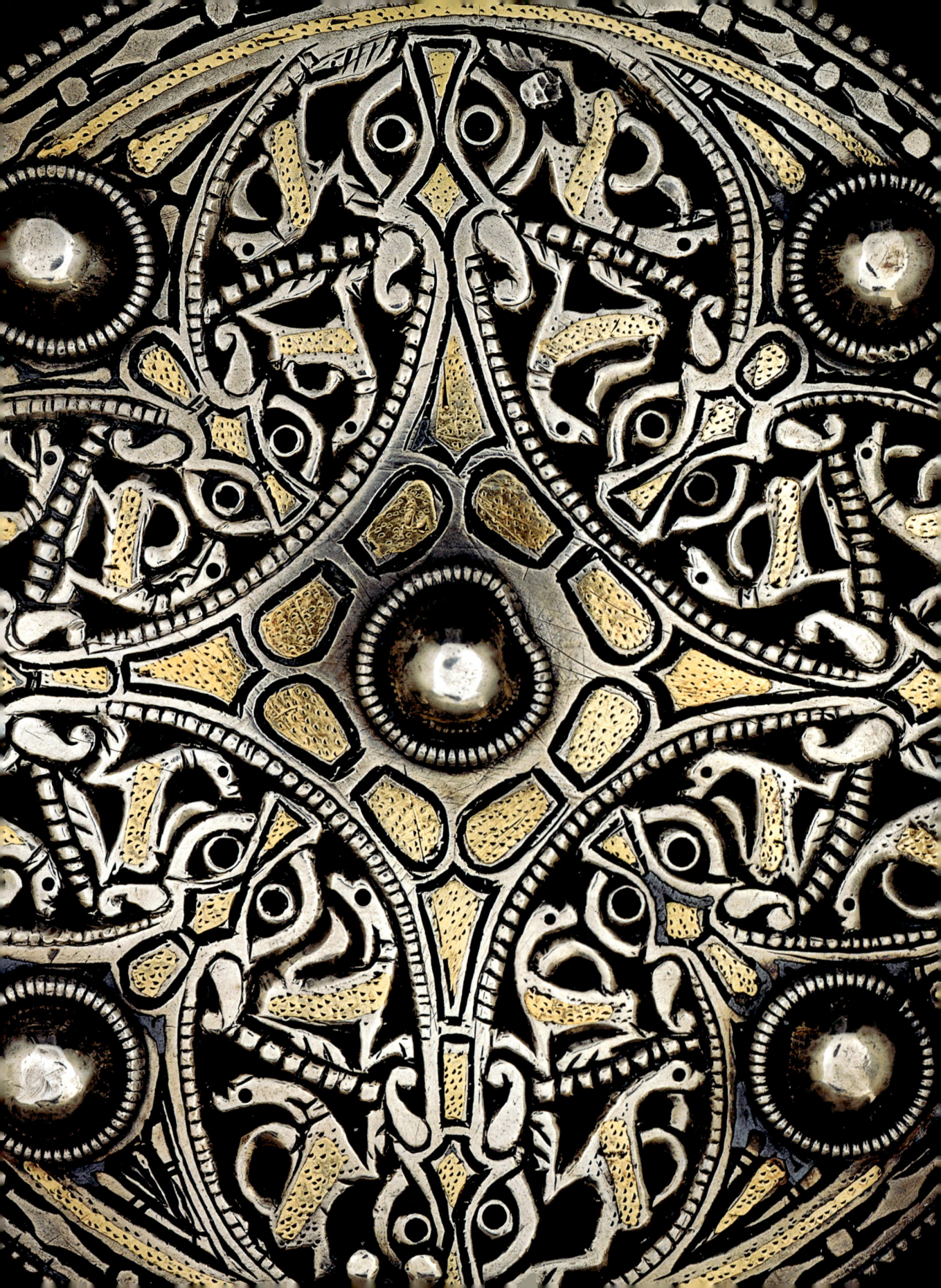

CHAPTER 1

Hrothgar spoke: he examined the hilt, that ancient
relic; on it was engraved the beginning of age-old war.
Afterwards the Flood, the rushing sea, destroyed the
race of giants; they fared badly. That was a people
estranged from the eternal Lord; the Ruler gave them
retribution in the surging of the water. On those bright
gold casings it was also properly marked in runic
letters, set out and stated, for whom that sword was
made, the best of blades, with its interlaced, snake-
patterned hilt.

Beowulf, lines 1687–98[1]

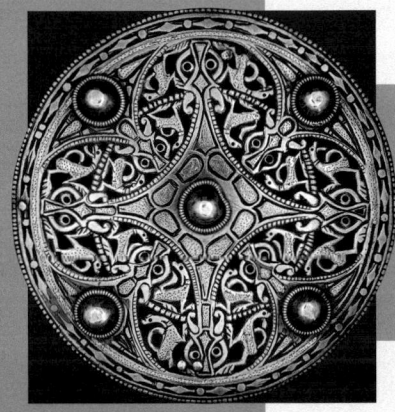

READING THE IMAGE,
SEEING THE TEXT

The Strickland Brooch:
silver disc brooch with
gold and niello inlays
and animal ornament
in the Trewhiddle style.
9th century. Diam. 11.2
cm (British Museum)

Telling stories

The Anglo-Saxon imagination was an intensely visual one: images contained
stories just as much as words. In the quotation above, the intricate patterns of
Hrothgar's sword-hilt tell a tale about the world of gods and men in the same
way that a gospel-book could convey its mysteries through images as well as in
words. To set the scene for the chapters that follow, this introductory section
explores the fundamental importance of visual literacy in Anglo-Saxon culture,
and shows how it underpins and shapes many of the enduring characteristics
of Anglo-Saxon art.

Visual understanding and communication was paramount in a society that was in transition from an essentially oral tradition to one where
literacy, though more widespread, remained the preserve of ecclesiastical and
secular elites. Though some of the fifth-century Germanic settlers who eventually became known as Anglo-Saxons would have had encounters with the
written word – mostly on Roman coins and medallions – they themselves had
little use for writing, which was confined to brief inscriptions in the runic

alphabet on high-status portable objects. It was only with the re-introduction of a romanized written culture through the Christian missions at the end of the sixth century that the radical new technology of pen, ink and parchment enabled complex information to be set down in written language. Until then, and for a long time after, this was transmitted orally, through formal and informal recitation and story-telling, and also through visual images, which were often complex and sometimes many-layered. These images conveyed celebratory, mythical and religious matter, often in symbolic form; their meaning would have been regularly articulated through tale-telling and their role in ceremonial enactments.

In the extract from *Beowulf* that opens this chapter, the Danish king Hrothgar scrutinizes the hilt of the mighty sword, the 'work of marvellous smiths' with which Beowulf has just beheaded the monstrous Grendel and his mother. Revealingly, it is first and foremost the pictorial message of the destruction of the race of giants that the hilt carries which captures the king's – and our – attention; the runic inscription which names the owner is secondary in terms of the information that the sword conveys. This is because the images on this powerful weapon deliver a message – of alienation, war and judgement – which rumbles throughout the poem. Although this is, of course, an imagined weapon, there are real-life swords which also tell stories, as we shall see later in this chapter. The narratives they encapsulate are compressed to fit the sword-hilt's limited space, so, like that described in *Beowulf*, they can only be understood through close examination and explanation by those who have the skills to read them. This is a theme we shall encounter many times over as the book progresses.

Reading images

The habit of reading images stretches back to the beginning of the Anglo-Saxon period. Throughout the fifth century, successive settlers brought with them a rich and complex visual vocabulary that had developed in northern Germany and southern Scandinavia in the later fourth and fifth centuries, and which can be seen on the surviving decorated metalwork from the later fifth and sixth centuries. The key – though by no means the only – element in this vocabulary was densely patterned ornament based on stylized animals, sometimes supplemented by human elements such as masks, or curious animal/man hybrids. This distinctive style lasted into the later sixth century, when it was gradually superseded by a more symmetrical and rhythmical kind of animal ornament; these successive phases are known as Style I and Style II (see Chapter 2). To our eyes the effect is at first glance baffling in its busyness, a seemingly impenetrable jumble of dismembered bits. For this reason, it was often described by earlier writers in language that emphasized strangeness and barbarism, for example, contrasting its 'aesthetic discord and restlessness'[2] with the comfortable naturalism of classical art. But, in fact, right from the earliest forms of Anglo-Saxon art, the artists worked to a carefully constructed artistic vocabulary and grammar; in the hands of all but the most unskilled craftsmen, this early animal art followed a clear aesthetic in its form and organization.

A splendid silver-gilt square-headed brooch from an Anglo-Saxon woman's grave at Chessell Down on the Isle of Wight is a good illustration of the way in which such complex decoration followed a set of rules, enabling the whole piece to be 'read' in discrete stages (fig. 1). By analyzing its decoration in detail we can interpret it ourselves, and so get an idea of how an Anglo-Saxon might have understood such ornament, and what such a brooch might have meant to its wearer. More broadly, this example also suggests how other later Anglo-Saxon objects might yield up their sometimes cryptic meaning.

The brooch is divided into a number of fields by frames with zigzag ornament and other subtler dividing motifs. On the rectangular head-plate a framed border runs around the top and sides, its upper side containing two back-to-back crouching animals separated by a short bar, their U-shaped, beaked heads and hindquarters clearly visible. Down the sides are scrolls of a kind derived from late Roman metalwork. So far, so good. But the inner panel of the head-plate is much harder to decipher at first glance. The panel is divided in two by a central motif composed of a human mask facing upwards towards a highly stylized animal. The mask is upside down in relation to the ornament on the lower part of the brooch. In the fields to either side of this dividing image is what appears at first glance to be a meaningless debris of animal parts. In fact, careful scrutiny reveals that each field contains two creatures, highly compressed to fit into the small space, and separated by a discreet S-shaped scroll. These are also to be read in the same orientation as the upward-facing mask. The creatures are, in fact, animal/man hybrids, with clearly legible human heads in profile, attached to stylized animal bodies.

Below the brooch's head-plate, the curving bow of the brooch is left free of ornament, though its ribbed construction leads the eye on down to the separate visual programme of the foot-plate below. Immediately below the bow two open-jawed animal heads, with tiny animal heads at each end of their jaws, curve gracefully down on either side of a central human mask, and are clasped by a horizontal bar below it. Their necks sweep down to merge into a frame which defines the central field of the foot-plate. At either side of this is a circular lobe containing an inward-facing human mask, bordered by the inner frame, but separated from the central field by a clasp. The brooch terminates in a similar geometrically decorated lobe, entirely separated from the central panel by its frame. On the lower edges of the foot-plate are two back-to-back creatures separated by a central ribbed element. They are severely compressed images, but a head and a leg are visible in each case, showing that

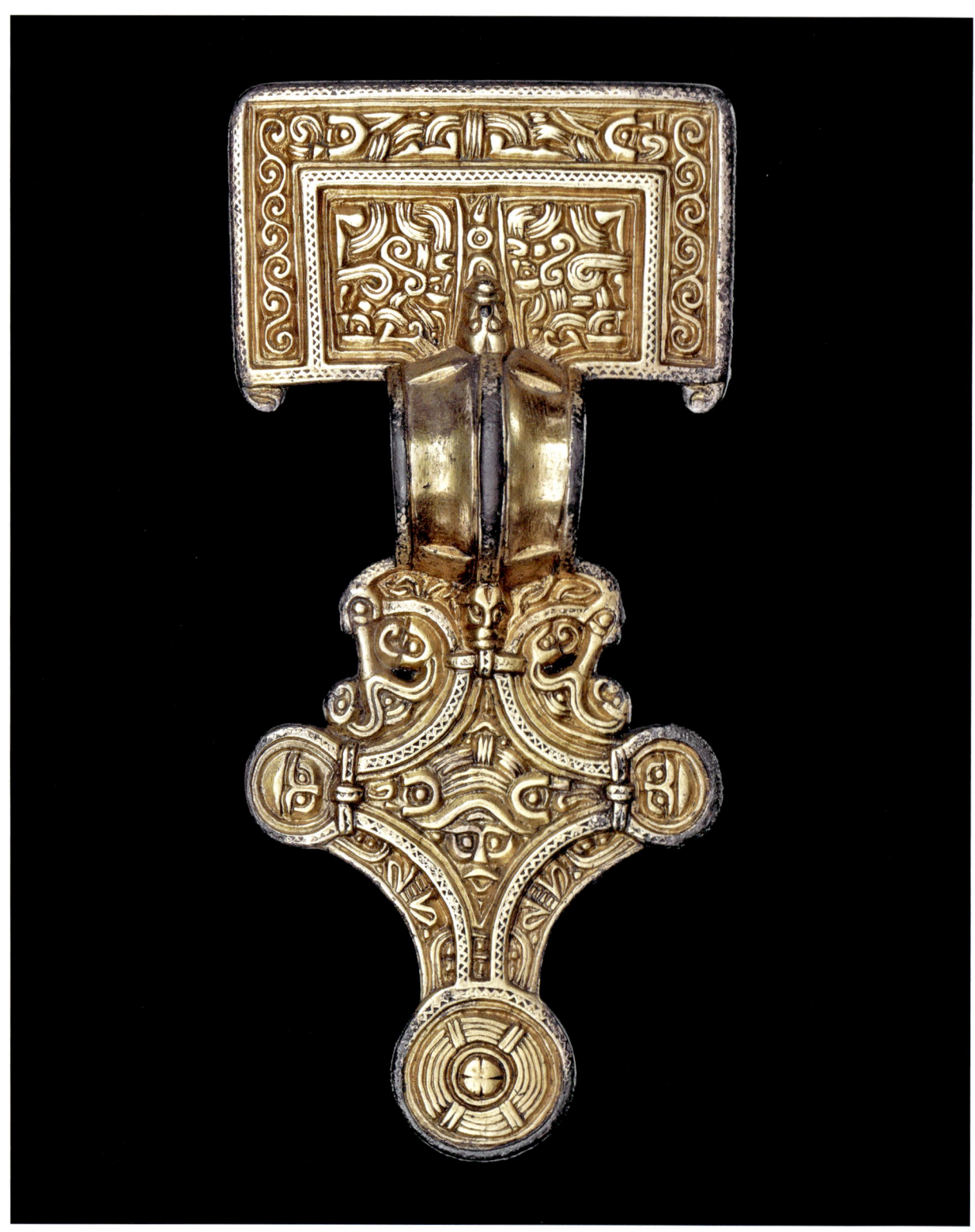

the two upper beasts face up towards the lobes with human masks, while the two lower ones face down towards the terminal disc. Finally, in the central field, above a bearded human mask with a helmet-like cap or hair are two conjoined bird heads with curving beaks which point towards the masks on either side, one with its head facing the top of the brooch, the other facing the foot. Above them is another clasped element, which may also be read in the opposite orientation as a stylized mask.

It takes a while to unpack this intricate decoration and, having deciphered each element, to see that the brooch contains a carefully articulated visual programme. This is controlled by a well-defined framework, in which animal and human images are set in a series of complex conjunctions and oppositions; we shall encounter such characteristics many times in later chapters.

This richly decorated and gilded silver brooch conveys several messages. At the most straightforward level, it would have signified wealth and power through the precious metal and craftsmanship invested in it. At another level, its form and decoration would have signified particular status and affiliation, both social and religious. Such grand brooches would have been worn on special occasions, including feasts and religious ceremonies, where the messages embodied in the miniature cosmos of their decoration would have had particular resonance. Finally, it probably assured protection and good fortune for the wearer through powerful images of gods, and of the dangerous natural world in which man and beast were at the same time enemies, yet interdependent. The central image on the foot-plate – the bearded face with bird-like creatures forming a protective shield above – is quite possibly to be read as an image of Woden/Odin, chief among the Germanic gods, accompanied by his two ravens, known from later Scandinavian sources as Huginn and Muninn. We can only guess at the intended meaning of the other images on the brooch. It is possible, however, that all the human images in some sense depict supernatural beings, and that its overall programme of protective oppositions had an important apotropaic function, warding off evil, as well as signifying wealth, status or 'ethnic' affiliation – as we shall see later.

Structuring the message

It is clear that the importance of being able to 'read' images continued throughout succeeding centuries; even texts could be presented to be seen as much as read. And though the stylistic vocabulary changes radically over time, the visual grammar underpinning decoration persists. Thus many of the same elements that signal content and guide interpretation on the sixth-century Chessell Down brooch are equally apparent in Christian art of the later Anglo-Saxon period. For example, the frameworks and other subtler dividers which help to organize the dense visual information on the brooch reappear time and again in later metalwork, sculpture and manuscripts.

Made some four hundred years after the brooch from Chessell Down, a ninth-century disc brooch, known as the Strickland Brooch after its donor, is decorated with equally intense patterns of animal ornament, carefully organized through elaborate frameworks punctuated by prominent and striking animal masks (see the illustrations on pp. 12–13). This product of a wholly Christian society does not carry the pagan symbolism of the earlier brooch, but it certainly uses a similar structural grammar, as well as a vocabulary of formulaic animal ornament which has its roots in the earlier animal styles.

The manuscripts and sculpture of the eighth and ninth centuries do something very similar, adapted to the conventions of Christian art. The great Northumbrian stone cross at Ruthwell, Dumfriesshire (discussed in Chapter 3; see fig. 59), carries a sophisticated programme which counterpoints images from Christ's life on the front and back of the cross with fruiting vine scrolls inhabited by lively animals on the sides. The inhabited vine scroll is a long-standing Christian symbol of Christ and his church, referring to the gospel description of Christ as 'the true vine' in which the faithful dwell (John 15:1–7). But it is also an image that draws some of its power and resonance from the long Anglo-Saxon tradition of animal ornament, and in this context it evokes in addition the living tree from which Christ's Cross was made. The figural and vine-scroll panels are enclosed by broad frames bearing inscriptions. Those accompanying the Christological scenes are scriptural labels, written in Latin and the Roman alphabet; but the sides with the vine tree are bordered by a very different kind of text, a poem in Old English, carved in runes. In this poem the tree that became the Cross speaks about the Crucifixion, echoing the accompanying image of the vine tree/cross. These inscriptions not only physically separate the two depictions of the Christian message on the cross, but, by using two different languages, alphabets and texts, they also emphasize the conceptual difference between the biblical figures and the symbolic vine. In framing the beast-inhabited vine tree within an Anglo-Saxon runic poem which is partly narrated by the Cross, and the classicizing figural scenes with Latin scriptural texts, a distinction is being made between two ways of embodying the Christian message, as well as two cultural traditions. Here, the word becomes a powerful image in its own right. As with the sixth-century brooch from Chessell Down, the highly structured message presented on this eighth-century cross requires visual literacy in order to be understood, as much as the ability to read texts; the prominent frameworks, with their different visual cues, help to guide the reading of this great monument.

Frames are used in a similar way in many of the Anglo-Saxon illuminated manuscripts of the seventh and eighth centuries, particularly in setting out the so-called carpet pages that introduce each gospel, which derive from eastern Mediterranean models. The concept of pages entirely covered with ornament – which embodies the Christian message in often intricate cross

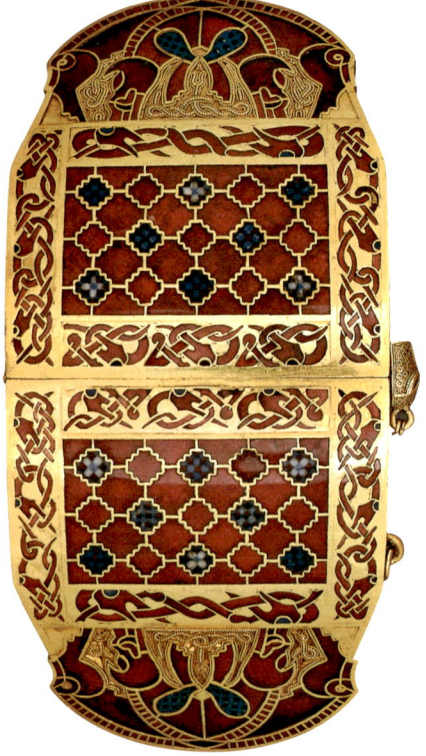

2 (*below*). Gold shoulder clasp with garnet and millefiori glass inlays, chequer cellwork and interlacing animal ornament. From the Mound 1 ship burial, Sutton Hoo, Suffolk, *c*. 620s. L. 12.7 cm (British Museum)

3 (*opposite*). The Book of Durrow: carpet page with processing animals. Probably *c*. 680. 24.5 x 14.5 cm (Trinity College, Dublin, MS A.4.5.(57), fol. 192v)

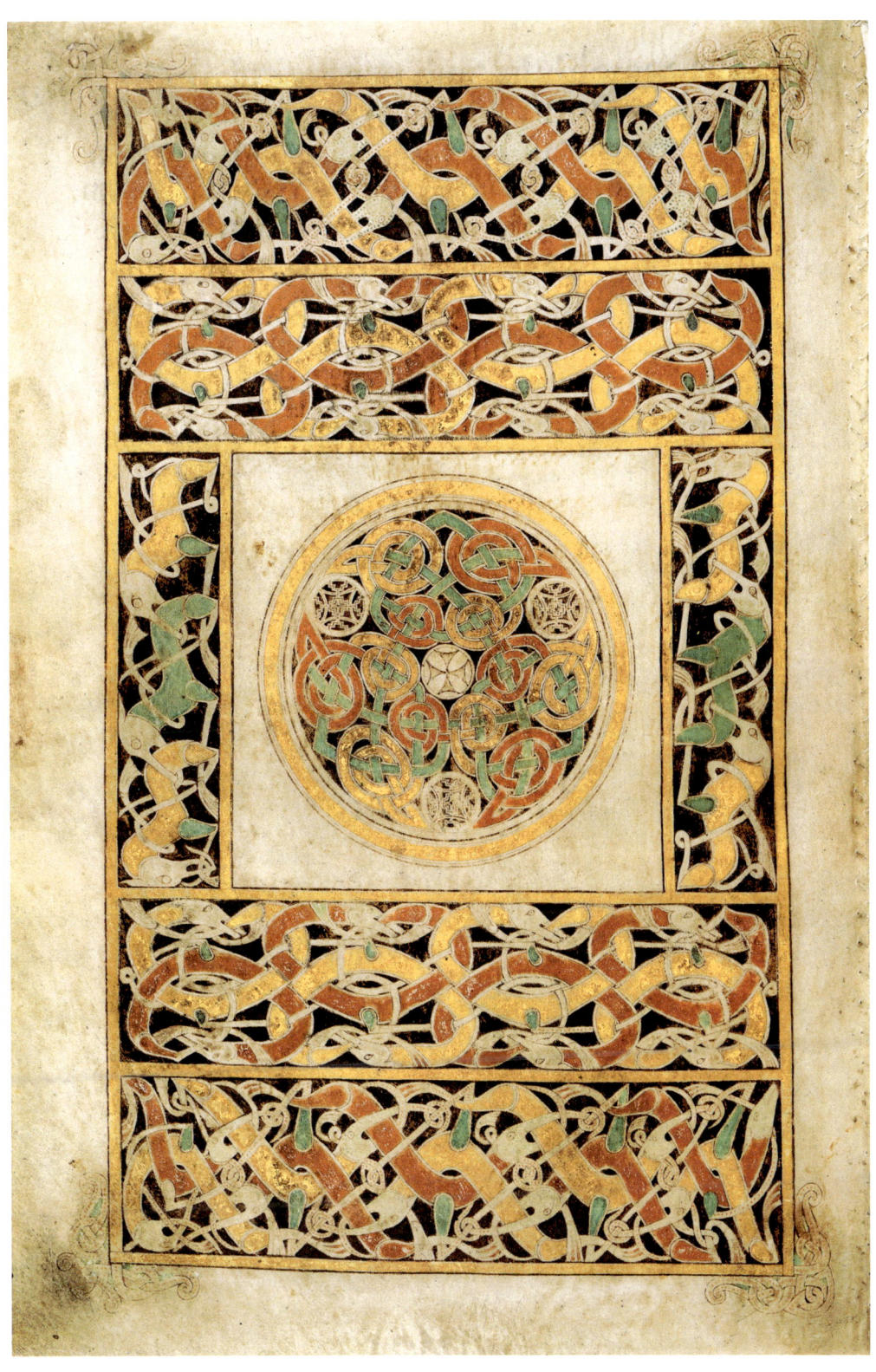

patterns – is faithful to their eastern exemplars. But the rich interlacing menagerie of birds and animals, and complex spiral decoration, is wholly Anglo-Saxon in its love of intricate pattern and meticulously ordered structures.

The Book of Durrow is one of the oldest surviving Insular gospelbooks, though we have no record of its date or place of origin. It has been ascribed to Northumbria, Ireland and Iona, and, more recently, even to East Anglia (see p. 78). It has been dated over an equally broad range, though most scholars would now place it around 680. One of its carpet pages has processing animals which could almost have trotted off the Sutton Hoo shoulder clasps – indeed, it has often been remarked that the central panels of the clasps themselves closely resemble carpet pages (figs 2 and 3). Both clasps and carpet page share a similar clear hierarchy of animal and other ornament. The evangelist symbols in this manuscript also owe a debt to Anglo-Saxon goldsmiths' traditions, particularly fine cloisonné inlay. All four evangelist symbols, as well as the processing animals on the carpet page, are defined by frames evoking the golden cellwork of cloisonné. The St Matthew image even has a body composed of chequer patterns, echoing the much-prized millefiori glass inlays of Romano-British, Anglo-Saxon and Celtic metalwork (see fig. 49). With their references to luxury metalwork, these images are intended both to enhance the precious nature of the text itself and to be familiar aids to its understanding (see Chapter 4, pp. 77–8).

Only a little later, from around the beginning of the eighth century, the Lindisfarne Gospels took the structuring of richly textured Anglo-Saxon animal ornament with a Christian theme to new heights.[3] In the carpet page opening to St John's Gospel (fig. 4), an exquisite turmoil of birds – an image of God's Creation – forms a cruciform background against which golden interlaced Greek and tau crosses stand out. The pattern is intricate and complicated, and it is only on closer examination that the overall scheme of crosses within a cross becomes apparent, guided by the brightly coloured frames which separate the different elements of the composition.

As with the symbolic texts on the Ruthwell Cross, we also encounter in such manuscripts formal presentations of text which make their initial impact entirely as images. For example, opening the account of Christ's birth at the beginning of St Matthew's Gospel in the Lindisfarne Gospels (fig. 5), a flamboyant Chi-Rho symbol (the first two letters of Christ's name in Greek) begins an elaborately ornamented text, *Christi autem generatio erat* ('Now the birth of Christ was on this wise'; Matthew 1:18). The virtuoso decoration of these keynote letters dominates the rest of the highly stylized text on this page. This is also characteristic of gospel openings in Hiberno-Saxon manuscripts, such as the text beginning St Luke's Gospel in the St Chad Gospels, with its angular stylized capitals that interplay with runic forms, which also have to be teased out from their coloured and decorated frames.[4]

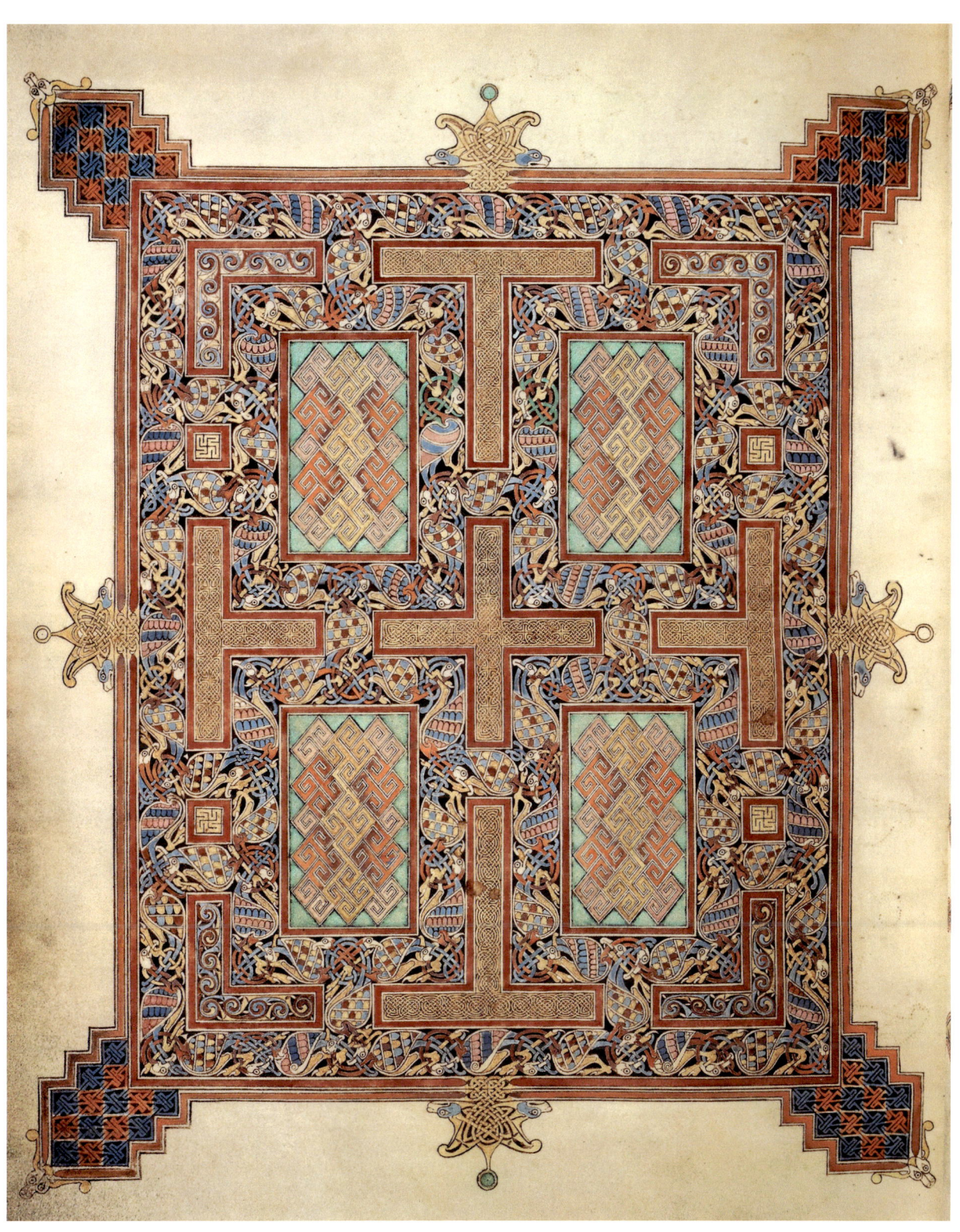

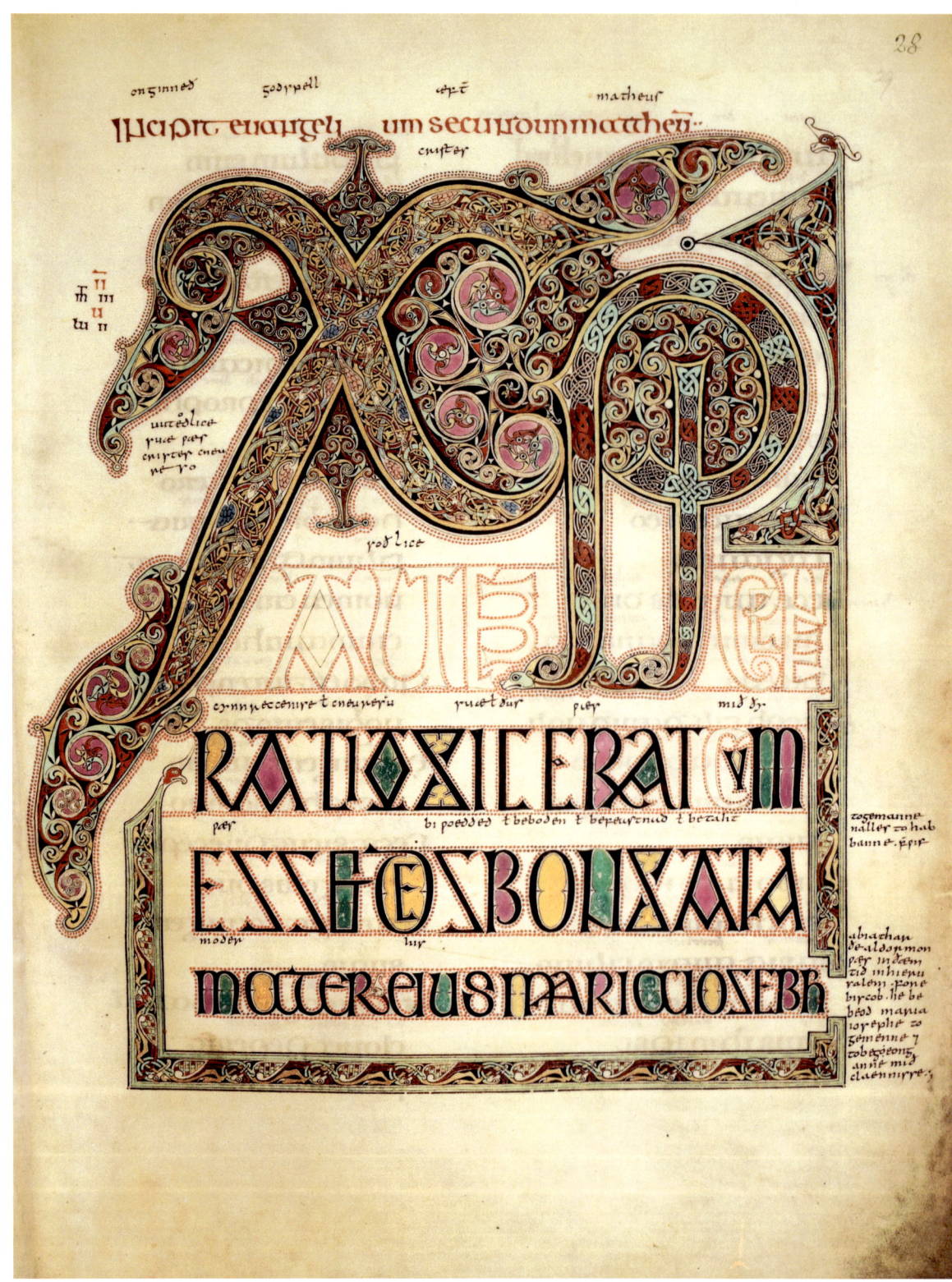

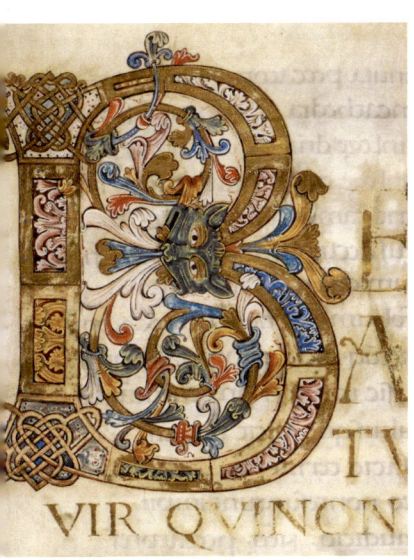

5 (*opposite*). The Lindisfarne Gospels: decorated Chi-Rho monogram from the beginning of St Matthew's Gospel. Early 8th century. 34 x 24 cm (British Library, Cotton MS Nero D.iv, fol. 29r)

6 (*above*). The Ramsey Psalter: detail of decorated initial B. *c*. 1000. Whole page 28.5 x 24.2 cm (British Library, Harley MS 2904, fol. 4v)

The Anglo-Saxon mastery of decorated text continues unsurpassed, as can be seen in the ornate *Beatus* initial which opens the first psalm in illuminated psalters of the tenth and eleventh centuries (fig. 6). The Latin word *Beatus*, meaning 'blessed', opens the verses which describe the happy destiny of the righteous compared with that of the wicked; in this context, and at the very beginning of the book of Psalms, it is a potent word indeed. Even in the learned and literate context of the monastery, these and other decorated initials and words were meant to be seen as much as read. Key texts that tell of the Incarnation, of the Godhead and humanity of Christ, are presented as images which proclaim the message in gloriously symbolic form; and yet, in this, they continue a tradition that began with the brooches and buckles of the pagan first settlers.

Visual formulas

Some of the examples discussed above reveal another enduring characteristic of Anglo-Saxon art – its frequent use of a formulaic vocabulary, familiar images which can guide and reinforce understanding. Conventionalized vine scroll, acanthus sprays, interlace and geometric motifs, as well as animal ornament, are particularly prominent. As we have seen in the case of the Chessell Down brooch, the zoomorphic ornament of early metalwork could convey highly compressed information. Many of its motifs – human masks, animal/man hybrids, crouching creatures with forelegs raised, conjoined beast heads in profile and so on – are the mainstays of decorative programmes in early Anglo-Saxon art (see Chapter 2).

This use of motif formulas is strikingly reminiscent of the way in which Anglo-Saxon poetry uses recurrent phrases to steer the narrative flow. Both poetry and visual art use particular formulas to create a rich and dense texture of metaphor and allusion. The profusion of formulaic phrases regularly used in vernacular poetry – *wuldres weard* or 'guardian of glory' for Christ, *banhus* or 'bone-house' for body, *swanrade* or 'swan-road' for sea, and so on – have their origins in the oral transmission of tales, where they aided memory as well as embellishing the verse. The equally stylized animal motifs of Style I and Style II resemble these literary formulas in encoding ideas in an ornate visual structure and, through repetition, reinforcing the message. In this way, even the most crudely formed or brutally elliptical reductions of animal motifs could be readily understood (see figs 7 and 36).

These allusive formulas in poetry and early metalwork also draw on a storehouse of images from a distant or mythic past – seventh-century boar-helmeted warriors and ring-swords in the tenth-century written text of *Beowulf*, for instance, or Woden images and totemic beasts in the case of the Sutton Hoo purse-lid (see fig. 77). It is equally striking that, just as formulas and other hints of orality have survived in the written versions of Old English poems – evocatively described by one scholar as 'visible song'[5] – so the use of visual formulas, patterns, models and templates persists in Anglo-Saxon metal-work and sculpture right up to the Conquest.

Texture, movement, colour and contrast

The dense textures shared by Anglo-Saxon verbal and visual art is one of their most striking, and persistent, characteristics. The busy surface of the Chessell Down brooch and the exuberant patterning of the carpet pages of the Lindis-farne Gospels have already illustrated how this passed from a pagan to a Christian context (see figs 1 and 4); and this delight in rich surfaces continues throughout the period. While the lush sprouting acanthus borders, turbulent clouds and agitated draperies that are characteristic of some late tenth-century manuscripts and ivories derive from Carolingian sources, they have been strik-ingly transformed into a distinctively Anglo-Saxon style (see p. 187). A miniature of the Baptism of Christ, for example, in a lavishly decorated benedictional made for Bishop Æthelwold of Winchester in the 970s, is closely related to the same scene on a Carolingian ivory casket (see figs 143 and 144). The design of the two scenes, with flanking angels and the River Jordan pouring from a vessel held by a river god in late Antique tradition, is almost identical; but the style is utterly different. In the Anglo-Saxon manuscript every detail of the setting is transformed into a turbulent pattern, far removed from the static, classicizing style of the ivory. This, in common with other manuscript painting of this period, vibrates with a nervous energy that seems to reflect the ardent spiritual renewal at the heart of the transforming Benedictine reforms of the tenth cen-tury (see pp. 173–4). In this fascination with all-over complex patterns and restless movement, such manuscripts reflect a long-standing aesthetic, visible in the glittering complexities of early metalwork (see figs 1 and 42), the swirl-ing creatures of gospel manuscripts (see figs 4 and 51) and the quivering cascades of draperies of some late Anglo-Saxon ivories. Restless surfaces such as these, glimmering in the firelight of the hall, or captured in the candle glow of church ceremonies, would have made a powerful visual counterpart to the formal recitation of both secular poetry and liturgical ceremony.

Alongside this goes a fascination with bold contrast: a tension between busy ornament and smooth plain surfaces is often present in early metalwork. It can be seen, for instance, in the visual interplay between the silver-plated lobes and panels which occur on some sixth-century brooches, and the bub-bling animal ornament which covers the rest of their surface (fig. 7); and in the plain bow which interconnects the highly decorated head- and foot-plates of the Chessell Down brooch (see fig. 1). Contrasts of movement and stasis are also frequent in manuscripts and sculpture of the Christian period. The sim-plified gravitas of the four evangelist portraits in the Lindisfarne Gospels, with their flattened blocks of colour, sits strikingly alongside the whirling animal and curvilinear decoration in other pages of the manuscript (see figs 4, 5 and 48).

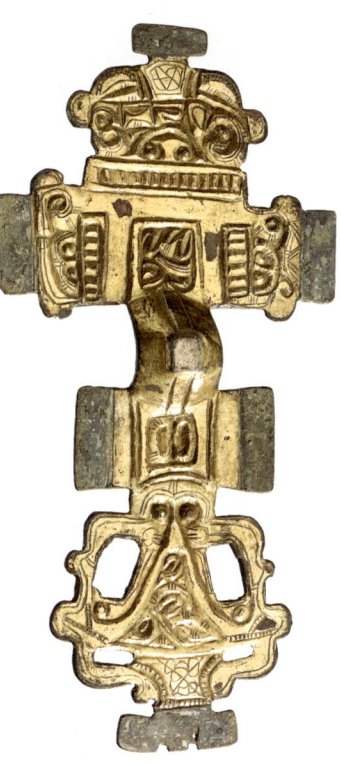

7. Gilded copper-alloy cruciform brooch, from a woman's grave. Longbridge, Warwickshire, late 6th century. L. 18.7 cm (British Museum)

In many later manuscripts this tension between stillness and agitation is taken to new heights, in the contrasts between the often tumultuous backdrops and leafy acanthus frames which surround the central figures, as in the Baptism miniature in the Benedictional of St Æthelwold (see fig. 143).

Other kinds of contrast are prominent. The opposition of light and dark is a regular theme in Anglo-Saxon poetry, in which the joys of the bright hall are contrasted with the outer world of darkness, cold and dangers; Bede's famous comparison of human life to a sparrow's brief flight through the warm, firelit hall where the king feasts, into the wintry darkness and storms from which it came, is apposite here.[6] This contrast is very prominent in metal-work, from the glitter of red garnets against gold in war-gear from the Sutton Hoo burial and the Staffordshire Hoard to the starker contrast of gold or silver against black niello inlays in ninth-century metalwork (see figs 79 and 115).

Anglo-Saxon gospel-books and Bibles repeat these contrasts on the painted page. The biographer of St Wilfrid describes a lavish Bible that he presented to his foundation at Ripon, illuminated with bright gold lettering on a purple ground, in the Roman manner. Though we cannot be certain that this particular manuscript was made in England, we know through the survival of the *Codex Amiatinus*,[7] one of three great Bibles produced at Bede's own monastery of Wearmouth/Jarrow, that the grand style of Italian manuscripts was emulated in Northumbria as early as the late seventh century (see p. 73). It contains three purple pigmented pages, some with orpiment yellow lettering and touches of silver, no doubt because gold was scarce. Some contemporary gospel-books in the Insular tradition also use yellow pigment contrasting with brightly coloured ornamental detail (see fig. 49). Much later, in the elaborate manuscripts of the late tenth century, the glitter of silver and golden frames and script is boldly set off by the cool greens, blues and pinks of the painted foliage borders, and the scenes contained within them.

In Anglo-Saxon art colour also takes on some very particular roles and meaning. The fashion for using garnets ultimately originated in grand late Roman and Byzantine jewellery: the deep purple-red of the precious stone was seen as the imperial colour, *purpura*. The vogue for bold garnet inlays in precious jewellery was adopted by many of Rome's Germanic successors, in Italy itself and in former imperial territories throughout Europe, including Frankish Gaul. Although its imperial connotations may have been half-forgotten by the time the fashion reached Anglo-Saxon England, the rich colour of garnet was prized beyond other coloured inlays such as blue or green glass, and dominated the finest jewellery in the sixth and seventh centuries (fig. 8).

Red is indeed one of the few colours that resonate in Anglo-Saxon literary culture, where references to hues are less prominent than those to darkness and brightness, glitter and dullness. If clerical condemnation is an indicator, red dyes were greatly prized as a sign of luxury and standing – in his

De virginitate, Aldhelm, writing in the later seventh century, rebuked certain nuns for wearing tunics of violet and crimson, and scarlet shoes, aping secular fashions. As we have already seen, purples and dark reds were used in some of the richest Bible manuscripts; not only was the purple-red colouring expensive and imperial in its connotations, but it also carried Christian significance, as Bede observed, through reference to the blood of Christ. Ambitious later examples of purple- and red-stained pages survive in the Stockholm *Codex Aureus*, an Anglo-Saxon gospel-book of the mid-eighth century, and the Royal Bible, made in Canterbury in the second quarter of the ninth century (see fig. 109). As late as 965, the richly painted preface to the Winchester New Minster Charter depicts King Edgar presenting his charter to Christ against a background of this deep imperial red (see fig. 141). The dual symbolism of the colour plays its part in this image of divine and secular power united.

8. Gold pendant with a Roman garnet cameo with the head of an oriental male. Ewell or Epsom, Surrey, mid-7th century. L. 3.2 cm (British Museum)

But the most widespread impact of colour was probably in monumental and architectural sculpture – including the lost body of wood carving, as well as stone – and in wall-paintings. The traces of original painting on Anglo-Saxon sculpture are few and faint, but there can be little doubt that much surviving sculpture was originally painted in bright colours, designed both to entice the eye and to glorify the message. Traces of blue and red paint on ivory carvings have shown that some of these, at least, were also brightly coloured. Others, such as a tau-shaped crozier head from Alcester, Warwickshire, originally had gold foil pressed into the recesses of the carved decoration to add rich contrast to the relief (see fig. 169). On much of the stone sculpture the range was probably limited to easily obtainable colours – black, red and white – as, for example, on the Ringerike-style carvings from St Paul's churchyard and Rochester Cathedral (see fig. 191).[8]

However, two recent studies have dramatically revealed the sophistication of painting on sculpture at certain ecclesiastical sites. During excavations in the cathedral at Lichfield, a major royal and ecclesiastical centre of Mercia, a sculptured fragment which probably depicts the archangel of the Annunciation was discovered beneath the floor of the nave (fig. 9).[9] It dates to around 800 and possibly formed part of the end of a shrine, perhaps that of St Chad (d. 672), the first bishop, who founded the monastery there in the seventh century. Because the shrine was demolished and buried about a century after it was made, the colours and crispness of the decoration are uniquely well preserved. A palette of red, yellow, white, black and probably gold was skilfully used to produce a modulated effect. The feathers on the angel's wings, for example, are delicately graduated from deep red through to yellow, ending in white at the tips, each feather outlined in black. The face is painted in pink

9 (*opposite*). The Lichfield Angel: carved and painted limestone sculpture, probably depicting the archangel Gabriel. *c*. 800. H. 60 cm (Lichfield Cathedral)

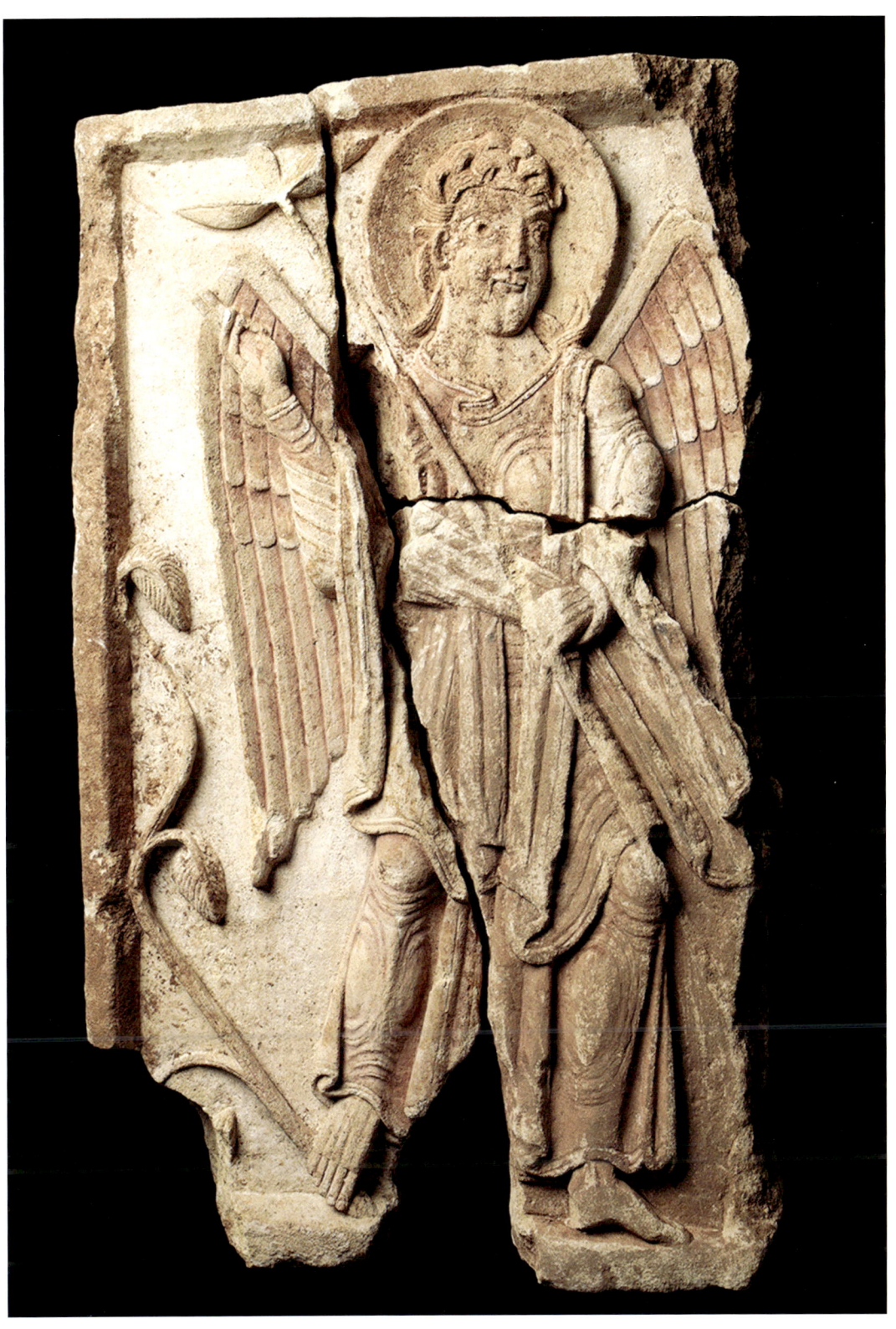

flesh-tones, with the features accentuated in black; the hair is a golden yellow, and the halo was probably bordered with gold. The garment is also yellow, the folds of its draperies outlined in red, and the background is painted white. This bright and bold palette, with its emphasis on rich red and golden yellow, may reflect contemporary ecclesiastical perceptions of the symbolism of these colours, expressed, for instance, in Bede's comments on the spiritual significance of gold, violet and red.[10]

Recent work on the sculptures at the Anglo-Saxon church at Deerhurst, Gloucestershire, have indicated a similar palette of red and yellow, most dramatically on the red, pink and yellow decoration of the ninth-century chancel arch.[11] In addition, paint traces on a figure of the Virgin have revealed that she had a yellow 'sunburst' halo with radiating red spokes, and a red robe; the background to the figure contains traces of purple and red, and the recessed cells below her feet are painted a bright yellow – perhaps in imitation of the coloured glass and metal insets that once adorned some other Anglo-Saxon sculptures. As this last example indicates, painting was sometimes employed to add features or decoration to a plain figure, and may also have been used to add inscriptions and other details.

Wall-paintings from the period are exceptionally rare, but fragments of painted plaster from archaeological excavations on a number of Anglo-Saxon ecclesiastical sites suggest that internal walls were often decorated with paintings. Some depicted figural scenes, as exemplified by fragments from Colchester and Winchester. The latter dates to before 903 and depicts a group of three figures with a broad border, painted in red ochre, yellow, white and black (fig. 10). Hints of more ambitious schemes exist, as indicated by the remains of an elaborate painting dating to around 1000 over the chancel arch in the parish church at Nether Wallop, Hampshire; damaged by later works, it must have originally consisted of four flying angels supporting a figure of Christ in Majesty.[12] Documentary accounts also give occasional glimpses of the existence of wall-paintings, confirming that some religious establishments had elaborately decorated walls. There were painted images of former abbots at Glastonbury, and a wooden chapel built by St Edith shortly before 984 at the royal nunnery at Wilton, Hampshire, was decorated with paintings of Christ's Passion, said to have been executed in many colours, including blue and gold.

Although the surviving evidence is slight, there is little reason to doubt that, in the later Anglo-Saxon period, the interiors of rich ecclesiastical buildings were widely embellished with wall-paintings, sometimes even enriched with gold. For secular buildings, mostly built in wood, there is even less evidence; but the fragments of brightly woven hangings in the Sutton Hoo Mound 1 ship burial, and allusions to costly hangings in the great hall Heorot in *Beowulf,* suggest that colourful wall adornments were to be expected in the interior of high-status buildings, so it is likely that they too had painted and carved walls.

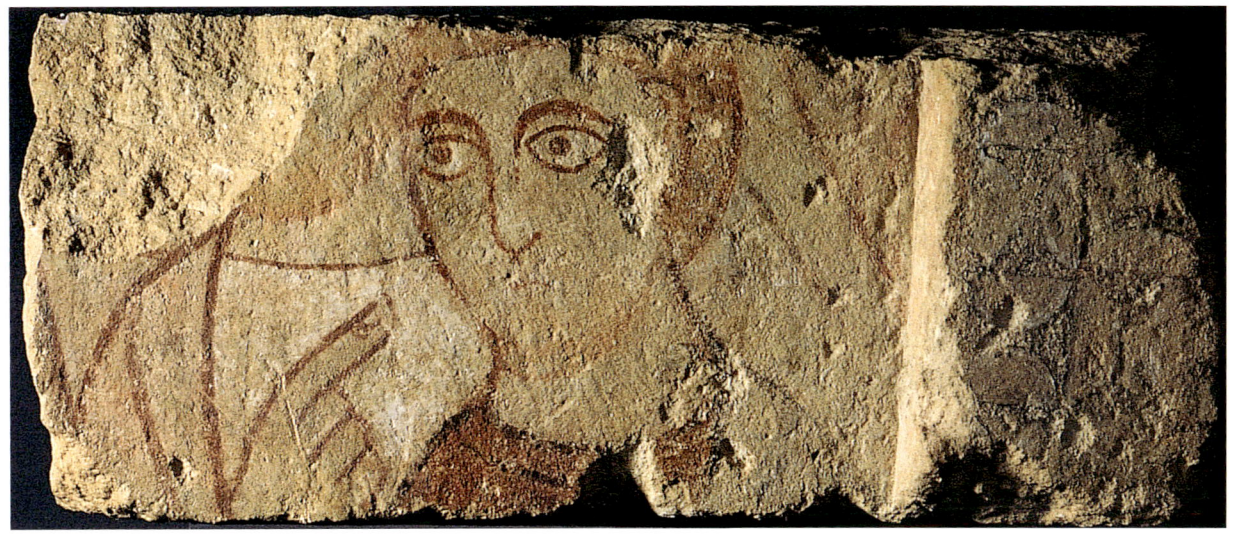

10. Wall-painting fragment with figures. Found during excavations at the Old Minster, Winchester. Before 903. L. 58.6 cm (Winchester City Museums)

Purpose and meaning

As these examples imply, in a society where relatively few outside the church and aristocracy were literate (even fewer before the Conversion), the reading of images was an all-important skill in negotiating one's way through social transactions. At a basic level, they could be as simple as an image on a coin, a flag, a ship's prow, or an emblem on a shield; at another, they could assert a complex origin myth, a protective charm, or a many-layered religious message – or all of these things. As the case of the brooch from Chessell Down illustrates, reading images at these more complex levels required patience to tease out the message. Christian writers called this process *ruminatio* – slowly chewing over the text or visual trope to extract every last nutritious bit – but pre-Christian Anglo-Saxons would have been long familiar with this concept. The knowledge required to understand the narratives embodied in the decoration of manuscripts, sculpture, and even rarer survivals such as the Franks Casket (see Chapter 3), was supported by a long tradition of image-reading.

A number of recent studies on Germanic bracteates (die-impressed gold sheet pendants) has shown that, although they are based on late Roman gold medals and coins depicting the emperor on his horse and other imperial themes, in the transposition to Germanic usage the meaning and appearance of the images is radically transformed.[13] Emperor and horse are reconfigured into an image of the Germanic god Woden/Odin and his attributes, sometimes accompanied by runic inscriptions which are clearly magical in intent (fig. 11). On these amulets, human and man/beast images represent not mortal men, but gods; sometimes depicted with attendant animals which both protect and threaten, the images also symbolize man's relationship with

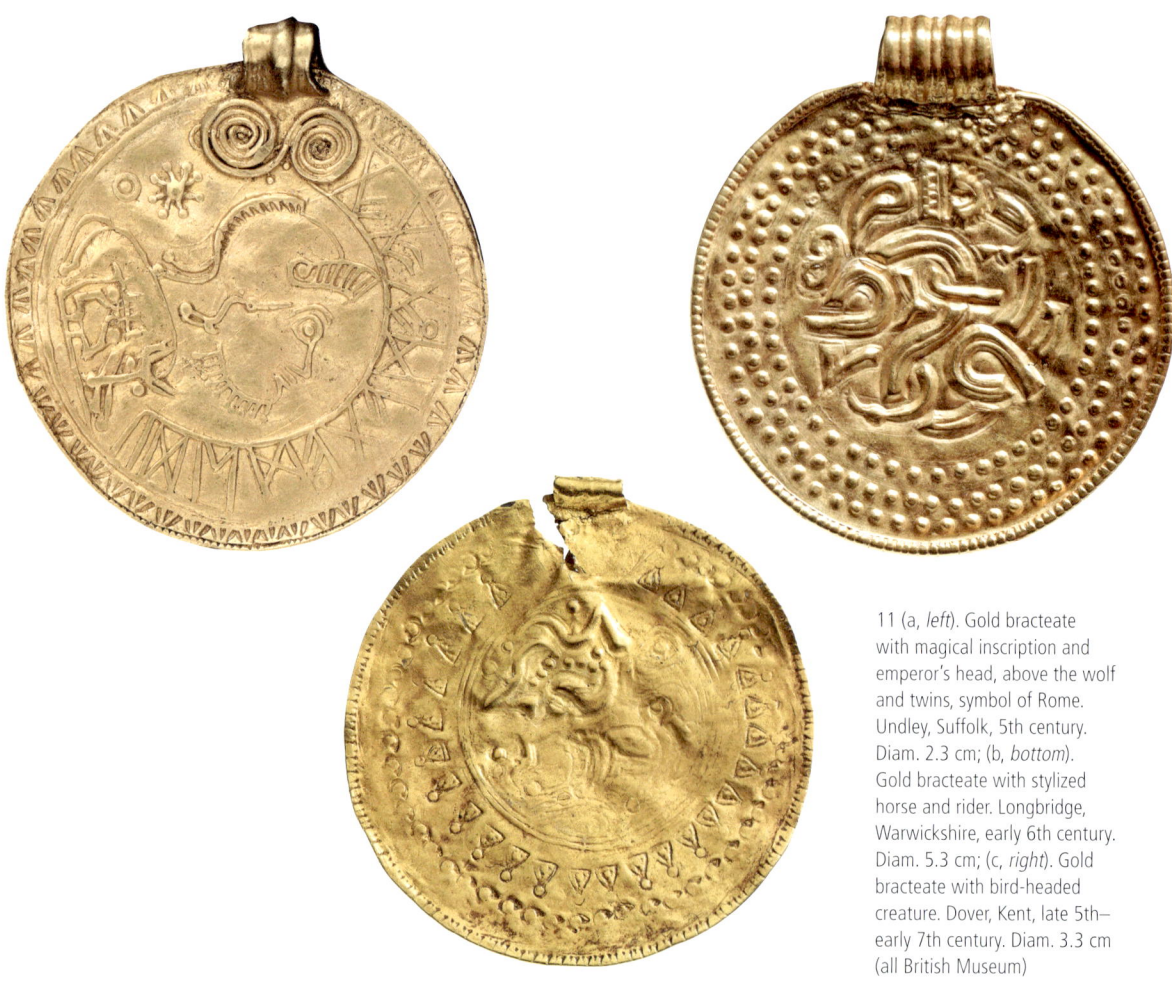

11 (a, *left*). Gold bracteate with magical inscription and emperor's head, above the wolf and twins, symbol of Rome. Undley, Suffolk, 5th century. Diam. 2.3 cm; (b, *bottom*). Gold bracteate with stylized horse and rider. Longbridge, Warwickshire, early 6th century. Diam. 5.3 cm; (c, *right*). Gold bracteate with bird-headed creature. Dover, Kent, late 5th–early 7th century. Diam. 3.3 cm (all British Museum)

the supernatural world, a source of protection, but also of danger. The decorative elements of the bracteates – helmeted heads, raised arms, crouching beasts, beaked birds and a variety of symbols – are clearly linked to Style I animal ornament on other high-status metalwork; and here, too, a mythic reading of the iconography has been suggested.

It has also been argued recently that the densely conceived zoomorphic decoration on Anglo-Saxon and Scandinavian high-status brooches and elite male gear is not only apotropaic – warding off evil and conferring protection – but may also refer to origin myths, signalling not just social identity, but where dynastic power actually originated. Recent Scandinavian studies have suggested that such objects, used by the elite, and decorated in the most extended and complex versions of this animal ornament, were displayed in cult and ceremonial contexts, which reinforced authority and social structures. Great square-headed brooches, related to the example from Chessell Down with which we began the chapter, sometimes appear worn prominently by women figured on some Scandinavian gold foil sheets which have a votive function. The images of gods and beasts on vessels used in communal feasting rituals may have proclaimed a lord's connection to mythic power, and in the shared act of drinking also signalled the protection given by him to his warrior retinue, in return for their loyalty (see fig. 34). On elaborately decorated shields, images of fierce creatures associated with the gods may have performed a similar role.[14] Complex messages about power, affiliation and protection are all here mediated through a gallery of mythic images.

The placing of symbolic ornament on high-status secular possessions did not end with the adoption of Christianity in the seventh century. A Christian message could be embedded in Germanic decoration, as a remarkable gold and garnet-inlaid sword pommel from Dinham, Shropshire, demonstrates (fig. 12). This object gives a new twist to the way in which Germanic tradition was adapted to the changing social and religious circumstances of the seventh century (see Chapter 5). At the centre of one side, the cloisonné inlay forms a central equal-armed cross, encircled within a halo composed of long and short cells, perhaps suggesting rays; at each corner of the pommel the eye gradually teases out the image of a round-eyed animal head in profile, with a long muzzle and a pointed ear. Animal heads in this position are known from other seventh-century sword pommels, and continue as a tradition on swords into the eighth century and later. But in this Christianized context it seems that they may represent not only a Germanic tradition of protective animal images, but also the creatures which, in early medieval Christian iconography, adored the figure of the Christ triumphant – as, for example, on the Ruthwell Cross (see fig. 59).

12. Gold and garnet sword pommel (both sides) with Christian motifs. Dinham, Shropshire, second quarter of the 7th century. L. 3 cm (Ludlow Museum)

Even more startling, on the other side of this sword pommel is an image dominated by a long-shafted cross in the centre, flanked by two smaller crosses on either side, and by mushroom-shaped garnets, perhaps suggesting trees. Above the central cross, a semicircular element containing a stepped garnet descends, in a manner reminiscent of the semicircular clouds from which the hand of God acknowledges his Son in early medieval convention (see also fig. 157). Flanking the foot of the central cross, and facing towards it, are two small beast heads, their mouths open, perhaps as if in praise, for this must also represent Creation's adoration of the risen Christ symbolized in the cross. The supplementary crosses are those of the two thieves crucified alongside Christ. The whole scheme is a subtle and wonderfully condensed image of the Crucifixion and its message of redemption. This highly compressed narrative is a contemporary Christian counterpart to equally elaborate pagan images seen, for instance, on the Sutton Hoo purselid (see fig. 77), and presented in a way which would have been wholly familiar to an Anglo-Saxon audience. Just like images in the Germanic tradition on which it draws, it is a powerful expression of religious belief and affiliation, but also gives protection to its owner. The idea of the Christian warrior, who is at the same time part of a long Germanic tradition, is one which recurs on prestige weapons throughout the Anglo-Saxon period.

An eighth-century helmet from Coppergate in York certainly belonged to a Christian warrior, as is made clear by a cruciform prayer which crosses its crown in a powerful invocation of divine protection (fig. 13). But the prayer is set in frames which terminate in fierce guardian animal heads, recalling similar creatures from earlier pagan metalwork; the eyebrows, too, end in apotropaic snarling beasts, just like those on the unequivocally pagan Sutton Hoo helmet. Other items of eighth- to ninth-century warrior equipment bearing Christian inscriptions and symbols alongside an older tradition of image-making include scabbard mounts from swords and seaxes; purely magical charms sometimes occur on these as well (see figs 105 and 108). The conflation of Christian ideas with older motifs resurfaces in the later tenth and eleventh centuries on a number of Anglo-Scandinavian stirrup mounts. They display an image of a male figure with outstretched arms, enveloped in interlacing bands, in which the idea of the binding of the Norse god Odin seems to be combined with the image of Christ crucified (see fig. 183).

The decorative schemes of grand religious manuscripts and sculpture very obviously invite close attention; but close reading can also be required for smaller-scale ecclesiastical artefacts. Items such as reliquaries and panels from book covers can embody complex iconographies, the smaller scale lending itself to more elliptical schemes, reminiscent of the way in which compressed narratives appear in some of the earliest Anglo-Saxon metalwork. This can be seen in a whale-bone chrismatory known as the Gandersheim Casket, which was probably made near Peterborough in the late eighth century (see fig. 100). It is covered with panels of delicate animal ornament, vine scroll and interlace, which at first glance seem to contain no obvious Christian message. Yet on closer study it reveals a subtle iconography of divine cosmology and redemption, expressed through the symbolic numerology of its precisely gridded structure, and the vine scrolls, crosses and images of God's Creation that populate its densely decorated surfaces (see p. 106).

Another even more condensed iconography is seen in the elaborate gold, rock-crystal and enamelled manuscript pointer known as the Alfred

13. Iron helmet with copper-alloy crest and other fittings. Found during excavations at Coppergate, York. Second half of the 8th century. H. 24.6 cm (Yorkshire Museum)

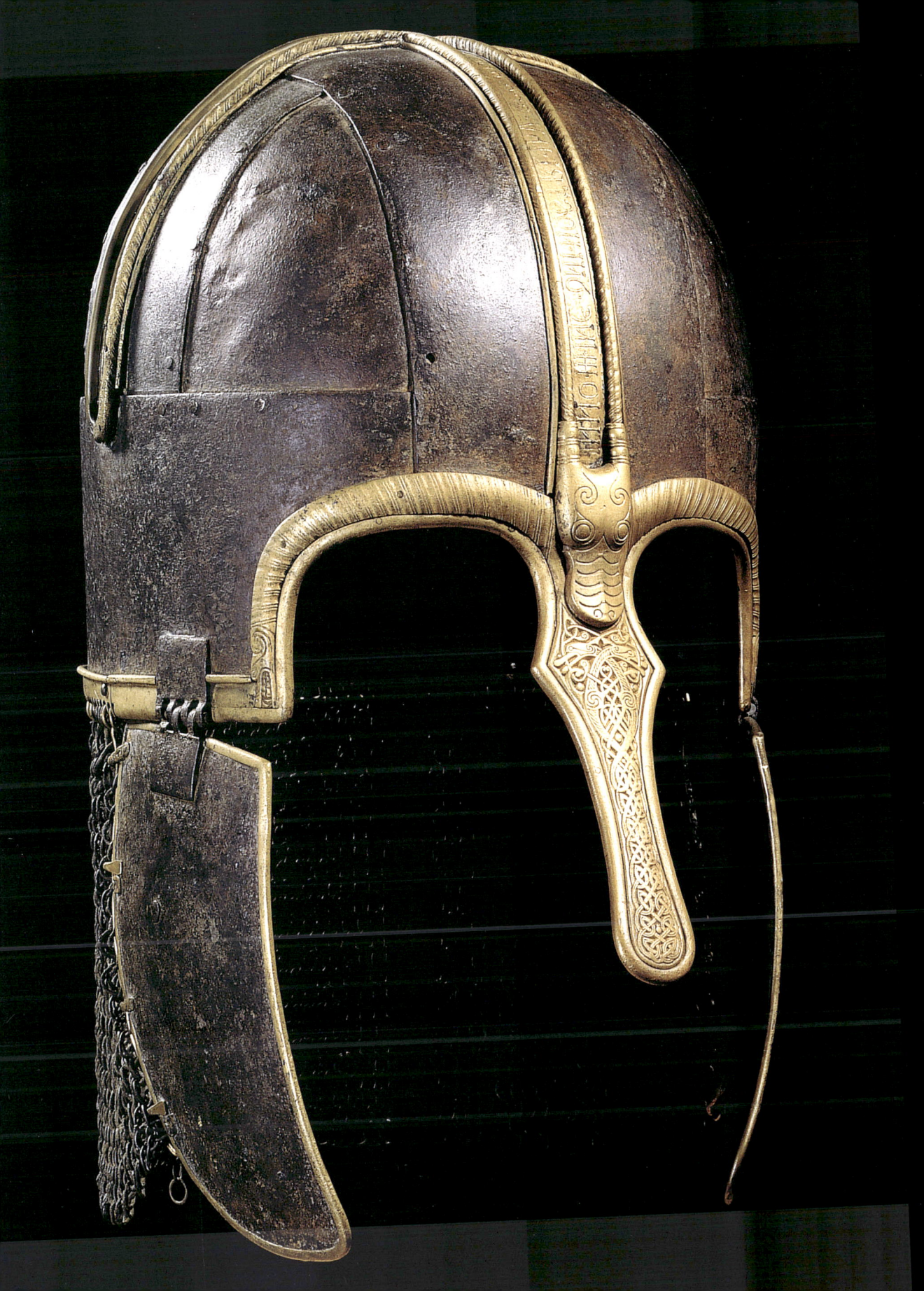

Jewel (fig. 114; see the detailed discussion on pp. 154–6). It is thought to be the handle of an ecclesiastical manuscript pointer, a function supported by its distinctive form and decoration. The enamelled image which dominates the jewel is of a wide-eyed figure holding two flowering wands; the subject of much debate over the years, it has been convincingly argued to be a personification of Sight as the conduit of Wisdom – a recurrent theme in texts that Alfred had translated and circulated, and a very appropriate image for an implement intended to aid the act of reading and learning.[15] The pointer has no need for an explanatory label; to the Anglo-Saxon user, understanding the connection between the image and the function of the pointer would have been an inseparable part of the act of studying the Bible and other religious works.

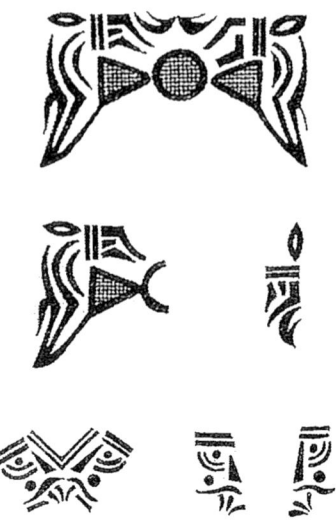

Riddles and ambiguities

Many of the examples given above have an intriguing, riddling aspect to their nature; indeed, ambiguities and paradoxes are threaded throughout Anglo-Saxon literary and visual culture. Early Anglo-Saxon metalwork abounds in visual riddles – images which can be read in more than one way.[16] On the head-plate of some sixth-century square-headed brooches of Kentish type, for example, the animals can be read as crouching beasts, or, by rotating the view, as human profiled heads attached to animal bodies; alternatively two of the profiled human heads can together make an animal mask (fig. 14). These ambiguous creatures are related to the hybrids seen on the Chessell Down brooch but, unlike them, morph from man into beast according to the orientation – rather like the shape-shifters of medieval legends. On one of the Taplow drinking-horn terminals of similar date, a pair of backward-looking crouching animals is seen when the horn is held horizontally; but if the horn is tipped up, they turn into a stylized mask with a scrolled mouth, like the masks on the horn's rim mount (figs 15 and 34). This is a message for the drinker, to see and ponder, as Hrothgar did with the sword that beheaded Grendel and his mother – another of those points where literature and art seem to walk a parallel path. Perhaps the most memorable of these shape-shifters, though, is the stern face of the Sutton Hoo helmet, with its heavy brows, long nose and bristling moustache, which on inspection turns into a flying dragon with wings outspread. This fierce creature, guardian of treasure and destroyer of homes in legend, would have both protected the wearer and sent fear into the heart of the enemy (fig. 16).

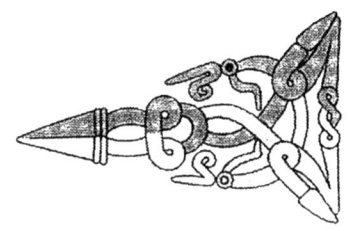

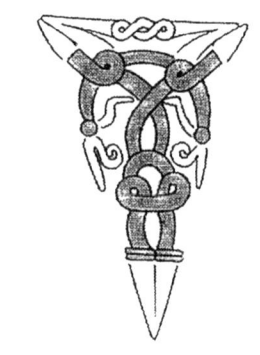

This distinctive and specifically northern taste for riddling images is one of the elements that marks out Anglo-Saxon art as different to the products of most other contemporary cultures. Nothing quite like this exists in early Irish or Pictish metalwork or sculpture, or in the naturalistic decoration of late Roman and Byzantine art, and it is a tradition which is continued into the art of later centuries. The extraordinary parade of stylized creatures that writhe and gape over the surfaces of an eighth-century silver-gilt sword pommel from near Woodeaton, Oxfordshire, are seen conventionally by the onlooker when the sword-blade points downwards, but become a sombre horned beast mask when the sword is held with the blade pointing outwards, as when fighting (fig. 17). More modest objects, such as strap-ends, can also show the same delight in puzzles which are perhaps simply for entertainment – the birds that become a beast head with a fox-like muzzle when the object is turned upside down;[17] or the conventional animal mask on a ninth-century strap-end that turns into an owl-like bird when looked at the other way up (fig. 18).

14 (*opposite*). Examples of Style I ornament showing riddling animal-men. *Above*) animals incorporating human profiles; *below*) animal mask formed of human profiles (Drawings after Leigh 1984)

15 (*opposite*). Style I riddling motif from a drinking-horn terminal, Taplow, Buckinghamshire. *Above*) as two animals, *below*) as a mask (Drawings after Webster 2003a)

16 (*right*). Helmet (replica) with an ambiguous visage formed from a dragon. Original from the Mound 1 ship burial, Sutton Hoo, Suffolk, early 7th century. H. 34 cm (British Museum)

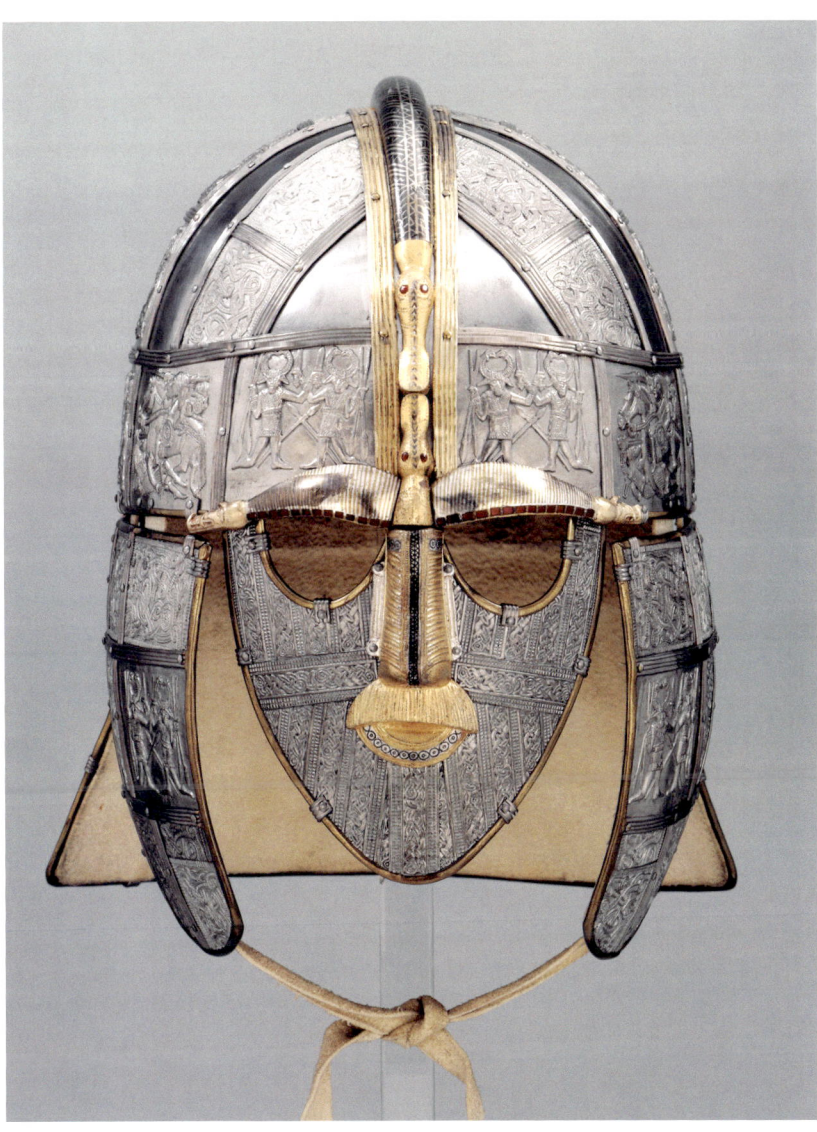

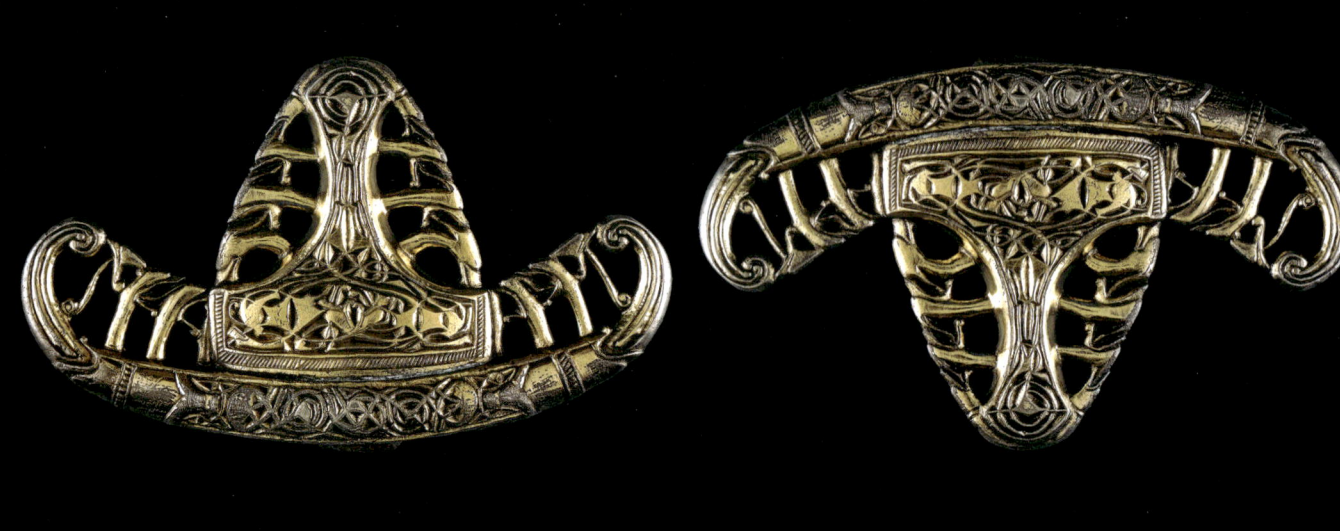

17. Two views of a silver-gilt sword pommel with animal ornament, showing a horned animal mask when inverted. Woodeaton area, Oxfordshire, late 8th century. L. 9.9 cm (British Museum)

Anglo-Saxon vernacular riddles were certainly used for entertainment, as the impressive compilation in the manuscript known as the Exeter Book suggests, and show a rich and diverting vein of wordplay and invention. But, like the Latin *enigmata* on which many of them were modelled, these would have also played an important role in the Anglo-Saxon classroom. They were intended to stretch the mind and hone its agility, as well as to instruct in Latin prosody, in the case of riddles in Latin. But they also taught the reader to discover 'the secret riddles of created things', as Aldhelm, the most prolific Anglo-Saxon writer of Latin riddles, wrote in his treatise *De metris*. In other words, they were, like their visual counterparts, an invitation to ruminate on the outward signs of the mystery of life. One of Aldhelm's riddles describes a chrismatory, similar in its house-like shape to surviving Anglo-Saxon examples;[18] and it is an interesting coincidence that the decoration on at least two of these, including the Gandersheim chrismatory mentioned above, itself contains visual riddles. Thus the inventive menagerie of the Gandersheim chrismatory at first glance conceals its biblical Christological and numerological symbolism beneath the sprightly elegance of the decoration, as do the puzzle inscriptions and the winged and prancing symbolic animals of another late eighth-century gilded copper chrismatory, discussed in Chapter 6 (see pp. 165–7).

Humans and animals

The long-lived Anglo-Saxon fascination with zoomorphic decoration is one of the most striking aspects of the art, unique in the early medieval period. The stylized formulaic creatures of early metalwork, the elegant animals of eighth-century manuscripts and sculptural inhabited vine scrolls, the quirky beasts of ninth-century brooches, and the birds and creatures that perch in the lush foliage of tenth-century strap-ends are all part of an unbroken tradition. As we have also seen, hidden man/beast hybrids and shape-shifters form part of the

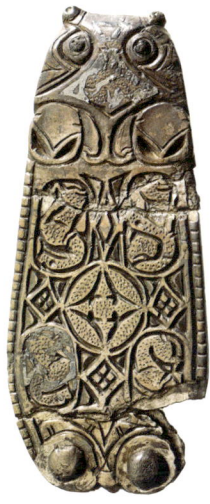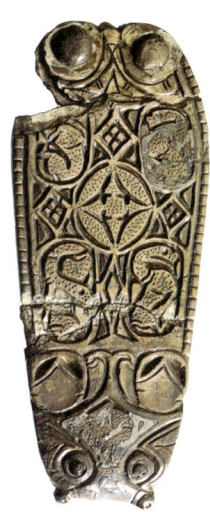

18. Dual reading of a silver strap-end: the orientation on the left shows an owl-like creature; when reversed (at right), the owl's head becomes that of an eared animal. Braughing, Hertfordshire, 9th century. L. 5.4 cm (British Museum)

riddling tradition that runs through Anglo-Saxon art. In these strange bondings, in later images of humans, beasts and vegetation intricately bound up with one another, and in the persistence of animal art itself, the interdependence of man and the natural world is a pervasive theme – whether expressed in terms of Christian iconography, as a reflection of pagan cosmology, or as pure diversion.

One of the particular characteristics of Anglo-Saxon manuscript art in the seventh and eighth centuries is, as we have seen, its wonderfully inventive animal decoration. By the end of the eighth century, one can see in the decoration of manuscripts such as the Barberini Gospels the further development of a playful, sometimes grotesque, mixture of animal, human and plant elements, in which classical and native motifs combine in exuberant display (see fig. 89 and Chapters 4 and 5). Very few decorated manuscripts survive from the ninth century, but the quirky creatures and occasional humans which combine to form initials in a range of late ninth- and tenth-century manuscripts show that the Anglo-Saxon fascination with the interplay of man and nature survived the troubled times of the first Viking wars. A tenth-century copy of Bede's *Ecclesiastical History* is one of a number of manuscripts from this period in which man and animals cavort together in the decoration of initials. It contains, among other lively decorated initials, one in which the bow of the letter is formed by a clambering acrobat, and which terminates in a biting beast and a bird (fig. 19). There is no contemporary Continental source for initials such as these, suggesting that Anglo-Saxon illuminators may have drawn on their own traditions when they developed these inventive ways of combining the human image with animal ornament (see Chapter 6, p. 175).

On the other hand, naturalistic human images are rare indeed in the early period. Those that do survive seem in every case to be connected with cult practices, and are to be seen as images from the world of gods, not of men. The unique brooding seated figure on a lid from a pottery cremation urn at Spong Hill, North Elmham, Norfolk, is in a real sense a watcher over the dead (fig. 20). His power is signalled by the throne he sits on, which is very similar to a fifth-century decorated wooden ceremonial chair from a Saxon chieftain's burial at Fallward, north Germany.[19] In recent years, a number of small gilded silver or bronze figures, both male and female, have also been found in England; two come from seventh-century burials, but most are without known contexts (fig. 21). Like the Spong figure, they are three-dimensional, and the silver figures in particular are carefully modelled in delicate detail. Most share a distinctive gesture, with one arm raised up across the body, the other pointing down to the genital area. On the more detailed figures, the breasts of the female figures and the penises of the men are emphasized, suggesting perhaps that they may represent deities associated with fertility. Similar figures from Denmark and Sweden have been found in buildings and deposits possibly associated with cult ceremonies at sites of power, and it is likely that these Anglo-Saxon versions were also intended for ritual or magical purposes.

Other rare depictions of human figures from this period also seem to refer to ritual activities. Images of a near-naked spear-carrying warrior with a horned headdress appear on two seventh-century buckles from opposite ends of the country. One comes from a man's grave at Finglesham, Kent (fig. 22), the other is a stray find from Ayton in the Scottish Borders (at that time in the Anglo-Saxon kingdom of Northumbria).[20] They are clearly related to the dancing warriors found on both the Sutton Hoo helmet (see fig. 16) and on contemporary Swedish dies for making foil plates for helmets. Their appearance on such high-status male objects may well have been protective in function.

The rarity of these human images, their stylization and their presumed pagan role make the rapid appearance of naturalistic human images in the manuscripts and sculpture of the earliest Anglo-Saxon Christian art seem at first all the more startling. Recurrent ecclesiastical concerns about the veneration of divine and human images, seen most spectacularly in the eighth-century iconoclastic controversy in Byzantium, were allayed by

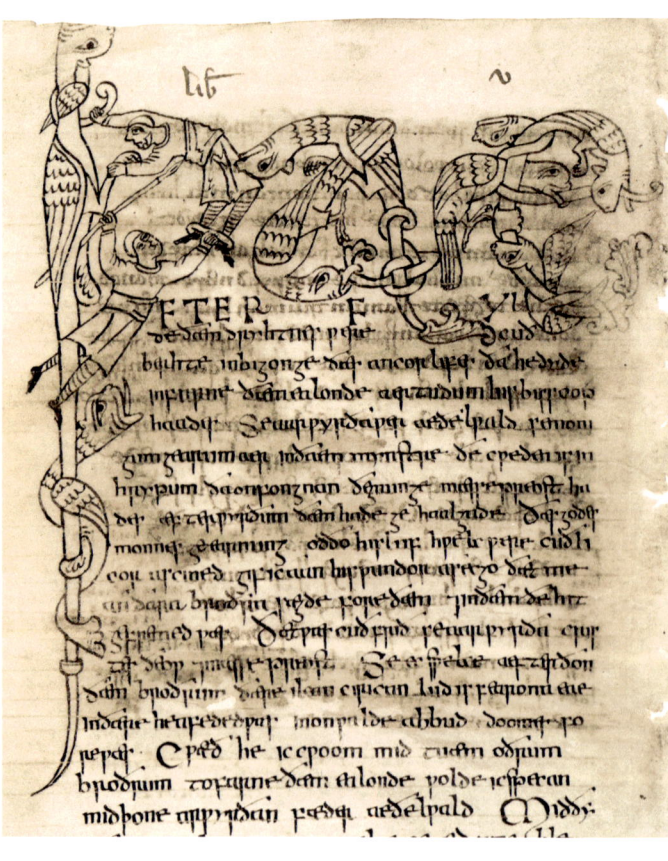

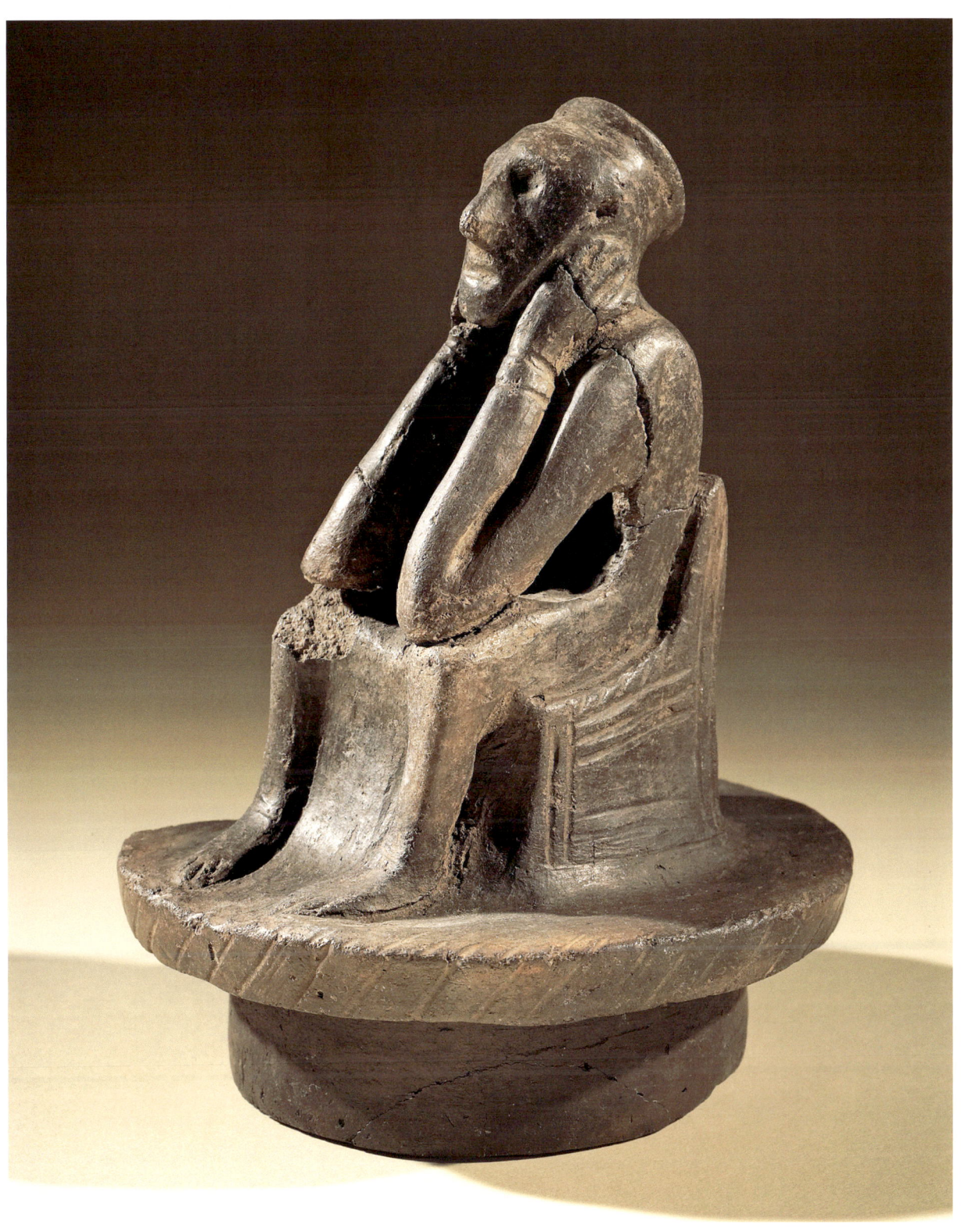

supportive commentaries on key biblical texts by Gregory III, Bede and others. The Anglo-Saxons embraced a more naturalistic, classicizing representation of the human figure with remarkable alacrity and sophistication. It has been suggested that the magisterial figures on eighth-century Northumbrian monuments such as the Ruthwell, Bewcastle and Otley crosses, with their realistic proportions and carefully modelled draperies, reflected the influence of Roman figure sculptures which were still to be seen throughout the former Roman frontier zone of the north. But even more influential must have been the contemporary imports from Gaul, Italy and Byzantium; not only illuminated manuscripts, painted panels, textiles and ivories, but craftsmen too – all of which reached even the far north of England in this period (see Chapters 3 and 4). As succeeding chapters will relate, manuscripts from the early eighth century onwards show how Italian and Byzantine models, and, later on, Carolingian versions, were influential in the figural art of Anglo-Saxons following the Conversion, though in the process of copying, these new models were also transformed into something recognizably within that older Anglo-Saxon tradition of surface patterning and movement.

A clash of traditions?

The rapidity of assimilation of Christian art forms noted above is important. Anglo-Saxon art has sometimes misleadingly been portrayed in terms of a barbaric tradition which, in its love of pattern, complex rhythms and fractured surfaces, was in opposition to a classical aesthetic. Kendrick, a wonderfully intuitive interpreter of Anglo-Saxon art, described it as 'a sustained struggle between fundamentally opposed types of artistic expression . . . the strange glittering brilliance of the lively mosaic pattern seen through the kaleidoscope, . . . [and] the familiar and friendly picture in a mirror held up to reflect the visible world'.[21] But as this introductory chapter has tried to show, and the following chapters will develop, this is a more complex and interesting story than one simply of tensions between opposites, as it has often been presented in the past.

One of the chief reasons why Anglo-Saxon art was able to assimilate so swiftly the new modes of depiction and iconographies shaped for Christian learning was because both traditions required images to be read. As we shall see, the earliest Anglo-Saxon art adapted the vocabulary of late Roman metalwork to its own grammar and meaning. When the introduction of Christianity brought new kinds of artefacts, new messages and new ways of communicating these messages, they too were absorbed and subtly transformed to fit the existing tradition – just as in Anglo-Saxon poetry, scriptural characters such as Judith and St Andrew were presented in terms which recalled the Germanic heroes of epic verse. This was a process of assimilation, not opposition. To return to the image with which this chapter opens, the mighty sword-hilt that

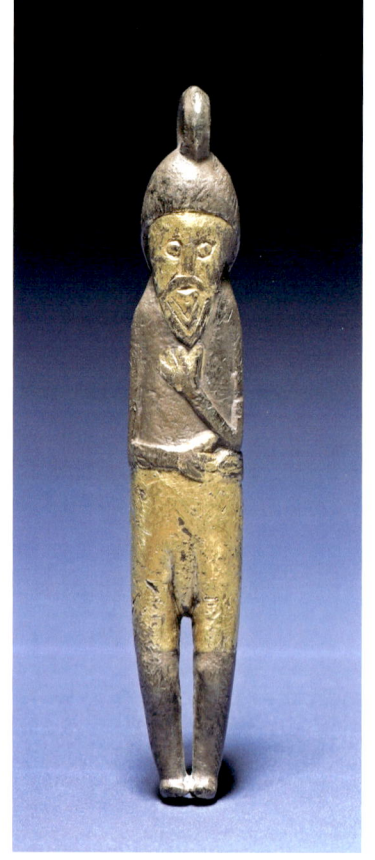

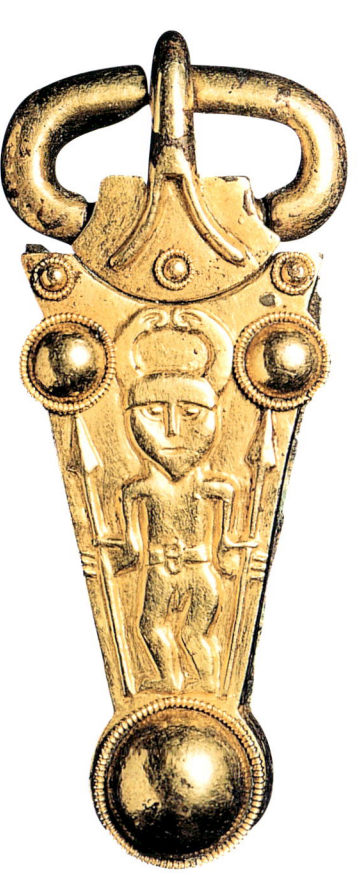

Beowulf presents to Hrothgar is portrayed as an antique relic, 'the ancient work of giants'. Yet its decoration, so carefully scrutinized by Hrothgar, tells a biblical story, in a poem which, although it records heroic deeds performed in a distant Germanic past, is suffused with Christianity and delivers a wholly Christian message. Arguably the most impressive aspect of Anglo-Saxon artistic and literary culture is that it was so receptive to external influences, yet was able to transform them in radical ways. The chapters that follow will trace the changing nature of Anglo-Saxon art as it adopted, adapted and reshaped these incoming influences within its own enduring traditions.

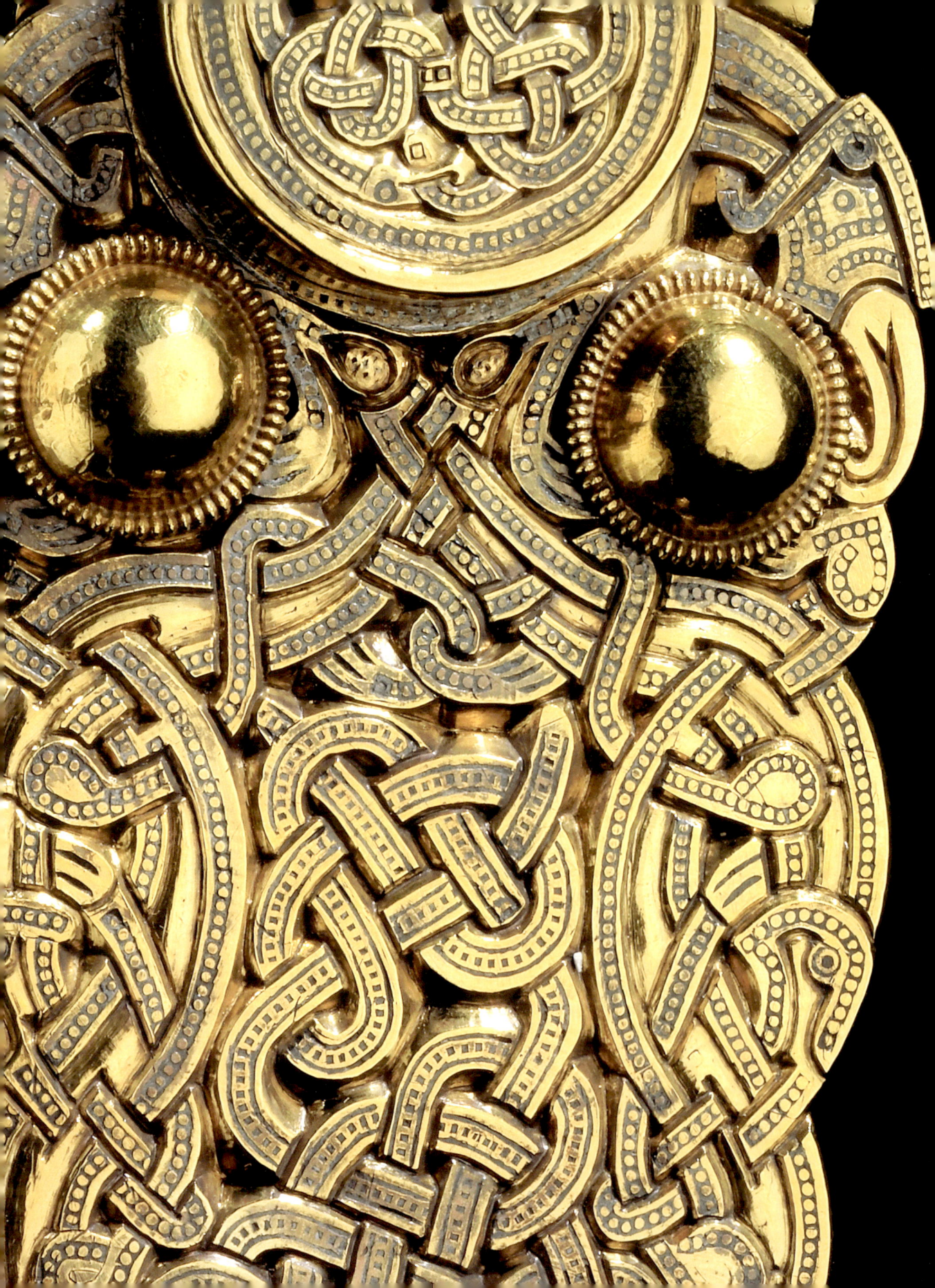

CHAPTER 2

I have been with the Franks and with the Frisians
and with the Frumtingas. I have been with the Rugas
and with the Glommas and the Romans. I have also
been in Italy with Aelfwine, son of Eadwine, who, I
have heard, had the promptest hand among mankind
in achieving praise, and a heart quite unniggardly in
giving out rings and gleaming collars . . . I have been
with the Greeks and with the Finns, and with Caesar
who held sway over festive cities, over riches and
desirable things, and over the empire of the Romans.

Widsith, lines 68–78[1]

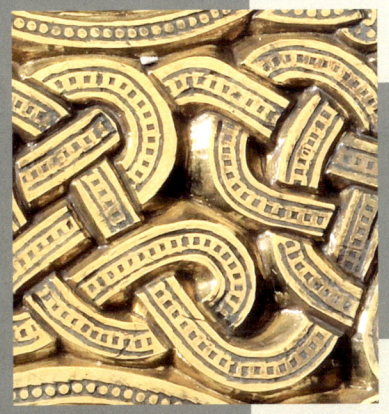

The Sutton Hoo gold
buckle (see fig. 42).

ROME REINVENTED: THE EARLY INHERITANCE

Rome and *Germania*

The popular image of the Anglo-Saxons (when not, as all too often, confused with the Vikings) is as being wholly Germanic from first to last. Films such as *The 13th Warrior* (1999), *Beowulf* (2007) and the adaptations of J.R.R. Tolkein's *Lord of the Rings* trilogy have been largely inspired by idealized literary constructs of Anglo-Saxon warrior culture. There is a hearty emphasis on dragons, monsters and treasure, drawn from tales of legendary heroism in *Beowulf* and other Anglo-Saxon, Norse and Germanic sources. Yet the reality was much more complicated. Conscious as they certainly were of their Germanic past, and its European background, Anglo-Saxons knew that they lived in the shadow of Rome. They were both heirs of the Romans who had preceded them, and – from the beginning of the seventh century – followers of Christianity, which had its focus in the eternal city of Rome.

The Old English poem known as *Widsith*, meaning the 'far-traveller', which may date back to the seventh century, is named after the bard who addresses the audience. He tells of the great lords whom he has served and who in turn have rewarded him with gifts of treasure, and he lists the many kings, tribes and peoples he knows of or has journeyed with. On one level, the poem acts as a memory aid for the professional poet, a sort of index of heroic themes for recital at lordly feasts and other such occasions. But, as a poem which is suffused by a sense of times and peoples past, it consciously evokes the sweep of ages of the great European migrations that took place in what we now call the early medieval period, and of the wider world context in which the past happened. Germanic names predominate in this list, yet Widsith's view of the world is not restricted to his own ancestors: Alexander and Caesar are mentioned, and Saracens and Greeks figure, as well as Medes and Persians, Hebrews and Egyptians. As the quotation at the opening of this chapter indicates, Romans and the Roman Empire are prominent. This is a Germanic view of the world, but it is also one which has seamlessly absorbed the Christian idea of universal history, in which the three histories of mankind known to the early medieval church – Germanic, Roman and biblical – all converged on Christ's Incarnation and on Rome, centre of Christianity.

The Germanic past was certainly important to the cultural identity of its peoples, Anglo-Saxons among them. Tacitus, in his *Germania*, the history of the Germanic tribes with which Rome was so embattled in the first century AD, writes that the songs of the Germans were their sole record of history. In a society in which writing (in runes) was confined to brief inscriptions on wood and metal, orally transmitted heroic tales and ancestral myths of the kind alluded to in *Widsith* were central to identity. Germanic identities in this early period also clearly manifested themselves through visual signals, including distinctive dress and hair fashions: Anglian women, for instance, wore long-sleeved dresses with decorated wrist-fastenings, the Frankish kings were famous for their long hair, and the Suebi of northern Germany sported a knotted hairstyle. Art, too, played a vital part in creating identities, as noted in the previous chapter. We see it chiefly in the animal art of surviving fifth- and sixth-century high-status metalwork, with its probable representations of origin myths; but it must also have existed in more perishable media, such as textiles, and bone and wooden artefacts.

But – as *Widsith* implies – the Germanic peoples who lived outside the empire, and then came to settle in it, were also very conscious of being, in a real sense, the heirs of Rome. This too was a part of their identity. When the Frankish king Childeric died in 482, he was buried at Tournai (in present-day Belgium) with all the panoply of both a Roman imperial officer and a Frankish warrior king. His burial was accompanied by grave goods in the Germanic tradition, among them many ostentatiously lavish gold and garnet-inlaid items, including magnificently decorated weapons, horse trappings and personal jewellery, as well as an array of slaughtered horses, another distinctive

Germanic custom. But the dead king was dressed in garments adorned with the gold cross-bow brooches that designated high imperial office, and he wore a Roman-style gold signet ring with his image and title in Latin, *Childerici Regis*, '[in the name of] King Childeric'. In the image on the ring's bezel, Childeric wears distinctive Roman body armour (the *lorica*) and carries a spear, but his hair is long and braided, in Frankish style. In addition, the purse he was buried with contained at least three hundred Roman gold and silver coins, a symbol both of Roman largesse and of kingly treasure.

Only a few years later, in 508, we see something similar, when the Byzantine emperor Anastasius (*c.* 430–518) conferred the imperial title of consul on the Frankish king Clovis (*c.* 466–511). The scene is vividly described by Gregory of Tours in his *History of the Franks* (Book 2, 38): the king rode through the streets of Tours dressed in a purple tunic and military cloak and crowned with a diadem, showering gold and silver coins among the multitude. The image neatly combines Roman imperial *largitio* – the distribution of gold and silver in coin, jewellery and plate to buy favour and foster allegiances – and the importance of treasure and gift-giving in the Germanic tradition. But, like the Roman insignia in Childeric's grave, it also makes a point about legitimizing the authority of a Germanic successor to Roman rule in the West.

These royal Frankish examples have clear echoes in Anglo-Saxon England, explored further in Chapter 5. Many Anglo-Saxon kingly trappings – their genealogies and coins, for example – deliberately evoke a Roman inheritance. Even their buildings occasionally perform this role, such as the tiered assembly place at the royal palace complex at Yeavering, Northumberland, which recalls the segment of a Roman amphitheatre. It is not by chance that the surviving East Anglian king-list, dated to the late seventh century, has Caesar as the ultimate progenitor of the dynasty, succeeded by a series of soundly Germanic names. But from even before the first settlers had left the Continental homelands, Rome was already an integral part of their history, its influence vividly expressed in the art of their metalwork.

The continuing sense of a Roman inheritance was further developed through the Anglo-Saxon adoption of Roman Christianity in the course of the seventh century, and then reinvigorated through contact with a reinvented Roman Empire under the Carolingian rulers (see Chapter 6). But, as with the Frankish kings and many other Germanic successors to Roman rule, and as *Widsith* so clearly shows, the potent image of Rome is assimilated to a Germanic version of the past. Roman largesse becomes the Germanic treasure hoard; the Roman emperor on a gold coin becomes a protective image of the god Woden on a Germanic gold bracteate; and on the extraordinary object we know today as the Franks Casket, the stories of Rome, of the Bible and of a heroic Germanic past intersect in one overarching Christian *exemplum*, or moral tale (see p. 96 and fig. 66). In the art of the Anglo-Saxons, as with the wider cultural tradition, the history and symbolism of the Roman world was inextricably bound up with its Germanic inheritance, and indeed was seen as part of the same history.

The fifth-century inheritance

The history of the Anglo-Saxon settlement of Britain in the fifth century is full of gaps and uncertainties, largely because of the paucity and unreliability of the written records. No near-contemporary account of the earliest settlers exists. The Northumbrian historian Bede's great *Ecclesiastical History of the English People*, written in the early eighth century, gives as authoritative an account of the fifth-century settlements as he was able to construct from the documents and oral sources available to him; but these were relatively few, certainly partial and sometimes contradictory. The art and archaeology of this fugitive period are thus a major source of information for understanding the nature of the early settlements and their relationship to the native Romano-British population, nowhere more vividly than through the earliest Anglo-Saxon metalwork.

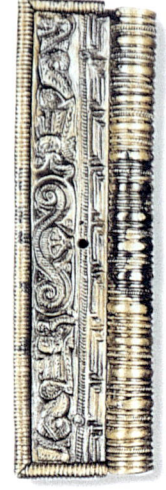
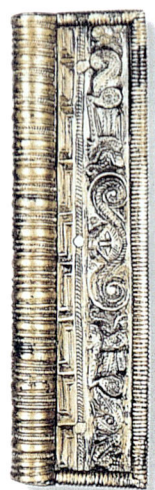

The first settlers arriving in fifth-century Britain from north Germany, southern Scandinavia and the Frisian coast encountered Roman cultural traditions in two quite different ways. As noted earlier, some of these settlers would have had contact with Roman culture, and especially with the Roman army manning the northern frontiers of the empire: from across the frontier, they were able to acquire gold coins, fine metalwork and doubtless much else. This came as booty from raids, but also from imperial payments intended to buy barbarian support; and a significant part came from Germanic soldiers who had served as troops in the army. Some may even have served and settled in Britannia, either under the Romans or under the Romano-British *civitates* who, left to manage their own affairs after the Roman army had withdrawn in 410, sought help from Germanic warlords, according to some sources. Certainly the prominent buckles worn by the late Roman military and other officials, with their distinctive glittering chip-carved geometric decoration (see p. 51 below), and mask and animal motifs, were much prized by Continental Germanic peoples and by Anglo-Saxons, as their appearance in high-status fifth-century male graves indicates (fig. 23). Copies of such prestige buckles, adapted to various native idioms, were also made in Scandinavia and Britain, for example the elaborate set from a male burial at Mucking, Essex (fig. 24).

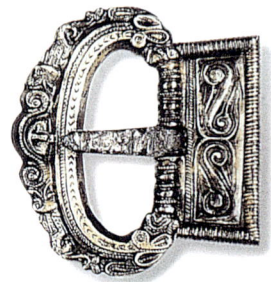

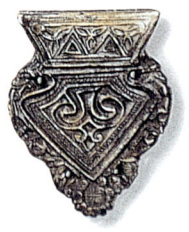

23. Silver-gilt belt-set of a late Roman military type, from a man's grave. Fallward, Lower Saxony, Germany, early 5th century. Max. L. 11 cm (Museum Burg Bederkesa, Bad Bederkesa)

Equally influential were the huge quantities of Roman gold medallions and coinage that circulated beyond the frontiers of empire, treasure paid out to the neighbouring tribes to buy peace, as well as acquired as loot. Much of this was transformed into prestige jewellery, such as the magnificent gold collars, bracteates and arm-rings found in Sweden, southern Norway and Denmark.[2] But thousands of these coins and medallions were also accumulated in huge treasure hoards and ritual deposits, particularly in Scandinavia. And, most significantly, they were imitated. The decoration of these imperial coins and medallions, and of the official issue metalwork, had profound effects on the art of these Germanic peoples. It was a key element in the creation of what we now call Style I animal art in Scandinavia and in the distinctive decoration of Saxon brooches (see p. 51). Transmitted through such routes, the influence of late Roman metalwork became an essential ingredient in the making of the earliest Anglo-Saxon art.

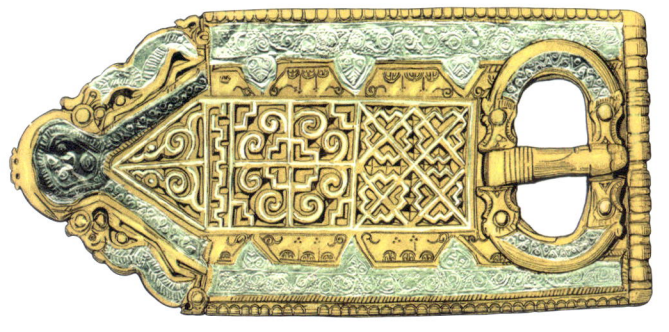

24. Copper-alloy and silver buckle (reconstruction drawing) from a late Roman-type military belt-set, from a male burial. Mucking, Essex, 5th century. L. 5.9 cm (buckle, British Museum; drawing by Judith Dobie, English Heritage)

Having crossed the sea, with their experience of Roman culture under and indeed worn on their belts, these early Anglo-Saxons, who had always lived beyond the frontier, encountered a rather different version of it in the former Roman province of Britannia. Regular attacks from barbarians on all sides – Picts and Irish, as well as Saxons from across the North Sea – had weakened the province over many years, and pressures elsewhere on the empire's frontiers caused Rome to finally withdraw its troops from the defence of Britain in 410. Nevertheless, in much of the country the population still kept up some form of Roman culture, including Roman Christianity.

Although it was a province in retreat, with a steady decline of active town and villa life that had begun back in the fourth century, Britain was still a rich and desirable land. This was especially the case in the prime areas in which the Anglo-Saxons settled – the lowlands of the east and south – where they encountered standing towns, monuments, large estates and villas. A number of late Roman gold and silver hoards of coins, tableware and jewellery buried in East Anglia and Kent in the early fifth century also testify to the wealth – as well as the fears – of some rich Romano-British families at this time.[3] The traditional accounts of the Anglo-Saxon settlement, based in part on the polemic of a sixth-century British writer, Gildas, suggest a violent series of assaults by the incomers, furiously driving the inhabitants westward out of their lands until stemmed by a British leader who may have been the ultimate inspiration for the King Arthur of legend. The archaeological evidence, on the other hand, hints that in the south and east, the principal heartlands of early Anglo-Saxon settlement, many Romano-Britons simply adopted the culture of the incomers. Most notably in the Thames estuary, in southern Sussex and in Kent, there is some evidence for the assimilation of Romano-Britons into Anglo-Saxon communities, adopting new burial customs, yet – sometimes – keeping their own costume styles, jewellery and possessions. In the north and west of England, British kingdoms continued independently throughout the fifth century and beyond; and even in the south-east, the continuing post-Roman survival of a Christian martyr cult at St Albans, and the lack of archaeological evidence for early Anglo-Saxon settlement in a great arc of land north of London from the Chilterns to Essex has suggested the existence of some British communities.[4]

The landscape provided another form of Roman inheritance. Although there is some archaeological evidence for casual Anglo-Saxon activity in Roman towns such as Canterbury and York, the fifth-century incomers, with their agrarian culture, had little use for urban structures, living instead in farmstead communities, which made good use of the Romano-British rural landscape and its resources.[5] The Roman inheritance was still tangible all around them: over 150 years later, when Pope Gregory's Christian missions introduced a new vision of Rome and what it was to be a member of the Roman Church, Anglo-Saxons readily acknowledged this Roman past, and its highly visible monuments. The Anonymous *Life of St Cuthbert* describes how, in the later seventh century, the saint was taken round the Roman town of Carlisle by a local official and shown a fine fountain in the centre. This was a city that still had meaning for the local people nearly three hundred years after the formal withdrawal of Roman rule in Britannia, a meaning which also had profound resonance for the Christian missionaries and saints who preached in these places. The Old English poem known as *The Ruin* describes, with a haunting regret for times past, a city of stone, fallen into decay, a city of hot springs where formerly there was feasting and joy:

> There were bright city buildings, many bathhouses, a wealth of
> lofty gables, much clamour of the multitude, many a meadhall
> filled with human revelry – until mighty Fate changed all that.
> *The Ruin*, lines 21–3[6]

The poem is a Christian meditation on the transience of earthly things, but its detailed physical description of the Roman city – its red-tiled roofs, its plastered walls and its baths fed by hot springs – reveals a sharp awareness of the Roman past that framed the Anglo-Saxon presence. Surrounded by the visible stamp of Rome on the landscape, intermingled with the descendants of a fifth-century Romano-British population and their culture, and bringing with them ideas of Roman tradition that their forebears had developed on the Continent, the early Anglo-Saxons developed an art which owed much to both these strands – and which was readily able to adopt and adapt new influences from Rome when they arrived with Christianity in the seventh century.

Understanding styles

Much of the surviving art from this early period, up to the seventh century, comes from burials: it occurs on personal or symbolic objects placed with the dead or, as in the case of cremation urns, specially made containers for their ashes. Since organic materials survive very poorly in such conditions, inevitably the evidence for the earliest phases of Anglo-Saxon art comes mainly from relatively small items of metalwork. Much scholarly discussion has been devoted to establishing object typologies, as well as a stylistic and chronological framework for this material, where precise dating evidence is limited. The study of style has therefore played a major part in the understanding of the earliest Anglo-Saxon art, between the fifth and seventh centuries, and remains an essential toolkit for navigating this complex and substantial material. So there are no short cuts here: to understand the role that Roman tradition played in Anglo-Saxon art, we must turn first to the key styles current in early Anglo-Saxon England.

The Saxon Relief Style

The first manifestation of a Germanic art style to appear in England is thoroughly romanizing in its elements.[7] Indeed, it is possible that in the Saxon homeland of Lower Saxony Roman craftsmen were employed in making some of the Saxon brooch types on which this style appears. In England these occur in areas associated with Saxon settlement and include the aptly named saucer brooches, equal-armed brooches and, much more rarely, supporting-arm brooches.

The Saxon Relief Style developed in the early fifth century in the Saxon heartlands of northern Germany, between the Elbe and the Weser rivers – an important focus of migration to England in the fifth century. It is distinguished by its exclusive use of geometric and animal motifs derived

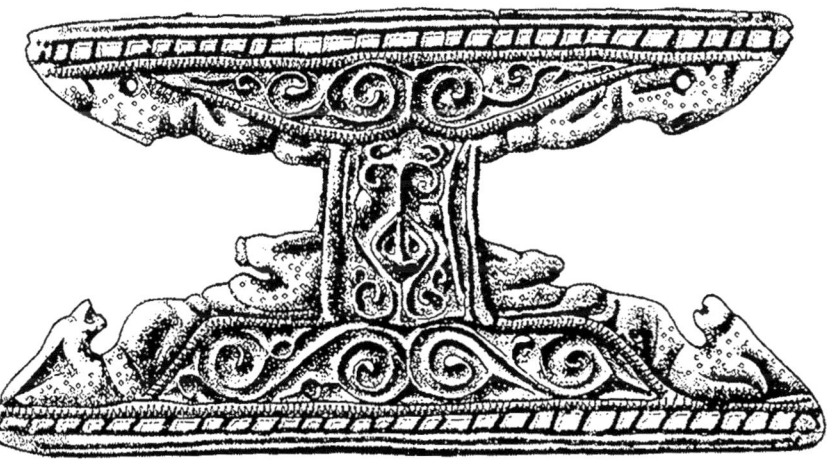

25. Copper-alloy equal-armed brooch, from a grave. Haslingfield, Cambridgeshire, 5th century (Drawing after Inker 2006)

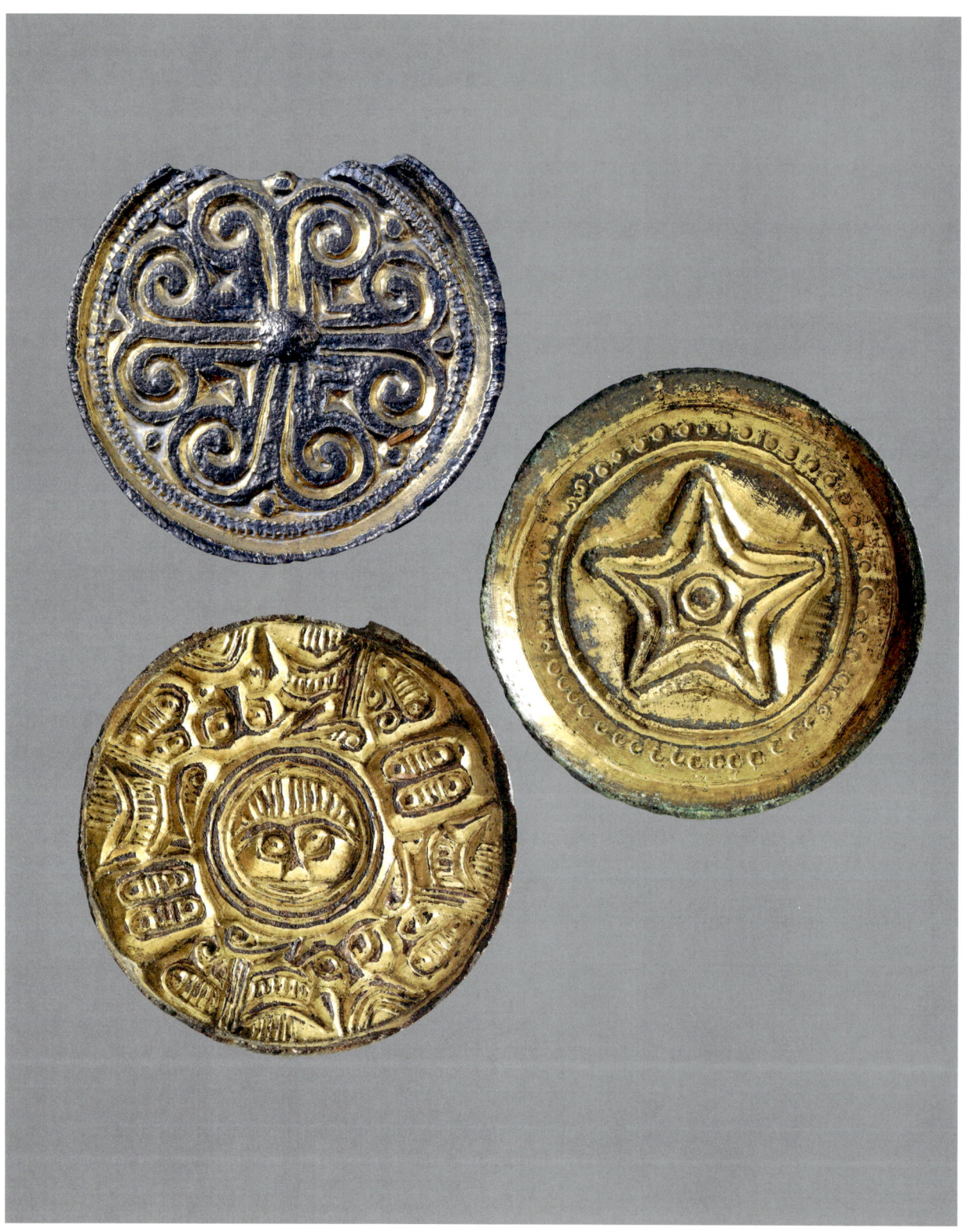

from the decoration on late Roman belt fittings, and other official and military metalwork such as sword mounts and by its use of the chip-carving technique (see below, and fig. 23). Thoroughly Roman motifs, such as bead and reel decoration, spiral and scroll motifs, cross patterns formed from palmette elements, and star-shaped designs, are typical of fifth- and early sixth-century saucer brooches from southern England. This type of brooch continued to be made and developed in England long after the earliest examples were brought from across the North Sea (fig. 26). Scroll decoration is also prominent on the more elaborate forms of equal-armed brooch in England, which in addition have relatively naturalistic crouching beasts along their edges, copied directly from Roman belt-sets (fig. 25). The very few examples of decorated supporting-arm brooches from England draw on this same repertory. The recognizable animals, modelled in rounded relief, are adapted from the hybrid creatures – such as sea-creatures and lions that morph into fish – that decorate this late Roman military metalwork. On the Roman originals, these motifs probably carried mythological and protective meaning, which was adapted in the Germanic versions.

This romanizing Saxon animal decoration does not, however, directly lead into the dominant Anglo-Saxon Animal Style I, discussed below. Unlike the saucer brooches, the equal-armed and supporting-armed brooches never took firm root in England and did not outlast the fifth century; along with the animal elements of the Saxon Relief Style, they were replaced by other brooch forms. The geometric aspects of the style, on the other hand, continued to develop on saucer brooches and other metalwork as a significant element in Anglo-Saxon art throughout much of the sixth century.

The chip-carving technique, which was central to this style, also remained very important in Anglo-Saxon art. It was originally developed for wood carving, for which angled knife or chisel cuts were made to produce a v-sectioned channel, the basic component of a design. The spectacular wooden furniture and elaborate containers from early fifth-century Saxon burials at Fallward, north Germany, show the chip-carving technique in its element.[8] It was easily adapted to metalworking: chip-carved wooden or wax templates were used to create the clay moulds for both cast Roman buckles and Saxon brooches. The technique continued to be used in metalwork for several centuries, spreading throughout Anglo-Saxon England, and as far as Ireland and Pictland by the eighth century. In gilded silver or bronze, the many glittering facets distract the eye with their dazzle, creating an impression of opulence, status and power. Indeed, it has been argued that the Saxon Relief Style, through its relationship to military metalwork, and perhaps to designs on Roman shields, is intimately associated with Saxon warrior culture.[9] It is possible that the decoration on brooches worn by women in Anglo-Saxon England, reflecting the ornament of Roman-style buckle-sets worn by high-ranking male ancestors, continued to reflect a military status acquired by their menfolk. Whatever its significance, apart from the geometric motifs that descended through saucer brooches, the style had a relatively short currency and was superseded by Style I zoomorphic designs from the later fifth century.

The Quoit Brooch Style

A rather different social significance may be seen in another style which took its inspiration from late Roman provincial metalwork.[10] It also occurs on high-status metalwork found in Anglo-Saxon graves, predominantly in south-eastern England and the regions south of the Thames. The rather archaically titled Quoit Brooch Style, named after a type of broad-rimmed ring brooch on which some of the finest examples of the style occur, developed in the first half of the fifth century, but seems to have all but vanished by its last decades, though the brooch type itself lived on for a while in a much humbler form. Although it partly overlapped chronologically with the Saxon Relief Style, and drew on similar sources, it is very different in appearance and in the types of objects on which it occurs. Instead of the high-relief chip-carved surfaces and rounded animal decoration of the Saxon Relief Style, it is characterized by flat surfaces, with lightly engraved ornament and simple punching, sometimes inlaid with silver (on bronze) or partly gilded (on silver). The decoration includes the same range of late Roman geometric motifs – spirals, bead and reel, palmettes and so on – and also processional animals and human masks. The animals are semi-naturalistic or sea-beasts, often with speckled bodies suggesting fur (fig. 27). They sometimes flank a simplified human mask, a motif again taken from some late Roman buckles which carry a mask of

27. Quoit Brooch Style, details: (a, *top left*). Brooch from Howletts, Kent; (b, *top centre*). Buckle from Mucking, Essex; (c, *top right*). Brooch fragment from Howletts, Kent; (d, *bottom*). Bucket mount from Bidford on Avon. a–c, approx. 2:1, d, approx. 1:1 (Drawings, C. Williams, British Museum)

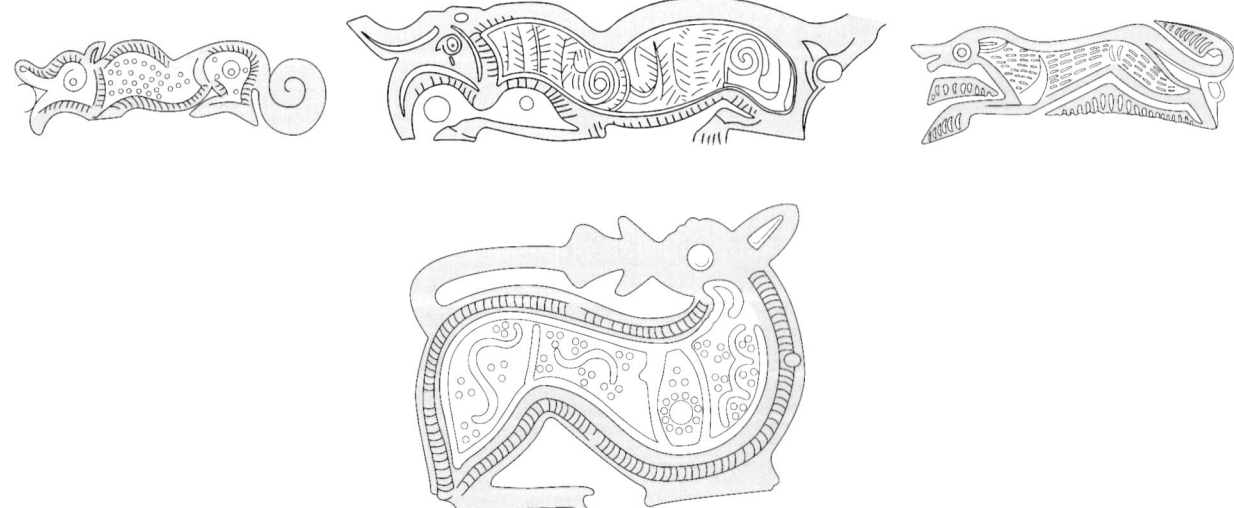

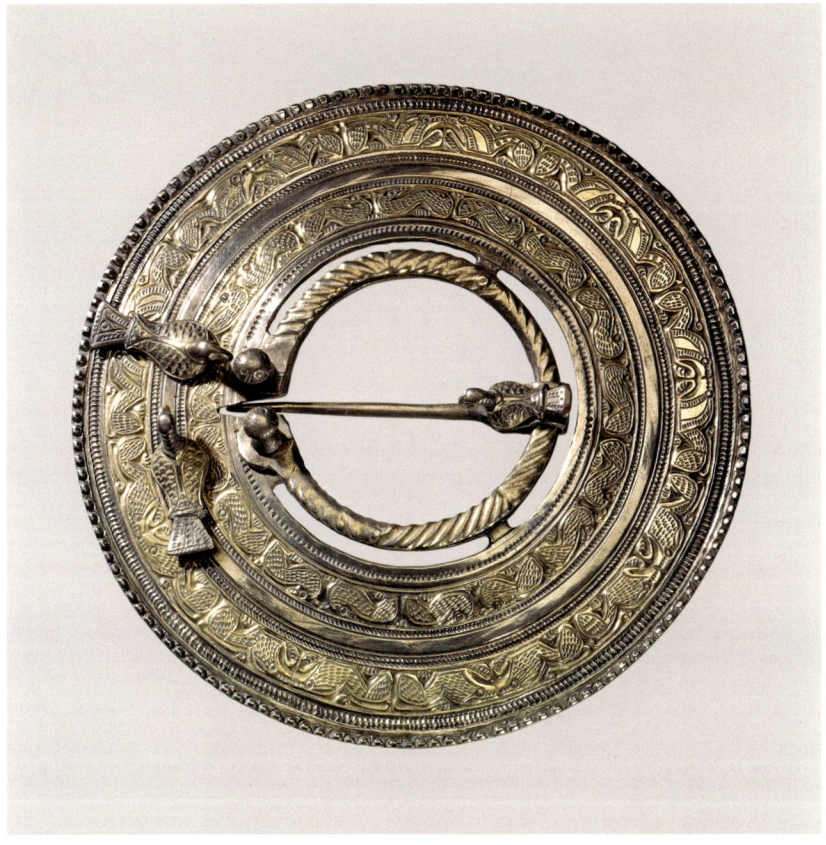

Oceanus supported by sea-beasts (figs 23 and 24). Some, such as the paired doves on the finest quoit brooches, are even modelled in three dimensions (fig. 28). The overall effect is of elegance and a delicate touch.

The style's debt to Roman military-style metalwork is clear; the speckled animals are cousins to the more naturalistically furred creatures on, for example, the Fallward buckle fittings (fig. 23), and the entire belt-set from a grave in the Anglo-Saxon cemetery at Mucking, Essex, is an obvious copy of a Roman model, although in a very different idiom. But the style seems to draw on other kinds of late Roman prestige metalwork as well. A decorated gold bangle from the Hoxne (Suffolk) gold and silver treasure hoard, which was deposited around 410, has a lightly engraved procession of lively running beasts with speckled bodies denoting fur, which are very reminiscent of the Quoit Brooch Style animals (fig. 29). As a product of a Romano-British workshop active in the early fifth century, the bracelet suggests an additional source of models for the later style.

The flat surfaces, light engraving and punching of the Quoit Brooch Style also recall some of the simpler fifth-century Roman-style buckles, which may have been issued by Romano-British civil authorities after the Roman

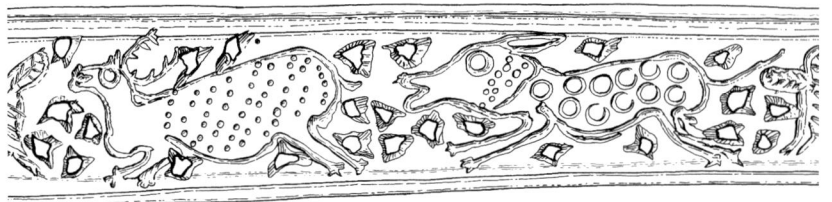

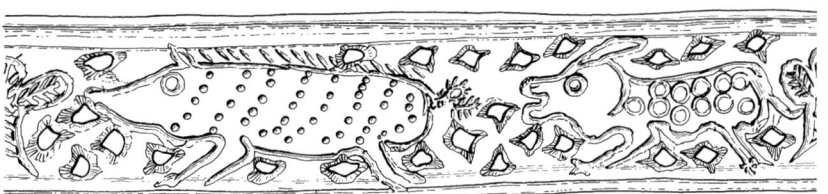

29. Details from a gold bracelet with hunt scene. Hoxne, Suffolk, late Roman (early 5th century). (Drawing, S. Crummy, British Museum)

garrisons were recalled (fig. 27).[11] In this context of Roman and Romano-British models, it is striking that not one of the objects decorated in this style is of Germanic type; instead, they consist of quoit brooches and other brooches of an innovative, non-Germanic form, belt fittings and bracelets derived from late Roman types, as well as tear-shaped pendants and decorative mounts from weapons.

Much animated debate has taken place over the years as to the origin of this style and the fine metalwork it adorned, and of the people who wore it. Gallo-Roman, Jutish or Frankish origins have all been advocated, but it is now generally agreed that it was produced within its south-eastern distribution zone, in Romano-British workshops that continued to work in a late Roman tradition during the first part of the fifth century. Its social significance, however, is intriguing. Although most of these highly prized items come from burials in Anglo-Saxon cemeteries, and were often buried with other objects of Anglo-Saxon origin, it does not follow that all were made for, or worn by, the Anglo-Saxon incomers. The archaeological evidence is not extensive, and often ambiguous, but the presence of Roman glass vessels in some of these burials, and occasional indications that some of the dead were buried in Roman costume, suggest that during the fifth-century heyday of this style at least some of the owners of this fine metalwork were of Romano-British, rather than Anglo-Saxon, stock and had simply adopted Anglo-Saxon burial custom. Equally, Anglo-Saxon owners of such objects may not merely have prized them, but have wished to signal, through wearing them, a relationship with Romano-British elites or authorities. This may have been through marriage, for example, or descent from Germans who had served in the late or post-Roman military. The fifth-century Roman-type belt-set from Mucking (fig. 24), which comes from a cemetery where there is other evidence of a close relationship with the indigenous population, may suggest something of the kind. Finally, it is also quite possible that objects in this style were simply produced by local craftsmen for the elite of both populations, and continued to be treasured and eventually buried for some time after their production. Quoit brooches themselves went on being made up to the end of the fifth century, and perhaps a little beyond, slowly declining into a greatly simplified form, without the elegant animal ornament. The other distinctive object types decorated in this style, mentioned above, do not seem to have been made much after the middle years of the fifth century, suggesting that the workshops and the tradition had finally come to an end. The Quoit Brooch Style, like the Saxon Relief Style, died out and played no part in the development of the Anglo-Saxon animal style which was to dominate from the later fifth century – although that, too, has clear Roman origins.

Animal Style I

The real and enduring Anglo-Saxon heir to the late Roman chip-carved tradition had its beginnings in Scandinavia some time early in the fifth century (fig. 30). First characterized and named by the Swedish scholar B. Salin, the origin and development of Style I and its immediate Scandinavian predecessors are now well understood, though a complete account of Anglo-Saxon Style I and its regional variations has yet to be written.[12] At much the same time as the Romano-Britons and the Saxons in northern Germany were producing their own romanizing styles, craftsmen in southern Norway and Denmark were also beginning to copy the motifs and techniques of late Roman metalwork, gradually adapting them to serve their own needs. The origins of Style I lie in the Nydam Style, named after the findspot of one of the great Danish sacrificial deposits of weapons and other warrior gear in lakes or marshes, mainly dating to the fourth and fifth centuries.[13] The Roman chip-carving technique predominates in this metalwork, known from several such battle offerings from Denmark, as do geometric, animal and

30. Style I, details:
(a, *top left*). Brooch from grave 41, Bifrons, Kent;
(b, *top right*). Brooch from grave 63, Bifrons, Kent;
(c, *bottom left*).
Drinking-horn rim from Taplow, Buckinghamshire;
(d, *bottom right*). Brooch from grave 97, Boss Hall, Ipswich. (Drawings, C. Williams, British Museum)

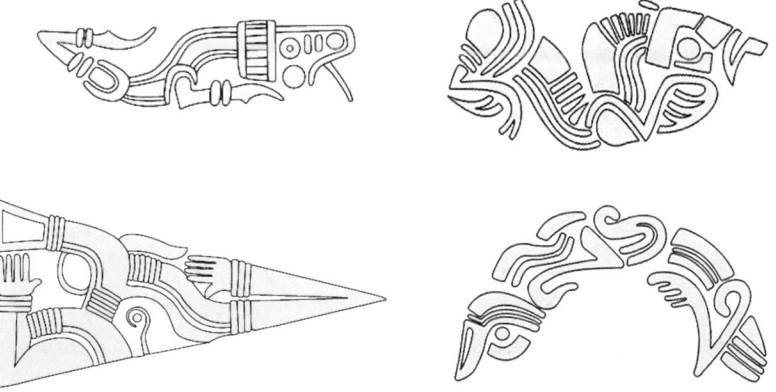

mask elements of the kind described above. But in the transposition of these motifs into a non-Roman context, the animal and human elements have become progressively more stylized and more prominent. While some buckles and strap fittings are faithful adaptations of the geometric style, other items reveal a growing taste for strange creatures – a response to a northern European aesthetic which drew on Germanic myths. The extraordinary gallery of human creatures with gesturing hands, strange birds and open-jawed fishy creatures, on a sword chape from the second Nydam find is an example of this new interest (fig. 31). Similarly, on a brooch fragment from Galsted in Denmark, spiral ornament, mask and animal decoration refer to the Roman tradition, but in a very altered way (fig. 32). The staring human head and its accompanying animals to either side, with their wide curving mouths and long tongues, have travelled a long way from the Roman image of the god Oceanus between dolphins from which they derive.

It was but a short step from this to a further stage in which the animals modelled in relief that had bordered the edges of the object in the Roman manner were transferred to inner fields of decoration, where the chip-carving technique was used instead. This was the beginning of true Style I, which emerged in the last quarter of the fifth century: rounded quadrupeds replaced sea-beasts, and contour lines were added to their bodies and used to define the individual limbs. These contour lines eventually developed into a characteristically ribbed way of representing these animal limbs and increasingly ribbon-like bodies, while the animals themselves lost their rounded forms and became flattened, two-dimensional creatures. Bird-of-prey elements became more prominent, as well as human/animal hybrids, which ultimately derive from images of the emperor and his horse, as they appear on late Roman gold medallions and coins (see p. 29, and figs 30b–c and 11a).

The style reached south-east England in the later years of the fifth century, probably first of all on silver square-headed brooches of a type known from Jutland in Denmark. According to Anglo-Saxon tradition, Kent was primarily settled by Jutes from this region. Although the archaeological evidence shows that this is only a part of a much more complex settlement history, the early presence of these Scandinavian square-headed brooches and other Danish brooch types in Kent, along with the continuing import of southern Scandinavian gold bracteates, does indicate a significant influence from southern Denmark (fig. 33). These brooches, with their processions of animals, human and animal masks, hybrid creatures and curved-beaked birds, rapidly inspired a distinctive Anglo-Saxon version of Style I. It soon spread from Kent into all regions of settlement; a late fifth- or early sixth-century saucer brooch from Aston Remenham, Berkshire, in the heartland of the saucer brooch fashion, shows how readily Jutlandic-type Style I ornament could be transposed from a square-headed brooch onto the small and circular

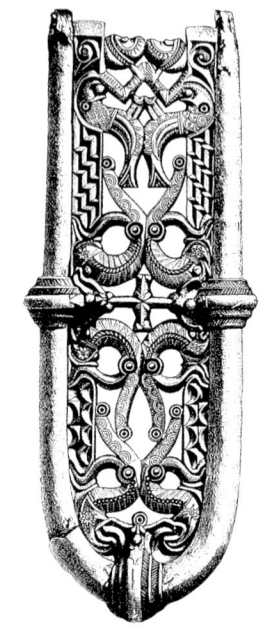

31 (*above*). Silver-gilt sword chape with early version of Style I. Nydam, Denmark, early 5th century (Drawing after Salin 1904)

32 (*opposite, top*). Silver-gilt square-headed brooch fragment. Galsted, Denmark, second quarter of the 5th century (Drawing after Salin 1904)

33 (*opposite*). Silver-gilt square-headed brooch. From grave 41, Bifrons, Kent, late 5th century (Drawing after Haseloff 1981)

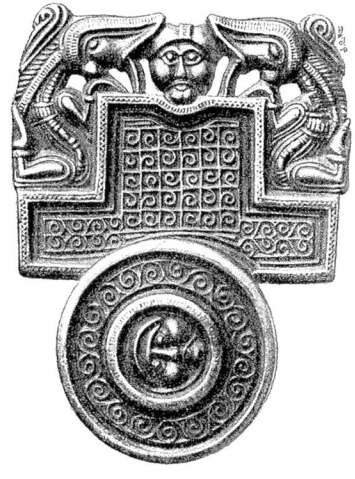

field of a saucer brooch (see fig. 26b). It also incidentally represents the beginning of a shift in the decoration of these Saxon-type brooches, away from the traditional geometric ornament to zoomorphic patterns, which were to become more pronounced as the sixth century went on.

The brooch from Chessell Down, which we examined in depth in Chapter 1, is a descendant of the Danish imports mentioned above, and a good example of how, by this period, the style had become wholly naturalized (see fig. 1). Some geometric elements continued to be used, as in the scrollwork on that brooch's head-plate, but the dominant ornament is riotously zoomorphic, covering most of the surface in dense patterns. The contour lines defining the animal components quickly vanished from the repertory, enabling the now ribbed individual body parts to be adapted in various formulaic ways. Additional elements could be grafted onto an animal, or it could be reduced to a few essentials – a head and a leg, for instance, or even just one representative part. It could be reassembled in an eye-teasing 'animal salad' of disconnected bits, in one writer's happy phrase.[14] Some motifs were especially influential. A particular version of a hybrid creature, the so-called 'helmet and hand' motif, was so widely adapted that Kendrick used it to rename Style I as the Helmet Style. It derives from imperial images via the Nydam Style and bracteate art (see fig. 30c). In Anglo-Saxon England its earliest and most legible versions occur on prestige Kentish metalwork, such as the early sixth-century drinking horn mounts which were buried as prized heirlooms in the early seventh-century princely grave at Taplow in Buckinghamshire (fig. 34). From this image others descended and were modified, but essential elements remained. Animals on a fine buckle-set from Howletts, Kent, for example, have the helmet-like head, and the forelimb is raised in the same gesture as the hand in earlier versions (fig. 35); while the saucer brooches of middle England and the later Anglian florid cruciform brooches exhibit many examples of helmeted animal/men which derive from the motif (fig. 36).

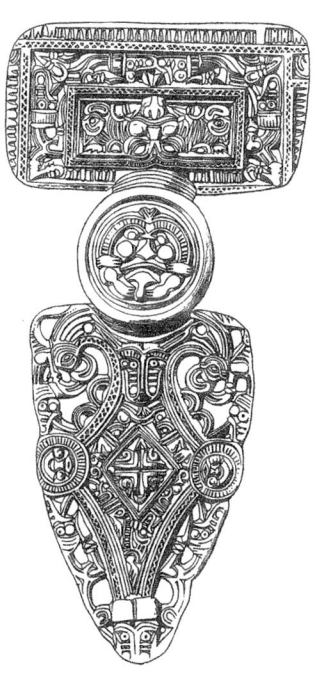

As these last examples indicate, just as brooch types and costume differed from region to region, so Style I developed distinctive regional versions over time. While still adhering to the form and basic template, a square-headed brooch from the east midlands looks distinctly different from its Kentish cousin – the decoration is more crowded, busy with individual elements rather than entire animals – yet it may still also employ sub-geometric motifs that contain distant reference to their late Roman origins. Some square-headed brooches from East Anglia have very little animal decoration, but plenty of spiral ornament; and some of the florid cruciform brooches have decoration that is hardly recognizable as animal ornament at all (see figs 7 and 36).[15] These regional distinctions, both of costume and of ornament, become more pronounced during the course of the later fifth and sixth centuries. This is one indication, among others, that across England the descendants of the

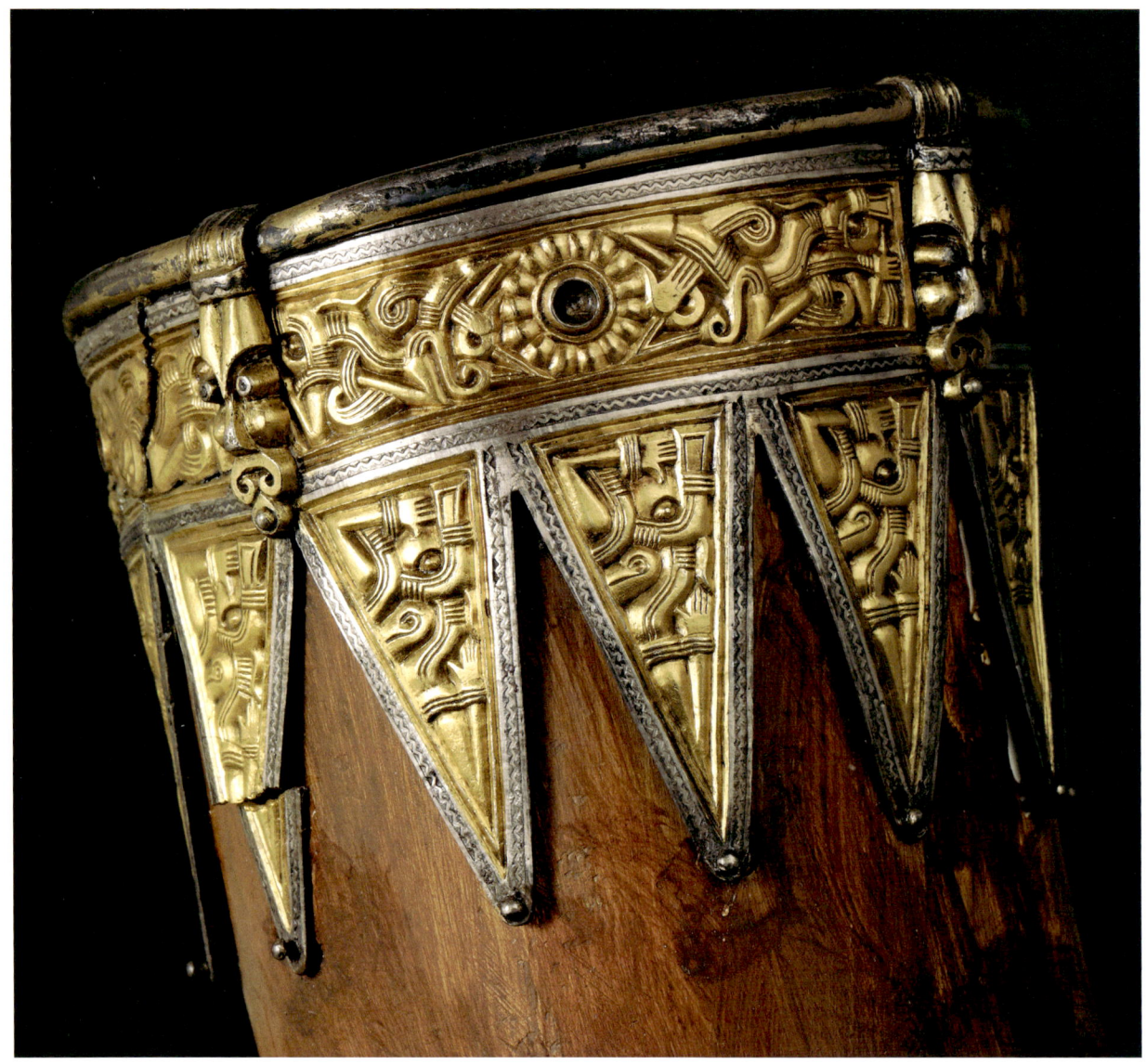

original settlers were developing fresh, regional identities, allied to the growing and competitive tribal power-bases of emerging kingdoms.

Nowhere is this sense of a developing regional identity more apparent than in the rich and powerful kingdom of East Kent in the sixth century. Here, close contact with mainland Europe, in particular through dynastic, trading and diplomatic alliances with Merovingian Gaul, helped to bring about new brooch forms, new techniques and a distinctive, extremely condensed version of Style I. The use of garnet inlays was a catalyst in this. They had long been used on southern and eastern European Germanic jewellery, following a Roman and ultimately Greek tradition of lapidary work, and

34. Silver-gilt mount from a drinking horn, showing Style I 'helmet and hand' motif. From the princely burial at Taplow, Buckinghamshire, early 6th century. Diam. (rim) 11 cm (British Museum)

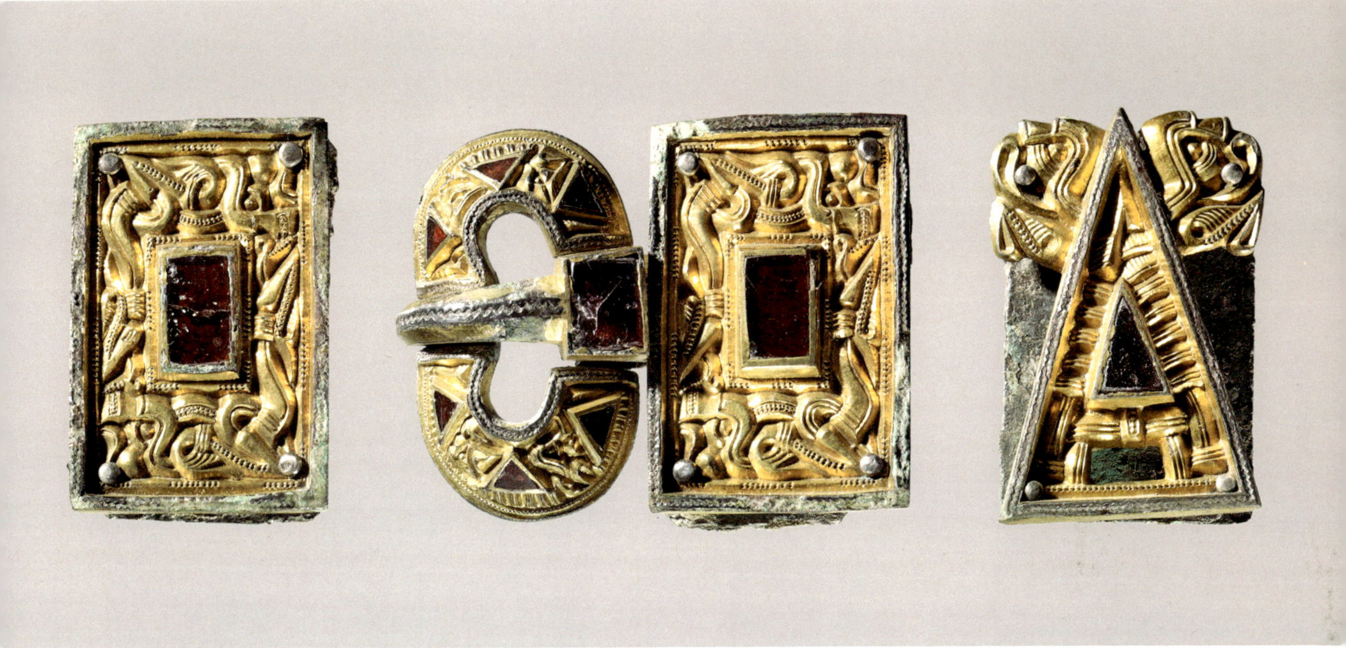

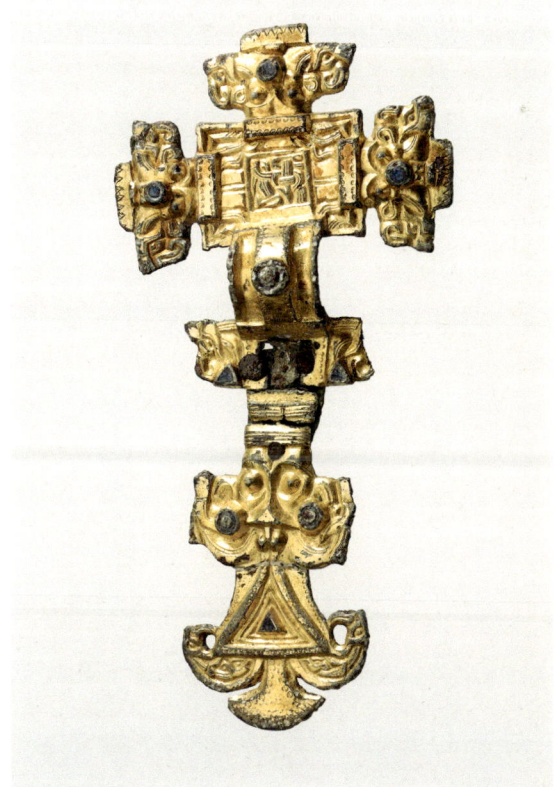

35 (*above*). Silver-gilt buckle-set with garnet inlay and Style I ornament, from a grave. Howletts, Kent, second quarter of the 6th century. L. (*left to right*) 4.3 cm, 5.3 cm, 4.3 cm (British Museum)

36 (*right*). Gilded copper-alloy florid cruciform brooch, from a grave. Sleaford, Lincolnshire, later 6th century. L. 16.8 cm (British Museum)

their bright red colour carried connotations of rank and wealth. Imported by way of the Frankish kingdoms of northern Gaul and the Rhineland, where they were used on small round brooches in all-over cloisonné inlay, in Kent, these small flat gemstones usually trapezoidal or round, were inlaid much more sparingly. Here they were used on large and small square-headed brooches and on a new, specifically Kentish type of gilded silver disc brooch, which had migrated from being a disc fixed to the bow of a square-headed brooch to having an independent life of its own. Squeezed into the small fields between the garnet inlays, highly compressed versions of Style I beasts, sometimes reduced to a mere leg or head, were invented (fig. 37). The garnet and other coloured inlay, with its exotic connotations, was to become more important still in the development of Style II.

Since stylistic variations were one way in which the identity of emergent regional powers was expressed, it may seem curious that much of the Style I metalwork, as it survives in burials, was in the form of female dress accessories, rather than in male equipment. However, we should perhaps be wary of making too much of this. While there are far fewer Style I objects from male burials, those that survive are often of very high status – decorated shield mounts, drinking-horn fittings, horse gear, elaborate belt-sets, and fittings from swords and scabbards – all objects which represent and sustain male warrior status. Such items may have often been considered too precious to dispose of in the grave in this early period, when precious metals were scarce, and instead been handed down as heirlooms.

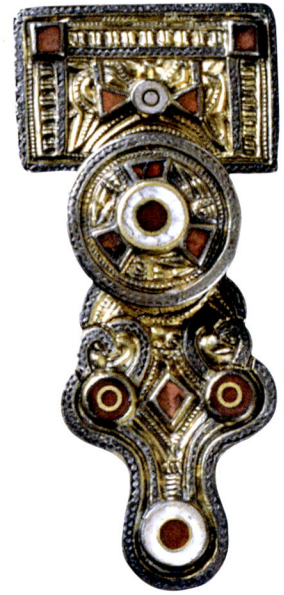

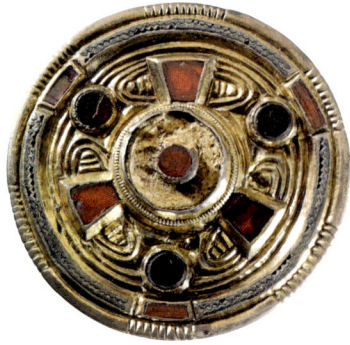

37. Two silver-gilt brooches with garnet and white shell inlays and Style I ornament: (*left*) Square-headed brooch with disc-on-bow. Howletts, Kent, mid-6th century. L. 9.4 cm; (*right*) Disc brooch. Faversham, Kent, mid-6th century. Diam. 4.7 cm (both British Museum)

Versions of Style I continued up to and perhaps beyond 600 in some areas, particularly in the north, but already in the later sixth century – perhaps as early as the 570s – its lineal descendant, Style II, had appeared in Kent and East Anglia.

Animal Style II

The origins of Style II have been much discussed, but there is a general acceptance that it emerged from late versions of Style I in southern Scandinavia, some time after the mid-sixth century, from where it subsequently spread to other Germanic peoples, including the Anglo-Saxons (fig. 38). A two-strand arrival of Style II in England has recently been suggested, one centred in Kent, and drawing on versions imported from the near Continent (themselves dependent on Scandinavian models), the other centred on East Anglia and coming directly from Scandinavia.[16] However, while Scandinavia was undoubtedly the crucible of Style II, the picture is probably more complicated. For example, in the versions of Style II used by the Langobards in northern Italy and the Alamanni of southern Germany, although there is a clear Germanic base, there is also evident input from the Roman and Byzantine tradition. This is seen most clearly in the use of symmetrical interlacing patterns with no zoomorphic elements, and in the eclectic decoration of the gold funerary crosses which were prominent in their culture. The interconnectivity of western Europe in this period enabled Scandinavian metalwork to be influential much further south, but it also brought goods from the Mediterranean to the furthest parts of the north, including Anglo-Saxon England. The influence of classical ideas of symmetry and of interlacing patterns played an increasing part in the development of Style II through the seventh century, and nowhere more so than in post-Conversion England, with its newly reinforced links to Rome and classicizing art traditions.

In Scandinavia, already before the middle of the sixth century, the ribbed bodies of Style I animals on chip-carved metalwork were becoming thinner and more elongated, sometimes interlocking with one another. Some Scandinavian brooches have non-zoomorphic ornament that approaches pure symmetrical interlace. The trend reached England early; the Taplow cast-silver horn terminals, made in the early part of the sixth century, are decorated with elongated, ribbon-bodied animals which intertwine with themselves and with other snake-like creatures (fig. 39). At the same time, gold filigree decoration came into fashion in Scandinavia, seen most dramatically on a series of filigree-encrusted sword-scabbard mounts from Norway and Denmark.[17] The ductility of gold lends itself very well to creating fine wirework, and these mounts are decorated with sinuous backward-turning creatures formed of beaded wire, sometimes interlocking, which echo the ribbon bodies of late phase Style I chip-carved creatures. It is a short step

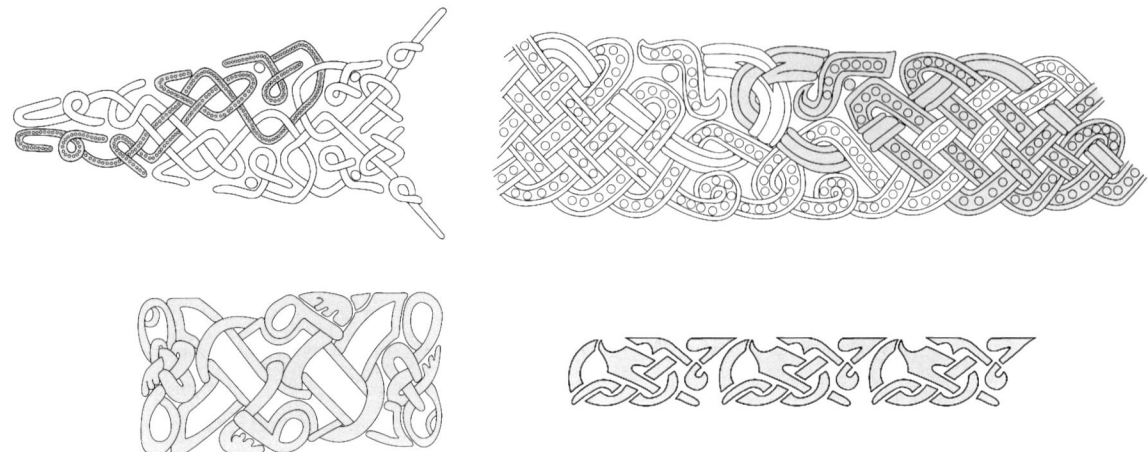

from metalwork such as this to true Style II, which is characterized by coherent, long-bodied animals that may interlace sinuously with other animals in pairs or in complex processions, or may turn back upon themselves to bite their own bodies with long jaws (fig. 38).

In Anglo-Saxon versions of the style, which begin to appear towards the end of the sixth century, as elsewhere the emphasis is on entire and clearly articulated animals in fluent, symmetrical structures, often interlaced. There are no man/beast hybrids or geometric decoration, but chip-carving continues, alongside the extensive use of filigree, impressed foils and garnet inlays. As well as on more traditional high-status male equipment, including swords, drinking vessels and horse gear, the new style now appears on a whole range of different object types, such as triangular buckles, large disc and composite brooches, and disc pendants, many inspired by Mediterranean models. Indeed, Style II represents a revolutionary change in the way people presented and saw themselves; nothing could seem more different from the densely packed, dismembered elements of Style I decoration on the now outmoded sixth-century buckle- and brooch-types. It seems to have been quickly adopted as one of the ways in which newly powerful elites chose to identify themselves – for example the royalty buried at Sutton Hoo, the Kentish puppet king buried at the gateway to Wessex at Taplow, the royal war-bands whose armour and weapon fittings form the Staffordshire Hoard, and the followers of the Christian king Æthelbert of Kent (r. *c.* 585–616), whom Bede describes as supreme among the kings of his day.

Anglo-Saxon Style II endured for about a hundred years; it was probably first developed in elite metalwork of the last quarter of the sixth century and lasted until the end of the seventh century. An early example of the new style is seen on the great gold and garnet-inlaid buckle from the

38. Style II, details: (a, *top left*). Kentish-style animals on a beaded wire buckle-plate from Wickham, Kent; (b, *top right*). Kentish-style animals on a repoussé foil cup mount from Taplow, Buckinghamshire; (c, *bottom left*). Anglian-style animals on a carved bone plate from Southampton; (d, *bottom right*). Anglian-style animals in garnet inlay on the shoulder clasps from the Sutton Hoo ship burial, Suffolk (Drawings, C. Williams, British Museum)

Taplow burial mentioned above, which was made in Kent, perhaps as early as the 570s (fig. 41). The triangular buckle is a Frankish type only recently introduced into Anglo-Saxon England, but it has an indented kidney-shaped loop and coarse cloisonné cellwork which look back to earlier sixth-century Frankish metalwork. It is one of only three solid gold buckles known from Anglo-Saxon England – the other two are from the Mound 1 ship burial at Sutton Hoo (see fig. 42) and the princely chamber-grave at Prittlewell, Essex; all three burials date to the early seventh century. Lavishly constructed filigree borders surround the central beaded wire decoration on the buckle plate, which consists of an animal that turns backwards to bite its S-shaped body, its jaws disintegrating into interlace elements. It is certainly a Style II animal, but its jerky, segmented construction lacks the fluency of the interlacing fili-gree creatures on the gold-sheeted clasps from the same burial, which are among the latest objects placed within it (fig. 40). The animal on the Taplow buckle was executed by someone who was feeling his way in the new style, and had yet to master the smooth symmetry seen in the decoration of the clasps.

Gold played a significant part in the genesis and development of the style. This was a period when it briefly became more available in England than it had ever been, due to an influx of considerable subsidies paid out by the Byzantine emperors to the Franks in the late sixth and early seventh cen-turies. Some of this travelled on to England in the form of Byzantine and Merovingian gold coins, which were readily recy-clable. Kent's proximity to northern France, together with its dynastic, diplomatic and economic relationships with the Merovingian kingdoms across the Channel, made it the main conduit for this incoming gold, and also for the first manifesta-tions of Style II in England in the later sixth century. Luxurious gold jewellery, often with garnet inlays, was the main showcase for the new style, and beaded wire decoration was, as we have seen, ideally suited to its sinuous creatures (fig. 40). The importance of this decoration in the development of Anglo-Saxon Style II is demonstrated by the way in which it is so frequently copied in other techniques, such as the

39. Silver-gilt drinking-horn terminal with Style I animal ornament. From the princely burial at Taplow, Buckinghamshire, early 6th century. L. (terminal) 24 cm (British Museum)

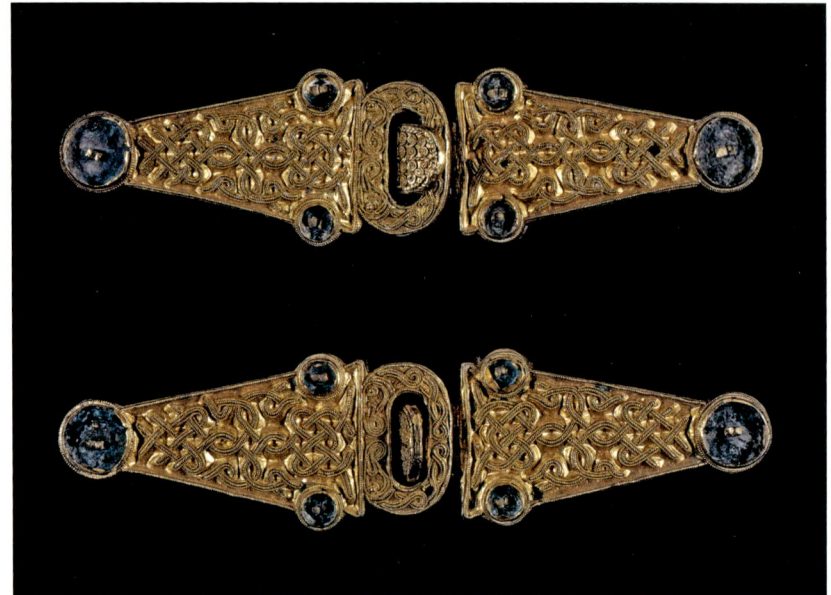

40. Gold-sheeted clasps with Style II animal ornament. From the princely burial at Taplow, Buckinghamshire, early 7th century. L. 13 cm (British Museum)

pelleted or ribbed imitations of beaded wire animals on die-impressed gold foils, or in cast ornament (fig. 38a–b). The supreme example of the imitation of beaded wire animal ornament is the representation of this in niello inlay on the cast great gold buckle from Sutton Hoo Mound 1 (fig. 42).

The so-called 'Anglian' version of Style II occurs particularly in East Anglia, Lincolnshire and (rarely) in Northumbria, though examples are also known from elsewhere in England, including Kent and Hampshire. These animals are rarely executed in filigree, although they follow the same back-ward-looking or interlocked, long-jawed formula; but these creatures often have distinctive lentoid eyes, and marked contouring (see figs 44 and 38c–d). Cast metal or foil-impressed versions are the preferred medium, and increas-ingly elaborate garnet cellwork, building on the simple shapes originally introduced from the Continent, is particularly prevalent. The relatively small number of Anglian Style II artefacts has until now inevitably been dominated by the stupendous jewellery from Sutton Hoo Mound 1, with its virtuoso displays of different versions of the style on the clasps and purse-lid, and on the great gold buckle. However, the many new examples in this style, some executed in elaborate garnet inlay, from the extraordinary hoard found in south Staffordshire in 2009 are now changing our ideas; this material is also best understood in some kind of royal context (see Chapter 5, figs 78–80). The Sutton Hoo royal jewellery and the best of the Staffordshire Hoard arte-facts are clearly in a league of their own compared with most 'Anglian' Style II metalwork, and even with surviving high-class jewellery from Kent. Never-theless, there is a clear kinship between the style of this superior metalwork,

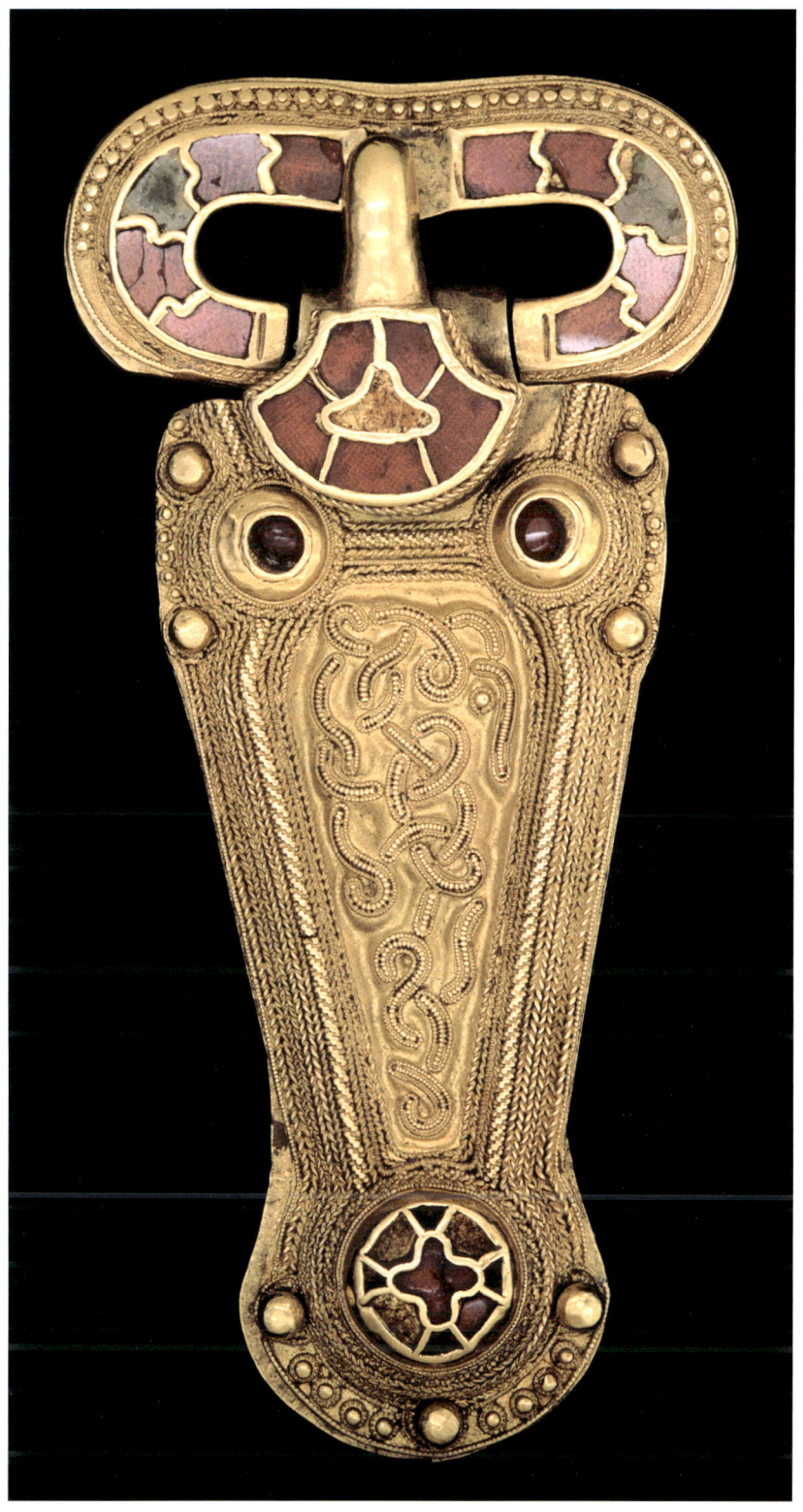

41. Gold buckle with Style II beaded wire animal ornament and garnet and glass inlays. From the princely burial at Taplow, Buckinghamshire, later 6th century. L. 9.8 cm (British Museum)

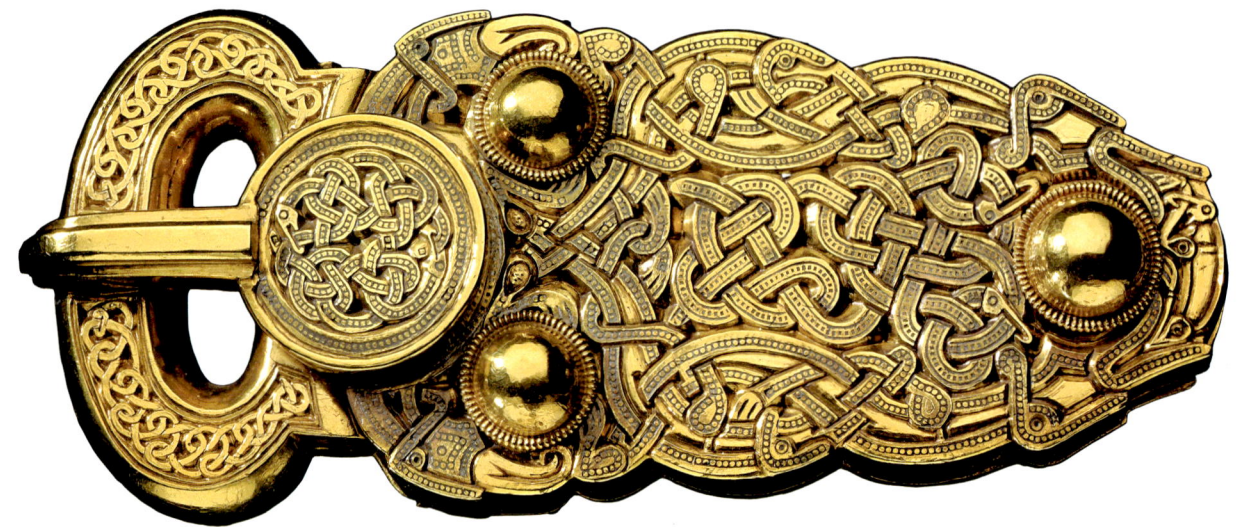

probably produced by peripatetic master-goldsmiths, and lesser versions, such as the wreathed snakes on the garnet-cloisonné pendant from Bacton (Norfolk), interlacing creatures on dies for impressing foil sheets from Icklingham (Suffolk), impressed foil inlays from Caenby (Lincolnshire), and a number of cast harness fittings from the Anglian regions.[18]

The 'Anglian' version of the style was to be especially influential in the development of Insular manuscript painting in the seventh century, discussed in Chapters 3 and 4. But the 'Kentish' version, with its emphasis on sinuous filigree animals, soon began to travel far and wide across regional boundaries: fine metalwork of this kind appears not only at Taplow on the remote Chiltern edge, but in Wessex, Essex, East Anglia, Mercia, Lindsey and even Northumbria. With an increase in internal mobility in the seventh century due to a variety of factors, it is really no surprise that Style II – and the object types it appears on – show less regional variation than Style I. It also occurs more widely on male equipment, especially large buckles, drinking vessels, musical instruments, swords, shield mounts and horse gear. Ostentatious princely burials, especially noticeable in the early years of the seventh century, as at Sutton Hoo, Taplow and Prittlewell, contain particularly lavish displays of such items, and it seems likely that one of the propellants for the new style was growing competition between emergent rival kingdoms – again, hinted at by the Staffordshire Hoard. Was the early spread of the Kentish version of Style II linked to that kingdom's domination in the early seventh century? And was it also linked to the activity of the Kent-based Augustinian Christian mission? In promoting the new religion throughout England this helped to extend access to influences from the south, including jewellery and manuscripts reflecting Roman and Mediterranean cultural

42. Gold buckle with Style II animal ornament, inlaid with niello in imitation of beaded gold wire. From the Mound 1 ship burial, Sutton Hoo, Suffolk, early 7th century. L. 13.2 cm (British Museum)

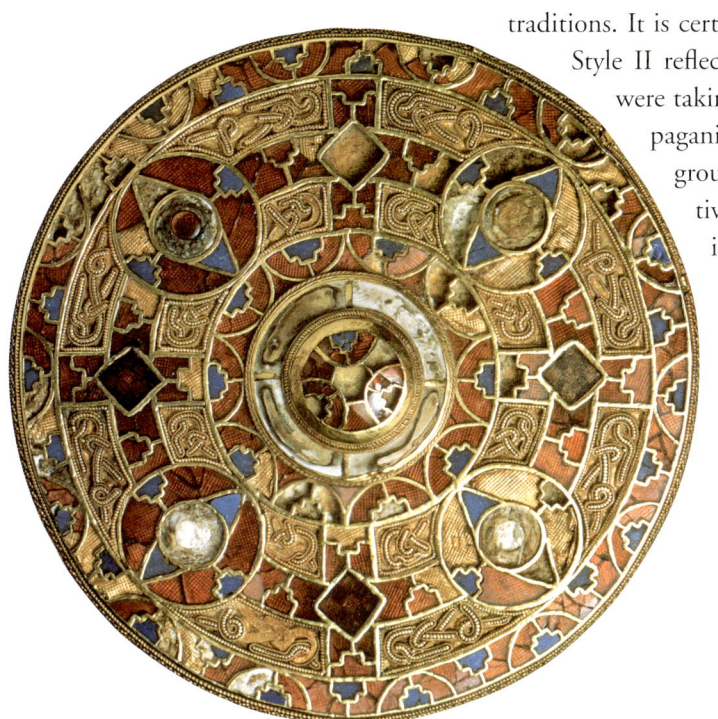

traditions. It is certainly the case that the widespread adoption of Style II reflects the major social and political changes that were taking place in this period of great transition: from paganism to Christianity, and from numerous regional groupings to a smaller number of highly competitive polities. How these changes, with the new influences from Rome, impacted on the Christian art of the seventh century is the subject of the next chapter.

43. Gold disc brooch with beaded wire Style II decoration and garnet and glass inlays, from a woman's burial. Kingston Down, Kent, early 7th century. Diam. 8.6 cm (World Museum, Liverpool)

44. Silver-gilt sword pommel, from a grave. Crundale Down, Kent. Later 7th century. L. 6.1 cm (British Museum)

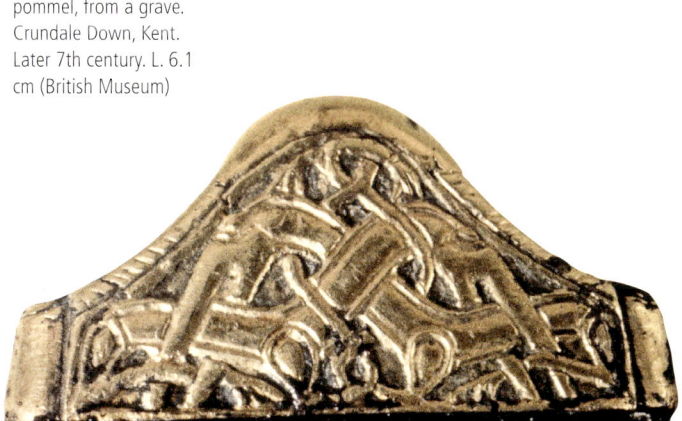

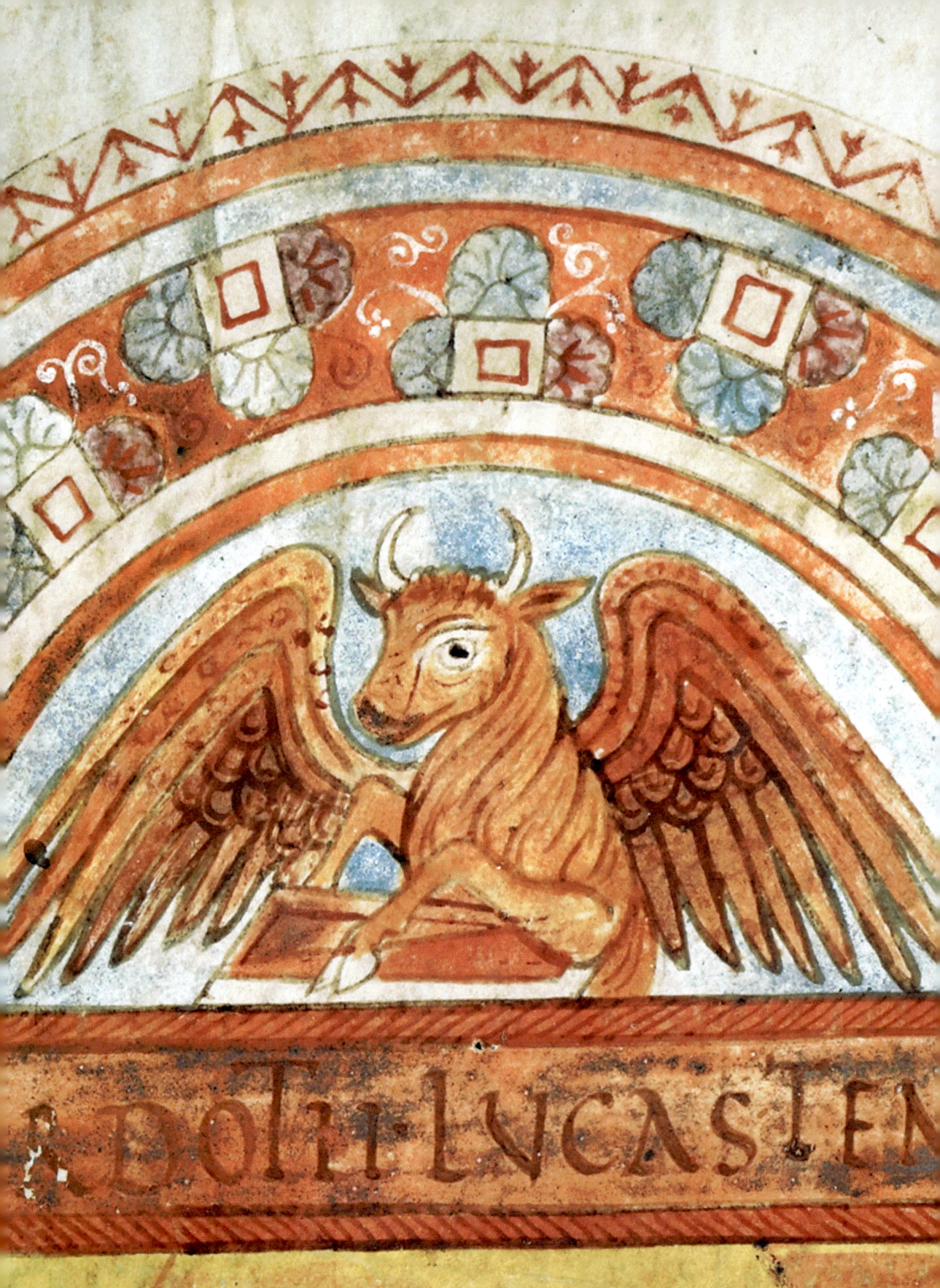

CHAPTER 3

My poor mind is quite at a loss to describe it –
the great depth of the foundations, the crypts of
beautifully dressed stone, the vast structure supported
by columns of various styles, and with numerous side-
aisles, the walls of remarkable height and length, the
many winding passages and spiral staircases leading
up and down. Without a doubt it was the spirit of God
who taught our bishop to plan the construction of
such a place, for we have never heard of its like this
side of the Alps.

Stephen of Ripon, *The Life of St Wilfrid*[1]

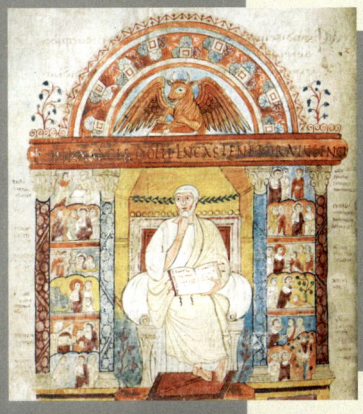

ROME REINVENTED: THE IMPACT OF CHRISTIANITY

The St Augustine Gospels,
opening page to St Luke's
Gospel (see fig. 47)

New ways of being Roman

Stephen's marvelling account of Bishop Acca's and St Wilfrid's great monastery at Hexham, Northumberland, founded in 671–3, gives some sense of the
powerful impression that grand Roman-style stone buildings had on a people
who until recently had known only single-storey wooden halls. This was a
wonder expressed in all the great Anglo-Saxon ecclesiastical foundations of
the seventh century. At Canterbury, centre of the Roman Christian mission,
the cathedral of Christ Church was reconstructed from what Augustine (archbishop, 597–604/9) and his fellows believed was a former Roman church.
Indeed, the idea of Canterbury as a Roman city was active enough for Augustine to locate his early churches within and without the remaining Roman
walls, in emulation of the location of churches with the same dedications in
contemporary Rome. In fact, all the early Anglo-Saxon bishoprics were set up
in former Roman towns, giving a physical validation and authority to the
Roman origin of Augustine's mission in England, and to the concept of the
universal Christian church centred on Rome.

At Hexham and Ripon (North Yorkshire), elaborate stone crypts were constructed from reused dressed Roman stone, their dark twisting passages and candle-lit recesses little changed today, and as evocative as they must have been in the seventh century, when relics were probably venerated there. Elsewhere, monasteries were built in former Roman forts, as at Reculver (Kent), Bradwell (Essex) and Burgh Castle (Norfolk). And at Wearmouth (County Durham), Bede tells us, in 674, Abbot Benedict Biscop built a church *iuxta more romanorum*, 'in the Roman manner', using masons from Gaul. Benedict, who had studied for two years at the island monastery of Lérins in France, travelled on many occasions to Gaul and Italy. He brought back to his twin foundation of Wearmouth/Jarrow (founded in 673 and 681 respectively) not only books, to build what was one of the most extensive Anglo-Saxon libraries of the age, but also liturgical vestments and vessels, relics and icons. Also from Rome he brought a precentor named John to teach correct ceremonial chant, as well as foreign glaziers and Frankish masons. Excavations on both sites have shown that these buildings had crushed-tile cement floors in the Roman manner (*opus signinum*), plastered and painted walls, Mediterranean-style architectural and standing sculpture, and elaborate coloured window glass, some of it depicting holy figures. They must have seemed astonishing and wonderful creations to the local people, compelling embodiments of the power and universality of the Church. Even today, one can get some sense of that at the *Bede's World* centre at Jarrow, where the Mediterranean style of the modern building in that dour northern setting dramatically evokes the shock of another, very foreign, culture.

We can see here how radically new perceptions of a late Roman tradition, focused on its art and architecture, its books and indeed the written Latin language itself, were all mediated through the Christian church. Yet as we shall also see, both in the art of the Church and in secular art, this new vision of Rome adapted to Germanic tradition, resulting in the production of distinctively rich and complex artefacts, whether manuscripts, sculpture or metalwork. To set this in context, we need first to understand a little more about the nature and history of the Christian missions to the Anglo-Saxons.

The Christian missions to the Anglo-Saxons: a melting pot of influences
The story of the conversion of the Anglo-Saxons is a complex one, because Christianity came to them initially from several sources. On the one hand, there was the mission sent from Rome by Pope Gregory the Great (*c.* 540–604), and led by Augustine, prior of Gregory's monastery of St Andrew in Rome. This arrived in Kent in 597, and spread north and west from there. Not long after, a separate Irish mission to the northern kingdom of Northumbria was sent from the monastery founded by St Columba on the Scottish island of Iona, through the request of Oswald of Northumbria (r. 633–41/2), who had

converted to Christianity during a period of exile in the Irish kingdom of Scottish Dál Riata. This mission was led by Bishop Aidan, who in 635 founded the famous monastery of Lindisfarne on a coastal island opposite the Northumbrian royal stronghold of Bamburgh. Aidan's followers went on to be active throughout Northumbria and elsewhere, including much of the midlands and eastern England, where they also founded monasteries, but they were not alone. Other Irish monks are known to have set up foundations in East Anglia and Wessex, and there were doubtless more who came from Iona and Ireland itself. Frankish clergy, such as Felix and Agilbert, were also active in eastern and southern parts of England.

Bede's generally hostile account of the existing British Christians in England and Wales, descended from Romano-British converts, suggests that though numerous, particularly in the west, they played little or no role in converting the Anglo-Saxons – but he is scarcely an unbiased source. There is documentary evidence of a thriving British Christian cult centred on St Albans, which remained active into the late sixth century. This may be associated with a church which archaeological investigation has shown continued to be an important centre of worship into the eighth century; it is unlikely that this had no contact with Anglo-Saxon communities, or with the Augustinian missions.

The Roman and Celtic Churches differed significantly in their organization, mode of operation, and most bitterly in certain doctrinal matters, especially in how the date of the major feast of Easter was to be calculated. This dispute was only eventually resolved at the Synod of Whitby in 664, after which the Roman model prevailed, and a unitary church was established throughout England. Cultural differences between the two churches were equally marked, but despite the momentous decision at Whitby, a fertile cross-pollination developed. This gave rise to a highly influential so-called Hiberno-Saxon or Insular style, seen especially in illuminated manuscripts of the seventh and eighth centuries. And long after the triumph of the Roman order, Irish and Welsh clerics continued to play influential roles in the Anglo-Saxon Church and state. The important influence of the Celtic Church on Anglo-Saxon art of this period will be explored further in the next chapter.

Gregory's missionaries had also been active in the north. One such was Paulinus (bishop of York, 625–33), who in 626 carried out a mass baptism at the palace of the Northumbrian king Edwin (r. 616–33) at Yeavering, in the remote foothills of the Cheviots. In Northumbria, the differences between Celtic and Roman Christian practice were particularly marked: Benedict Biscop's twin foundation of Wearmouth/Jarrow was as unlike the Ionan traditions of Lindisfarne – only ninety or so kilometres up the Northumbrian coast – as could be. Benedict's successor, Ceolfrith, commissioned three magnificent single-volume copies of the Vulgate version of the Bible,

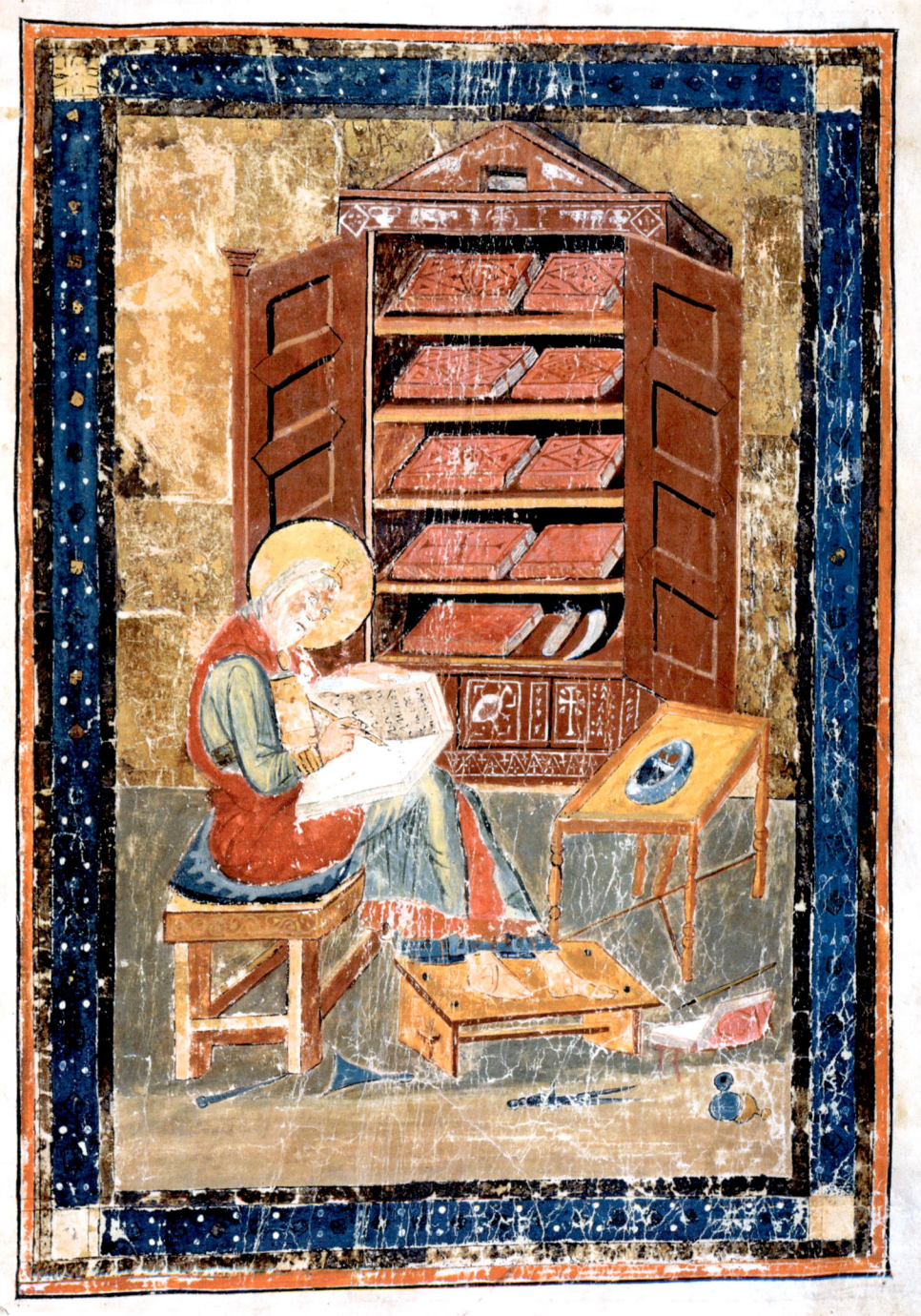

CODICIBVS SACRIS HOSTILI CLADE PERVSTIS
ESDRA DŌ FERVENS HOC REPARAVIT OPVS

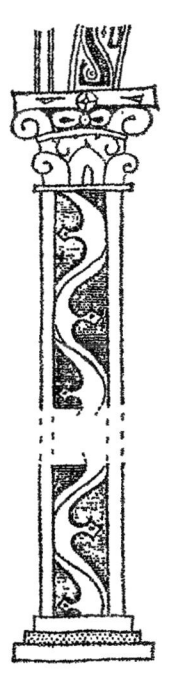

known as pandects, to be made in his monastery. Each book contained around
1030 pages; it has been calculated that each one required the hides of some
1550 calves, a vivid indication of the resources controlled by these wealthy
monasteries. One of these pandects, the *Codex Amiatinus* (fig. 45), survives, as
well as the remains of twelve leaves of another.[2] The *Codex Amiatinus* also
incorporates material from an Old Latin Bible, the *Codex Grandior*, written at
the monastery of Vivarium, founded by Cassiodorus (*c*. 490–583) near Squil-
lace in southern Italy; this Bible had been brought to Northumbria around
679. Ceolfrith intended to present his dauntingly huge volume – a quarter of
a metre in thickness and the weight, apparently, of a fully grown female Great
Dane – to the Pope, but he died on the way at Langres, France, in 716. Nevertheless, this great codex certainly reached Italy, where it came to rest in the
monastery of San Salvatore at Monte Amiata, from which it entered the Lau-
rentian Library in Florence after the dissolution of the monastery in 1782.

Until the late nineteenth century, this stupendous manuscript was
thought to be Italian because of its impeccable uncial script, classicizing decoration and pure text. It was only when later alterations to the dedication were
observed that it was realized that this was a part of Ceolfrith's great offering to
the Church of Rome: a Northumbrian manuscript so Italian in style that no
one imagined it could have been made by Anglo-Saxons in the remote north
of England – a 'barbarous fierce and unbelieving nation', as Gregory had
thought at the time of the conversion, hardly a century before. In its purple
and gold- and silver-decorated pages, its elegant script, and its classicizing
figure painting, the manuscript is indeed very Italian in style, and clearly faithful to its sources. However, hints of Insular taste can be seen in the Celtic-style
pelta decoration of the canon tables (fig. 46). This is a manuscript in which,
at the beginning of the eighth century, a Roman ideal is poised to assimilate
elements of an Insular style.

Although this is the only surviving Northumbrian manuscript in a
purely Italian manner, others certainly existed. Stephen of Ripon, Bishop
Wilfrid's biographer, tells of a sumptuous gospel-book that Wilfrid, that most
quarrelsome and grandiose of seventh-century prelates, had commissioned for
his great church at Ripon:

> a marvel of art hitherto undreamed of . . . a book of the gospels
> done in letters of purest gold on parchment all empurpled and
> illuminated, and had ordered jewellers to make a case for them
> also of the purest gold, and set with precious gems.

Continental models for these Bibles and other religious manuscripts, such
as gospel-books and psalters, were certainly entering the country in considerable numbers to serve the teaching and the liturgy of the church. One such

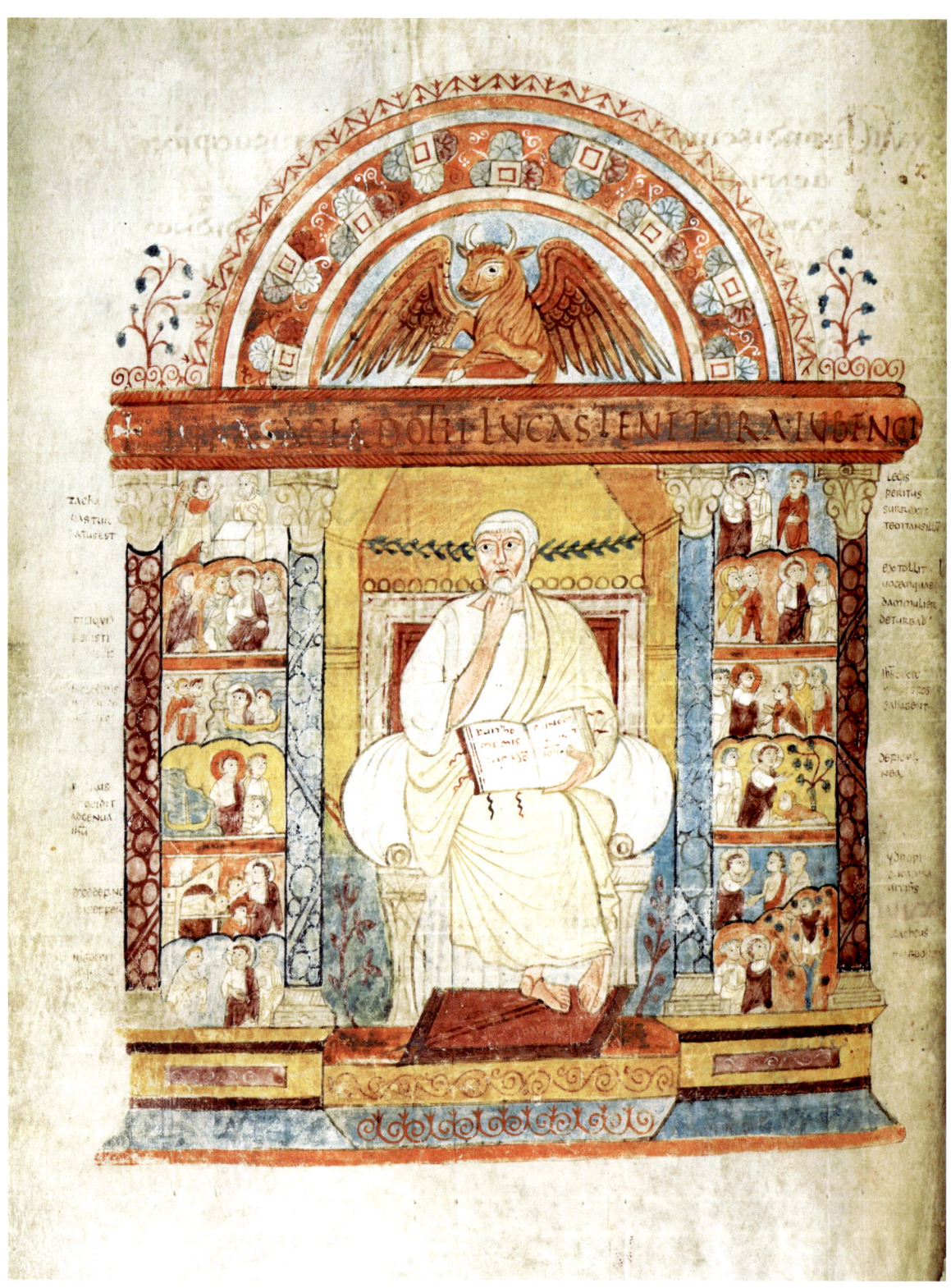

47. The St Augustine Gospels: portrait of St Luke. Italy, later 6th century. 24.5 x 18 cm (Corpus Christi College, Cambridge, MS 286, fol. 129v)

survives today, the so-called St Augustine Gospels (fig. 47), a late sixth-century Italian manuscript which is traditionally said to have been among the books sent by Gregory to Augustine himself. It had certainly reached England by the late seventh or early eighth century, when captions in an Insular hand were added to its illustrations. In the eleventh century further additions suggest that it was kept at St Augustine's Abbey, Canterbury. Whether or not the association with Augustine is true, this fine example of a late Roman illuminated gospel-book is certainly of the right date, origin and provenance to have been among the earliest such books to reach England. Reflecting this status, it is used in oath-taking at the installation of every new Archbishop of Canterbury. Although only two brightly coloured illuminated pages survive today – a portrait of the evangelist St Luke, flanked by small scenes from scripture, and a page with scenes from the life of Christ – it would have originally contained all four evangelist portraits with their symbols, each prefacing the accompanying gospel, probably a set of decorated canon tables, and at least one further page of scenes from the life of Christ.

The Christological cycle apart, this format formed the basis of many of the earliest Anglo-Saxon gospel-books. These also included the distinctive Insular additions of the densely ornamented carpet pages that prefaced each gospel; decorated *Incipit* pages with the title and opening words of each gospel; and decorated initials of increasing complexity, including the great Chi-Rho which begins that part of Matthew's Gospel describing the Incarnation of Christ. The rich colouring of the St Augustine Gospels, its linear yet still classical figural style, its architectural settings and its narrative sequences are all typical features which were to be very influential in the development of Anglo-Saxon art – and not only in manuscripts. Indeed, this particular manuscript continued to be echoed in Canterbury products up to and after the Conquest, reminding us that many other influential models, now lost, must have reached England at this time.

Even manuscripts produced at foundations with strong Irish/Ionan connections, such as the Lindisfarne Gospels, show evidence of the influence of Mediterranean manuscripts, alongside the exuberant animal, geometric and curvilinear decoration associated with the Hiberno-Saxon style of the later seventh and eighth centuries. The Lindisfarne evangelist portraits show a strong Italo-Byzantine influence (and, indeed, are accompanied by Greek-derived inscriptions) based on models from the Wearmouth/Jarrow monastery. The distinctive St Matthew figure (fig. 48), for example, clearly shares – albeit at some degree of separation – the same model as that of the Ezra portrait in the *Codex Amiatinus* (fig. 45). Its rich palette also indicates access to a wider range of pigments than the predominant reds, greens and yellows of the seventh-century manuscripts of Irish or Ionan inspiration, which echo the colouring of Coptic and early Frankish manuscripts. The fertile interchange of models and motifs from the two traditions is very clearly seen here.

Like the *Codex Amiatinus*, the Lindisfarne Gospels can be closely dated to the early eighth century on the basis of an inscription added in the tenth century by the glossator Aldred. This records that it was written and illuminated by Eadfrith, Bishop of Lindisfarne from 698 until his death in 721. With its immaculate script, virtuoso decoration, expensive pigments, and its binding of precious metal and gemstones made by Billfrith the anchorite (now lost, but also described by Aldred), the Lindisfarne Gospels was made as a supreme object of honour and veneration. The manuscript was without doubt associated with the cult of St Cuthbert, who was initially Bishop of Lindisfarne and then, in the latter part of his life, a holy recluse in the Irish tradition. It may well have been conceived in connection with Cuthbert's enshrinement in 698, at the beginning of Eadfrith's incumbency. Because of this close association with Northumbria's foremost saint, its history is known from its inception to the present – exceptional for any early medieval manuscript. This is the grandest of books, made for a special purpose, and that has helped to keep it safe through the centuries. But other less magnificent manuscripts also reflect the new Continental influences, fused with more traditional Anglo-Saxon zoomorphic elements, and with curvilinear and spiral motifs familiar from Celtic art (see Chapter 4).

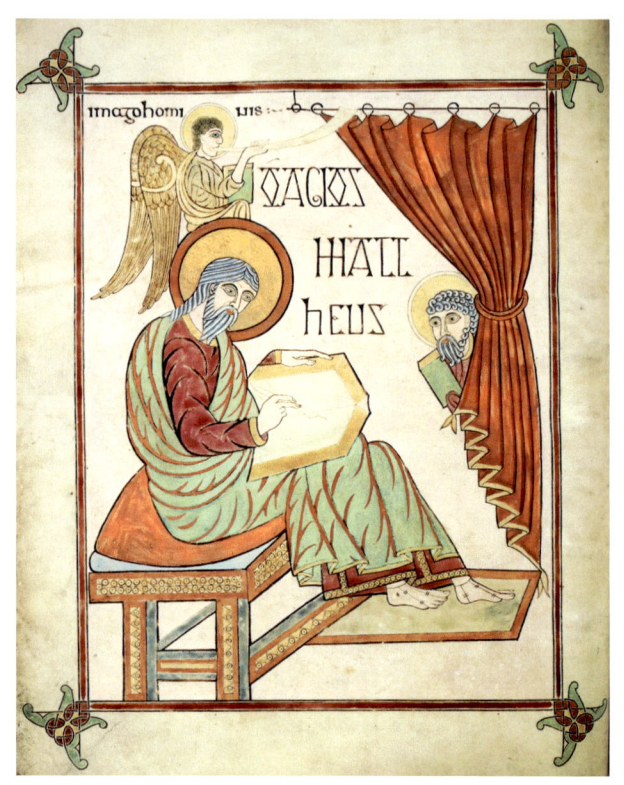

48. The Lindisfarne Gospels: portrait of St Matthew. Early 8th century. 34 x 24 cm (British Library, Cotton MS Nero D.iv, fol. 25v)

One of the very earliest surviving Insular gospel-books, the Book of Durrow, which was probably made in Iona or Northumbria around 680, elegantly assimilates Mediterranean, Celtic and Anglo-Saxon models in its decoration. Its elaborate carpet pages (see fig. 3) show eastern Mediterranean influences, probably Coptic and Syrian, drawing on manuscript models such as a copy of the *Diatessaron* of Tatian (*c.* 160–75). But these pages also incorporate Celtic curvilinear scroll and spiral ornament, and Anglo-Saxon interlacing animal decoration (closely related to the Anglian version of Style II), alongside classicizing grid decoration and interlace. So Mediterranean did some of this decoration appear that it has even been suggested that some of the carpet pages drew inspiration directly from Roman mosaic pavements, of types still to be seen throughout much of England. Insular influences are apparent in the Book of Durrow even where the model is Mediterranean in origin, as in the evangelist's animal symbols. The lion of St Mark and the calf of St Luke, with their distinctive curving delineation of the musculature, are strikingly similar to animal symbols on early Pictish sculpture, and it has been

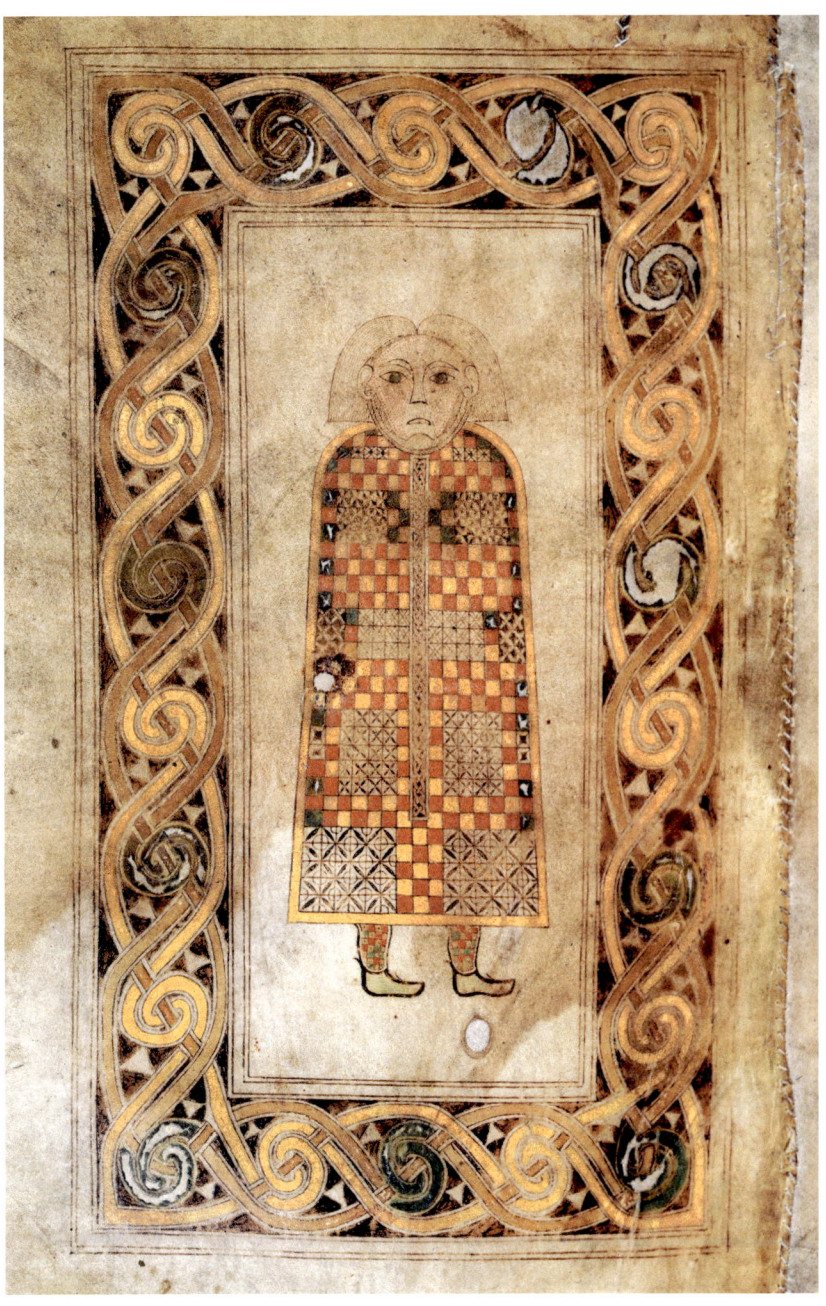

49. The Book of Durrow: portrait of St Matthew. Probably *c.* 680. 24.5 x 14.5 cm (Trinity College, Dublin, MS A.4.5.(57), fol. 21v)

argued that they could derive from them rather than vice versa.[3] Such exemplars were certainly not far from Iona, or Northumbria.

Yet this small manuscript is particularly important to the understanding of the development of the Hiberno-Saxon or Insular style because of its striking relationship to Anglo-Saxon metalwork of the mid-seventh century. The colourful chequerboard garment of the man symbolizing St Matthew (fig. 49) and the yellow frames that define his outline and those of the other evangelist symbols, echo Anglo-Saxon metalwork techniques of millefiori glass and cloisonné cellwork, as seen for instance, in the royal jewellery found at Sutton Hoo. More echoes of Anglo-Saxon cellwork are apparent in the rectangular and roundel patterns of some of the carpet pages. These recall seventh-century cloisonné belt buckles and 'button' sword fittings, best known from Sutton Hoo, but also from sites across England, which perhaps inspired the later enamelled stud inlays on eighth-century Irish metalwork, such as the 'Tara' chalice and the Derrynaflan paten.[4] As noted earlier, one of its pages recalls in its layout the gridded panels of the Sutton Hoo shoulder clasps, with its framework of Style II interlacing creatures surrounding a central decorated panel. The processing animals that dominate the same page have close Style II parallels on other seventh-century metalwork, including sword pommels from Crundale Down, Kent, and the Staffordshire Hoard, as well as the great processional cross from the hoard (see figs 3, 44 and 80). As we shall see, the cross, astonishingly, uses the identical model used to create the animal motifs on the Sutton Hoo maple-wood bottle mounts (see fig. 81). This even raises the outside possibility that the Book of Durrow itself might have originated in an Irish foundation in East Anglia, such as that founded by the monk Fursa in the Roman fort at Burgh Castle in Norfolk.[5]

     This is not the only instance in which objects from the extraordinary Staffordshire find are challenging our understanding of the art of the period. In the process, we are reminded once more of the great gaps in the surviving evidence, and the lack of certainty surrounding the localization and dating conventionally assigned to many of the earliest Insular manuscripts, and their relationship to secular metalwork (see Chapter 5). But whatever its precise date and origin, the Book of Durrow vividly exemplifies one of the ways in which newly introduced Mediterranean traditions of manuscript design were married with a Celtic, Anglo-Saxon and Pictish decorative vocabulary, to produce a quite new Insular style.

     Other surviving early Insular gospel-books – including two fragmentary Northumbrian manuscripts now in Durham Cathedral,[6] the Northumbrian Echternach Gospels, associated with the Anglo-Saxon

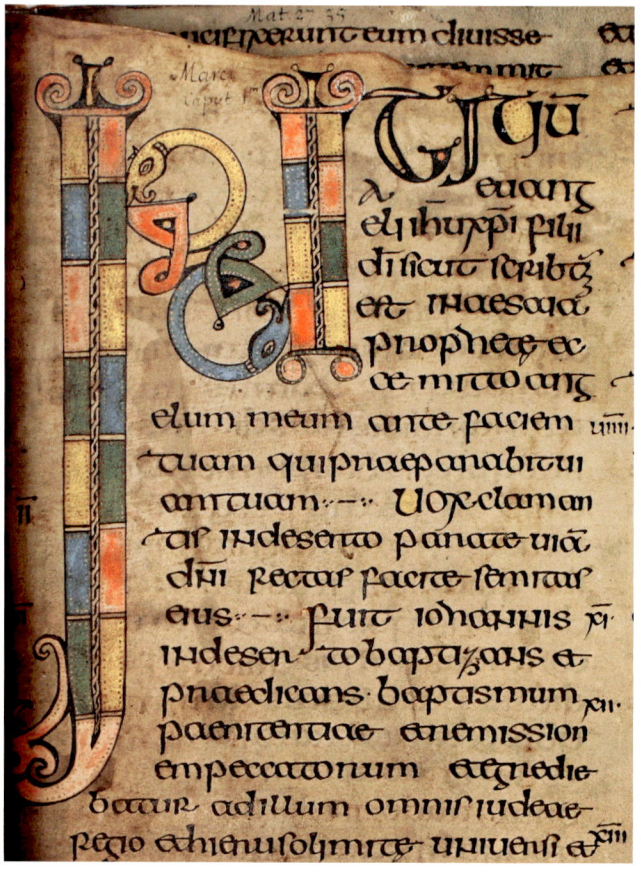

50 (*above*). Gospel fragment: detail of initial with animal head decoration from the beginning of St Mark's Gospel. Mid-7th century. Whole page 38.5 x 25 cm (Durham Cathedral Library, MS A.II.10, fol. 2)

51 (*opposite*). The St Chad Gospels: carpet page with interlacing animals preceding the Gospel of St Luke. Second quarter of the 8th century. 30.8 x 23.5 cm (Lichfield Cathedral Library, MS I, fol. 220)

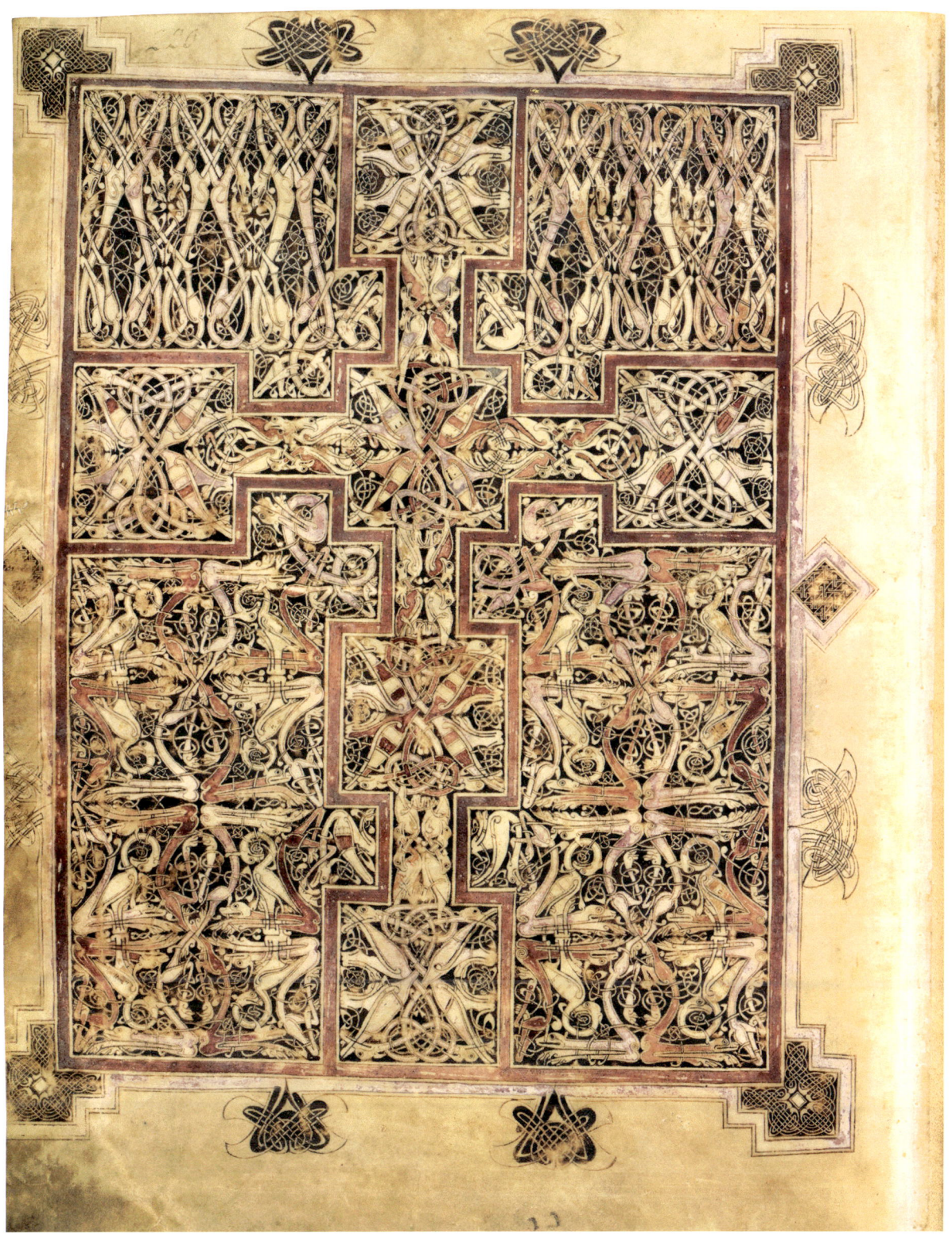

missionary St Willibrord[7] and the possibly Mercian St Chad Gospels (figs 50 and 51) – also testify to the heady mixture of Celtic, Germanic and classicizing cultures which were particularly active in Northumbria and its sphere of influence during this period. Stray metalwork finds, and excavations at secular and ecclesiastical sites from Pictland and the Scottish kingdom of Dál Riata down to Mercia, East Anglia and even Kent, have produced further evidence of the extent to which decorated artefacts from these different traditions circulated among the elite of the secular and ecclesiastical world. From this Insular melting pot, a hugely influential artistic tradition grew, which was to dominate Anglo-Saxon art for at least a century, and spread far beyond England itself.

The assimilation of new classical iconographies to native traditions appears in other media too. At Monkwearmouth, the earlier of the twin Wearmouth/Jarrow monasteries, much of the architectural sculpture is emphatically Roman or Gaulish in style. There were stone seats with arms in the form of crouching lions which would not have looked out of place in a Merovingian church, as well as turned stone columns and miniature baluster-patterned friezes. Alongside these, in one of the most Roman buildings of the north, there were also late seventh- and eighth-century sculptures in Insular style. These include a panel, perhaps from a screen, with interlacing long-beaked animals; great open-jawed animal-head terminals from chairs or other furnishings; and remarkable intertwining long-jawed beasts carved on the inner faces of the west entrance to the church (fig. 52). These creatures derive from a long line of older Anglo-Saxon protective images; here they guard the threshold between the sacred and profane space. Wilfrid and Bishop Acca's great church at Hexham was equally decorated in the manner of Gaul and Rome, almost to the exclusion of Germanic or Celtic elements – but even there, some Insular decoration occurs. However, perhaps nowhere is the mingling of traditions more clearly seen than in the sudden and extraordinary development of the depiction of the human figure and of visual narratives, in Anglo-Saxon art of this period.

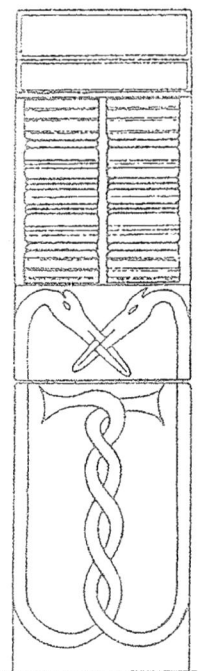

52. Interlacing creatures inside the porch at St Peter's church, Monkwearmouth, County Durham. Late 7th century (Drawing after Bruce-Mitford 1969)

A new figural tradition

Among the many items that Benedict Biscop brought back from his successive visits to Rome to install in his churches at Wearmouth and Jarrow were a number of panel paintings containing a wealth of figural illustration (described by Bede in his *Historia Abbatum*). At Wearmouth the church was hung with images of the Virgin and Apostles, scenes from the gospels and the Apocalypse, and depictions of the life of Christ. At Jarrow, images of events in the Old Testament were juxtaposed with images of events from the New Testament, which they were interpreted as prefiguring. These Roman icons and figural narratives (and no doubt there were many others in England) were quickly absorbed and imitated. A century later the monk Æthelwulf, describing a Northumbrian dependent house of Lindisfarne, referred to its richly furnished interior which included, among much else, banners or hangings depicting the miracles of Christ.[8] Such descriptions give a striking insight into the prominence of images in the early Anglo-Saxon Church, and to their importance as aids to worship, meditation and teaching. Along with manuscripts, textiles and ivory carvings, the imported icons were a key source of influence on the art and iconography of early Anglo-Saxon Christianity, and especially on the figural images which now began to play such an important role.

One manuscript example dating to the second quarter of the eighth century illustrates the assimilation of new ways of depicting the human form. Cassiodorus's *Commentary on the Psalms* is a large but now sparsely decorated book which is evidently based on a sixth-century Italian manuscript probably housed at Wearmouth/Jarrow.[9] The decoration of the two extant pages is competent, but far from the exquisite imagination and execution of the Lindisfarne Gospels; it must have been typical of many manuscripts produced to serve the needs of the growing church in this period.

The two surviving full-page images from Cassiodorus's *Commentary* are clearly drawn from a Mediterranean tradition. The first is of King David the psalmist seated on a throne, composing with a lyre of a Germanic type well known from seventh-century Anglo-Saxon contexts at Taplow and Sutton Hoo. This type of image of the psalmist king is of Continental origin and occurs widely in early medieval sculpture and manuscripts. The figure has a green halo, and his mauve robes swathe him in a pattern of narrow bands and angular folds. His hair is crisply curled and his green eyes are prominent. The other image is of a haloed standing figure in a mauve cloak holding a spear, and an orange halo bearing the name of David; beneath his feet is a snarling twin-headed beast (fig. 54). The boldly delineated folds of his clothing loop around the body to make arching patterns that merge into the shape of the torso. His hair is arranged in a series of tightly coiled spirals around the face, and he stares beyond the viewer with an otherworldly gaze. It is clear from the pose and the attributes that, although this figure is labelled as David, it also represents the widespread image of the risen Christ, trampling the beasts of sin and death (Psalm 91), a depiction which also occurs in later psalters. Here Christ is manifested as the new David, the warrior king from whom he was descended. The pose has a classical feel to it, as do the hard-edged stylized draperies, drawn from a distinct late classical linear style.[10] But in both these pages we can see how the style and iconography has been subtly adapted to incorporate Anglo-Saxon-style animal and interlace motifs, and how the marked stylization in the depiction of the figural images of Christ and David draws upon earlier Anglo-Saxon traditions of abstraction and pattern-making.

The animal ornament in the manuscript reflects these two contrasting strands. In the borders that frame the image of David playing the lyre, interlace panels are juxtaposed with ones containing animals of Anglo-Saxon pedigree, and others with lion-like beasts adapted from classical sources. The fierce animal-head decoration of David's throne, and the twin heads of the beast below Christ/David, are completely Insular in style, while the dual nature of the Christ/David image, intended to be read at more than one level, speaks both to the native Anglo-Saxon taste for riddles, verbal and visual, and to the contemporary Anglo-Saxon cult of the heroic Christian warrior king.

The two powerfully emblematic figures seen in the Durham Cassiodorus – King David, ancestor of Christ, and composer of the Psalms that played such a major part in the daily rituals and teaching of the Church; and David's descendant, Christ, the triumphant victor over sin and death, and embodiment of the salvation promised by the new faith – simply drawn though they are, represent something new and astonishing in Anglo-Saxon art. The new faith imported images in human form by the hundreds and possibly thousands, in manuscripts, ivories, icons and metalwork. Through the Christian message, such figural depictions introduced a new way of presenting ideas and narratives to Anglo-Saxon England. The idea of the human image as a means of telling a deeper truth, often through complex narratives, took Anglo-Saxon art in dramatically new directions.

As we saw in Chapter 1, the depiction of the human form seems to have been rare in Anglo-Saxon art of the pre-Christian period, and largely confined to particular cult or talismanic contexts. Highly stylized animal ornament was the main portal through which ideas about the cosmos, ancestry, life and death were transmitted visually. Even allowing for the distorting impact of the loss of wooden sculpture from that period, such human images as have survived from the fifth and sixth centuries are distinctive in not being naturalistic. And the rather less stylized figures of warriors on early seventh-century male gear, such as the Finglesham buckle and Sutton Hoo helmet also come from a tradition which is very different from the grave images of Christian manuscripts (see figs 16 and 22).

However, there may nonetheless be a relationship between some human figures glimpsed in this early metalwork and the sacred depictions of Anglo-Saxon Christian art. A clue may lie in the small three-dimensional silver and bronze cult figures discussed in Chapter 1, datable to the earlier part of the seventh century. The best of these are slim, stylized figures with formal gestures, delicately modelled in silver with gilded faces or clothing (see fig. 21). They may be influenced – at some remove – by small Roman bronze figurines of gods, or possibly their cruder Scandinavian counterparts. Yet their sudden appearance at much the same time as the first Christian missions suggests that their inspiration may lie further afield, through increasing contacts with

53 (*below*). Detail of the Virgin and Child, from St Cuthbert's coffin. *c.* 698 (Drawing after Battiscombe 1956)

54 (*opposite*). Cassiodorus's *Commentary on the Psalms*: Christ/David. Wearmouth/Jarrow, second quarter of the 8th century. 42 x 29.5 cm (Durham Cathedral Library, MS B.ii.30, fol. 172v)

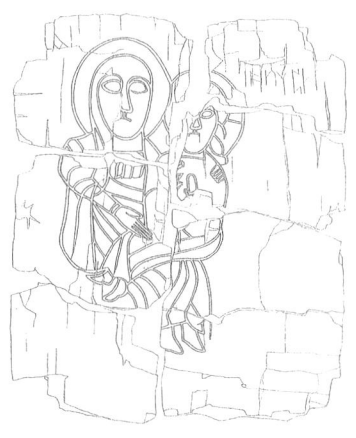

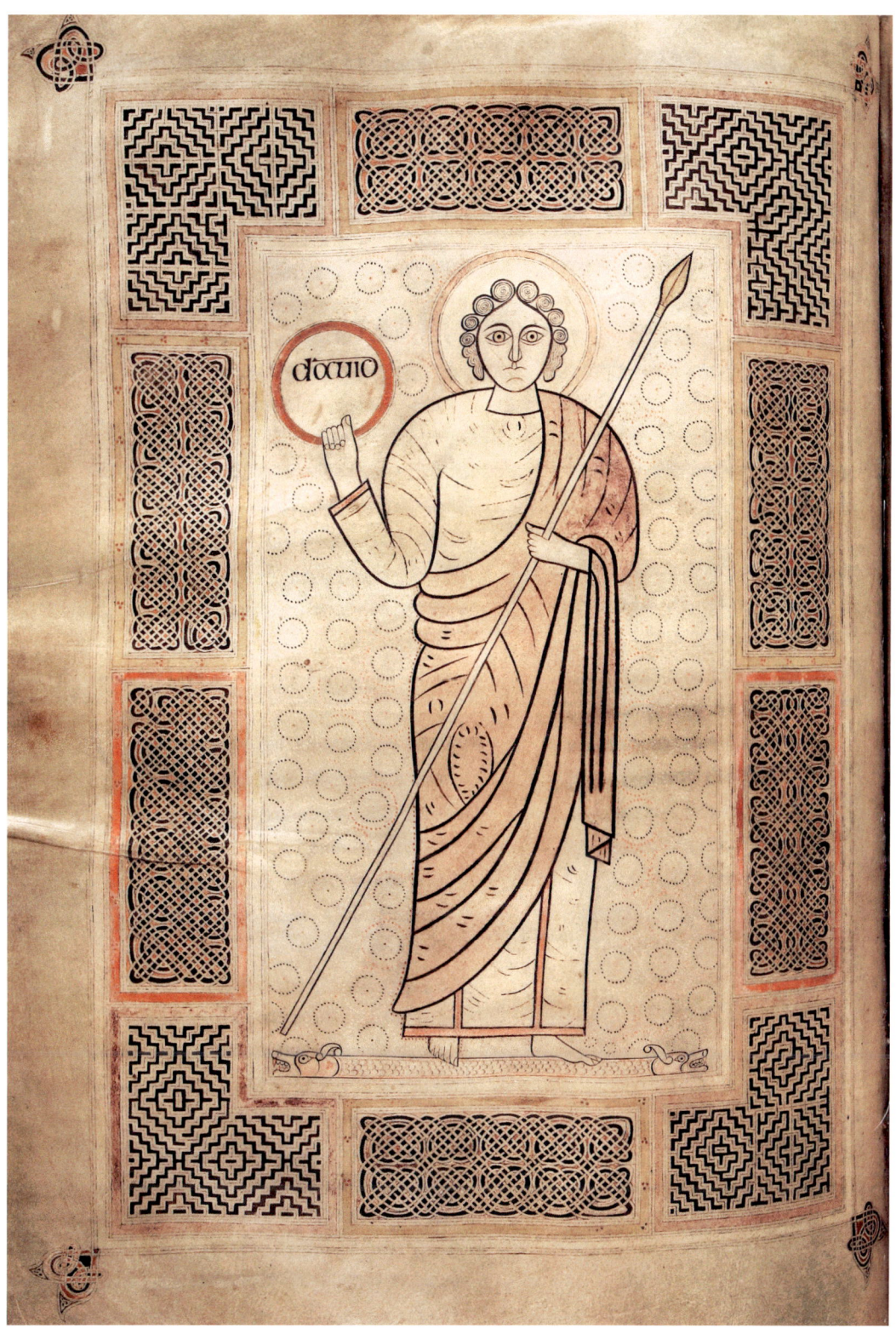

Christian Gaul and Italy. A shared Mediterranean influence may explain some of the similarities between these pagan figures and Anglo-Saxon Christian images. Their elongated, linear treatment and distant frontal gaze reflect a similar tendency to stylization in early medieval sacred images from Italy, Gaul and their Christian Germanic neighbours. This had its own impact on Anglo-Saxon Christian art, alongside that of the more naturalistic classical tradition. Visiting Anglo-Saxon pilgrims and clerics would have seen mosaics and paintings in some of the great early medieval churches in Rome and Ravenna which treated the human form in this much more stylized way. The icons and manuscripts that they brought back with them would certainly have included examples of this less naturalistic style – like the miniature scenes from the life of Christ in the St Augustine Gospels. At the same time, the traditional Anglo-Saxon taste for highly stylized ornament, favouring dynamic surface patterning and linearity rather than naturalistic modelling, also fed into the new depictions of the human image.

Certainly, the two different sets of human images – pagan and Christian – convey a similar message. As in the pagan cult figures, the stylization and otherworldly gaze of the figures seen in manuscripts, sculpture and metalwork of the period emphasize spiritual, not earthly matters. Images such as those of Christ in the Durham Cassiodorus (fig. 54) and Durham Gospels,[11] of the Virgin, Christ, apostles and other figures on St Cuthbert's coffin (fig. 53), and the figures of St Luke and St Mark in the St Chad Gospels are icons, not corporeal beings.[12] The abstract patterns of the clothing that covers Christ delineate not the tangible human body underneath, but an unimaginable divinity. Likewise, the human depictions – the Virgin, David, saints, apostles and evangelists – are all intermediaries between God and man, embodiments of the divine message rather than their earthly, three-dimensional selves. At its most accomplished – as on St Cuthbert's coffin, made around 698 for the saint's enshrinement at Lindisfarne, the evangelist portraits of the near-contemporary Lindisfarne Gospels (fig. 48), or the delicately drawn bust of St Gregory in the St Petersburg Bede manuscript dating to about 746 (fig. 55) – this figural stylization conveys this spiritual message with great eloquence. In less skilled hands, as on the little silver plaque from a shrine or book cover from Hexham (fig. 56), or the somewhat later St Andrew Auckland cross shaft,[13] it has an arresting simplicity. It was also highly influential: in its emphasis on line, rather than volume,

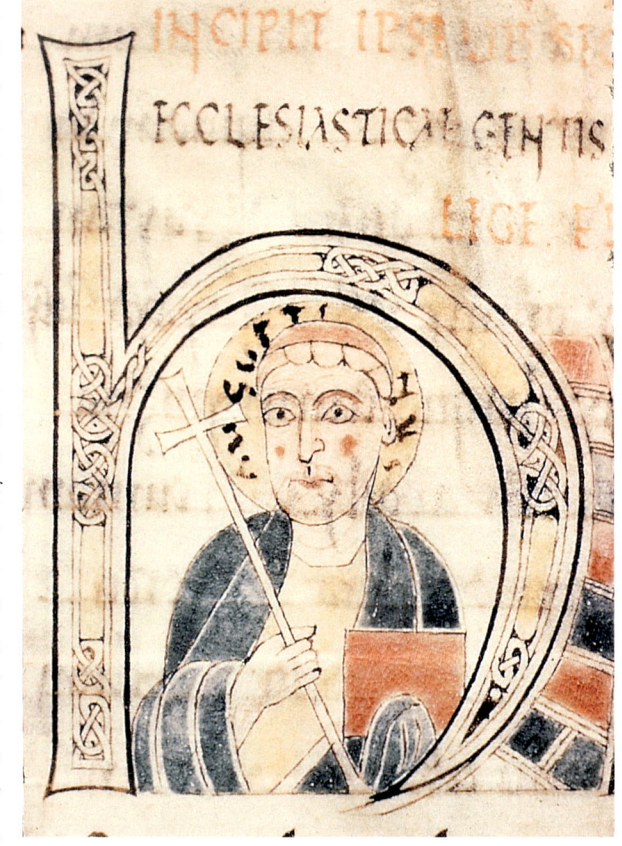

55. The St Petersburg Bede: detail of an initial and Gregory the Great. Wearmouth/Jarrow, c. 746. Whole page 27 x 19 cm (National Library of Russia, St Petersburg, MS Cod. Q.v.1.18, fol. 26v)

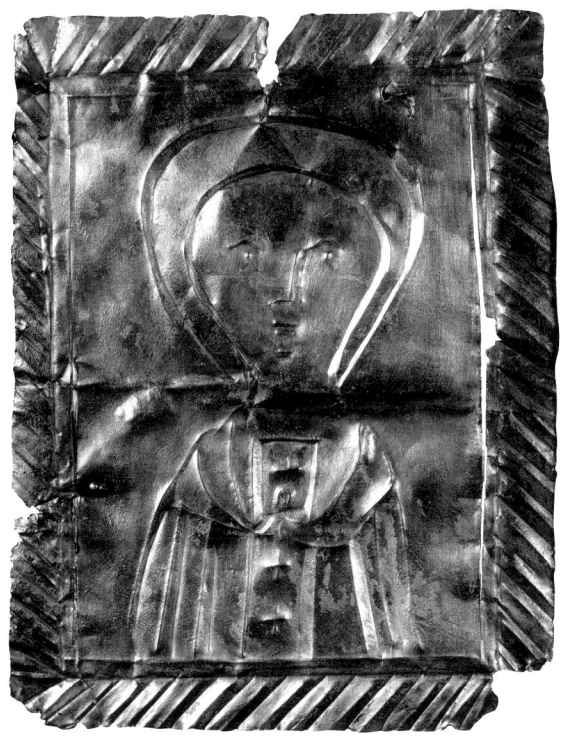

56. Silver plaque depicting a saint, from a book cover or shrine. Hexham, Northumberland, first half of the 8th century. H. 9.9 cm (British Museum)

this treatment of the human form was to become a distinctive and enduring element in Anglo-Saxon figural art.

A Canterbury manuscript tradition

But Hiberno-Saxon manuscripts do not tell the whole story of manuscript art in the seventh and earlier eighth centuries. Although we know little about art and learning at Canterbury until the later years of the seventh century, when Theodore of Tarsus (602–90) and Hadrian (*c.* 635–709/10) established a highly influential school of learning there (see p. 111), it is clear that it must have had libraries and scriptoria from the time of St Augustine. It was certainly a well-established centre of learning by the 630s, when Sigeberht, king of East Anglia (630/1–?), who had become a Christian while exiled in Gaul during the reign of Rædwald (d. *c.* 625), imported teachers from Canterbury when he wished to set up a religious school in his kingdom. No decorated Kentish manuscripts survive from the seventh century; but from the first half of the eighth century two distinctive, superbly ornamented manuscripts suggest that Canterbury had its own well-established tradition of manuscript painting, strongly influenced by Italian models.

The early eighth-century Vespasian Psalter (fig. 57) and the slightly later Stockholm *Codex Aureus* (fig. 58) are close in style and were probably decorated in the same scriptorium. A strong Italian influence is evident in the script and decoration; the image of David composing the Psalms in the psalter, and those of the evangelists Matthew and John in the *Codex Aureus* combine a degree of naturalistic modelling. This can be seen especially in the faces, hands and feet of the figures, where it is combined with a boldly defined linear treatment of the garments, whose dynamic and painterly patterning has little to do with the human body within. The colours are rich and densely applied, the tones skilfully modulated. The *Codex Aureus* in addition has purple-stained pages with gold, silver and white script of exquisite quality, and an exceptionally lavish use of gold, seen most magnificently on the Chi-Rho page (fig. 76). This was a manuscript of exceptional, perhaps even royal, splendour, unmatched by any other from this period – although the Vespasian Psalter shows that Canterbury clearly had the capacity to produce other manuscripts of the highest quality. The psalter also contains rich gold detailing in its frontispiece, and two surviving decorated initials with images of David, which can claim to be the first surviving historiated initials in a Western manuscript – a remarkable innovation in itself (fig. 57). But the lively figure tradition reflected in both manuscripts is also combined with other elements taken not from Italian tradition, but from the Hiberno-Saxon repertory. These include swirling hairspring spirals, peltas, trumpet scrolls and, particularly in the *Codex Aureus*, Insular-style animal ornament. It shows just how seamless, even in so Roman a context as Canterbury, the melding of the native and classical traditions had become by the early eighth century, creating a new and distinctively Anglo-Saxon aesthetic.

Northumbrian stone sculpture

Alongside the firmly defined, linear figural style that runs through these manuscripts, another much more naturalistic classical tradition can be seen in Anglo-Saxon sculpture of the eighth century. The great Northumbrian stone crosses, such as those at Ruthwell, Bewcastle, Rothbury and Otley, embody the message of the Roman Church in their imposing classical-style figures, skilfully carved in high relief, as well as in their complex iconographies. The origins of these great Anglo-Saxon standing crosses are unclear; they may owe

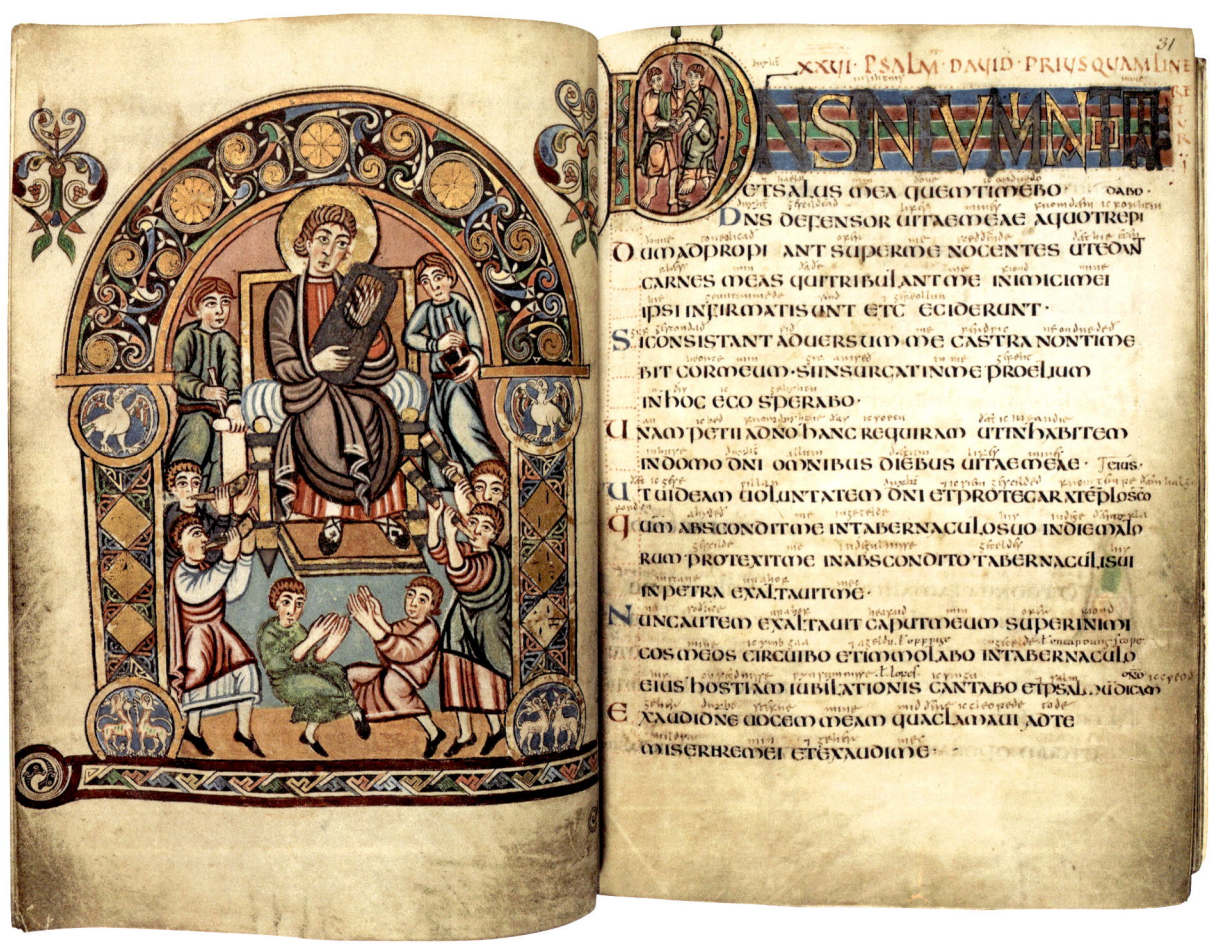

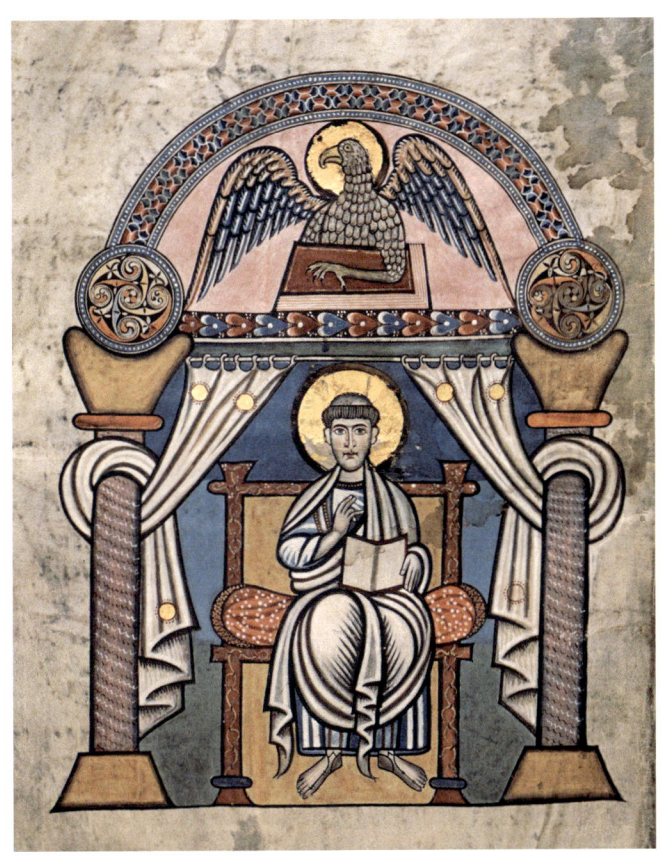

something to a native tradition of carved wooden monuments, but it is certain that the skills for stone carving were brought to England in the seventh century by masons and sculptors from Gaul and Italy.

The earliest Anglo-Saxon stone carvings are mostly architectural in nature and, as we have seen, very much based on Continental models; they are associated with the building of churches and monasteries that were needed to house the monks and spread the new faith. Only at a slightly later date, it seems, did the first stone crosses begin to appear in Northumbria, probably in the earlier part of the eighth century. The use of stone as a material, both for the churches and for the freestanding crosses, had a special significance. It signified the enduring nature of the Roman Church, in much the same way that the Roman Empire had used its own stone monuments – still widely visible in northern England – as statements of its authority to govern its outposts according to the civilized standards of Rome. But stone also had a particular Christian significance for clerics of the Conversion period in England. Christ's words to his apostle Peter (whose Greek name, πετρος, means 'rock' or 'stone') were 'You are Peter, the Rock; on this rock I will build my church' (Matthew 16:18); according to tradition Peter, with Paul, established the See of Rome, and was its first bishop. So the church built in stone (and many early Anglo-Saxon ones, including Benedict Biscop's foundation at Wearmouth, were dedicated to St Peter) embodied both the foundation of the Christian church, and its authority from Rome. The early stone crosses, mostly associated with monastic foundations where they served as focal points for prayer, meditation, instruction and ceremony, reinforced the same message.

This brief digression on the symbolism of stone serves as a reminder of the deeply meditated nature of such monuments, and their evocation of a Roman authority. This is also clearly seen in the decorative programmes on the crosses, articulated in often complex iconographies with accompanying texts in Latin and, sometimes, Old English. The great cross at Ruthwell, Dumfriesshire, which in the earlier eighth century was part of the kingdom of Northumbria, is the most elaborate surviving monument of this early period. It gives a remarkable glimpse into the sophisticated ways in which religious ideas were presented in eighth-century Northumbrian sculpture (fig. 59). Broken up and buried by Protestant iconoclasts in 1642, it was subsequently

57 (*opposite*). The Vespasian Psalter: David the Psalmist with musicians (left), and an initial with David and Jonathan (right). Canterbury, early 8th century. Each page 23.5 x 18 cm (British Library, Cotton MS Vespasian A.i, fols 30v–31r)

58 (*above*). The Stockholm *Codex Aureus*: portrait of St John. Canterbury, mid-8th century. 39.5 x 31.4 cm (Kungliga Biblioteket, Stockholm, MS A.135, fol. 150v)

restored to an approximation of its original grandeur, although its cross head is largely missing and some parts are badly defaced. Its decorative programme is ambitious. One of the two broad sides is carved with depictions of Christ's life on earth: the Annunciation, the Visitation and the Crucifixion, together with the miracle of the healing of the blind man as an image of conversion, and the woman bathing the feet of Christ as an image of repentance. The second broad side displays images relating to Christ's sacramental body: the return of the incarnate Christ child from exile in Egypt; the heavenly bread broken by the first monks, Paul and Anthony, in the desert; the risen Christ treading on beasts, symbols here of sin and death; and Christ adored as the Lamb of God. The references to the desert (the monks and the return from exile) connect the cross firmly to a monastic community. Monasteries were seen in contemporary thought as emulating these early monks by retreating into a symbolic desert, represented by the establishment of monasteries in remote and marginal parts of Northumbria, such as St Cedd's foundation at Lastingham on the edge of the North Yorkshire moorland, and Lindisfarne itself.

These biblical scenes are accompanied by explanatory labels mostly in Latin, and in Roman capitals. The narrower sides carry the early Christian motif of fruiting vine scrolls, here inhabited by birds and beasts which feed upon them, in an allusion to the true vine as a symbol of Christ nourishing his church (see p. 18 above). But the accompanying inscriptions are from a version of a poem known as the *Dream of the Rood*, composed in Old English and here carved in runes. In it, the Cross addresses the dreamer/poet in a dramatic account of the Crucifixion which falls into two parts: the Cross accepting Christ and his suffering, and then delivering his body to its keepers. These two halves of the poem are matched in the scenes on the broad sides; the first, beginning with the Crucifixion, narrates events from Christ's life and ministry; the second focuses on his sacramental body. The images through which this complex meditation on the Christian message is conveyed display, like the poem, a sophisticated gravity and mastery of the craft which speaks directly to the onlooker. The figures of Christ are clothed in garments which fall in cascading folds of impeccable classicism, acknowledging the human form within. This new Roman naturalism, seen in both the figural style and the elegant scrolling vine and its inhabitants, is here dramatically combined with the runic poem which comes directly from Germanic vernacular tradition, in a triumphant re-rendering of the Christian message for an Anglo-Saxon audience. And in the context of the learned, literate and monastic audience for which this cross was made, it may be significant that the Old English word for a runic letter, *run*, can also mean a mystery, something hidden, to be teased out – another instance of the marriage of theological *ruminatio* (see p. 29) with Anglo-Saxon modes of expression.

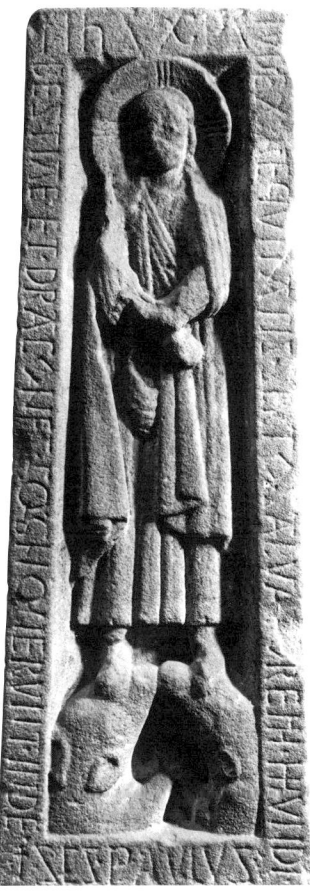
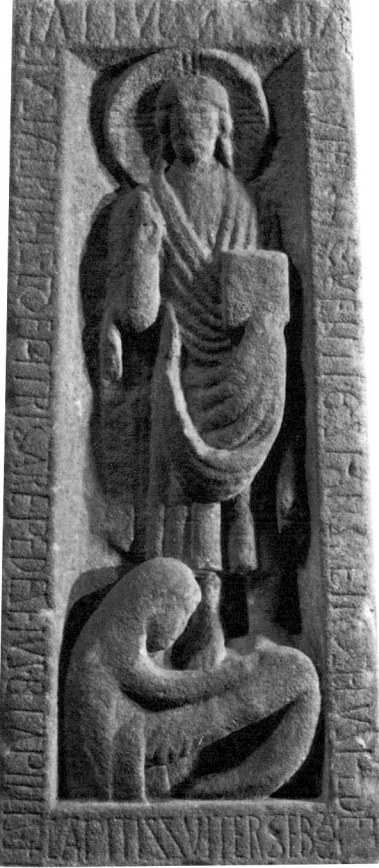
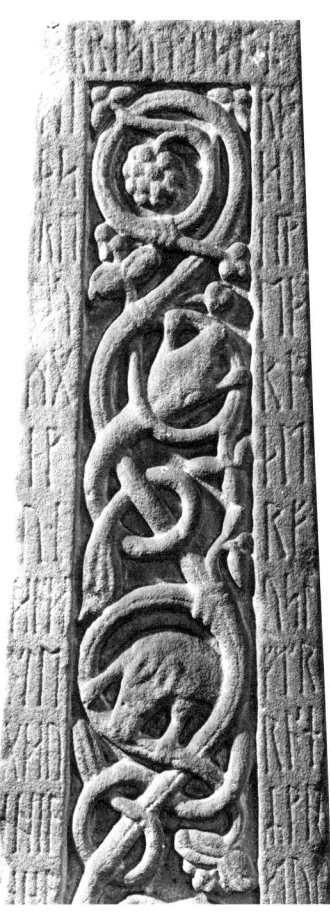

59. The Ruthwell Cross, details: (*left*) Christ triumphant; (*centre*) Christ and Mary Magdalene; (*right*) inhabited vine scroll with runic inscription. Mid-8th century. H. (whole cross) approx. 500 cm (Ruthwell parish church, Dumfriesshire)

Other crosses perform a similar function, using different combinations of image, text, and abstract animal and plant ornament. The near-contemporary Bewcastle (Cumbria) cross shaft still occupies its original position by a church on a lonely fell side, significantly sited within what had been the central administrative and religious complex of a former Roman frontier fort (fig. 61). One side depicts Christ in Majesty and John the Baptist, very similar in style to the images on the Ruthwell Cross. There is also a secular image of a cloaked man with a hawk, perhaps the person by whom, or in whose honour, the cross was erected – as a now extremely weathered runic inscription above is said to have originally recorded. The decoration of the other sides is composed of panels of lush and complex vine scroll, some with creatures feeding on it, interlace and chequer patterns of typical Insular type, and a sun-dial for keeping the hours of worship.

This Northumbrian tradition of a fully absorbed and reinvented *Romanitas* in figure-carving lasted into the early ninth century, as stone crosses such as those from Rothbury, Easby and Otley show. Their busts of saints, apostles and evangelists, often under classical arches, continue to be combined with lively animal and vine-scroll ornament in the now familiar interchange between classical and native in the art of the region (fig. 62). And as has recently been argued, the cross head at Rothbury is even carved with images of Christ and the consular *mappa* and sceptre, insignia of Roman rule that must ultimately derive from a late Roman consular ivory diptych.[14]

Only a little later, equally striking references to the power of Roman models can be seen in a number of monumental cylindrical columns, originally topped by cross heads, which survive in Northumbria (Masham and Dewsbury, Yorkshire), Mercia (Wolverhampton, Staffordshire) and Kent (Reculver; fig. 60). As with much other Anglo-Saxon sculpture, their dates have been vigorously debated, but a production period centring on the late eighth and early ninth centuries seems possible for all of them. The Masham and Wolverhampton columns are now severely weathered, but it is still possible to discern elegant arcades, frames and plant scrolls with figural or animal images which can be paralleled in Mercian sculpture at this period. The Reculver column is a formidable piece of classicizing figure sculpture, made for a rich early foundation which was built with an apse and *porticus* (small side chapels) in fifth-/sixth-century Italian style; it clearly belongs within the romanizing orbit of Canterbury in much the same way as the Vespasian Psalter and the *Codex Aureus*. These splendid columnar crosses, it is suggested, make clear reference to the triumphal and Jupiter columns which were set up across the empire, even in remote Britannia, of which Trajan's Column is the best known.[15] As with the stone crosses, the message is that of the new and everlasting imperium of the Church of Rome.

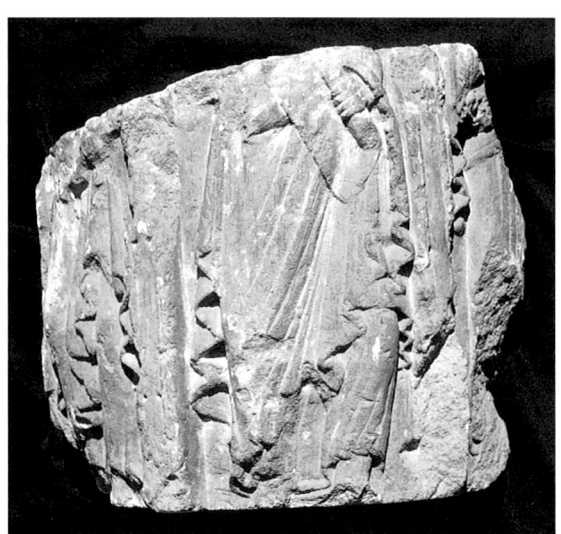

60 (*right*). Column with figures of saints or evangelists. Reculver, Kent, late 8th or early 9th century. H. approx. 32 cm (Canterbury Cathedral)

61 (*far right*). The Bewcastle Cross: side with elaborate vine scroll and interlace. Mid-8th century. H. 440 cm (St Cuthbert, Bewcastle, Cumbria)

62 (*opposite*). The Easby Cross: side with Christ in Majesty and haloed busts of apostles. Easby, North Yorkshire, late 8th or early 9th century. H. 250 cm (Victoria and Albert Museum, London)

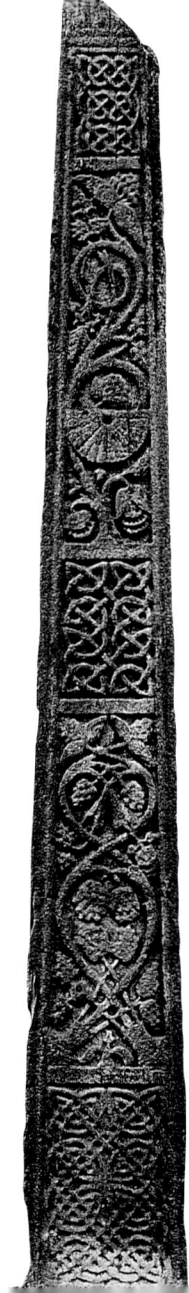

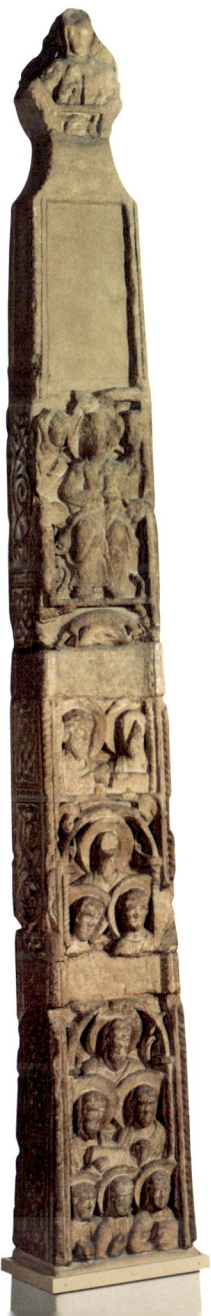

Secular art in the seventh and eighth centuries

The Christian images seen in ecclesiastical manuscripts and sculpture do not tell the whole story, however (though the apparently secular figure with a hawk on the Bewcastle Cross hints at another dimension). It is evident, in spite of the limited range of surviving artefacts, that there was a sturdy tradition of making secular images for secular purposes. The new Continental dress fashions that became current from around the beginning of the seventh century – which replaced the old-style paired brooches with single large disc brooches and decorated pendants and pins (figs 43 and 63)– also seem to have helped the spread of Style II around the country, along with new types of garnet inlay, including cabochons and simpler, 'honeycomb' cellwork. The grandest of this garnet ornament is to be seen in the royal jewellery of Sutton Hoo, and on the sword fittings and other accoutrements of the warrior elite, such as those in the Staffordshire Hoard (see Chapter 5). These new jewellery styles took their inspiration from Roman and Byzantine models, as did some of the earliest Anglo-Saxon coins – in gold and later, silver – which began to appear at the same time.

The history of early Anglo-Saxon coinage is complicated and uncertain, not only in terms of where and when it was made, but by whom and for what purpose. Nevertheless, it is clear that the seventh- and early eighth-century moneyers copied some designs from Roman sources as well as from contemporary Merovingian and Byzantine coins (fig. 65). But they were also increasingly experimenting in their silver coinage with combinations of images drawn from Germanic as well as a wide range of classical and Byzantine sources – not all of them copied from other coins. The silver coins known as sceattas, the Anglo-Saxon penny of this period (fig. 64), have a particularly inventive visual vocabulary, which includes vine scrolls, interlacing animals and plain interlace, prancing creatures, centaurs, snakes, birds, wolves and lions. Figural busts also occur, some of which, it has been argued, may be part of linked sequences, such as those apparently depicting each of the five senses. Some of this coinage may possibly have been minted by bishops, in the context of controlling the revenues of the large ecclesiastical enterprises which many monasteries had become by the end of the seventh century; but many were royal issues, as their inscriptions often make clear. Here, then, is a body of largely secular art, albeit on a very small scale, which makes use of the full range of traditions and influences that were now established in England by this time. There is much still to be understood here, as the study of their iconography, still in its infancy, unfolds.

But the most remarkable piece of secular art – albeit probably made in a religious milieu and for a moral purpose – to have survived from the Anglo-Saxon period is the Franks Casket (fig. 66). Named after its donor to the British Museum, the great collector and curator Augustus Wollaston

Franks (1826–97), the casket is a whale-bone box of Northumbrian origin and dates to the early part of the eighth century, not very distant in time from the making of the Ruthwell and Bewcastle crosses.[16] Yet it could hardly be more different in both appearance and content from these assured interpretations of classical style; indeed, there is really nothing else like it in the surviving art of the seventh and eighth centuries.

The casket was originally fitted with silver or gilded mounts, some possibly jewelled, and it is likely that the bone was originally painted, which would have given it a much richer, less austere appearance than that which it presents today. Each of its five faces is densely carved with scenes from Germanic and Roman legend, and from the Judaeo-Christian tradition. The Adoration of the Magi and the Germanic tale of Weland the Smith are paired on the front of the box; the Germanic hero Egil's defence of a stronghold is on the lid; the destruction of Jerusalem by the Roman general Titus on the back; Romulus and Remus fed by the wolf on the left-hand end; and a scene from a lost Germanic tale about Hos and Erta on the right-hand end. These are accompanied by explanatory texts which frame the scenes, and some smaller labels, in Old English and written in runes. There are two exceptions: the main runic inscription on the front describes not the two scenes it frames, but the physical origin of the casket itself, in the form of a riddling verse on the stranded whale from whose bones it was made; and the inscription describing the Roman sack of Jerusalem on the back shifts at one point into Latin and the Roman alphabet. In addition, the runic inscription on the enigmatic right-hand end, also in verse, is partly encrypted to conceal its meaning at first glance. The idea of riddles and multi-layered messages is central to the scenes on the casket, and how its overall programme is to be understood.

The human figures, animals and plants which crowd each scene are carved in marked relief, as are the inscriptions; and though the scenes clearly draw on very different classical and Germanic models, the style is consistent. The figures are clad in a variety of deeply grooved garments, their faces and

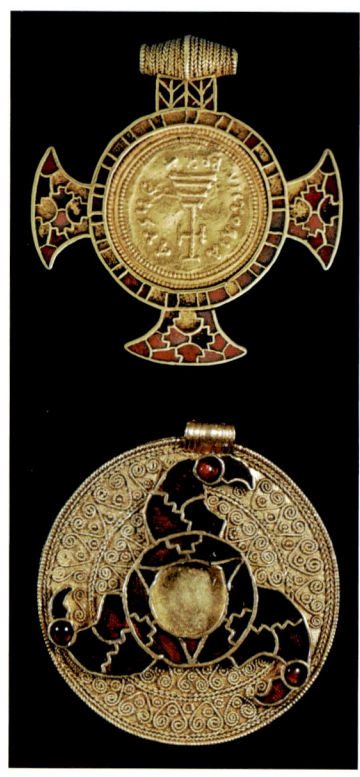

63. Two gold and garnet pendants: (*above*) Cross pendant with a coin of the Byzantine Emperor Heraclius datable to between 613 and 630. Wilton, Norfolk, early 7th century. H. 4.7 cm; (*below*) Pendant with triskele of birds. Faversham, Kent, early 7th century. Diam. (with loop) 3.7 cm (both British Museum)

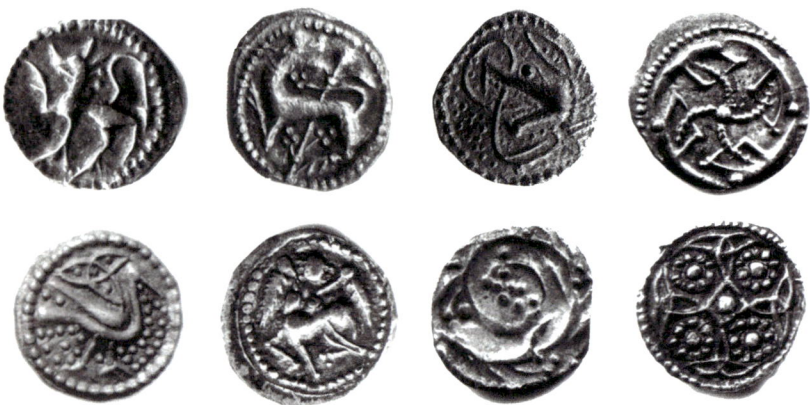

64. Silver sceattas, showing a variety of artistic motifs. Early 8th century. Average diam. 1.2 cm (After Gannon 2003)

65. Anglo-Saxon gold coins dating from the second half of the 7th century: (*top*) Shilling minted at London, based on a coin of the emperor Crispus. Diam. 1.2 cm; (*centre*) Shilling, clasped hands type. Diam. 1.3 cm; (*bottom*) Shilling with two emperors. Diam. 1.4 cm (all British Museum)

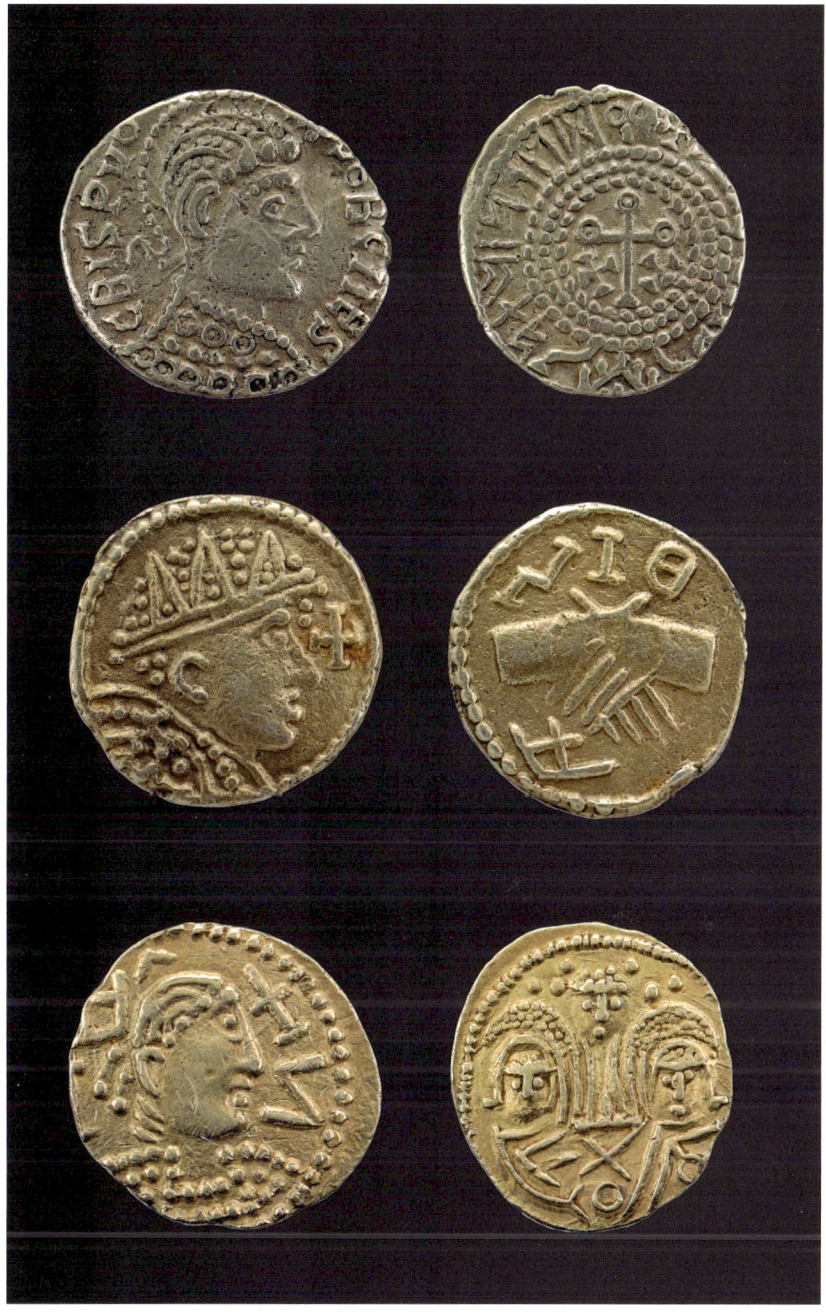

hands are stylized, and their gestures strongly accentuated. Even in those scenes where the figures are in static poses, the overriding impression is dynamic, charged with movement. In this linear style, and in the general busyness and gesturing, particularly in the Germanic scenes, there is a kinship with earlier Anglo-Saxon art, especially the stylized figures which appear on

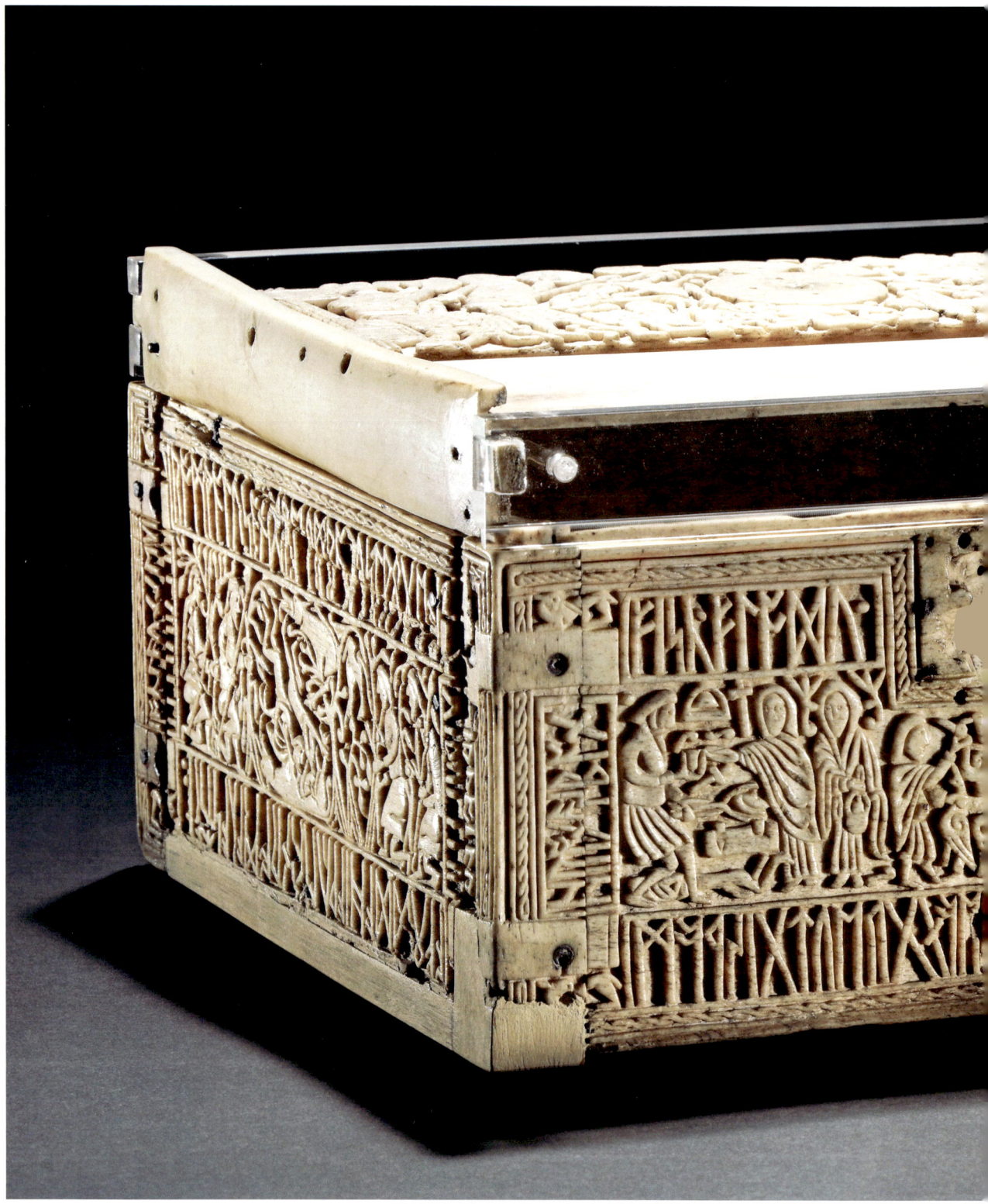

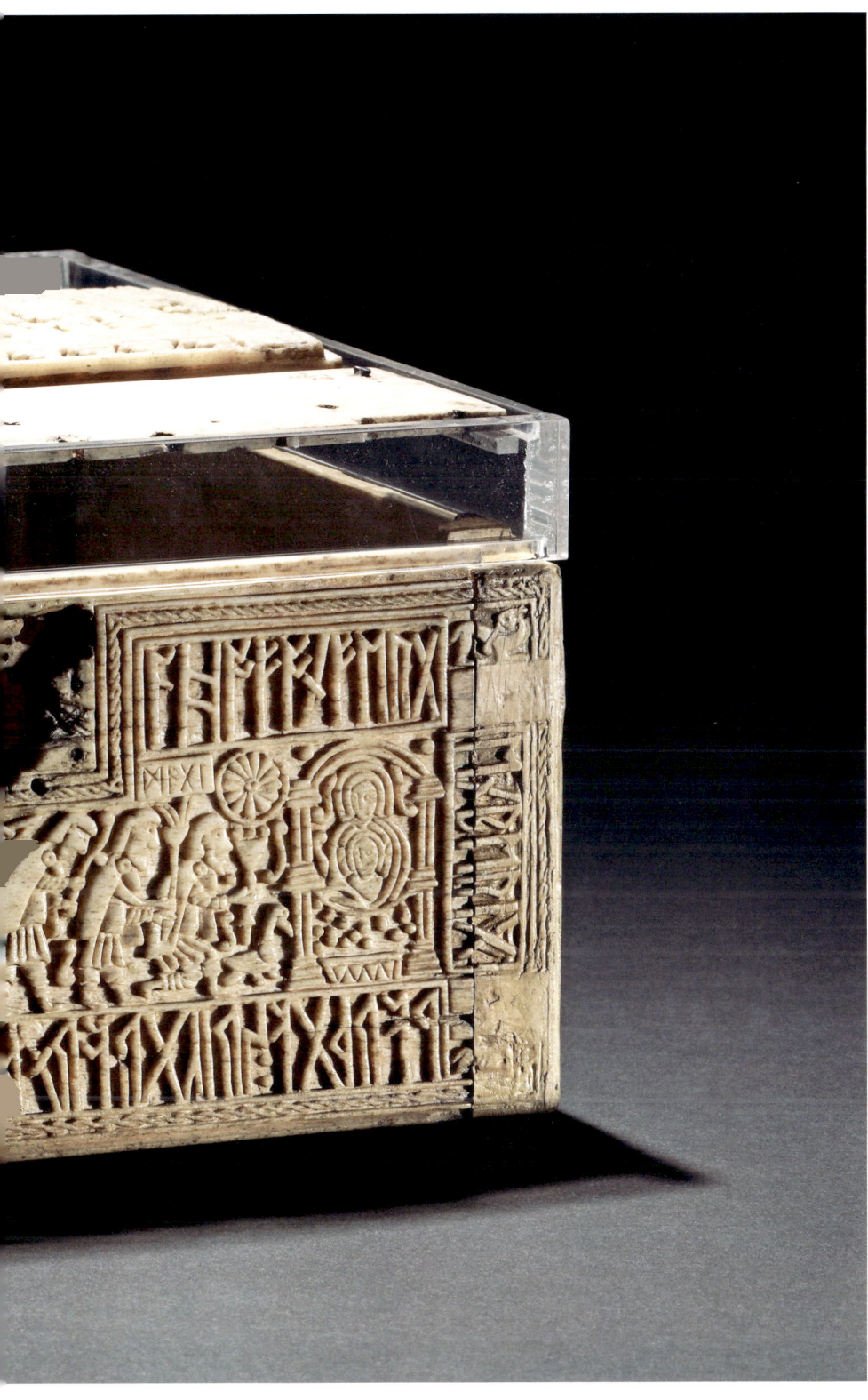

66. The Franks Casket: carved
whale-bone box. First half
of the 8th century. L. 22.9 cm
(British Museum)

helmets and other warrior gear from the late sixth and seventh centuries, most memorably at Sutton Hoo and in the Staffordshire Hoard. A traditional Anglo-Saxon stylistic strand is seen in other elements. Birds of a recognizably Insular character make their appearance in a number of scenes, and a variety of creatures – a horse, wolves, crouching dog-like beasts, winged lions and bird-headed snakes – also show a clear debt to the Hiberno-Saxon manuscript tradition. Forests and symbolic buildings with arches and masonry form the backdrop to these carefully orchestrated scenes, while any remaining space is filled with sprigs of foliage and roundels; elements of these, too, show a close relationship with Insular manuscript art of the period.

Nevertheless, the casket has an impeccable Roman pedigree, both in the iconography of the non-Germanic scenes, and in its very form and layout, which is based on an early Christian ivory reliquary chest similar to the fourth-century example that survives at Brescia in northern Italy.[17] This, too, has a programme of contrapuntal scenes – drawn, like the icons at Jarrow, from the Old and New Testaments – surrounded by frames which comment upon the main scenes, although in this case using images, not texts. A similar casket must have been available in Northumbria in the seventh and eighth centuries, among the many treasures brought back from Rome and Gaul by Benedict Biscop, Ceolfrith and other prelates and pilgrims.

The maker of the Franks Casket clearly possessed great learning and ingenuity, to construct an object which is so visually and intellectually complex. Its meaning continues to be much discussed, but it is generally accepted that the scenes, drawn from contrasting traditions, were carefully chosen to counterpoint one another in the creation of an overarching set of Christian messages. What used to be seen as an eccentric, almost random, assemblage of pagan Germanic and Christian stories is now understood as a sophisticated programme in perfect accord with the Church's concept of universal history. According to this, events or tales of the past, in all their diversity, were part of that greater history which culminated in God's message, incarnated in Christ, and which would achieve its end at the Second Coming, when all the nations had been converted. We know that cosmographies – world histories embodying this perceived truth – circulated in late seventh- and eighth-century England, because the Northumbrian king Aldfrith (r. 685–704) gave land to the monastery at Wearmouth/Jarrow in exchange for just such a prized manuscript. And the use of stories drawn from the Anglo-Saxon tradition, far from being at odds with a Christian message, is very much in step with Pope Gregory the Great's instruction to his missionaries that they should adapt pagan Anglo-Saxon temples and festivals to the service of the new religion, using that which was familiar to make Christianity more attractive and accessible to the heathen populace. Here once again, we see the past used to inform understanding of the present.

The carefully structured message of the Franks Casket is a highly moral one, about the nature of kingship, and of good and bad rule in a divinely ordered world, where salvation comes through devotion and obedience to Christ. It is likely that the casket was made to contain an exemplary text of some kind, very possibly a psalter. Alongside the gospels, the psalter has always been a central text; because of its daily recitation in services, it was also a book through which the key skill of reading was learnt. Because the Psalms were thought to have been composed by King David, they were also perceived as an inspiration for rulers. A fine psalter would be a very suitable gift for an Anglo-Saxon prince, especially one who was learning to read the sacred texts. The casket is unquestionably an object with a Christian message, made in a learned and probably monastic milieu; and its very distinctive iconography, lavish decoration, and rare and costly material, all point to an intended secular, probably royal, recipient.

To us the Franks Casket seems an extraordinary object, but it is not likely to have been unique in its mixture of cultural traditions, or in its ambitious and complex use of narrative. In many ways it is typical of the intellectual ferment of the age, in which traditional modes of expression were transformed by the new ideas and models brought from Italy, and Mediterranean styles and iconographies were adapted to an indigenous culture. What is more extraordinary is that such a supremely literate and sophisticated object could have been made only a hundred or so years after the first Roman missions began their work in England: a testimony, like the great gospel-books and standing crosses of this period, to the powerfully creative interaction of these different traditions which came together in new art forms, new ideas and new modes of expression.

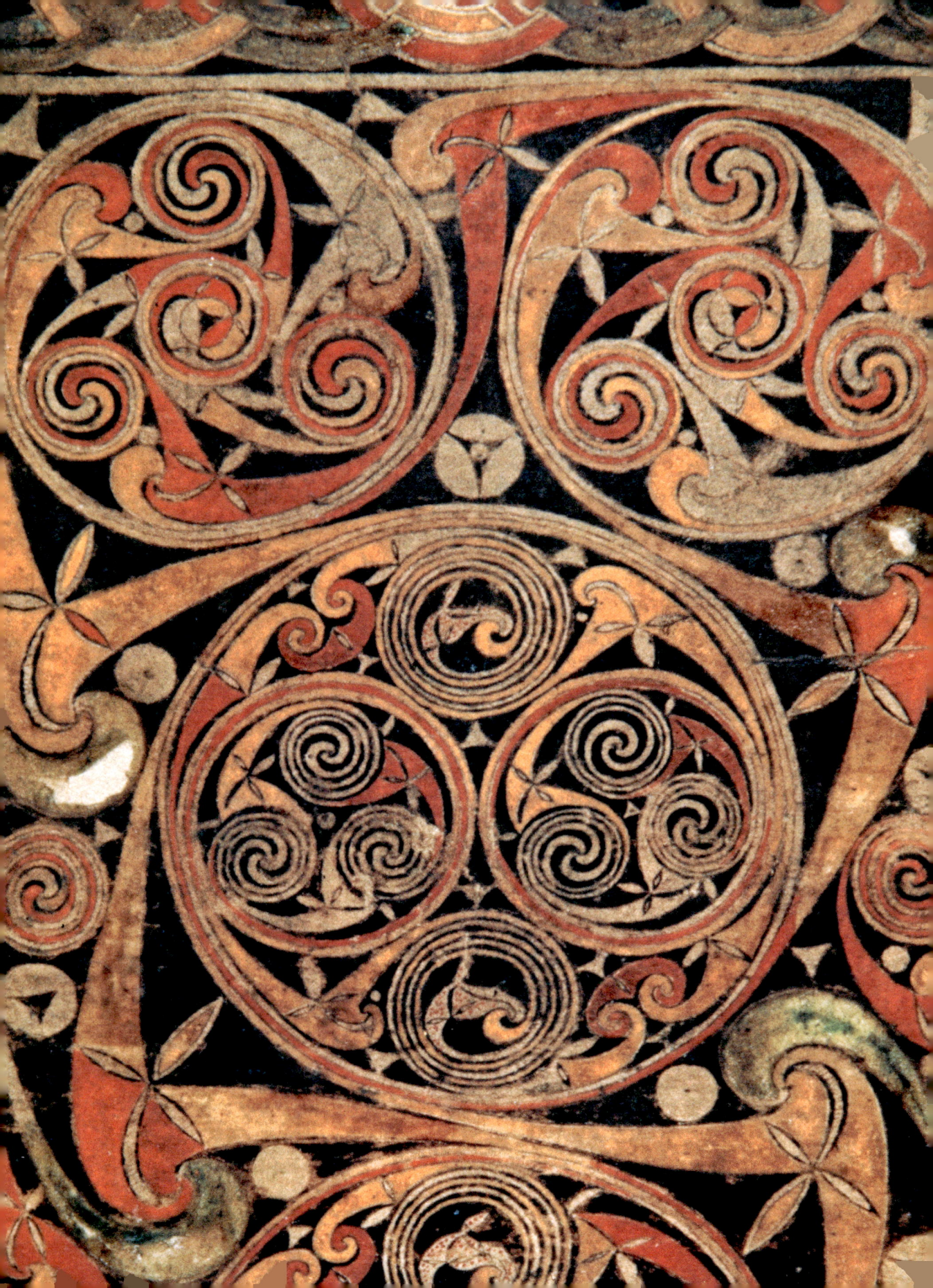

CHAPTER 4

The fame [of the monastic cell established by Eanmund]
impelled many to enter the perfect life. Ultan was one of
them . . . a blessed priest of the Irish race, and he could
ornament books with fair marking, and by this art he
accordingly made the shape of the letters beautiful
one by one, so that no modern scribe could equal him;
and it is no wonder if a worshipper of the Lord could
do such thing, when already the creator spirit had fired
his dedicated mind [to journey] to the stars.

Æthelwulf, *De Abbatibus*[1]

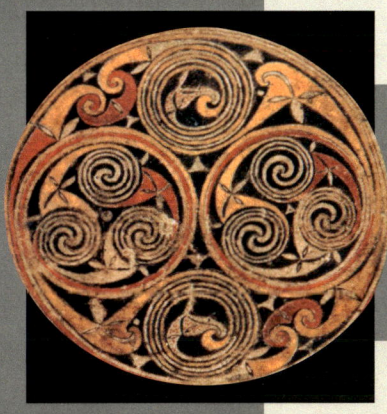

CELTIC CONNECTIONS, EASTERN INFLUENCES

SIXTH TO NINTH CENTURIES

The Book of Durrow, detail
from fol. 3v (see fig. 69)

This quotation describing Ultan, the gifted Irish scribe and artist, illustrates one of the most important strands that went into the making of Anglo-Saxon art in the pre-Viking period. Working in an unnamed daughter-house of Lindisfarne in the early eighth century, Ultan provides a rare glimpse of the activity of Irish artists in some of the Anglo-Saxon scriptoria during the seventh and eighth centuries. There must have been many such Ultans, especially, though certainly not exclusively, in the north of England, and their stamp is marked in the distinctively Insular style of manuscripts such as the Lindisfarne and St Chad Gospels. Alongside Ultan and his like, we also hear from Bede of many Anglo-Saxons who travelled to Ireland for instruction and the ascetic discipline – some, like the Northumbrian king Oswiu (d. 670), even earning Irish names.

The previous chapter dwelt on the enduring influence of Roman tradition, and of Italian models, on the development of a new Insular style, and examined how classicizing styles were assimilated into the native artistic traditions. This chapter will examine in more detail the key role of early medieval Celtic art in this fusion, together with other more distant influences from

Byzantium and even beyond, which also played their part in the shaping of Anglo-Saxon art between around 650 and 850.

The Celtic background to Insular art

The relationship of the Celtic inhabitants of Britain and Ireland to the Anglo-Saxon incomers was a close and complex one during the pre-Viking period. Despite the lurid accounts of Anglo-Saxon colonization by British chroniclers, the native British population was not decimated, nor all of it driven back to the western sea, as Gildas stated. As noted in Chapter 2, documentary and archaeological evidence across England suggests various degrees of British continuity, acculturation, and integration, rather than the hostile takeover of tradition.

The British records for this period are patchy and often difficult to interpret, and Anglo-Saxon accounts of Britons are scant and biased. However, fleshed out by the archaeological evidence, a picture emerges of kingdoms in the west and north of Britain which retained considerable power, and were capable at times of delivering crushing blows to the Anglo-Saxon kingdoms to the east (witness the Welsh king Cadwallon's ruthless attacks on Northumbria in the 630s). Offa's Dyke, on the English/Welsh border, and its associated earthworks visibly embody a political divide, as do other, less well-understood early medieval earthworks such as Wansdyke in Wiltshire and the Devil's Dyke in Cambridgeshire. The British Pennine kingdom of Elmet survived until its capture by Edwin of Northumbria in 616, and Cornwall and Devon only came under Saxon control in the ninth century. North of the present Scottish border, the Picts and the Scottish (Irish) kingdom of Dál Riata in Argyll were always powerful rivals to Northumbrian power in the region, and the Picts were later allies of the ascendant Mercian kings. Exiled Northumbrian kings, including Oswald and Aldfrith (himself half-Irish), sought refuge in Ireland and Dál Riata, and were fluent in the Irish language. In the south-east, as noted in Chapter 2, there is some evidence for a British presence in a swathe of territory extending from the Chilterns to north-west Essex, into the sixth century; while descendants of Romano-British populations may have transmitted some native metalworking traditions, including enamelling, in other parts of east and southern England. Other hints from the historical record suggest deeper connections: British personal names, for example, feature quite prominently among the early Wessex kings, and even in the densely anglicized south-east, some place-names, such as Eccles (from the Latin word *ecclesia*, 'church'), indicate an awareness of the institutions and customs of Romano-Britons and their descendants. In the Northumbrian royal dynasty, intermarriage with both Irish and Pictish royalty is attested.

Such evidence suggests close contact, and eventual integration, between British populations in England and the Anglo-Saxon incomers and their descendants, alongside close, if often stormy, relationships with long-lived independent neighbouring polities in Ireland, Wales and north Britain. When not in conflict with each other, there is plenty of evidence to show that this two-way contact was cemented through trade and exchange in luxury items and gifts. Anglo-Saxon glass drinking vessels and fine metalwork, for example, travelled to Wales and Scotland; and enamelled hanging-bowls became the burial accompaniment of choice for high-status Anglo-Saxons. At the height of its power, Northumbria controlled much of southern Scotland as far as Edinburgh (an Anglo-Saxon version of the earlier Celtic name) and the Forth. Northumbrian secular and monastic sites in this region, such as those at Dunbar, Hoddam and Jedburgh, have yielded ample evidence of Anglo-Saxon activity, including at some of them fine eighth-century sculpture in the Insular style. The contacts between the Anglo-Saxons and their Scottish, Irish and Pictish neighbours were a fertile conduit both for Celtic influences on hybrid Insular art, and for Continental and Anglo-Saxon influences travelling in the reverse direction, where they contributed to new developments in the art of Ireland and Pictland.

But the origins of the influence of Celtic art on the Anglo-Saxons have earlier roots, in England. A distinctively Celtic art style, based on fluid, curvilinear elements, had reached England and Ireland in the later Iron Age (c. 50 BC–AD 100), and had gone on to be influential in Romano-British provincial art. By the fifth century, fine red-enamelled brooches and pins with distinctive curvilinear decoration were being produced in British workshops in the south-west of England, fashions which were also exported to Ireland (fig. 67). During the sixth century yet more elaborate versions of this curvilinear style – involving the hairspring spirals, pelta motifs and trumpet scrolls that were to become such a feature of Insular manuscript decoration – appeared on the enamelled suspension mounts, and other decorative attachments of many of the hanging-bowls which are mainly known from rich Anglo-Saxon burials of the later sixth and seventh centuries (fig. 68).[2]

Despite earlier arguments in favour of an Irish origin, the archaeological evidence strongly points to Britain as being the main focus of manufacture of hanging-bowls during this period. Although there are close similarities between the decoration of some bowls and Irish metalwork (for instance, the great hanging-bowl from Sutton Hoo), only four fittings from bowls are known from Ireland before 700, while some 150 bowls or bowl fittings are known from Britain in the same period, most of them from England. And such direct evidence for local manufacture as there is also points to workshops in Britain: in the Pictish region, in Scottish Dál Riata and in the south-west of England. From this, it has been argued that in the sixth century the majority of bowls were made by Celtic populations within Britain, from the Severn valley in the south-west, up to the Moray Firth in Scotland; and that from the 620s or thereabouts, as the Anglo-Saxon kingdoms extended

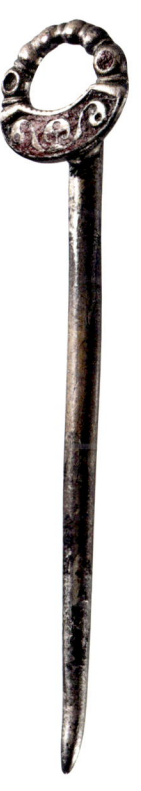

67. Copper-alloy pin with red enamel inlay and curvilinear ornament. Oldcroft, Gloucestershire, early 5th century. L. 6 cm (British Museum)

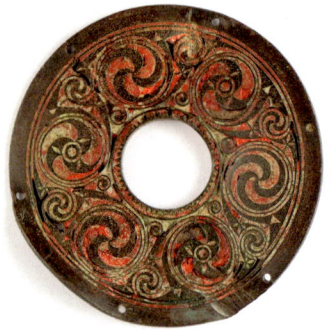
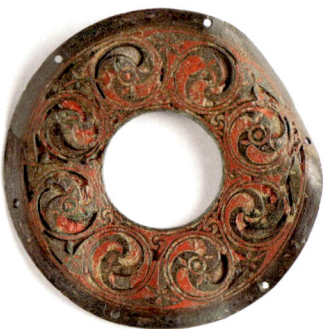

68. Copper-alloy
hanging-bowl mounts
with red enamel inlays
and curvilinear ornament.
Hockwold, Norfolk, 7th
century. Diam. (max)
5.6 cm (Norwich Castle
Museum and Art Gallery)

their territory west and north, the principal centres of production shifted north to Dál Riata, British Strathclyde and Pictland.[3] Hanging-bowls may well have been produced originally for use in the rituals of the British church, for it seems they were intended to contain water; but those from Anglo-Saxon graves – treasured luxury items which were often repaired before burial – had no doubt been used in more hazardous secular contexts, such as feasting.

Their distinctive, often beautiful, enamelled ornament was thus widely known in England in the seventh century and, indeed, there is also evidence of reciprocal Anglo-Saxon influence – gilding, ribbon interlace, foil mounts – on some of the bowl fittings from this period. As has recently been pointed out, the distinctive trumpet-scroll ornament which graces many of their attachments is exclusive to bowls from Britain, where it presumably originated, since it does not appear in Irish metalwork until around 700 (fig. 68).[4] A key element in Insular manuscript decoration, the trumpet scroll thus represents a British Celtic contribution to the inception of the style, alongside the impact of the decorated Irish service books and other manuscripts associated with the Ionan missions to the Anglo-Saxons.

Celtic influence in Insular manuscripts

As the account of Ultan's skills shows, it was to a very great extent the activities of the Irish missionaries and their followers – some from Iona, like Aidan and Colman, others direct from Ireland, like Fursa in East Anglia, and Maildubh, the founder of Malmesbury – which spread the script and decoration that contributed to the distinctive style of the manuscripts that witnessed the new faith. The late Roman invention of the codex, supplanting the fragile scrolls of the classical period, played a vital part in the work of the early missionaries, both Roman and Irish, because of its robustness and portability. The book became a central vehicle by which Christianity, the new religion of the Book, transmitted its ideas and its art.

From the beginning of the seventh century, the earliest surviving Irish manuscripts – the Cathach or Psalter of St Columba and two manuscripts written at the Irish foundation at Bobbio, Italy – show the beginnings of Celtic manuscript art in elegant flourishes, including simple trumpet patterns that were applied to initials introducing sections of the text.[5] The Cathach was by tradition closely identified with Columba, founder of Iona, and is an example of the kind of Irish manuscript that must have reached England with the earliest Ionan missions; its use of decorated initials was to be especially influential.

Somewhat later in the seventh century, as the Book of Durrow and a slightly earlier Northumbrian gospel fragment show,[6] the more extended decoration of the earliest surviving Insular manuscripts also took inspiration directly from contemporary metalwork ornament, both Anglo-Saxon, as we have already seen, and Celtic (see figs 3, 50 and 69). The Book of Durrow has six prefatory carpet pages, four of them decorated with ribbon interlace and/or grid patterns, and a fifth with interlacing Style II animals drawn from an Anglo-Saxon repertory (see p. 20). All of these pages have a cross at the heart, emblem of the Christian message. The sixth carpet page stands alone in having a magnificent pattern of six roundels with swirling trumpet scrolls, surrounded by a framework of dynamic interlacing circles which echo the Celtic discs (fig. 69). This has aptly been described as a page of hanging-bowl mounts, and the Celtic hairspring spirals in the elaborately decorated initials of this manuscript also show a clear debt to that metalwork tradition. At this early stage in the development of the Insular style, curvilinear motifs are completely separated from zoomorphic and grid decoration, and almost completely from the interlace, which in its endless rhythms seems to echo the spiral ornament.

In the Lindisfarne Gospels, made perhaps thirty or more years later, these features were elaborated with great virtuosity. In its carpet pages, canon tables and grand decorated initials, Celtic-style curvilinear decoration goes a step further (see figs 4 and 5). Here it is not separate, but smoothly integrated with rhythmically interlacing Anglo-Saxon animals, geometric grids and pure interlace of Mediterranean descent but Insular ingenuity. This is a remarkable synthesis; the bird and animal life of the Lindisfarne and St Chad Gospels, and other related manuscripts, is based mainly on dog-like animals and liberally feathered birds of prey, clearly derived from the Anglo-Saxon Style II menagerie (fig. 51). However, in their compass-constructed dizzying swirls, these animal patterns also visibly owe much to the Celtic tradition. Patterns of this kind in turn migrated into later eighth-century Irish metalwork and manuscripts, such as the 'Tara' brooch and the Book of Kells. The more elaborate new versions of grid, fret and interlace decoration seen, for example, in the Lindisfarne Gospels also seem to borrow from the Celtic tradition in their

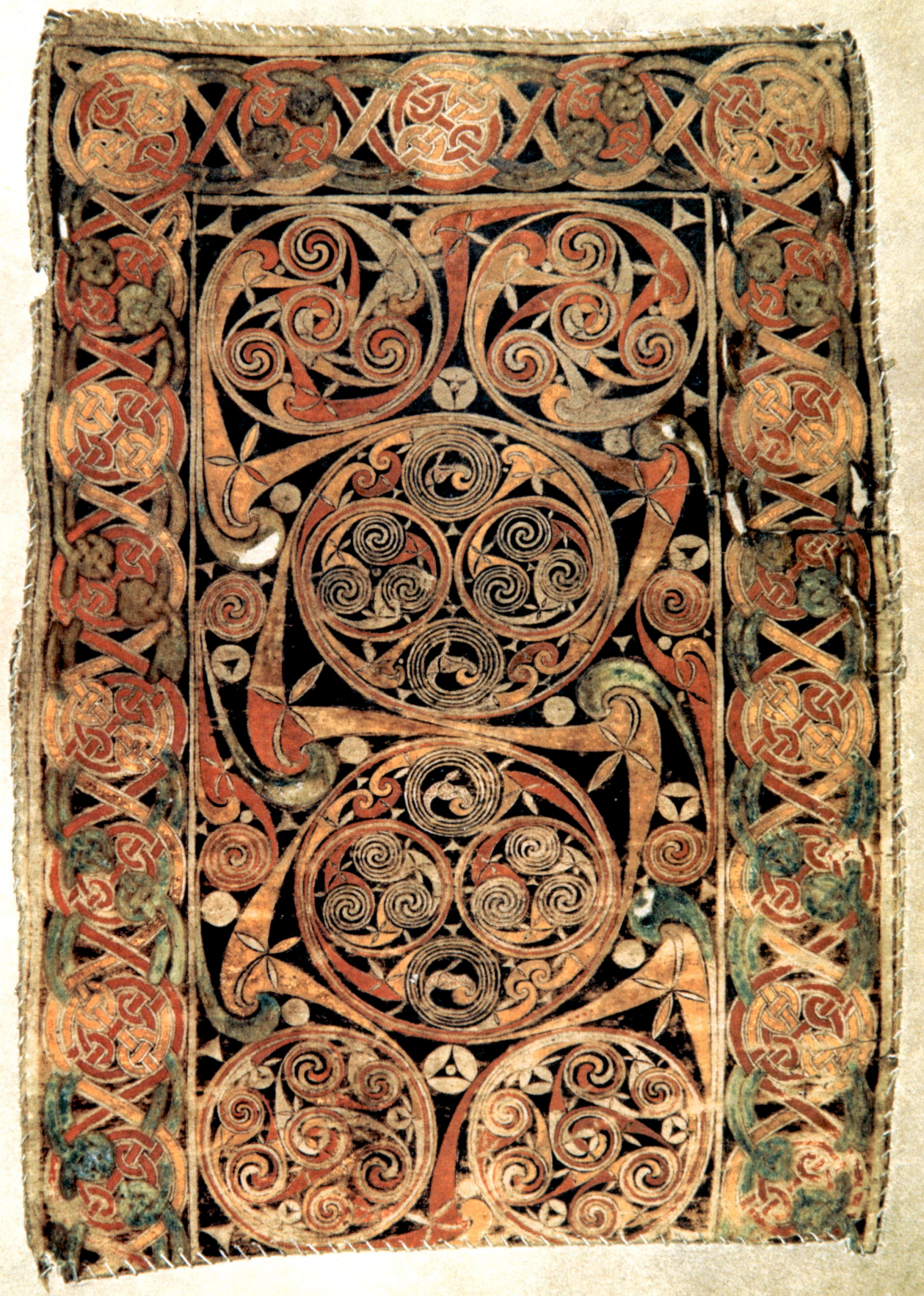

rhythmic complexity and subtle variation of type and colour, covering the surface in a never-ending continuum of pattern.

But some Celtic curvilinear ornament appears to project a special significance. The Book of Durrow carpet page with Celtic ornament is the only one not to be centred on an image of the cross. Instead the interconnected patterns made by the six main trumpet-scroll roundels play upon a theme of threes and fours, all symbolic numbers in early medieval Christian theology.[7] Numerology played an important role in this, and in the visual expression and interpretation of the Christian message in Insular art[8] – as exemplified by a number of early medieval house-shaped shrines which have arrangements of three large decorated roundels, sometimes alternating with four-sided settings. The number three evokes the Trinity, and four refers not only to the shape of the cross itself, but also to the divinely constructed universe with its four corners, and of course to the evangelists whose testimony to Christ is encapsulated in the four gospels. The prominence of patterns playing on these sacred numbers in the Durrow roundel page forms a parallel to the overt cross shapes which are central to the other carpet pages.

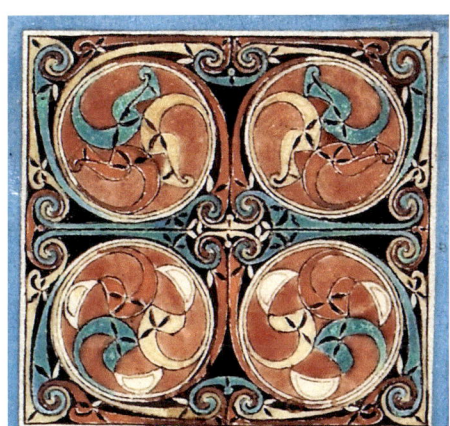

Roundels with continuous scroll decoration based on the interplay of three and four elements also appear frequently in the Lindisfarne Gospels, for example, and most strikingly on one of the great carpet pages, at the heart of which four Celtic-style roundels construct a cross in the space between them (fig. 70). They recur in many other Hiberno-Saxon manuscripts, and indeed in manuscripts from the south of England, such as the Vespasian Psalter (fig. 57). They continue even into the late eighth century, in such classically adept manuscripts as the Barberini Gospels, and their final vestiges can still be seen in the canon tables of the last grand Anglo-Saxon manuscript to survive from the troubled early ninth century, the Royal Bible.[9]

Celtic influence in Anglo-Saxon sculpture and metalwork

The influence of Celtic-style ornament was not confined to Anglo-Saxon manuscripts; it also appears on eighth-century sculpture and metalwork, albeit fairly rarely. In sculpture it can, for instance, be seen in the appearance of scroll decoration alongside zoomorphic knotwork and plant ornament on the elaborate late eighth- or early ninth-century font at Deerhurst (Gloucestershire), and on architectural elements from churches at South Kyme (Lincolnshire), Bradford on Avon (Wiltshire) and Breedon (Leicestershire).[10] Intricate Celtic-style scrolls and fretwork also appear – usually in conjunction with animal ornament – in a range of eighth-century secular metalwork, from dress-pins and pin-suites, to brooches and sword fittings, such as those from the St Ninian's Isle hoard and Fetter Lane in London (see figs 105 and 107); but here, again, it seems relatively uncommon compared with the prevailing zoomorphic and plant-scroll ornament of the day. Two notable late eighth-century Anglo-Saxon survivals which incorporate this tradition, however, are a great free-standing cross now in Salzburg, Austria (the Bischofshofen or Rupertus cross) and a whale-bone chrismatory known as the Gandersheim or Braunschweig Casket. These two great works of religious art are discussed further in Chapter 5 and 6, but their relevance here is in their use of spiral roundels – again, as with the Insular manuscripts, in highly symbolic ecclesiastical contexts, where the Christian message was expressed as much through image as through the Word.

The cross is formed of a maple-wood core covered with decorated gilt-bronze sheeting, into which were set at least thirty-eight dark blue glass insets, with white and yellow inlays (fig. 71). The metalwork is decorated with vine plants inhabited by sprightly animals, and spiralling vine scrolls and interlace of Anglo-Saxon type, but it is the glass insets that concern us here; the five largest were round, and set at the ends of the arms of the cross, and at its centre. The three that survive all bear a Celtic design of six running spirals, inlaid in white on the dark ground of the roundels. This quincunx of large glass settings is intended to represent the five wounds of Christ crucified, traditionally associated in early Christian thought with the idea of the *crux gemmata*, the jewelled cross. This image became widespread in Christian art after the finding of what was believed to be the true cross by St Helena, mother of Emperor Constantine, in the early fourth century. Again, the special nature of the spiral design is prominent, only occurring on these large roundels, and evidently deliberately selected for this purpose. Its six running spirals also reflect the cosmic symbolism of the number six, associated, among other theological themes, with the six days of creation and the six ages of the world.

The chrismatory, which may have been an Anglo-Saxon gift to Gandersheim Abbey, is made from whale-bone held together with bronze mounts (see fig. 100). It is exquisitely carved with a complex iconographical scheme of animals, interlace and inhabited vine bushes, set in frameworks composed of the symbolic numbers six and twelve. On its back, in the bottom centre of a grid of six squares, is a panel which contains, instead of the animals which occupy the other squares, a roundel composed of six running trumpet scrolls emerging from a central seventh, forming three triskeles as they do so (fig. 72). From these never-ending Celtic scrolls, four small embryonic creatures crawl towards the corners of the square in which the circle is set. In the overall decorative scheme of the *chrismal*, which is full of cosmological symbolism referring to the Creation, the circle and the square are here both

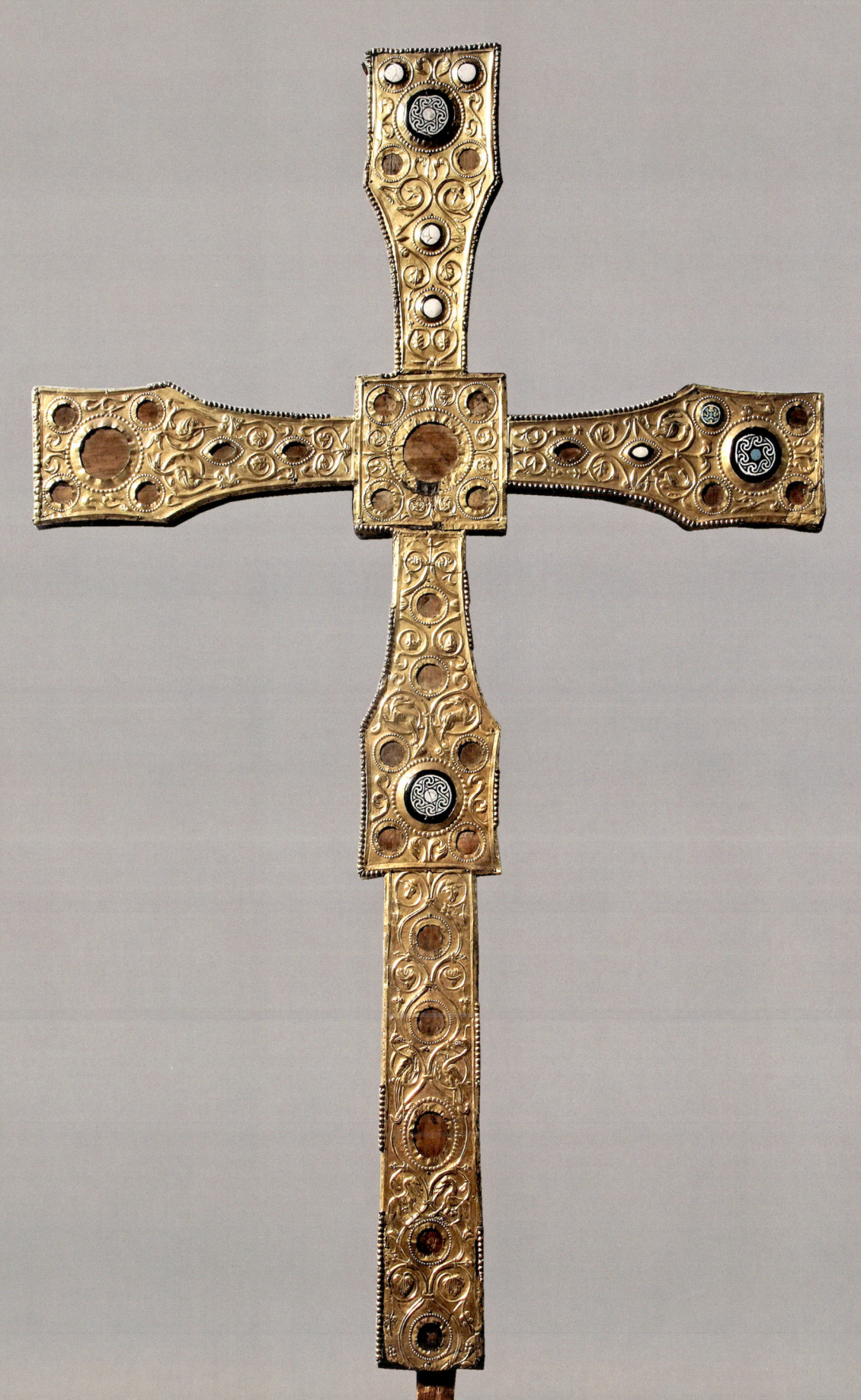

images of a divinely created world, in which the four creatures emerge from the whirling cosmos to inhabit the four corners of a symbolic earth.

Such extensive use of symbolic decoration echoes much earlier Anglo-Saxon art, with its fascination with visual riddles and encryptions but, as noted in Chapter 1, it also draws on a theological tradition of *ruminatio*. These are both likely reasons why trumpet-scroll patterns and other numerically interesting motifs from the Celtic repertory enjoyed such prominence in Insular manuscripts and other artefacts of the seventh and eighth centuries.

Contacts with Byzantium and the East

The use of visual metaphors as a way of explaining theological doctrine to a largely illiterate audience came by way of both the Celtic and the Roman tradition; but an equally influential set of connections brought Christian scholarship from further afield. This came from the Byzantine Empire, which

72. The Gandersheim Casket: whale-bone chrismatory (back panel). Late 8th century. H. 12.6 cm (Herzog Anton Ulrich-Museum, Braunschweig)

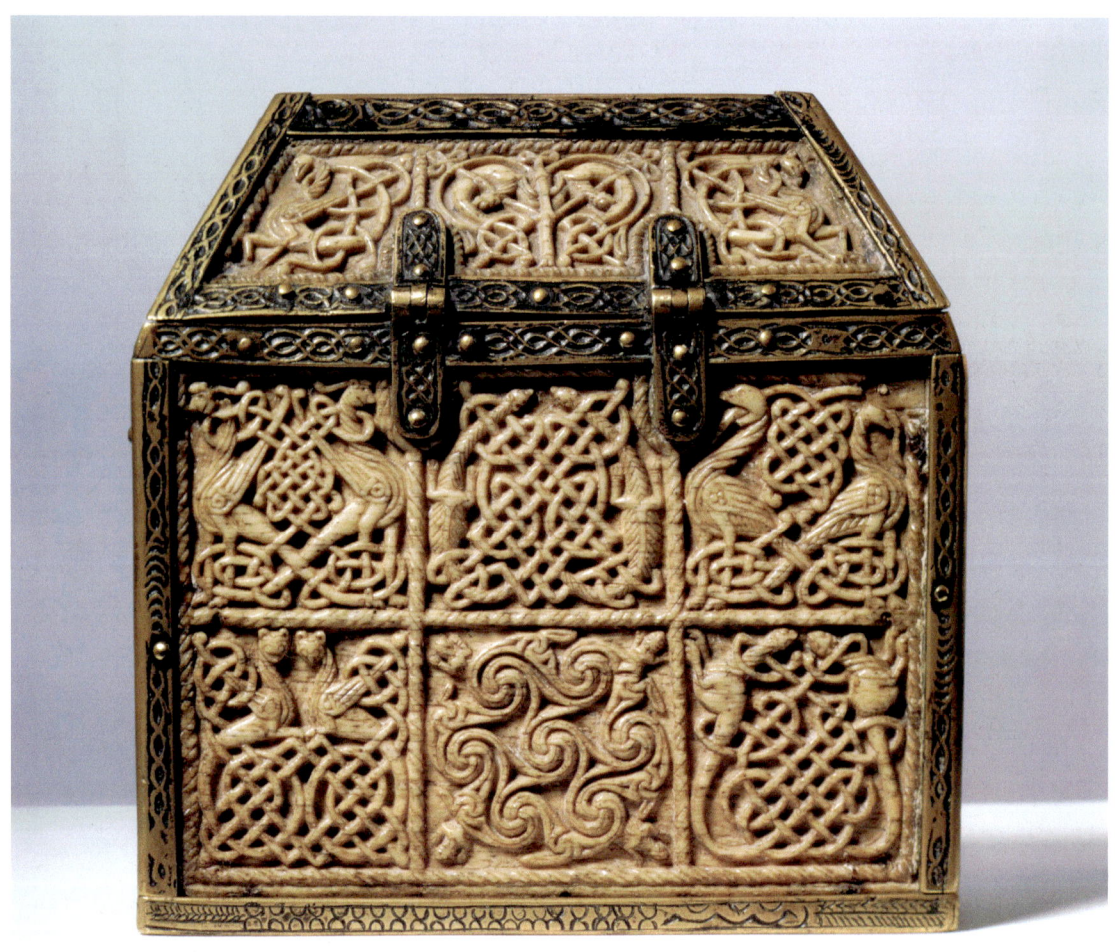

included Turkey, Syria and, until the early seventh century, much of North Africa. This brought access not only to Greek texts and their translations into Latin, but also to artefacts. Although the Empire in the eastern Mediterranean may seem very distant from Anglo-Saxon England, its influence was felt through the Augustinian mission and the route which these new contacts opened up to centres of Byzantine influence in Italy, including Rome and Ravenna. In fact, contacts between the Anglo-Saxons and Byzantium went back at least to the early sixth century, and from the later part of that century they seem to have existed on a regular basis, though mainly through a chain of connections, rather than through direct travel to the eastern Mediterranean. The Byzantine historian Procopius, who wrote in the mid-sixth century and was closely associated with the court of the Emperor Justinian, had certainly gleaned a wealth of curious information about Britain, probably from some Anglo-Saxons whom he describes as accompanying a Frankish embassy to Byzantium (later Constantinople) in about 553.

Apart from this slim evidence of an Anglo-Saxon presence in Byzantium itself, there is much more to suggest other contacts of various kinds. Late in the ninth century, King Alfred had contact with the Patriarch of Jerusalem, who sent him healing remedies. Merchants travelled, and so did their goods. In the tenth-century schoolboy text known as Ælfric's Colloquy, the character of the merchant describes how he sails to far places and brings back many exotic goods: 'costly textiles and silks, precious gems and gold, a range of garments, spices, wine and oil, ivory and brass, copper and tin, sulphur and glass'.[11] Trade and exchange were key propellants of cultural contact. Slaves and hunting dogs were just two of a number of valuable Anglo-Saxon commodities regularly sold abroad, in the markets of Frankish Gaul and Italy. In return came Byzantine gold coins, *solidi*, and no doubt many other prized goods including oil and wine, small glass mosaic cubes (*tesserae*) for melting into glass vessels, beads, and millefiori insets, like those found at the Anglo-Saxon monasteries at Jarrow and Whitby. Other luxury goods followed the same route – Byzantine decorated textiles and fine cast bronze vessels (so-called 'Coptic' bowls), as well as amethyst beads and ivory from North Africa, not to mention the coveted garnets, many of which had travelled overland from sources in the Indian sub-continent. Other fine goods from the Eastern Empire seem to have arrived in England through the mechanisms of gift exchange, some no doubt in dowries, others as diplomatic gifts. The grand late Antique and Byzantine silver dining equipment in the Sutton Hoo ship burial must represent the end product of some such process. The vast majority of these items, whether traded or exchanged, arrived not direct from Byzantium, but through intermediaries, and over several stages; but they nevertheless represent a relationship with and awareness of the Eastern Empire, long before the arrival of the Christian missions from Rome.

The British and the Irish had their own relationship with the eastern Mediterranean. This is signalled by the presence on high-status secular sites in Ireland and the west of Britain of imported sixth-century pottery from Turkey and North Africa, including amphorae for wine and oil. This sea-borne trade seems, however, to have been intermittent. The travels of the Irish monk Columbanus, and his later followers, to Francia, Alamannia and Italy resulted in the foundation of Continental monasteries in the Irish tradition from the later sixth century onwards. Merovingian, Frankish and Italian influence is evident in early manuscripts from such Irish foundations. But through their wide travels these missionaries also came into contact with the practices of the eastern Mediterranean, particularly the Coptic Church. The specifically Columban brand of monasticism, which owes much to the eremitic tradition of the first monks, the Egyptian Desert Fathers, is evidence of some such contact. And as noted in Chapter 3, it seems that an illustrated manuscript of the Syrian-born theologian Tatian's *Diatessaron* may lie behind the origin of

73. Front cover of the St Cuthbert Gospel of St John. Late 7th century. 13.8 x 9.3 cm (British Library, Loan MS 74)

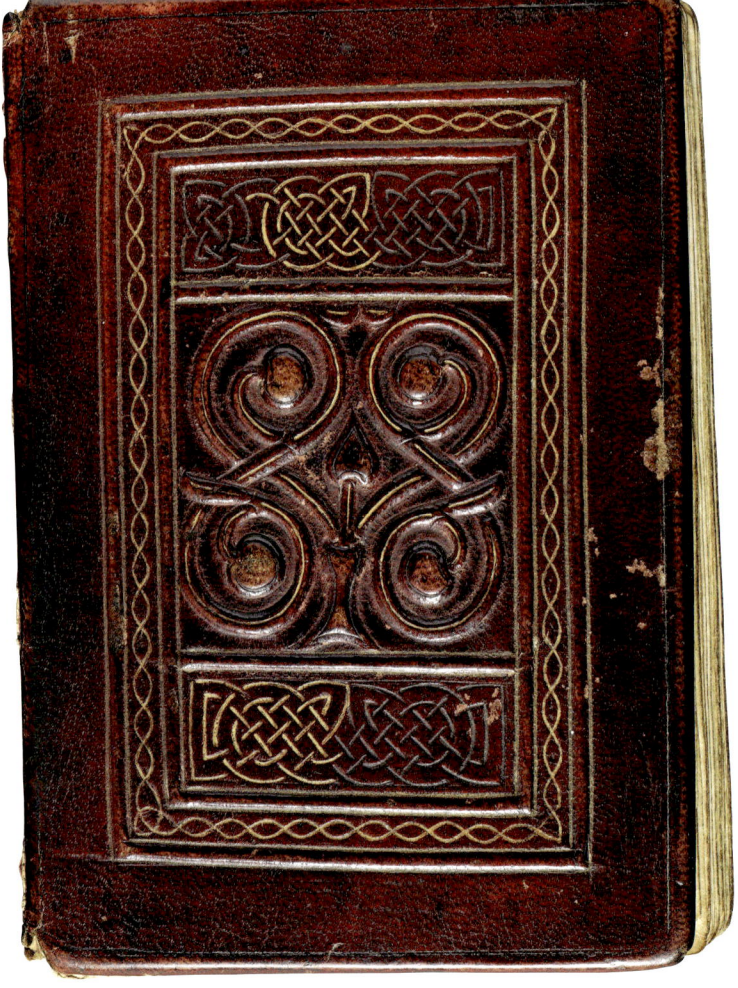

the carpet pages, which are a distinctly Celtic contribution to the earliest Insular gospel-books – a rare glimpse of a likely model from the East. Even more strikingly, an Irish psalter dated to about 800, which was found in 2006 in a bog at Faddan More, County Tipperary, has been shown to have a binding of Coptic type, with a lining of Egyptian papyrus – a tangible witness to such contacts. This, together with possible Coptic influences in the Book of Durrow and the binding of the late seventh-century St Cuthbert Gospel of St John, suggest that Eastern manuscripts arrived in Britain and Ireland via missionaries and travellers who had journeyed further afield (fig. 73).

One glimpse into direct contacts with distant Byzantium and beyond comes from around the beginning of the eighth century, when Abbot Adámnan of Iona welcomed the Frankish bishop, Arculf, who was shipwrecked there in the course of his return from pilgrimage to the Holy Land. Arculf gave a detailed account of the holy sites, as well as descriptions of Constantinople, Damascus and Alexandria. Adámnan used this account, with other information gleaned from Latin sources, in his influential book, *de Locis Sanctis* (On the Holy Sites), which he presented to his friend and pupil, King Aldfrith of Northumbria, 'through whose generosity', wrote Bede, 'it was circulated for lesser folk to read'. So impressed indeed was Bede by this that he devoted two chapters of his *Ecclesiastical History* to excerpts from the book, and himself wrote a summary version, describing the original as 'a work of great value, especially to those who live at a great distance from the places where the patriarchs and the apostles lived'. Here we gain a direct insight into some of the mechanisms by which information from the distant world of the eastern Mediterranean was disseminated at that period, not only by the pilgrim himself, but by the church and also, significantly, by the king's own decree.

Byzantine influences on Anglo-Saxon art

But the most important conduit of Byzantine influence on Anglo-Saxon art in the later seventh century was the immensely influential school established at Canterbury by the great scholar Theodore of Tarsus and his close colleague Hadrian (see p. 85). Theodore was a native of Greek-speaking Cilicia, now part of modern Turkey, and had been trained at Antioch and Edessa in Syria, and Constantinople, before moving on to a Greek-speaking monastery in Rome. From there he was eventually sent to England as Archbishop of Canterbury in 669 at the age of sixty-seven. It was due in large measure to Theodore and his drive for reform that the still fractured Anglo-Saxon Church was able to operate at full strength and in orthodoxy, but it is for the scholarship of the school of Canterbury that he is most remembered.

Hadrian was also a renowned scholar, born around 635 in a Greek-speaking part of North Africa, from which he had fled to Naples after the Arab conquest. He subsequently served as an ambassador for the Byzantine Emperor Constans II in Gaul, accompanying him to Rome. His experience of Europe beyond the Alps no doubt served him well among the Anglo-Saxons. At the Pope's insistence, Hadrian was due to accompany Theodore to England, but was delayed until 670, having been detained by the Frankish authorities who suspected him of carrying a message from the Byzantine emperor to the Anglo-Saxon kings.

The monastic school that the two churchmen founded at Canterbury established Greek and Latin learning and scholarship in England. This included, in addition to knowledge of the scriptures and exegetical material, Roman law, astronomy, poetry, *computus* (calendrical computation), medicine and sacred music. It had no equal in western Europe in its time. It was probably through this route that the Greek titles (in Latin lettering) of the evangelist portraits, and Greek letter forms in the grand display scripts of the early eighth-century Lindisfarne Gospels, came about, along with distinctively Byzantine influences which appear in the figure style of this manuscript. It seems that Byzantine manuscripts also provided likely models for the three-quarter profiles of three of the evangelist portraits in the Lindisfarne Gospels, and that contemporary Byzantine ivories, similar to a group of ivories said to have come from the throne of St Mark in Alexandria, also influenced the style of the portraits.[12]

Syriac Bibles, and Byzantine panel paintings and church vestments were also plausibly among the many other artefacts that were imported in this period, whether directly from the East or, more probably, acquired from Rome; and they were certainly disseminated onwards. Tellingly, this also happened at a humbler level; a small Byzantine censer of late sixth- to seventh-century date found near the Anglo-Saxon abbey precincts at Glastonbury is another indicator of the range of material from the East which was already finding its way into England in the early seventh century.[13]

Despite the Iconoclasm crisis which raged in eighth-century Byzantium, other sources of eastern Mediterranean influence became important towards the end of that century. Under the ambitious Mercian kings of the eighth and early ninth centuries, especially Offa (r. 759–96), Anglo-Saxon connections with the East deepened through their contacts with the rising Carolingian dynasty, which

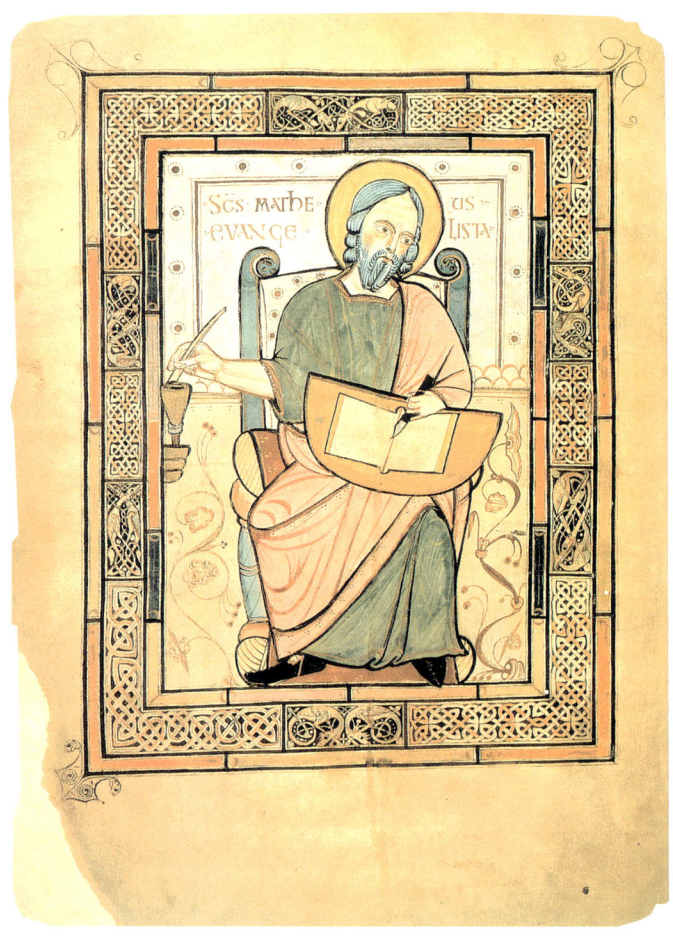

had its own relationship with Byzantium and the East. The sumptuous Barberini Gospels, probably made in the Mercian monastery of Medeshamstede (Peterborough) towards the end of the eighth century (fig. 74), shows a supremely confident mastery of three-dimensional illusionistic style in its evangelist portraits and in other figural details; it betrays an Italo-Byzantine ancestry mediated through Carolingian models. These are all elegantly dovetailed into a visual programme which, even at such a relatively late date, makes full use of the Insular repertory, from Celtic scrollwork to animal ornament, interlace and inhabited vine scrolls. Like the earlier Lindisfarne Gospels, Vespasian Psalter and *Codex Aureus*, it uses a rich and varied palette of colours, with subtle graduations of colour and tone to give movement and substance to its images. Luscious pinks, oranges and crimsony purples, as well as subtle blues and greens, contribute to a sophisticated and graduated tonal vocabulary. Some of the pigments used in Insular manuscripts, such as gold, and lapis from distant Badakshan, were very costly. The purple dyes used in imitation

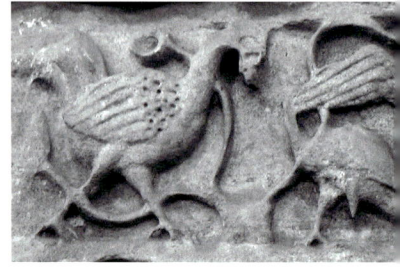

74. The Barberini Gospels: portrait of St Matthew. Late 8th or early 9th century. 34 x 25 cm (Biblioteca Apostolica Vaticana, Vatican City, MS Lat.570, fol. 11v)

of Italian and Byzantine manuscripts, in the *Codex Amiatinus* and the famous Bible presented by Wilfrid to Ripon, copied the use of Tyrian purple, the renowned and hugely expensive shellfish dye used in the Mediterranean. Intriguingly, it seems that the Barberini Gospels is one of only two possible Insular manuscripts to have used this or a similar whelk dye in its pigments – the other being the slightly later and very grand Royal Bible (see fig. 109) – in certain imitation of Mediterranean manuscript painting, and perhaps even employing the costly imported dye itself.

Sculpture and ecclesiastical metalwork of the eighth century also reveal strong currents of Byzantine influence. This is evident in figural images and in a new vocabulary of exotic creatures that decorate the architectural sculpture of some of the great Mercian religious houses. One of these, at Breedon on the Hill (Leicestershire), has a particularly extensive surviving set of animal friezes (fig. 75). The original impact must have been very powerful, especially given the likelihood that these sculptures were brightly painted. The lively beasts and birds that sport in Breedon's plant scrolls include griffins, lions, centaurs and peacocks, all inspired by creatures of oriental derivation which figured in the prized Byzantine silks and other textiles that were reaching England in the seventh and eighth centuries. Surviving written accounts of vestments and church furnishings made of fine decorated Byzantine silks, such as those acquired by Wilfrid and Benedict Biscop, the chasuble decorated with peacocks sported by Aldhelm, are supported by scraps of material evidence from the later Anglo-Saxon period. They reveal just how sought after and influential these textiles became, easily portable as they were, and readily visible in a church context. Some, like the 'Goddess' silk from the shrine of St Cuthbert, incorporated figural designs, similar to other seventh-century silks that still survive in the Vatican. The 'David' silk – one of the eighth-century Anglo-Saxon textiles now at Maaseik in Belgium – which carries texts in the Latin alphabet, may even represent a Western copy of a Byzantine original. The exotic creatures that appeared on some of these silks were also widely imitated, only slightly adapted to Anglo-Saxon taste, in ecclesiastical metalwork – on the Bischofshofen cross, for example, and on the closely related Anglo-Saxon silver-gilt ecclesiastical bowl found in a Viking grave at Ormside, Cumbria (see figs 71 and 93).

75. Stone friezes with animals. Late 8th–early 9th century. H. 23 cm. (Church of St Mary and St Hardulph, Breedon on the Hill, Leicestershire)

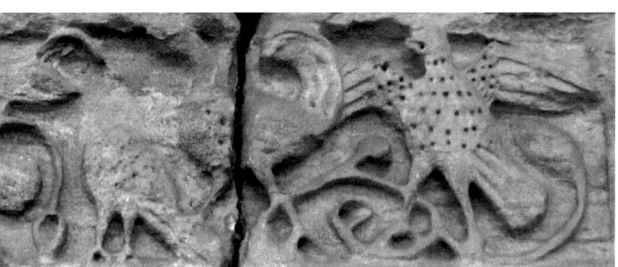 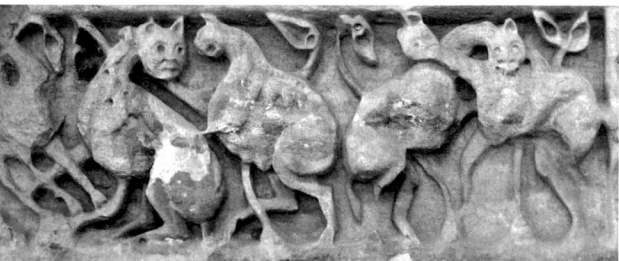

A more direct influence of Byzantine church textiles appears in a rare survival of Anglo-Saxon fine embroidery of the eighth century – textiles associated by tradition with two Frankish female saints, and formerly kept at the monastery of Aldeneik in Belgium; they are now in the church of Saint Catherine at Maaseik (see fig. 94). They may have reached Aldeneik through gifts to Anglo-Saxon missions in the Liège region in the eighth century. Their particular interest lies in the colourful gold-embroidered and (originally) pearl-embellished arcades and roundels with elegant interlace, bird and animal ornament, which clearly relate to similar decoration at Breedon and elsewhere in eighth-century Mercia. Their general style and content, as well as the luxurious use of gold and pearls, clearly draws inspiration from Byzantine textile art. Such grand textiles, made to adorn the interiors of churches, give an additional perspective on the rich polychrome decoration that was – as we now know – also used in architectural sculpture of eighth-century and later churches.

The remarkable flowering of such sculpture in Mercia in the eighth and early ninth centuries is discussed in more detail in Chapter 5. However, in this context of influences from the eastern Mediterranean, mention should be made of the new styles of figural sculpture attested at major monastic sites in the eastern midlands, such as Lichfield, Castor, Peterborough, Fletton and Breedon. Like the evangelist portraits of the Barberini Gospels, they show a visible debt to Byzantine illusionistic depictions of the human form, in their delicately modelled figures of angels, apostles and saints, often under elegant arcading. They are characterized by a sense of lightly floating motion, emphasized by the free-flying folds of their garments (see figs 85 and 87). The continuing Anglo-Saxon fascination with the play of movement and line in rhythmic patterning finds new impetus and new forms of expression here. It has been suggested that the transformative style of these figural sculptures may reflect an importation of Greek craftsmen, who are known to have been present at the court of Charlemagne.[14] The close ties of the Mercian kings Offa and Coenwulf with their Carolingian neighbours certainly provided a bridge to enhanced contacts with the East, including the Arab world (see p. 129 and fig. 83).

But there is another side to this Byzantine influence which is seen elsewhere in Mercian sculpture, this time from the west of the kingdom, and dating to the early ninth century. The important series of painted sculptures at the church of St Mary, Deerhurst, Gloucestershire, includes a prominent image of the Virgin, of a kind unique in England and very rare in western Europe. She originally displayed a full-length depiction of Christ in an oval frame, a representation which must have been taken from a Byzantine-inspired model; early examples occur on an icon from the monastery of St Catherine at Mount Sinai and in Syriac and Armenian manuscripts, among others.[15] One of the rare examples of this image in the West occurs in a mid-eighth-century Byzantine-style wall-painting in the Roman church of Sta Maria Antiqua, where it would certainly have been seen by Anglo-Saxon pilgrims to Rome. As it happens, one such pilgrim, a local nobleman named Æthelric and a patron of the church at Deerhurst (he was indeed buried there), made just such a pilgrimage to Rome between 802 and 807, comfortably fitting within the timeframe for the creation of the Virgin image at St Mary's Church, thought to be in the first part of the ninth century. The dominant placing of the image of the Virgin on an intermediate wall of the porch and overlooking the entrance may also reflect an image of the Virgin that Æthelric would have encountered in an eighth-century oratory of St Mary at St Peter's. Indeed it has been suggested that Æthelric may have brought back from his visit to Rome a painted Roman or even Byzantine icon of the Virgin for his church, as Benedict Biscop and other pilgrims had done a century earlier.[16] The sculpture as we see it today is bare and devoid of detail, and had long been thought to have been deliberately scoured of most of its defining features, until recent analysis of vestiges of paint which survive in its crevices revealed a very different story. It now appears that all but the broad outline details of the Virgin and the figure of Christ that she originally displayed were painted, not carved, on to the flattish surfaces that survive today, deliberately echoing those colourful painted and mosaic images that Anglo-Saxon pilgrims would have encountered in the churches of Italy and Byzantium.

Connections with the East, direct and indirect, continued to make their presence felt in the art of the later Anglo-Saxon period, not only through Carolingian influences, but also from Viking contacts with Byzantium and beyond, to the Muslim Caliphate and Baghdad. But the Celtic presence, so powerful in the shaping of the Christian conversion and its art in the seventh century, diminished in influence in England, although for a while it continued to have impact abroad, through the many Irish foundations scattered across western Europe. With the acceptance of the Roman model of Christianity at the Synod of Whitby in 664, the Anglo-Saxon Church shifted its focus south and eastwards, as did the new generations of Mercian and Wessex kings who were to put their stamp on art, as well as politics, in the next two centuries.

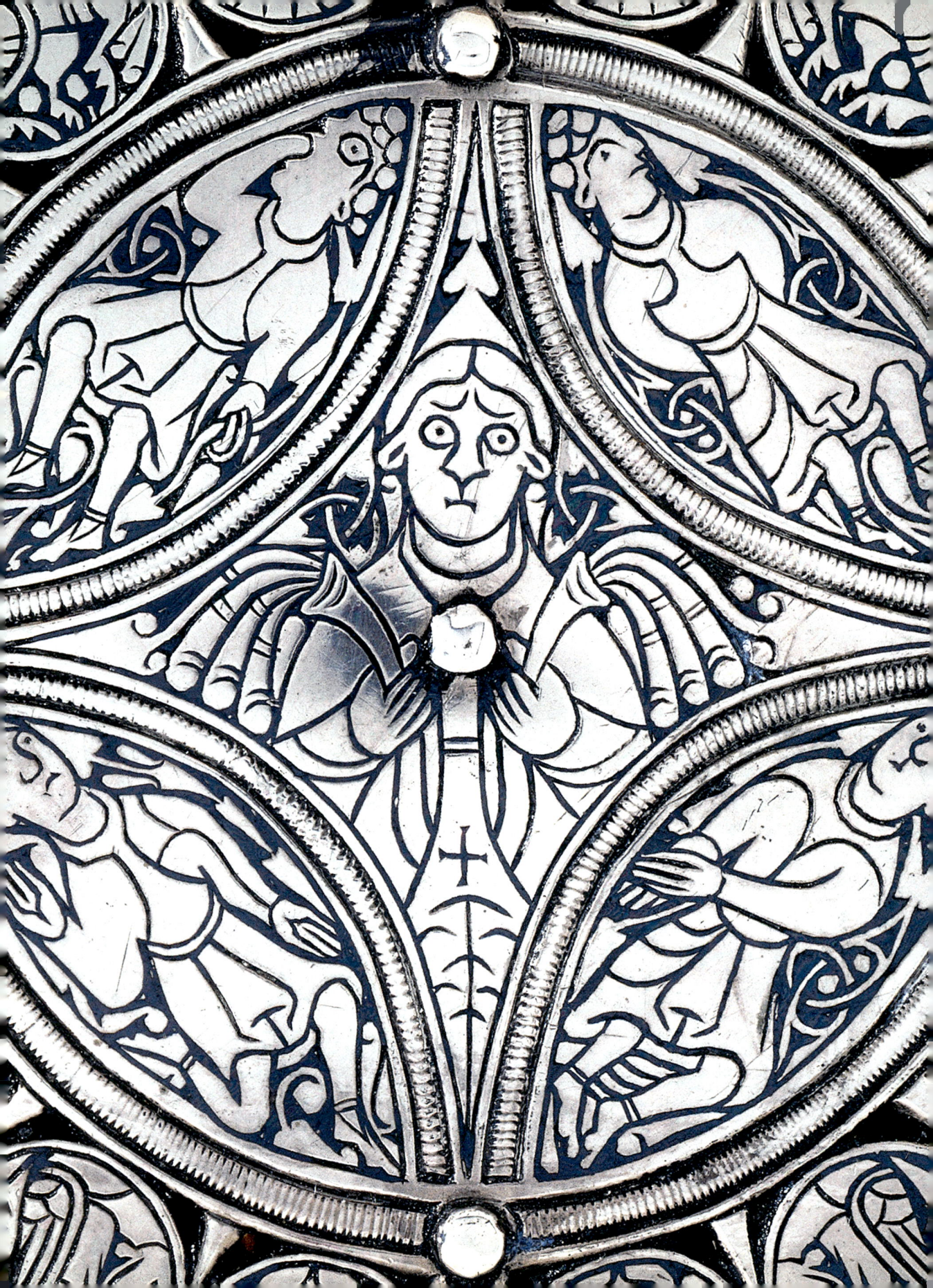

CHAPTER 5

What shall I say . . . of the treasures incomparably
fashioned in gold and silver at his instigation? And
what of the royal halls and chambers marvellously
constructed of stone and wood at his command?
And what of the royal residences of masonry, moved
from their old position and splendidly reconstructed
at more appropriate places by his royal command?

Asser's *Life of King Alfred*, chapter 91[1]

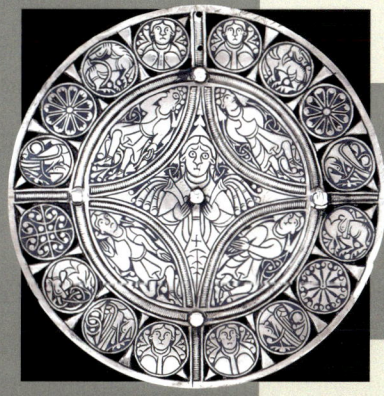

ART AND POWER

FROM SUTTON HOO TO ALFRED

The Fuller Brooch
(see fig. 115).

Art, wealth and power

This chapter explores some of the ways in which the creation of splendid and
beautiful objects, both secular and ecclesiastical, was intimately linked to the
expression and exercise of power in the early medieval period. For King Alfred
the expression of royal power went hand in hand with his devotion to God,
and his commitment to a revival of learning and religion. The incomparable
treasures with which his biographer Asser tells us he filled his churches were
essential to the renewal of religious life, but they also played a part in putting
his stamp on the kingdom. Political and religious power were always closely
intertwined in the Anglo-Saxon period, and as we shall see later in this chapter, they were exemplified by the many magnificent gifts given by kings and
nobles to the church, in the hope of conferring divine protection and success
in this world, and the soul's salvation in the next. In both the giving and the
display, these impressive donations manifested the givers' authority and power.

A striking illustration of the complex relationship of art to power in
this period is the case of the magnificent *Codex Aureus* gospel-book, which was

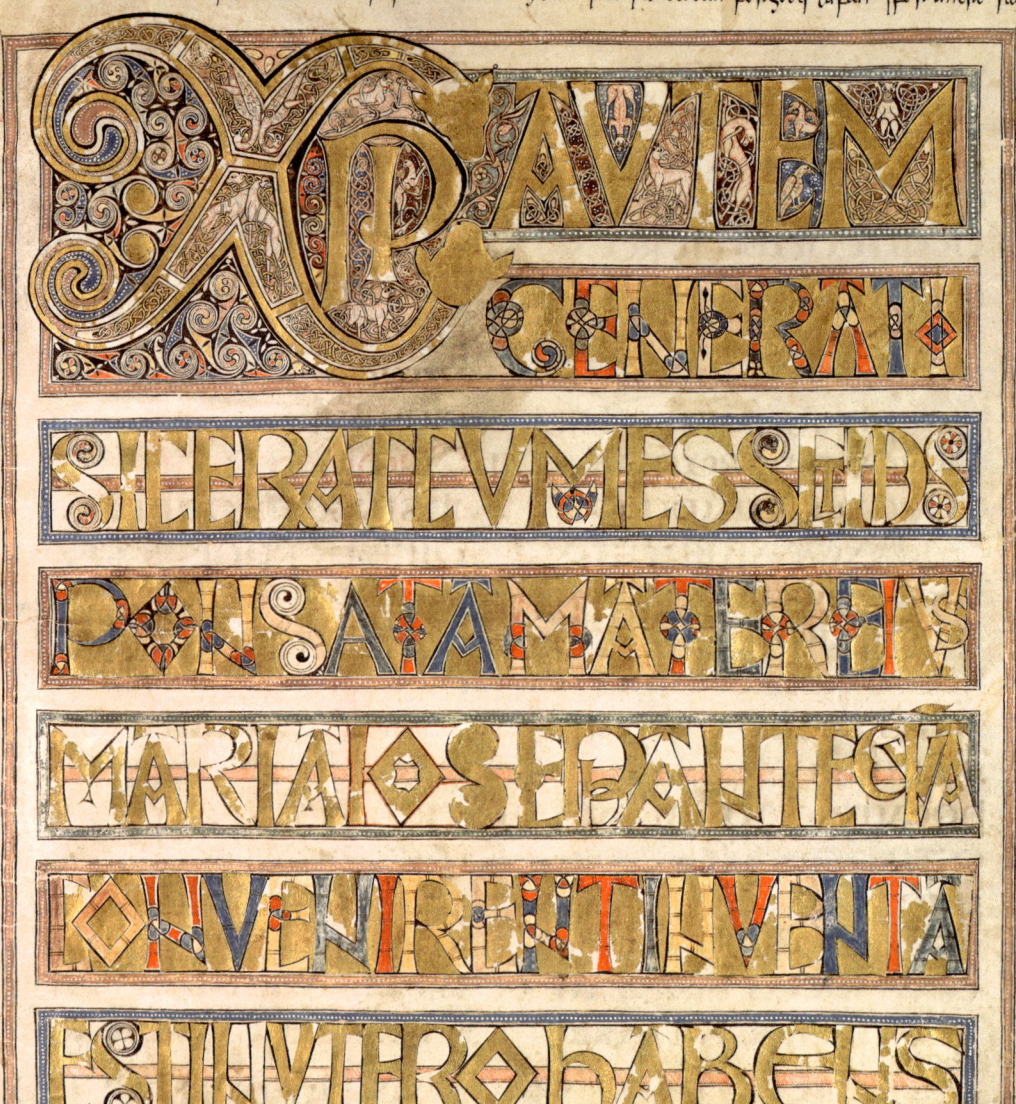

probably made for a Canterbury church. It was made above all to honour God – but it also reflected the standing of the church, its clergy and its patrons (see figs 58 and 76). It was certainly a book so highly regarded that when it was seized by a Viking war-band towards the end of the ninth century, the high-ranking nobleman Alfred and his wife Wærburg bought it back from the raiders and presented it to the priory of Christ Church, Canterbury. In an inscription (fig. 76) which they added on the gold-adorned page celebrating the Incarnation of Christ in St Matthew's Gospel – a symbolic choice for this presentation to a church dedicated to Christ – they carefully record that they redeemed it:

> from the heathen army with our pure money, that was with pure gold, and this we did for the love of God and for the benefit of our souls and because we did not wish these holy books to remain longer in heathen possession.

Of course, the Vikings who had held it to ransom also clearly recognized the value and the power of this sumptuous book – a treasure of the church, worth far more than the gold it contained. The splendour of this gospel-book, and its supreme artistry, made it a powerful possession even to these unbelievers, as well as a precious religious icon to the aristocratic couple who paid the price to save it – an act of patronage and redemption in which treasure, status and supreme artistry all played a part.

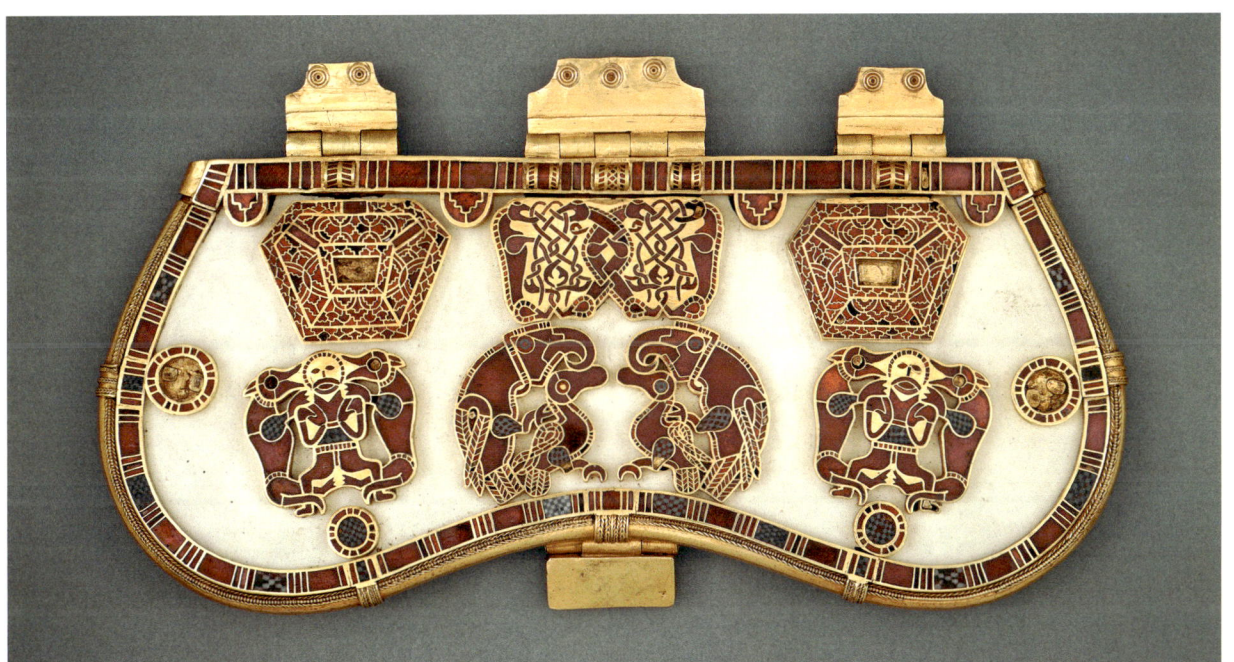

The seventh-century background: the Sutton Hoo ship burial and the Staffordshire Hoard

In order to set in context the relationship of art to power in the eighth and ninth centuries, it will be helpful to take as a starting point the extraordinary gold and garnet treasures of the seventh century, in which the secular and the sacred were so often closely intertwined as Christianity became established across England. This was a period when nascent Anglo-Saxon kingdoms, formed from earlier and smaller affiliations, were consolidating their identities and vying to extend their power-bases in violent wars. In the process, most kings were not slow to avail themselves of the protection of the new religion, which, from the moment that Æthelbert of Kent gave his support to the Augustinian mission in 597, became integral to their political ambitions. As we saw in Chapter 2, the early part of the century was also a period when gold was more plentiful, arriving in the form of Byzantine and Merovingian coinage that was rapidly recycled into Anglo-Saxon coin issues and high-status jewellery and other personal possessions. As Anglo-Saxon poems such as *Beowulf* and *Widsith* vividly illustrate, the gaining and dispensing of treasure was a vital part of an early medieval king's business, his campaigning and the maintenance of his court; how else was he to form alliances, or keep loyal his fighting band, without the reward of gold? The sources of treasure took many forms; but looting, booty and capture, as well as tribute and other payments exacted from enemies, such as Danegeld (see Chapter 7), were certainly prominent among them.

With all this in mind, the Sutton Hoo Mound 1 ship burial, with its grand enactment of wealth and power, can be seen as a dramatic expression of the aspirations of East Anglian royalty in the first third of the seventh century. Debate continues as to who was buried in the great ship burial, and when, although Rædwald, who succeeded the Kentish king Æthelbert as the most powerful Anglo-Saxon ruler of his day, remains a strong contender. The massive boat and its burial mound, the opulence of the gold and garnet warrior kit, the grand Roman-style silver dinner plate and quantities of other feasting equipment – not to mention the purseful of gold coins, recalling Roman largesse – all are statements of a king's right to rule and his ability to maintain it. The insignia spell out the message: the deep crimson of the lavish garnet inlays carries a distant echo of Roman *imperium* (see p. 25), and the helmet, sceptre and shoulder clasps, from a leather tunic, are also ultimately derived from Roman precursors, projecting an identity which consciously refers to a Roman inheritance. As noted in Chapter 2, this is also signalled in the East Anglian genealogy, where Caesar is inserted at the head of the ancestral king-list. Like many other Germanic successors to the rule of Rome, this was a dynasty concerned to emphasize that its authority was inherited from the former power; but it was also ready to invoke the power of the new religion,

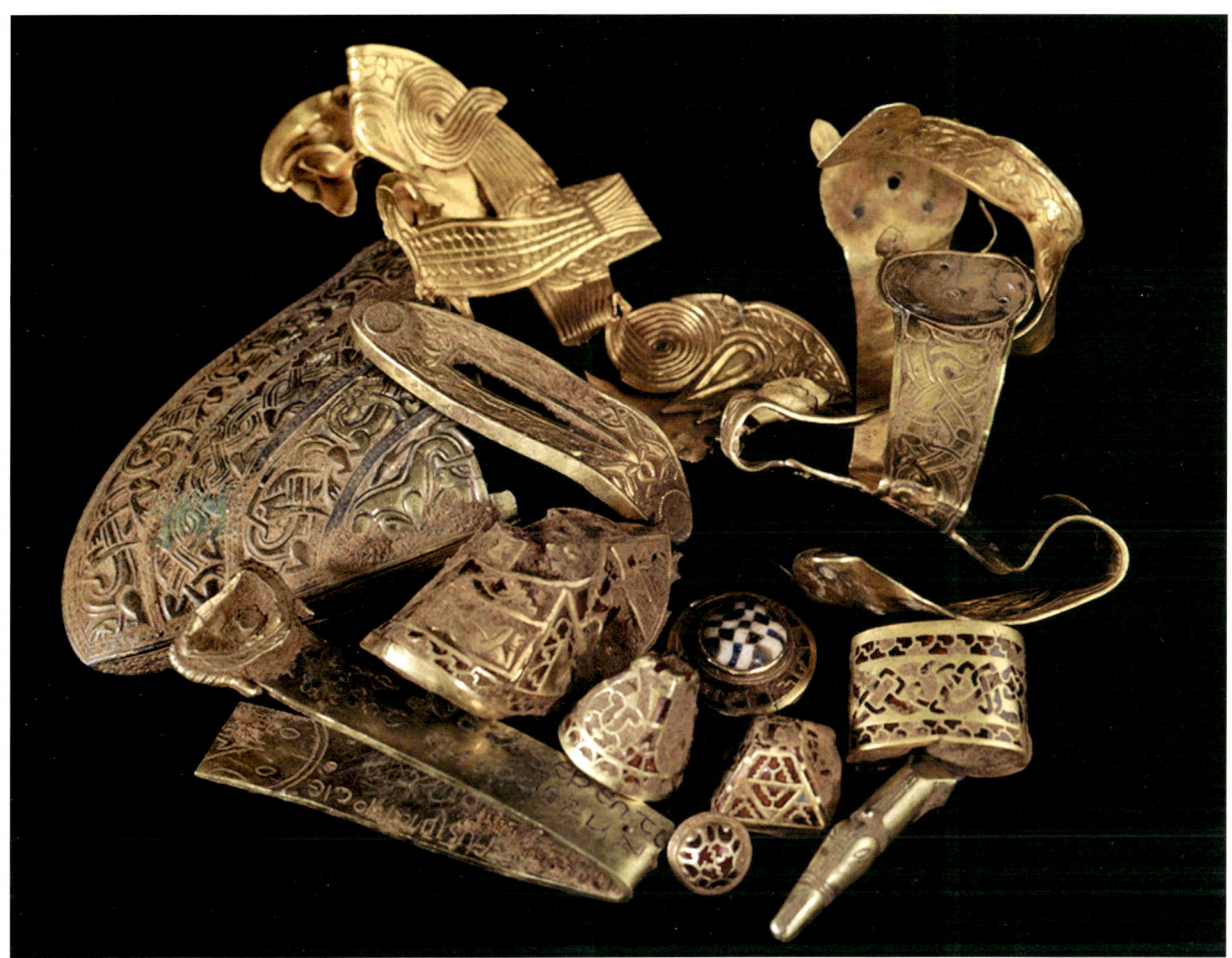

78. Pieces from the Staffordshire Hoard, including the silver-gilt helmet cheek-piece and animal-head crest terminal, and decorated seax guard. 7th century (Birmingham Museums and Art Gallery/Potteries Museum and Art Gallery, Stoke on Trent)

as Bede's story of Rædwald setting up twin altars to Christ and Woden make clear, and as the Christian elements in the burial also hint.

At the same time the complex zoomorphic decoration omnipresent in these images – the animal ornament and figural scenes of dancing and victorious warriors which cover the helmet; the men, monsters and birds of prey on the purse-lid; and the interlocking boars and snakes of the clasps – represents the rich Germanic cosmological tradition explored in Chapter 2 (see figs 2, 16 and 77). This entire regalia is a careful construct; it situates its owner in a dual inheritance of coin-distributing, sceptre-wielding late Roman consuls, and Germanic warrior culture, with its rich iconography of powerful animals, gods and victors. Its magnificent craftsmanship is as much an integral part of that message of power as its artistry. The exquisitely precise shaping and setting of an immense variety of gemstones, from minute inlays on the purse-lid and pyramidal fittings (fig. 77), to complex facetted and curving forms, is finer than anything that the courts of the Merovingian or Langobard kings, or any other European ruler at this time, could produce. This is the work of a master goldsmith at the height of his powers, manifested in the smooth precision of the large gold buckle and the other moving fittings; the regularity of the geometric inlays; and the ingenuity of the lidded-cell garnet inlay seen on the clasps – where free-flowing animal forms give the illusion of being inset directly into solid gold. The use of the finest and most expensive materials, the supreme technical skill, and the brilliantly inventive galaxy of geometric, animal and human decoration, are all united in a vivid evocation of the inheritance, authority and power of the East Anglian dynasty.

Since its excavation in 1939, the superbly crafted and decorated personal jewellery and war-gear from this grave has been seen as the pinnacle of early Anglo-Saxon artistic achievement; but now its pre-eminence can be seen in an unexpectedly different light. Seventy years later, the 2009 discovery of a massive hoard of over 3,500 pieces of gold and silver sword fittings, and other war-gear, near Hammerwich in south Staffordshire – the Staffordshire Hoard, as it has become known – is now radically changing our understanding of the art of early Anglo-Saxon England, and its relationship to secular and ecclesiastical power in the seventh century (figs 78–80 and 82).[2]

The hoard was buried towards the end of that century, in what was then the rising Anglo-Saxon kingdom of Mercia, not far from what were, by that time, important centres at Lichfield and Tamworth. It had been buried in wooded scrub and heathland, close by the great Roman thoroughfare of Watling Street, which remains to this day an arterial road, the A5. It was originally part of a much larger assemblage, possibly battle booty or tribute, from which it had somehow become separated. Many fittings in the hoard were damaged and twisted when wrenched from the objects to which they were originally attached, and some have been bent or folded – perhaps indicating that they were destined for the melting pot. Others have been reduced by both pre- and post-deposition processes to very small fragments. But even in this depleted and damaged state, it is an astonishingly rich assemblage of decorated fine metalwork. The hoard contains superb garnet-inlaid and filigree-decorated gold pommel caps and other hilt fittings from at least ninety-two swords and seaxes; richly ornamented elements from at least one gilded silver helmet; elegant garnet-inlaid gold mounts which probably come from saddles; and many kinds of as yet unidentified objects – not to mention numerous other fragmentary gold and silver items (fig. 78).

The Staffordshire Hoard is also remarkable in other ways. It contains none of the ironwork associated with weapons and fighting – no sword-blades,

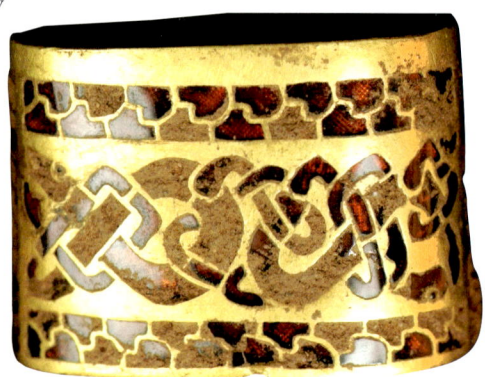

79. Gold and garnet seax hilt fitting, from the Staffordshire Hoard. First half of the 7th century. L. approx. 3.2 cm (Birmingham Museums and Art Gallery/Potteries Museum and Art Gallery, Stoke on Trent)

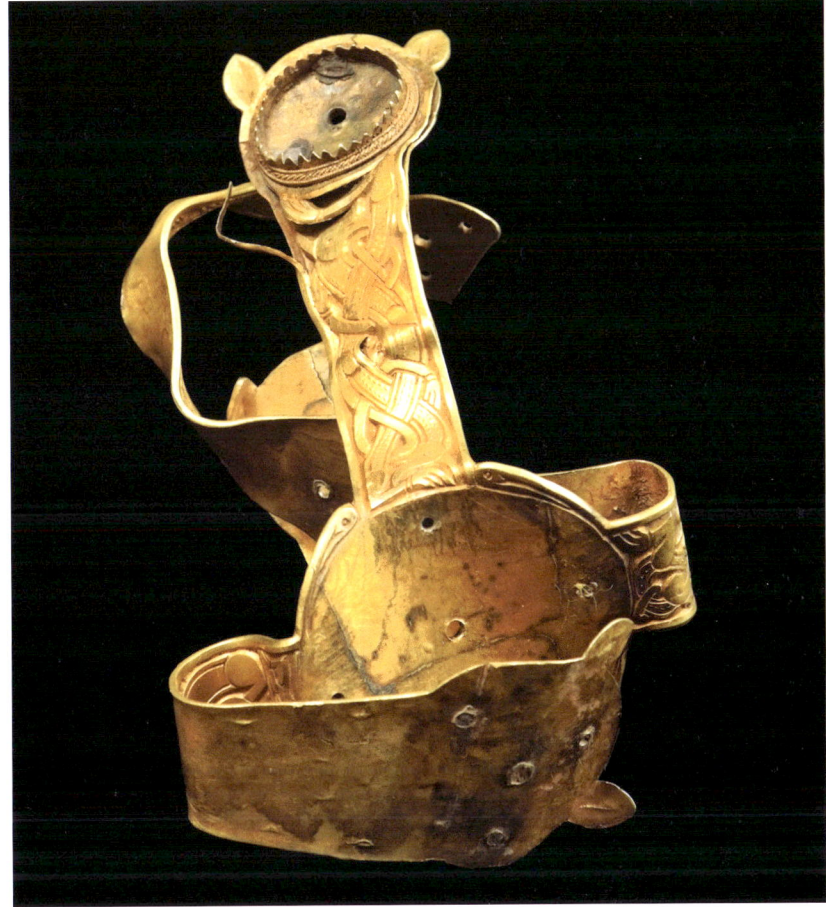

80 (*right*). Gold processional cross, from the Staffordshire Hoard. Late 7th century. H. 11.4 cm (Birmingham Museums and Art Gallery/Potteries Museum and Art Gallery, Stoke on Trent)

81 (*below*). Detail of rim-mount from a maple-wood bottle. From the Mound 1 ship burial, Sutton Hoo, Suffolk, early 7th century (Drawing, British Museum)

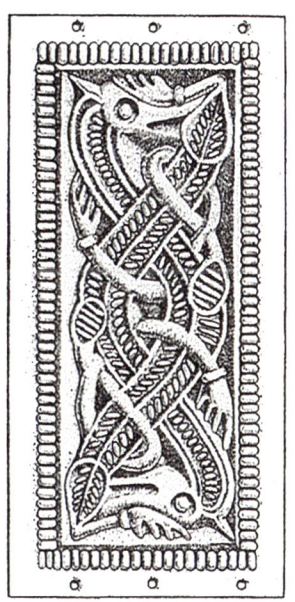

no spears, no shield bosses. Even more strikingly, it contains no coins and no objects associated with women, such as brooches or decorative pendants. But it does contain elements of at least three impressive gold crosses (figs 80 and 82). In total, over 5 kilograms of gold and 1.4 kilograms of silver were retrieved during metal detecting and excavation. The programme of conservation, investigation and research is at an early stage at the time of writing; but preliminary observations are already beginning to question some of our conventional views of art and society in the seventh century[3] – not least, how we should interpret super-rich burials such as those at Sutton Hoo Mound 1, Taplow and Prittlewell. Nowhere is this more strikingly seen than in our understanding of how art relates to power and status during this period.

One of the immediately surprising aspects of metalwork from the Staffordshire Hoard is the outstanding quality of the garnet-inlaid and incised or cast decoration in gold and silver, much of it decorated with Style II animal ornament or elaborate geometric patterns – some with cross-shaped motifs embedded in them. The finest garnet-inlaid decoration includes suavely interlacing animal motifs and sophisticated techniques such as lidded-cell inlays (fig. 79). These are so close to similar ornament on some Sutton Hoo metalwork, such as the purse-lid and shoulder clasps, that they could have been made in the same workshop – or even by the same master goldsmith. Their presence in some quantity invites many questions. Are we seeing here, as at Sutton Hoo, the traces of East Anglian and/or other royal warriors, and among the many other fine fittings, the presence of their personal war-bands, lesser nobility? Does this fine metalwork reflect the mobility of master crafts-men serving more than one high-status Anglo-Saxon patron? We certainly know such goldsmiths existed from early medieval written sources. Was the kind of splendid goldwork seen at Sutton Hoo actually much more wide-spread than we had thought? Another conundrum relates to whether the stylistic differences between the fine filigree sword fittings and the garnet-inlaid mounts arise from different origins – the products and insignia of different kingdoms, for instance – or from different dates; or are even the result of different techniques (the same animal executed in filigree can, for example, look very different to one executed in garnet inlay, or in cast metal). There are also different versions of Style II animal ornament in the hoard which, in current thinking, would be ascribed to opposing 'Anglian' and 'Kentish' traditions (see Chapter 2), yet, like some of the elegant back-biting beasts on the helmet cheek-piece and the large gold cross, actually share some distinctive features (see fig. 78). Such examples suggest that the history of stylistic variation in the seventh century may in fact have been more compli-cated and more entangled than has so far been thought. We certainly cannot yet say if the inventive and varied decoration that characterizes the many fine pieces in the hoard represents parcels of booty or tribute from Northumbria, East Anglia and Kent, or even includes products of the royal workshops in Mercia itself – though particular stylistic motifs, and the recurring use

82. Silver-gilt cross arm inscribed with niello, from the Staffordshire Hoard. Late 7th century. L. 9 cm (Birmingham Museums and Art Gallery/Potteries Museum and Art Gallery, Stoke on Trent)

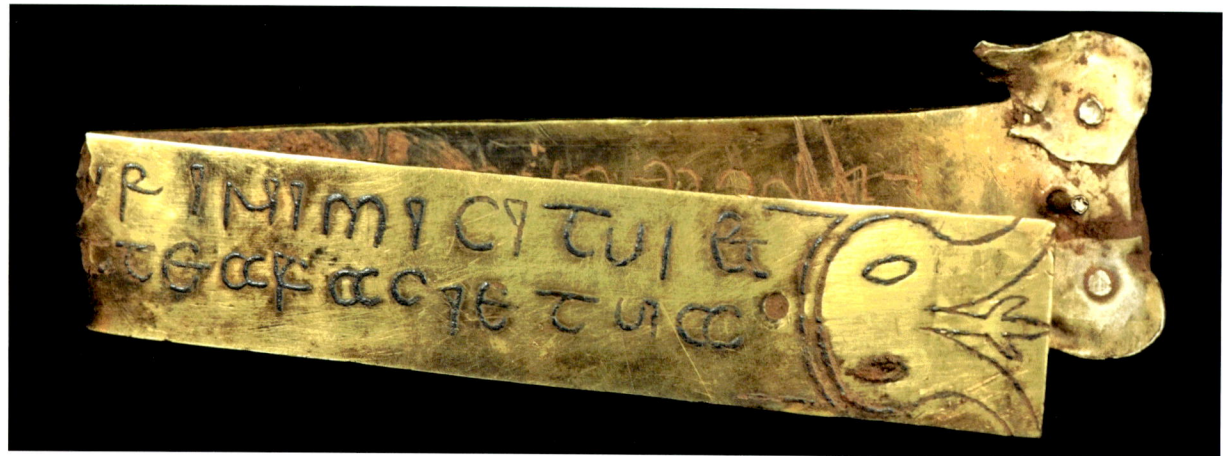

of bird-of-prey, snake, boar and fish iconography in the hoard may hint at differing allegiances. It is, however, clear that the wealth and quality of the art and craftsmanship displayed in this war-gear is not just a matter of status, but reflects the fiercely competitive politics of the age – the power of kings, and their ability to maintain the loyalty of their kinsmen and their close-knit fighting bands.

Sacred art and secular power in the seventh century

The large gold cross from the Staffordshire Hoard (fig. 80) – probably originally mounted on wood as a processional cross – takes us into yet more fascinating territory. It has already been noted (see Chapter 3, p. 78) that its intertwining Style II animal decoration is very close in style to the Book of Durrow and the Durham gospel fragment,[4] both nowadays dated to the second half of the seventh century. Yet it copies an identical model to one used in making the mounts of the maplewood bottles at Sutton Hoo, made in the first third of that century (fig. 81).[5] This has significant implications for the dating and origin of the cross and thus for these two surviving seventh-century prestige manuscripts – should they all be dated around the 620s, like much of the Sutton Hoo metalwork, or was the model for the cross and the bottle rims simply in use for many years?

Equally intriguingly, these intricate links between high-end secular metalwork and religious artefacts confirm the development of an intimate relationship between sacred and secular power in the changing world of the seventh century. The presence in the hoard of the great gold cross, a pendant cross, and the inscribed arm from another cross which may have been mounted on a shrine, is no accident in this otherwise wholly military assemblage.[6] If the hoard does indeed represent booty from one or more battles, the crosses look completely at home in such a context. The cross-arm fragment is inscribed with a fierce biblical text invoking the scattering of God's enemies (Numbers 10:35), framed within the body of an equally fierce creature with a triple-forked tongue (fig. 82).[7] This combination of text and image, both designed to ward off evil, and the iconography of the more complete processional cross, refer to victory and divine protection. Thus, the five great blood-red garnet cabochons which were originally mounted on the large cross represented in Christian tradition the five wounds of Christ, an image of his battle on the Cross and ultimate victory over death; while its animal decoration derives directly from pre-Christian motifs that held an apotropaic meaning, protecting the bearer. Word and image, as so often in Anglo-Saxon art, combine in these objects to reinforce the new Christian message, even on the battlefield itself. These images of religious faith were at the same time instruments of secular power, borne into battle to bring the forces of God to the assistance of temporal kings.

Certainly many of those seventh-century battles, as described by Bede and later sources, reflect a sacred aspect to such conflicts. At Heavenfield, near Hexham, Oswald of Northumbria set up a cross before the battle in which he defeated the British king Cadwallon in 634, with which many miracles were associated. At the Battle of Maserfelth, where Penda of Mercia in turn slew Oswald in 642, miracles were also performed with the aid of soil from the spot where the martyred Christian king died. At the Battle at the River Winwæd in 655, when Oswald's successor, Oswiu, eventually defeated and killed Penda, the modest Northumbrian army was allegedly far outnumbered by the Mercian forces and their East Anglian and other allies. However, after Oswiu had pledged to God the 'incalculable and incredible store of royal treasures' that he had originally offered to buy peace with Penda, the Northumbrians, we are told, 'went to meet the foe trusting in Christ as their leader' – that is, at the head of the Northumbrian army. Even in defeat, a Christian warrior king could not lose; victorious or martyred, he was an example to the faithful. Christ himself, in the *Dream of the Rood*, is portrayed as a warrior, victorious on the Cross. Some Anglo-Saxon saints, such as the eighth-century Mercian nobleman Guthlac, who gave up the life of a successful warrior to battle with demons on his remote Fenland hermitage at Crowland, were portrayed as soldiers for Christ. Strikingly, Guthlac is said by his biographer to have twice used the same biblical quotation as that used on the Staffordshire cross fragment; once to dispel his devilish tormentors, and a second time to reassure – correctly, of course – the exiled Æthelbald (r. 716–57) that he would dispel his enemies and gain the kingdom.

The superbly crafted metalwork in the Staffordshire Hoard shows us that, in a world which was at the crossroads between a pagan past and a Christian future, the power of the secular and sacred still merged seamlessly. Just as, under the old religion, warriors carried images from Germanic lore on their helmets, fierce creatures on their shields and magical runic texts on their swords – all in the name of victory and protection – now they might carry Christian images or texts on their weapons and body armour. The Dinham pommel (fig. 12), with its Crucifixion imagery, and a boar-crested helmet from Benty Grange, Derbyshire, with a Christian cross on the nasal,[8] are both of similar date to the hoard. A number of later weapon fittings with Christian inscriptions show that this tradition did not die out in a hurry; most impressive among them, the eighth-century Anglo-Saxon helmet discarded in a pit at Coppergate, York, bears an prayer inscribed crosswise across its crown, invoking God's protection for its owner (see figs 13 and 108). Taking crosses and shrines into battle, like later accounts of reliquaries being carried before armies, was only one step further in bringing Christ onto the battlefield. All these artefacts – weapons, helmets and crosses – unite secular and sacred power in densely imagined images and texts. Similarly, a number of

Anglo-Saxon poems, including *Beowulf* – which may possibly have been written down in something like its present form in eighth-century Mercia – also use traditional poetic formulas to place Germanic warrior culture, with its loyal fighting bands, its battle ethos, its treasure-seeking and gift-giving, in a Christian context. Even Anglo-Saxon poems with specifically biblical subjects often use similar heroic language to deliver a Christian message, such as the *Dream of the Rood*, described above, and *Judith*, in which the feisty apocryphal heroine who beheads the wicked Assyrian Holofernes is depicted in terms befitting an Anglo-Saxon warrior.

Battles themselves – the ultimate triumph of power – were also celebrated not just in poems and song recited in the halls of the victors, but in the visual arts as well. The Bayeux Tapestry is the most famous example of a splendid work of art created to celebrate a notable victory, and was probably intended as a visual accompaniment to sung or recited accounts of the victory. Another such is mentioned in the *Liber Eliensis*, which describes how, after the burial of Byrhtnoth, ealdorman of Essex, who died in a heroic defeat by the Vikings at the Battle of Maldon in 991, his widow donated to Ely Cathedral an embroidered hanging celebrating his deeds. Given the importance of heroic tale-telling in Anglo-Saxon culture, it seems very probable that many such visual aids – embroidered wall-hangings, but also wood carvings and even stone sculptures – accompanied the recitation of heroic deeds and battles won and lost.

83. Mercian coins: (*top, right*) Gold coin of Offa imitating *dinar* of Caliph al-Mansur (obverse and reverse). Diam. 1.9 cm; (*left*) Silver penny of Offa (obverse only). Diam. 1.2 cm; (*bottom, right*) Gold *mancus* of Coenwulf (obverse and reverse). Diam. 2 cm (all British Museum)

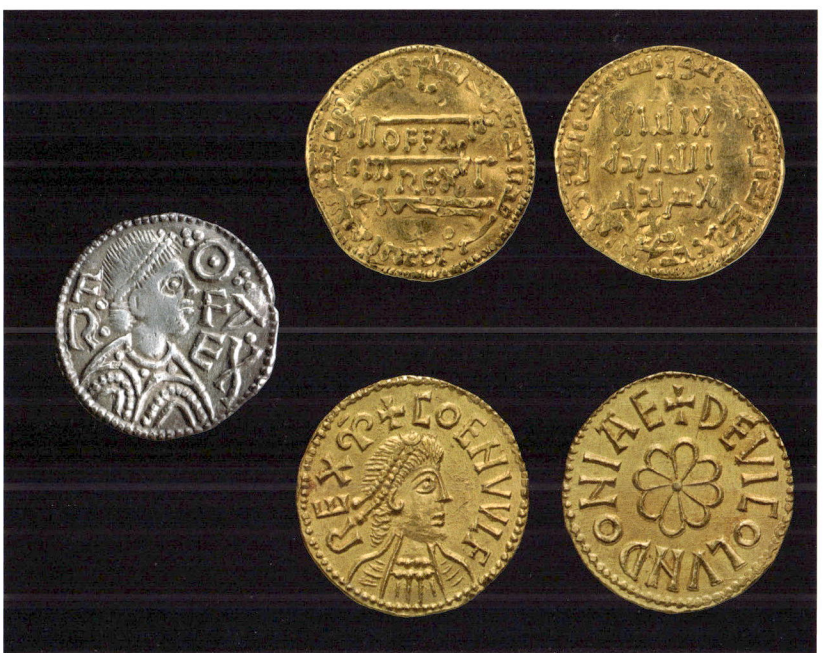

One further image of art, wealth and power brings us back to the indivisibility of the sacred and secular in the seventh and eighth centuries. We have already encountered St Wilfrid, bishop of Hexham and Ripon, as a lavish donor of the finest manuscripts and magnificent furnishings to his monastic foundations at York, Ripon and Hexham. But his biographer, Stephen of Ripon, also takes great pains to portray him as a noble accompanied by his own followers, 'arrayed and armed like a king's retinue'. He also describes how, on his deathbed, the saint shared out treasure of gold, silver and precious stones. This amassing, display and distribution of treasure is strikingly reminiscent of secular kingship. In his ostentatiously aristocratic bearing, Wilfrid (who passed at least two long spells in Mercia in the later seventh and early eighth centuries, around the time that the Staffordshire Hoard was buried) may have been exceptional as a prelate. But Stephen's account seems to confirm the impression given by the magnificent warrior gear and splendid Christian talismans seen in the Staffordshire Hoard and elsewhere, that the division between high-status military and ecclesiastical culture could often be hard to distinguish during this period.

Power and patronage in the art of the Mercian ascendancy

The Staffordshire Hoard gives a brief, if enigmatic, glimpse of the nature of wealth, power and art in the Mercian kingdom as it began its ascendancy under the kings Penda (r. *c.* 632–55), Wulfhere (r. 658–74) and Æthelred (r. 675–704). However, the shape of art in the eighth century, as Mercia secured its dominance over most of England south of the Humber, took a very different form. Already by the mid-seventh century the gold supplies that had fuelled the sumptuous metalwork of Sutton Hoo and the Staffordshire Hoard were failing, and by 700, silver had largely replaced gold as the metal of choice both for coinage, and for much fine secular and ecclesiastical metalwork. The showy combination of gold, filigree and garnet that had dominated the prestige jewellery of the seventh century gave way to a subtler, but no less accomplished, style based on cast and engraved silver, sometimes gilded. It was increasingly intricately inlaid with niello, enabling a fluidity of decoration which at its best approaches manuscript ornament in its fluency.

At the same time sculpture and manuscripts – essentially the products of ecclesiastical centres – benefited from the patronage of kings and noblemen. They exhibit the wealth and new influences brought about by diplomatic and ecclesiastical contacts with the Continent, as well as by expanding trade, now fostered through trading bases known as *wics*, such as London (*Lundenwic*), Ipswich (*Gippeswic*), York (*Eoforwic*) and *Hamwih* (at Southampton), as well as towns and major markets. During the eighth century the increasing dominance of Mercia was reflected in a distinctive and influential art which has its main focus of distribution across all those areas of England it controlled

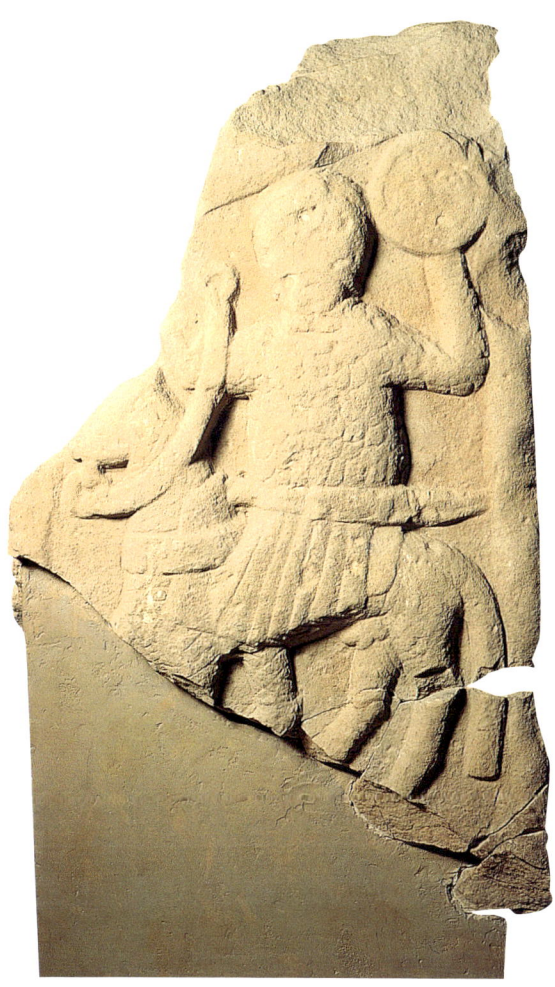

84. Stone figure of a warrior. From St Wystan church, Repton, Derbyshire, probably late 8th century. H. 91.2 cm (Derby Museum)

– at its greatest extent, almost all of England south of the Humber, except for Wessex and the extreme south-west. Only with the decline of Mercian power from the 820s, and the corresponding rise of Wessex, did this give way to an even more widespread and equally distinctive style which dominated the art of the ninth century, discussed later in this chapter.

The richness, quality and influential nature of Mercian art in this period prospered during the long reigns of the two ruthless and ambitious kings who largely created this Southumbrian super-kingdom, Æthelbald (r. 716–57) and Offa (r. 757–96). In 731 Bede described the former as ruling all England south of the Humber, and Offa built remorselessly on this; the extraordinary resources that he had at his command can still be seen in the construction of the great earthwork known as Offa's Dyke, which runs from the River Dee to the River Severn, forming a formidable barrier to the Welsh kingdoms beyond. Confident of their domination, these kings were happy to underscore it by sometimes styling themselves, respectively, as 'king of Britain' and 'king of the whole country of the English'. Offa in particular liked to represent himself as a player on the world stage, engaging like an equal in gift exchanges with Charlemagne. Through a radical reformation of the coinage, introducing for the first time the broad silver penny into England, he also made it an instrument of political as well as economic domination, stamping his authority throughout his realm with an outward and visible sign of imperium. These often handsome romanizing coins created an image of power allied with considerable artistic quality and invention (fig. 83). The grandest of these was a remarkable gold coin (*mancus*) imitating an Arabic *dinar* of Caliph al-Mansur, ruler (754–75) of the Islamic Abbasid dynasty, which was probably issued for trading purposes in the Mediterranean (fig. 83a). Offa's successor, Coenwulf (r. 796–821), the last of the successful Mercian kings, also made a political point in issuing a superb gold *mancus* from the mint of the great emporium of London – *Lundenwic* – perhaps to outdo a rather less impressive gold coin of Charlemagne, issued from his own equivalent trading centre at Dorestad, at the mouth of the Rhine (fig. 83c). These powerful kings brought, if not peace, at least a degree of stability across much of England for much of the time. Along with the increasingly wealthy developing economy indicated by the new coinage, this created a climate in which royal and aristocratic patrons, as well as the Church itself, could enrich existing ecclesiastical foundations, and foster the creation of ambitious new buildings, with elaborate sculptured and painted interiors (sometimes also exteriors), as well as magnificent manuscripts, textiles and metalwork. What survives of this today is almost entirely ecclesiastical in nature. But, like their much grander and more powerful Carolingian neighbours, the eighth-century kings of Mercia would also have aspired to richly furnished, handsomely decorated and well-equipped palaces and halls, even if these may not have been quite on the level of Charlemagne's great stone palace at Paderborn (Germany), revealed by excavation, with its glazed windows and decorative tiling. It seems from a letter of Charlemagne to Offa that the Frankish king sent his English ally a gift of fine black marble from his family estates, perhaps meant for the decoration of Offa's palace, though a favoured church is perhaps a more likely destination.[9] The small amount of material evidence that does survive, however, gives a hint of the grandeur of royal aspiration during the period, and how it was also emulated by noble donors and patrons.

A few examples suggest the scale of this ambition. At Repton in Derbyshire, in the heartland of Mercia, a double monastery had been established in the later seventh century which had attracted noble acolytes such as Guthlac (whose *Life* is a major source of information on Mercia in the early eighth century). A remarkable eighth-century crypt survives to this day; originally perhaps built as a baptistery, it was later modified to become a royal mausoleum housing the tombs of Æthelbald and a number of his successors. Its present appearance, incorporating elegant columns with spiral decoration, dates to the early ninth century, the closing years of Mercian hegemony. Excavations adjacent to the crypt have produced fragments of an exceptional sculpture of a mounted warrior sporting an Anglo-Saxon shield and seax, and more significantly, a distinctively Germanic moustache (fig. 84); there is a scene of the Last Judgement on the other side. It can probably be dated to the eighth century. The warrior's pose carries echoes both of the monuments commemorating Roman cavalrymen which are well known from Britain, and of the related victorious mounted warrior images seen on earlier Anglo-Saxon helmet panels, including those from Sutton Hoo and in the Staffordshire Hoard. These earlier images invoke victory and domination, and their owners' place in a world ordered by the gods. The later, Christian, context at Repton suggests that this striking sculpture may represent a warrior for Christ. But the location, next to the royal Mercian mausoleum where the victorious Æthelbald and other kings were buried, strongly suggests that a royal Anglo-Saxon patron lies behind the commissioning of such a work, and may even be depicted on it, in a graphic icon of secular power integrated into a Christian iconography.

Other ambitious projects are connected with the Mercian supremacy, including the great basilican church at Brixworth in Northamptonshire, larger than any other surviving Anglo-Saxon church and probably dating to the later eighth or first half of the ninth century.[10] We know almost nothing of its early

85. Stone panel with figure of an archangel. Late 8th–early 9th century. H. 91 cm (Church of St Mary and St Hardulph, Breedon on the Hill, Leicestershire)

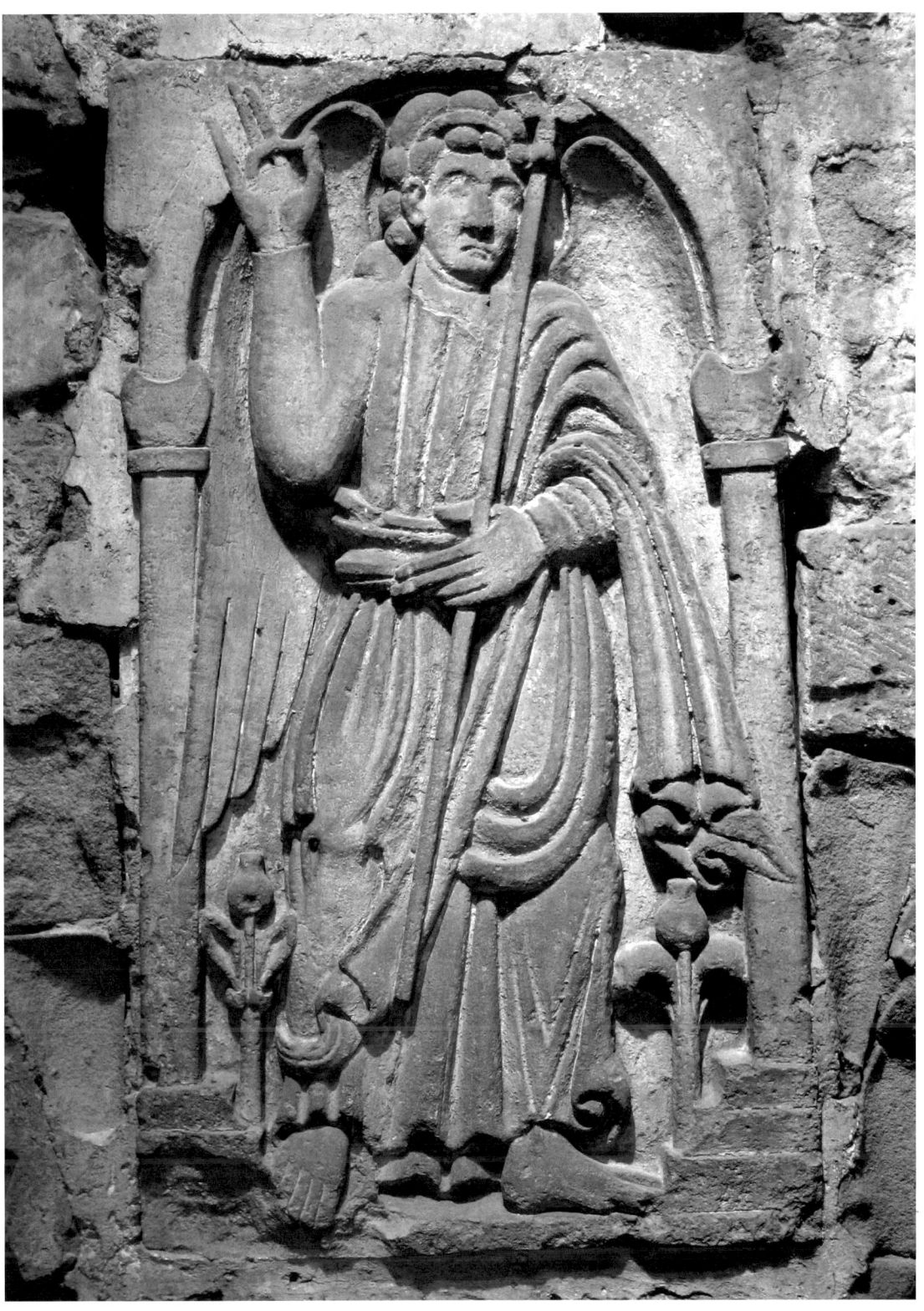

history, but it is evident that it must have been built by powerful and wealthy sponsors, whether ecclesiastical or aristocratic/royal, and very possibly with contemporary Carolingian examples in mind. Perhaps even more remarkable is the case of the cathedral church at Lichfield, a Mercian royal and ecclesiastical centre from the seventh century. Originally founded as a monastery by the Northumbrian missionary Chad in 669 on land donated by King Wulfhere, in the early eighth century a new church was built to house the shrine of St Chad, much visited by pilgrims. Later in the century, its importance was augmented when Offa transferred the archbishopric from Canterbury to Lichfield in 787 (it reverted to Canterbury sixteen years later, in 803). Offa no doubt brought in works of art and craftsmen from the Continent, to equip the new archiepiscopal seat in a grand and worthy manner.[11]

Nothing structural of this Anglo-Saxon cathedral survives, but the recently discovered painted sculpture of an archangel, buried beneath the floor of the nave, gives an insight into the quality and magnificence of the furnishings of this major church at the centre of the Mercian power-base (see fig. 9). The panel dates to the late eighth century, and was possibly part of a stone housing for the shrine of the founder, St Chad. It depicts an angel who seems to be in the act of alighting on the ground, his wings still half-spread, a staff of authority with leaf sprigs in his left hand, and his right hand raised in blessing. This is the archangel Gabriel, God's messenger, and the panel is part of a sculptured Annunciation scene which would originally have been completed by the figure of Mary, learning that she is to bear the son of God. The figure of Gabriel, as noted in Chapter 4 (p. 114), owes much to eastern Christian models, in common with other figures in Mercian sculpture and manuscripts. The crisply modelled draperies ripple naturalistically, giving a sense of the physical body underneath, and the curled hairstyle and pose of the angel are also inspired by late antique images. The sprouting plant at the angel's right derives from similar sources, and is probably to be interpreted as a symbol of the flowers of Paradise; similar plants appear elsewhere in sculpture and manuscripts of the period. Because the stone was buried during the later Saxon period, such surface detail is exceptionally well preserved, including much of the original painting which subtly emphasizes the carving (see Chapter 1). This superlative piece, unmatched by any other contemporary stone sculpture from Europe, is a witness to the creativity of Mercian sculptors.

Figural art in Mercian sculpture and manuscripts

None of the other fine sculptures of this period that survive in churches across Mercia retains its original crisp surface and its paintwork to the same degree as the panel from Lichfield, and many have suffered the ravages of time, warfare and weather. Nevertheless, a vivid impression of the vitality and wealth of early foundations such as Medeshamstede (Peterborough), Castor (both royal

86 (*opposite, left*). Stone panel with figure of the Virgin. Early 9th century. H. 53 cm (Church of St Mary and St Hardulph, Breedon on the Hill, Leicestershire)

87 (*opposite, right*). Stone panel with two apostles. Late 8th–early 9th century. H. 49 cm (Church of St Mary and St Hardulph, Breedon on the Hill, Leicestershire)

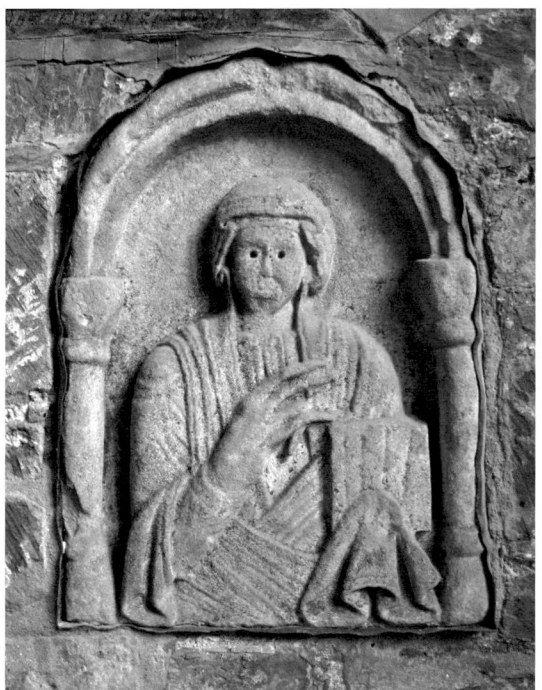

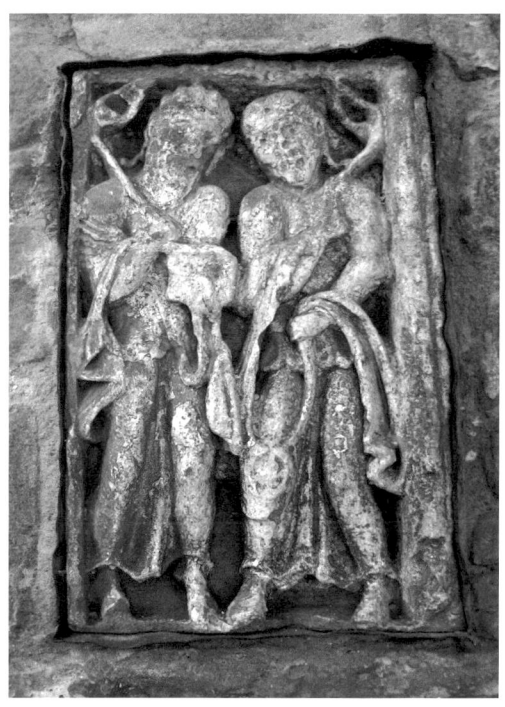

foundations), Fletton (Huntingdonshire) and above all – for the wealth of its surviving sculpture – Breedon on the Hill (Leicestershire), is immediately apparent from the outstanding tradition of figural sculpture which they share. Architectural friezes, screens, or panels from sarcophagi and shrines form the majority of this material (e.g. figs 9 and 85–7). It is also noteworthy that all these minster churches, though seventh-century in origin, like Lichfield, were rebuilt or refurbished in the late eighth or early ninth centuries, in the years of greatness before Mercia's decline.

88. Details from the 'roof' of the Hedda Stone, showing animal decoration. Late 8th century. (Stone, Peterborough Cathedral; drawing after Plunkett 1998)

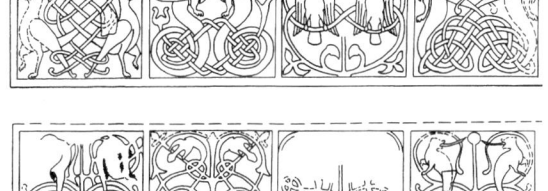

Like the Lichfield Angel, some of these figure sculptures originally belonged to Annunciation scenes. At Breedon, an imposing Gabriel figure under an arch represents a more stylized version than that at Lichfield (fig. 85). Although a tenth-century date has been suggested for it, this angel's distinctive bun-like hairstyle recalls that on the king's head on some of Offa's coins.[12] Furthermore, the cusped column heads of the framing arch also appear in the early ninth-century Book of Cerne (fig. 90) and in other Mercian sculpture of the later eighth and early ninth centuries. Many of these figures – for instance, an archangel and a saint at Fletton, an evangelist at Castor, two possible soldiers at Peterborough, two apostles and friezes of small figures of saints at Breedon – share a distinctively light, almost floating

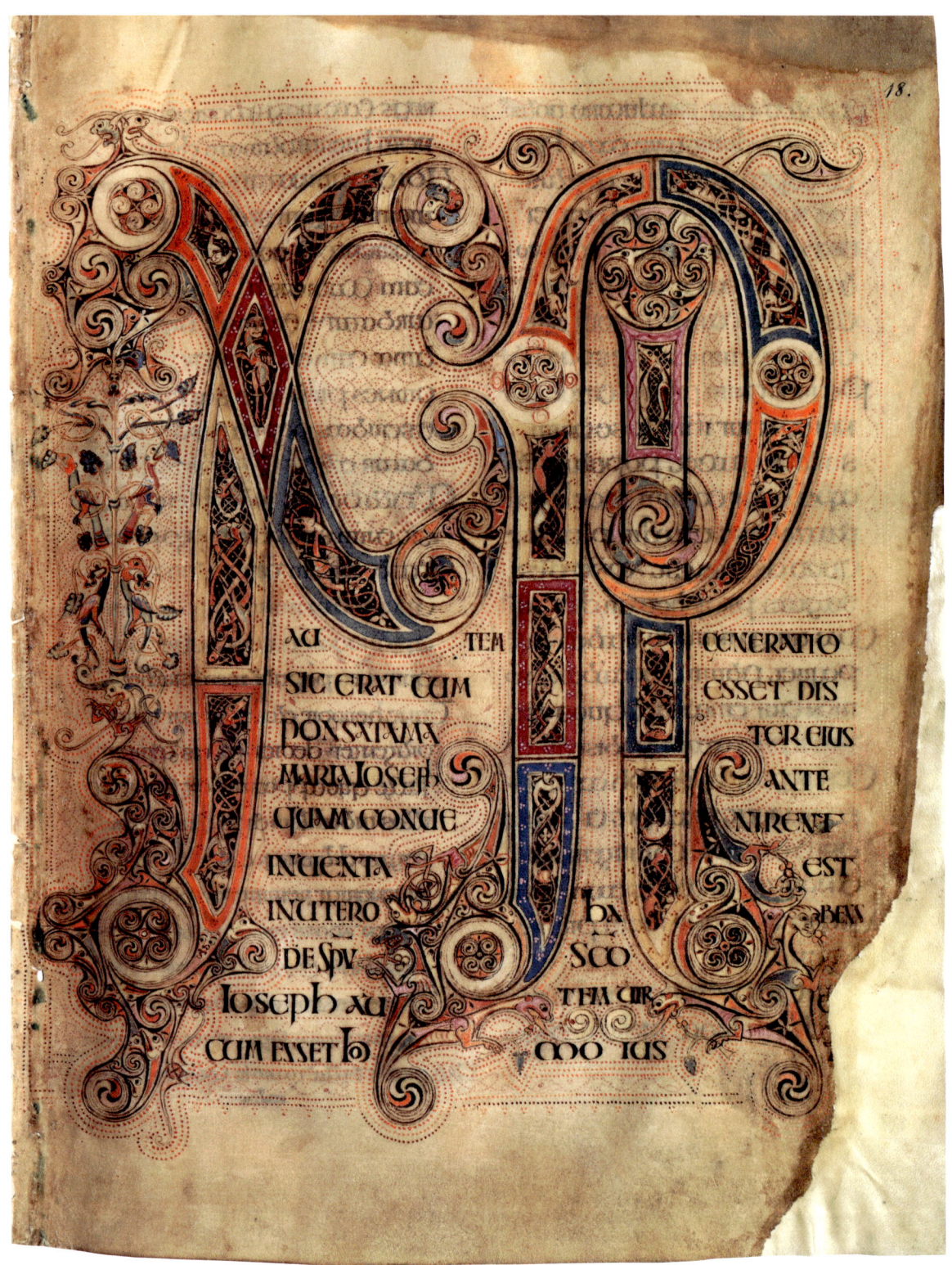

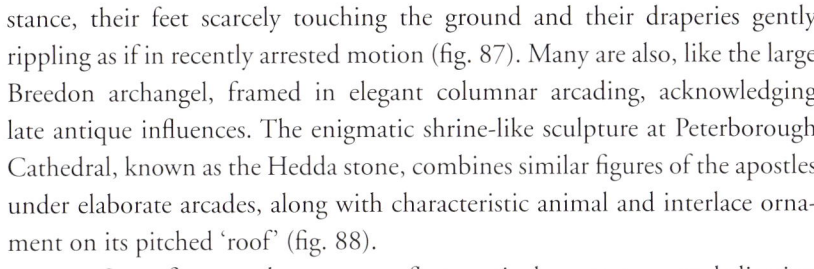

89 (*opposite*). The Barberini Gospels: Chi-Rho page. Late 8th or early 9th century. 34 x 25 cm (Biblioteca Apostolica Vaticana, Vatican City, MS Lat.570, fol. 18r)

90 (*below*). The Book of Cerne: the symbol and portrait of St Matthew. *c.* 820–40. 23 x 18.4 cm (University Library, Cambridge, MS Ll.1.10, fol. 2v)

stance, their feet scarcely touching the ground and their draperies gently rippling as if in recently arrested motion (fig. 87). Many are also, like the large Breedon archangel, framed in elegant columnar arcading, acknowledging late antique influences. The enigmatic shrine-like sculpture at Peterborough Cathedral, known as the Hedda stone, combines similar figures of the apostles under elaborate arcades, along with characteristic animal and interlace ornament on its pitched 'roof' (fig. 88).

Some figure sculpture may reflect particular patronage or dedication traditions; the Synod of Chelsea in 816 decreed that churches should contain an image of the saint to which they were dedicated. At Breedon, the solemn female figure holding a holy book – perhaps the Book of Life in which the deeds of the faithful are recorded – is probably an image of the Virgin Mary in her role as an intercessor for souls.[13] The church is dedicated to St Mary and St Hardulph, and the image may also reflect a re-dedication in the early ninth century (fig. 86). At St Mary's Priory at Deerhurst in Gloucestershire, another church rich in sculpture of this period and also within the Mercian orbit, the painted sculpture of the Virgin over the entrance to the church proper, which dates to the first half of the ninth century, may be linked to the church's dedication.[14] It might also reflect the patronage of a local nobleman who chose to be buried there, hoping for her intercession at the time of death and on the Day of Judgement (see also Chapter 4, p. 115).

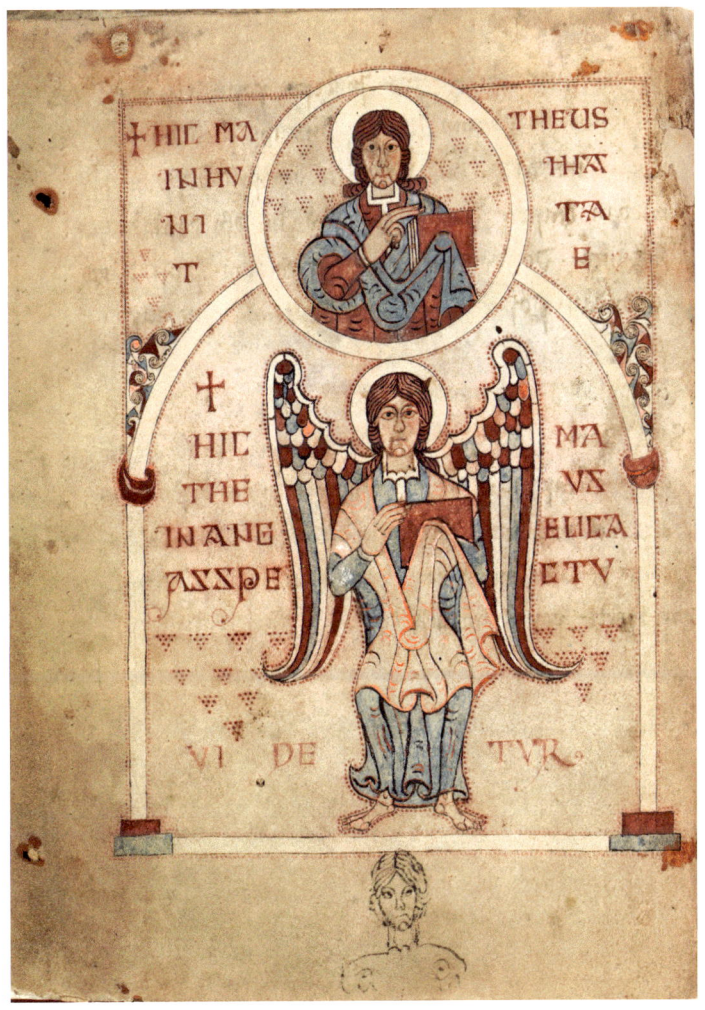

The finest of these sculptures are of the highest quality and originality; although they clearly owe something to Byzantine traditions, they are unlike anything else in contemporary western Europe, except, as we shall see, in Pictland. The royal and aristocratic patrons who commissioned these major works, from Offa at Lichfield to the nobleman Æthelric at Deerhurst, sought not only to earn salvation in the afterlife, but to demonstrate publicly their wealth and standing in the wider social and political world.[15]

As the ransom inscription on the Stockholm *Codex Aureus* so graphically illustrates (see p. 119), the grandly decorated manuscripts associated with the Mercian supremacy were, like their Northumbrian predecessors, all too susceptible to the predations of Viking raiders, not to mention the despoliations of the Norman Conquest and the Reformation. But among those that do survive are some that equal contemporary sculpture in sophistication and grandeur. The sumptuously decorated Vespasian Psalter and the Stockholm *Codex Aureus* (figs 57, 58 and 76), though made in Kent (most probably at Canterbury), were created towards or around the middle of the eighth century, as the star of Mercia rose under Æthelbald, described in the Ismere charter of 736 as lord of the southern English. By then, Kent was certainly part of the Mercian sphere of influence, if not definitively under Mercian control. Drawing on an Eastern Christian tradition in their rich palette, their use of

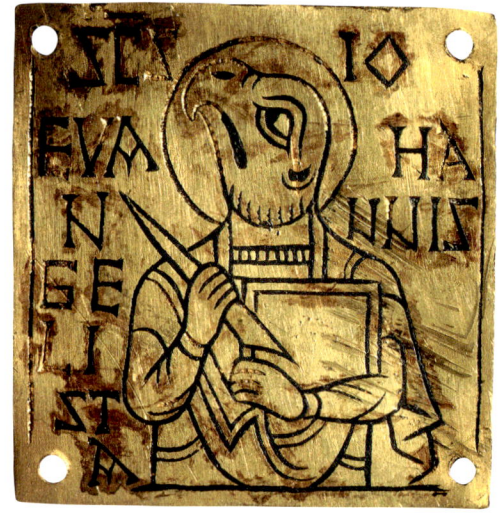

91 (*above*). Gold plaque from a cross or book cover, inlaid in niello with the symbol of St John. Brandon, Suffolk, early 9th century. H. 3.4 cm (British Museum)

92 (*opposite*). The Tiberius Bede: detail of initial and text with animal embellishments. Early 9th century. Whole page 27.2 x 21.6 cm (British Library, Cotton MS Tiberius C.ii, fol. 5v)

gold, the subtly modelled depictions of the human figure, and orientalizing animal motifs, manuscripts such as these, if not made in Mercia, were certainly influential in the development of a distinctively Southumbrian manuscript style during the eighth and early ninth centuries. An outstanding example of this, and now thought to be specifically Mercian in its origins, is the Barberini Gospels, described in Chapter 4 (see p. 112, and figs 74 and 89). It has a good claim to be a product of one of the oldest and most important monastic foundations in Mercia, that at Medeshamstede (modern Peterborough), allegedly founded in the 650s by two Mercian kings with the aid of its abbot, the nobly born Seaxwulf, later bishop of the Mercians. Probably made to honour this great minster some 150 years later, the Gospels' brilliant display of illusionistic figure painting, elegant plant decoration and playful animal ornament, assimilating up-to-the-minute Carolingian influences, is an equally prestigious counterpart to the great Mercian sculptural creations, such as those at Lichfield and Breedon.

Another Mercian manuscript, the so-called Book of Cerne, dated *c.* 820–40, exhibits a less naturalistic, more linear figure style (fig. 90). It does, however, make use of elegant arcading with cusped capitals and distinctive triangular falls of drapery, which is also seen in some Mercian figure sculpture, such as the 'Lechmere' stone[16] and the Breedon panels with small figures of saints.[17] Less ambitious in both execution and tonal range than the splendours of the Barberini Gospels, the Book of Cerne is a devotional compilation probably made for Bishop Æthelwald of Lichfield (818–30); it suggests a less formal, and perhaps more intimate, level of artistic patronage in this period. Another glimpse of this more linear figure style can be seen in a small gold plaque found at a high-status – perhaps also ecclesiastical – site at Brandon, Suffolk, dating to the later eighth and ninth centuries, a time when Mercia

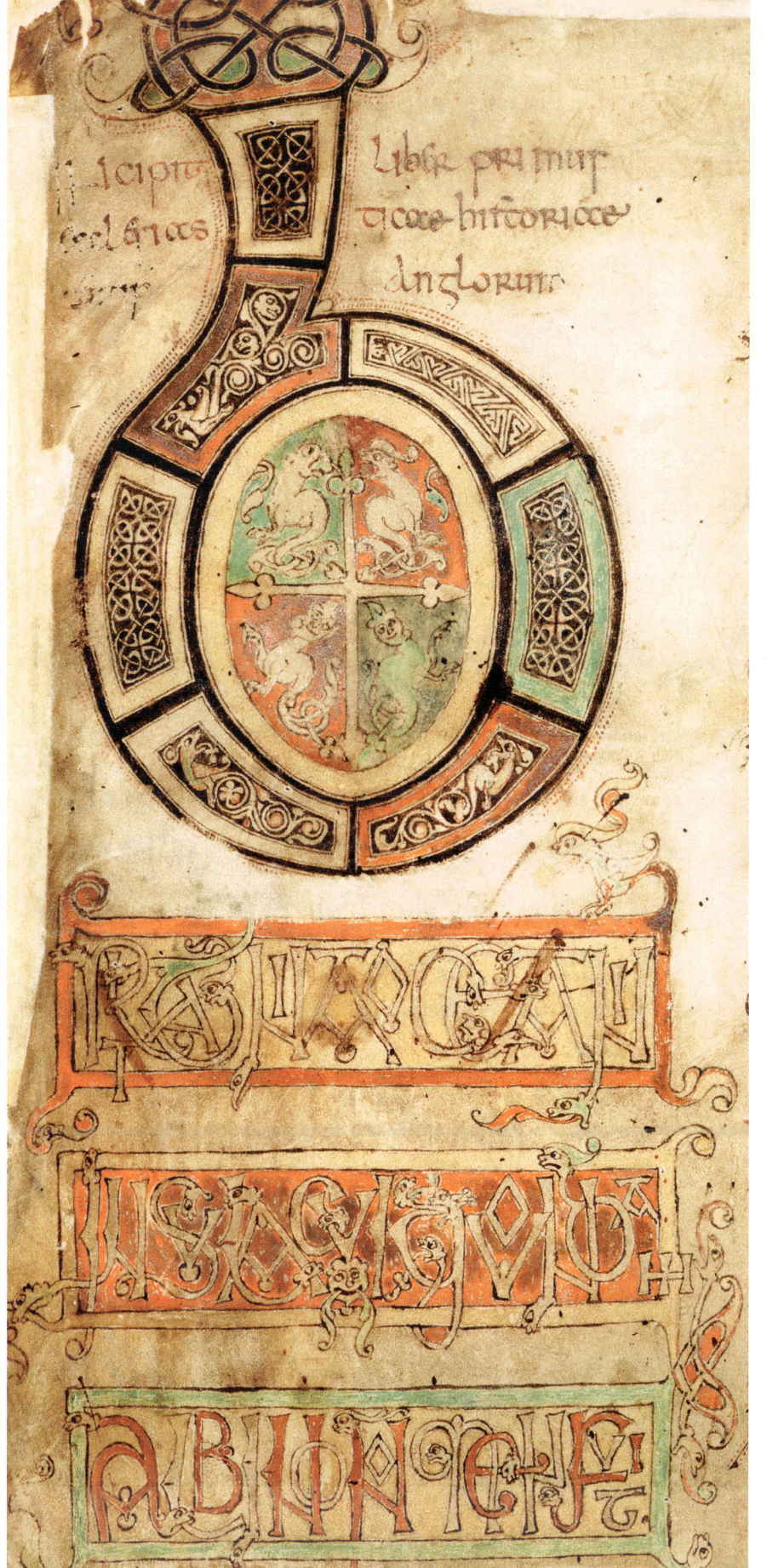

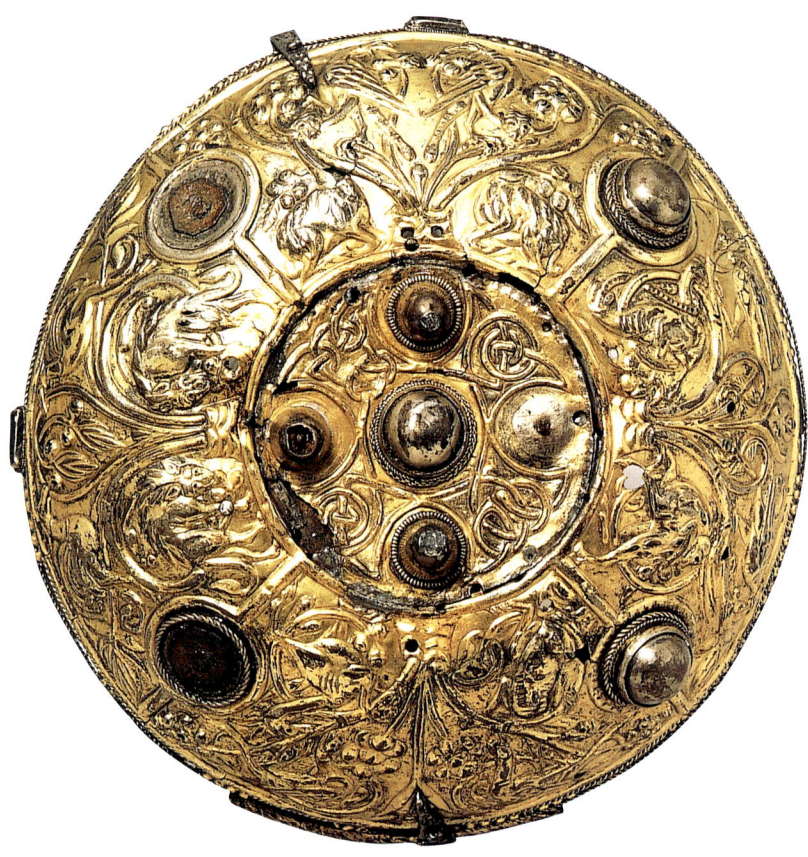

controlled East Anglia (fig. 91). It bears an image of St John the Evangelist, unusually portrayed as an eagle-headed figure, holding a sharpened quill and gospel-book. Although the figure and its accompanying inscription are incised in metal, and inlaid with niello, they have all the sharp fluency of a pen drawing on the page. This beautifully executed image, presumably one of four such evangelist images from a cross or a book cover, was clearly made by someone totally familiar with manuscript conventions. It gives a rare glimpse of the creative relationship between the ecclesiastical metalworker and the scribe and illuminator in the scriptorium.

Animal art of the Mercian supremacy

However, the most widespread and characteristic aspect of the art of the Mercian supremacy, whether in the decoration of manuscripts, sculpture or metalwork, is its distinctive animal ornament. It is an important distinguishing

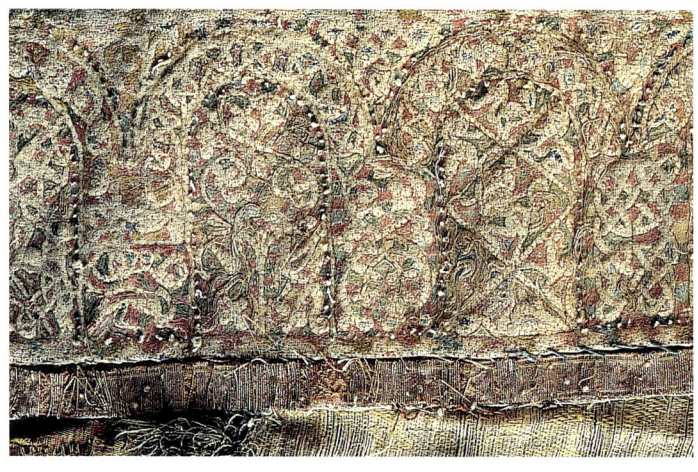

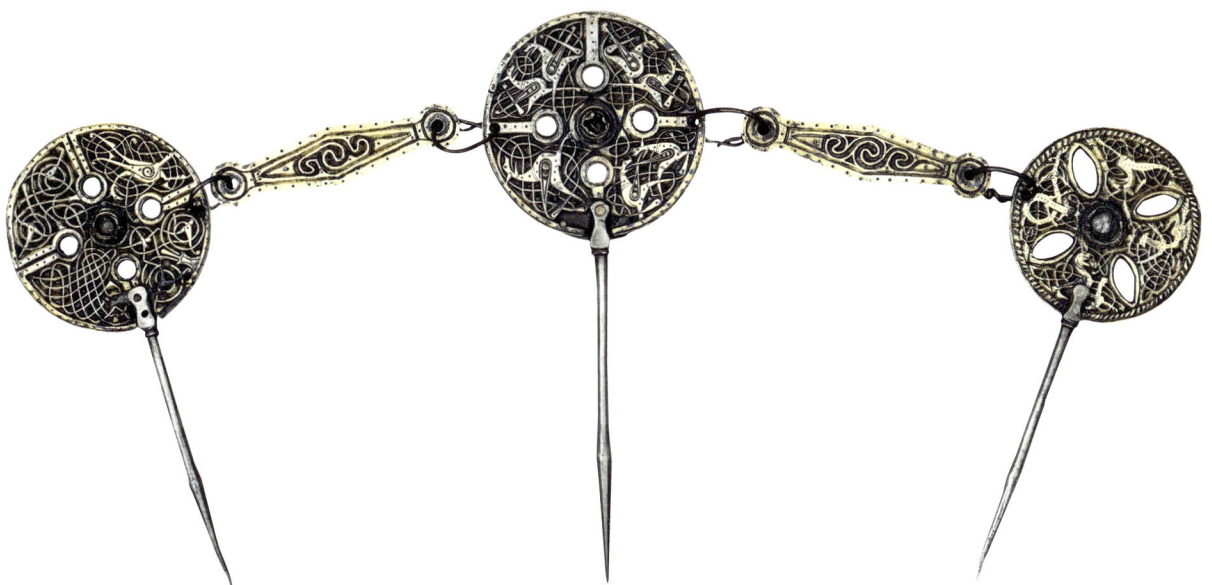

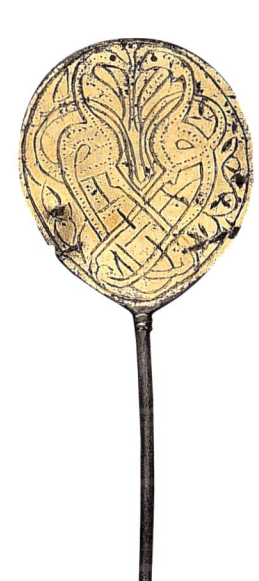

feature of the Southumbrian manuscript tradition, which flourished between the mid-eighth and mid-ninth centuries. and encompassed the script and decoration of manuscripts made at a variety of Mercian or Mercian-dominated centres, including Canterbury, as well as scriptoria in Mercia itself.[18]

Central to this animal ornament is the so-called Tiberius group of manuscripts, which takes its name from an early ninth-century Bede manuscript written at Canterbury (fig. 92). It includes grand and ostentatious manuscripts, such as the Barberini Gospels and the somewhat later Royal Bible fragment, as well as more personal and informal devotional compilations, such as the Book of Cerne and a number of prayer books (see figs 74, 89, 90 and 109). The quirky, playful animals that prance, bite and snap in initials and entwine in the columns of canon tables display a new range of stances and attitudes, far removed from the sinuous interlacing animals that dominated the zoomorphic art of the seventh and early eighth centuries. As noted in the last chapter, the influence of Eastern models – especially textiles and ivories – is an important element in the genesis of these new beasts. The exotic birds, chimeras, lions, centaurs and unicorns that frisk in richly ornamented ecclesiastical furnishings – such as the sculptured friezes at Breedon (fig. 75), the Bischofshofen cross (fig. 71), the liturgical water bowl found at Ormside in Westmorland (fig. 93) and the gold-embroidered crimson Anglo-Saxon altar cloths now at Maaseik (fig. 94) – have all escaped from a Byzantine menagerie. But their fondness for entwinements and oppositions of every kind, and their invasive habit, also look back to earlier Anglo-Saxon traditions. The fertile union of the Anglo-Saxon zoomorphic tradition and the new Eastern influences visible in ecclesiastical contexts swiftly gravitated to secular metalwork such as strap-ends, rings, pins and brooches, widely occurring throughout the area of Mercian dominance (e.g. fig. 96). Elaborate gilded brooches and pin-suites, such as that found in the River Witham at Fiskerton, Lincolnshire, display the style flamboyantly, as badges of wealth and status (fig. 95). Characteristic of this hybrid animal decoration, where animals are often enmeshed in fine interlace, are prancing creatures, beasts and birds with furled or pricked wings, sometimes with lolling tongues, lizard-like animals seen from above, and most of all, paired creatures that confront or turn their backs on one another, usually dissolving into deftly intertwining tails.

Sculptural versions of these lively little beasts are also widespread in Mercia, for instance in the vine scrolls of an early ninth-century cross head from Cropthorne, Worcestershire, with its animated birds and lion-like creatures (fig. 99). A particularly distinctive element in this style is the so-called 'Mercian' beast, with its heraldic stance and lolling tongue. It often appears in confronted pairs, as on some of the fine metalwork from high-status eighth- to ninth-century sites at Flixborough, Lincolnshire (fig. 97), and Brandon, Suffolk; and on a pair of large silver disc brooches from Pentney, Norfolk, the rising fashion of the early ninth century (see fig. 112). It is also a popular motif on stone cross shafts across the Mercian heartlands, including fine examples at St Oswald's in Gloucester, St Alkmund's in Derby,[19] and Elstow, Bedfordshire (fig. 98), all dating to the late eighth or early ninth centuries.

A few rare examples of this Mercian animal style in other media have survived. The most perfectly preserved is an intricately carved Anglo-Saxon whale-bone house-shaped chrismatory known as the Gandersheim Casket (see also Chapters 4 and 6, pp. 106 and 167), which reveals this artistry at its subtlest and most exquisite (see figs 100 and 72). It is decorated on the back and front with a complex scheme in which the divinely created animals of earth, air and water – quadrupeds, birds, and serpents or lizard-like creatures – are framed in grids of six and twelve. These are significant numbers in Christian cosmology, in which they are linked to God's Creation. They connote, among other things, the days of Creation, the hours of the day and the months of the year – the framework of a universe shaped by divine purpose. On the ends are sinuous lizard-like beasts snaking through interlace from delicate fruiting vine bushes, while on the gabled lid are more of the same menagerie along with vine sprigs, and a complex interlace, in the voids of which crosses are created. With its vocabulary of prancing and heraldic attitudes, opposed and twisting bodies dissolving into interlace, pointed wings, and animal and human features, the animal life on the casket is very close to larger-scale carved animal and interlace ornament at a number of major Mercian sites. These include the sculptured animal friezes at Breedon and especially the gables of the shrine-like Hedda stone in Peterborough Cathedral (see figs 75 and 88). One of its

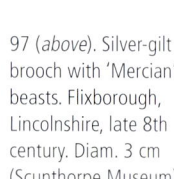

97 (*above*). Silver-gilt brooch with 'Mercian' beasts. Flixborough, Lincolnshire, late 8th century. Diam. 3 cm (Scunthorpe Museum)

98 (*below*). Cross shaft with confronted winged creatures. Elstow, Bedfordshire, late 8th or early 9th century. H. 56 cm (Elstow Abbey)

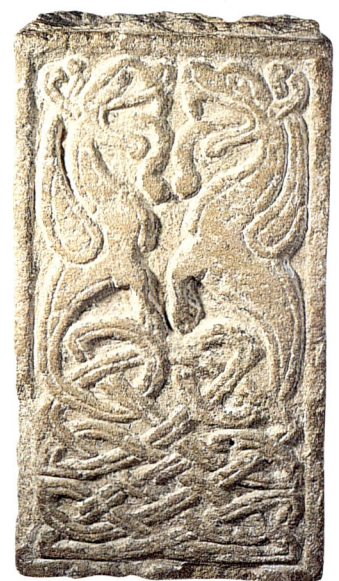

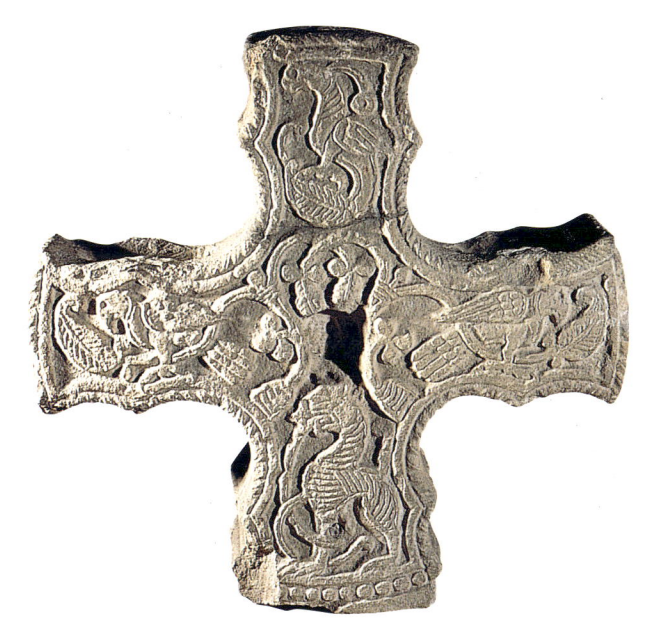

99 (*right*). Cross head with animals feeding on a vine. Late 8th or early 9th century. H. 84 cm (St Michael's church, Cropthorne, Worcestershire)

100 (*below*). The Gandersheim Casket: whale-bone chrismatory. Late 8th century. H. 12.6 cm (Herzog Anton Ulrich-Museum, Braunschweig)

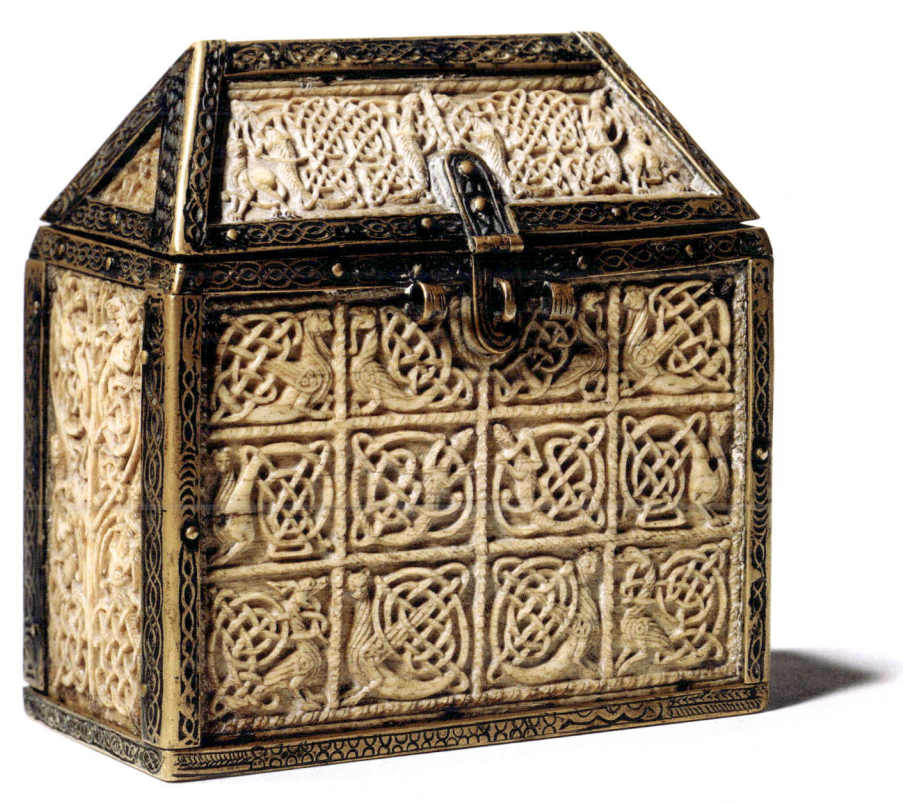

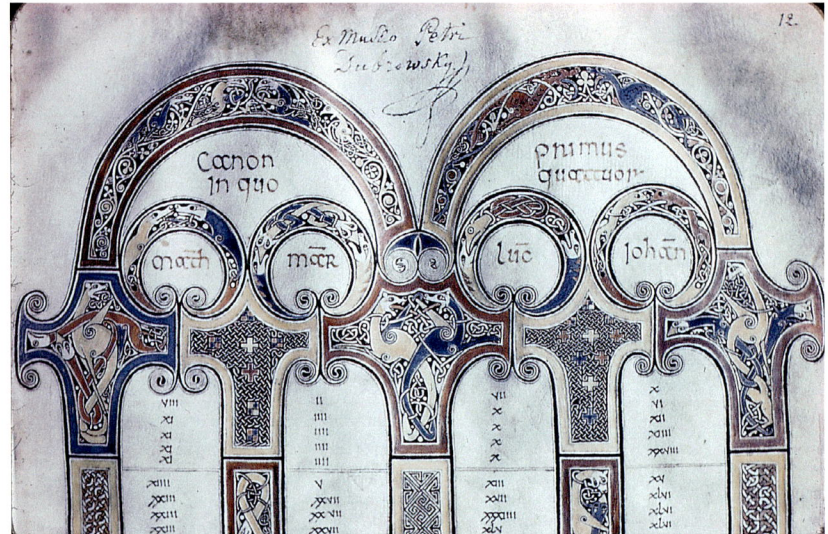

101. The St Petersburg Gospels: canon tables (detail). Late 8th century. Whole page 34.9 x 24.2 cm (National Library of Russia, St Petersburg, MS Cod. F.v.1.8, fol. 12r)

creatures, with a prancing posture and pointed wing, appears in identical form on a sculptured stone fragment at Castor, near Peterborough, suggesting that the same model was used for both.[20] It therefore seems plausible that the casket, like the closely related Barberini Gospels, was made at the great monastery of Medeshamstede.

More northerly versions of these classic creatures can be seen in the splendid prancing animals of the mid-eighth-century St Petersburg Gospels, a manuscript which, despite the Northumbrian exemplar used for its text, may have been written in Mercia (fig. 101). Very similar entwined beasts appear on the nasal of the contemporary helmet from Coppergate, York (fig. 13). The helmet also has distinctive snarling animal heads at the eyebrow ends and at the ends of its crest, which have many parallels in Southumbrian metalwork and sculpture where they are a recurring motif. Recent finds from across Mercian territory include a number of silver-gilt fittings of eighth-century date that have similar three-dimensional heads, with ribbed muzzles and gaping, sometimes fanged, jaws (fig. 102). Sculptured versions of this motif also occur, for instance in the powerful carved animal heads – their snouts and eyes originally picked out with red and white paint – that decorate the arches in the west porch and chancel of the early ninth-century church at Deerhurst, Gloucestershire (fig. 103). Intricate miniature versions of these appear in the four beast heads with inlaid eyes of blue and amber glass which decorate an imposing gold ring in the collections at nearby Berkeley Castle, which lies by the site of an Anglo-Saxon monastery (fig. 104). The muzzles and eyes of the creatures on the ring are delicately defined with niello markings very similar to the painted details of the stone heads at Deerhurst, suggesting local tradition linked by aristocratic or high ecclesiastical patronage.

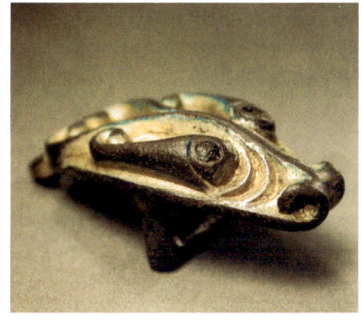

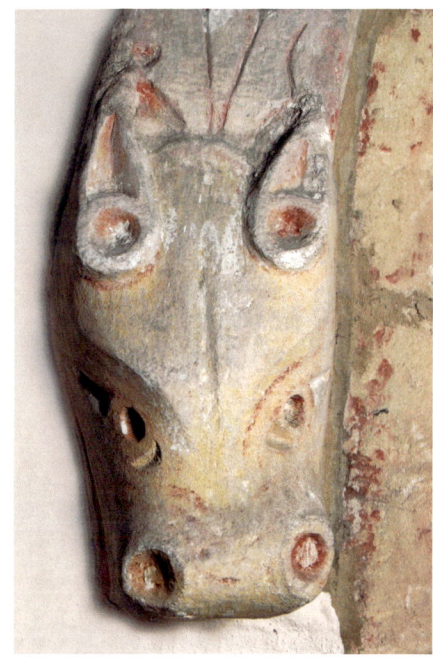

102 (*far left*). Silver-gilt strap-slide with animal-head. Early 9th century. L. approx. 2 cm (Private owner)

103 (*left*). Painted animal head on a chancel arch. Early 9th century. H. 43 cm (St Mary's church, Deerhurst, Gloucestershire)

These examples from across greater Mercia show how this particular style came to dominate the whole of the Mercian area of control, almost as if it signified some kind of regional identity. It is noticeably less common in Wessex, or Northumbria, beyond the limits of that supremacy. Even the distribution of highly portable personal items decorated in this style, such as weapon fittings, brooches, finger-rings and dress-pins, which could easily travel far from their point of manufacture, is largely confined to the area of Mercian influence, a trend that is confirmed by recent metal detector finds.[21]

The Pictish connection

One important exception to this style's general reluctance to travel beyond the borders of greater Mercia is its influence on high-status Pictish metalwork and sculpture. Some of the finest and most remarkable Pictish stone sculpture has features shared with Mercian sculptural and manuscript tradition, brilliantly integrated into their own native tradition of stone carving, as recent studies have shown.[22] The artist who carved the magnificent shrine at St Andrew's was certainly open to influences from beyond the Humber. This virtuoso piece, with its elaborate foliage, gallery of snakes and exotic creatures, and fluent, naturalistically modelled figures, is dominated by the powerful figure of David. He is portrayed as the hunter king, clothed in fluttering classical robes like an evangelist from the Barberini

104. Gold ring with four animal heads with niello decoration and coloured glass eyes. Early 9th century. W. (bezel) 4 cm (Berkeley Castle, Gloucestershire)

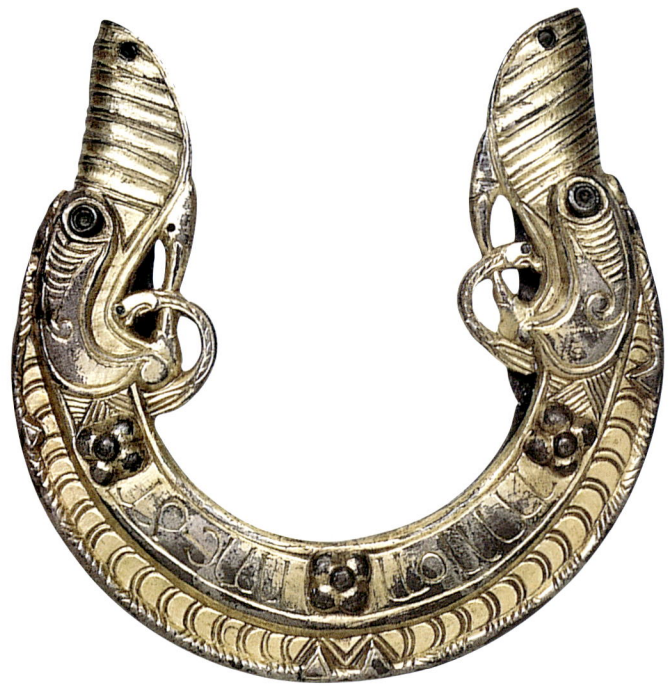

105 (*left*). Silver-gilt sword chape with animal heads biting fish, and an inscribed Christian prayer. From a hoard buried at a chapel on St Ninian's Isle, Shetland. Late 8th century. W. 8.2 cm (National Museum of Scotland, Edinburgh)

106. St Andrew's Sarcophagus: detail of David rending the lion's jaws. Late 8th century. L. (whole sarcophagus) 177 cm (St Andrew's Cathedral/Historic Scotland)

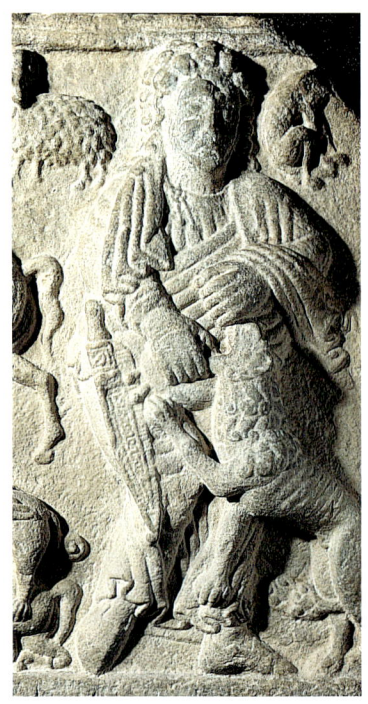

Gospels, but sporting a distinctive Anglo-Saxon seax at his waist (fig. 106). The influence of eastern Mediterranean art on Mercian taste is clearly reflected in the exotic animals and in the dynamic figure style of this imposing shrine, made for a royal centre, perhaps even for a Pictish king. The very idea of the stone shrine itself may have been adopted from Mercian examples, such as that at Lichfield. This Southumbrian influence is visible elsewhere in Pictish sculpture – most elegantly in the delicate scrolls of the vine tree framing a magnificent cross slab at Hilton of Cadboll (Easter Ross).[23] These are inhabited by sprightly birds and animals with pointed wings that could have sprung directly off the lower edge of the Woodeaton pommel, the Breedon friezes or the Ormside bowl (see figs 17, 75 and 93).

Whether these influences arrived in the north through the movement of sculptors themselves, or via gifts of manuscripts, bone and ivory carvings, and metalwork – or probably all of these – remains a matter for discussion. However, it is certain that fine metalwork in Mercian style was available in Pictland in the later eighth century, perhaps through the exchange of prestigious gifts between Mercian and Pictish kings – Æthelbald of Mercia was in the 740s and 750 in alliance with the Pictish king Oengus mac Fergus (r. 732–61). As the earlier Staffordshire Hoard implies, weapons are among the objects which travelled most widely in the early medieval period, as their owners undertook long journeys to join forces in attacking rival kingdoms.

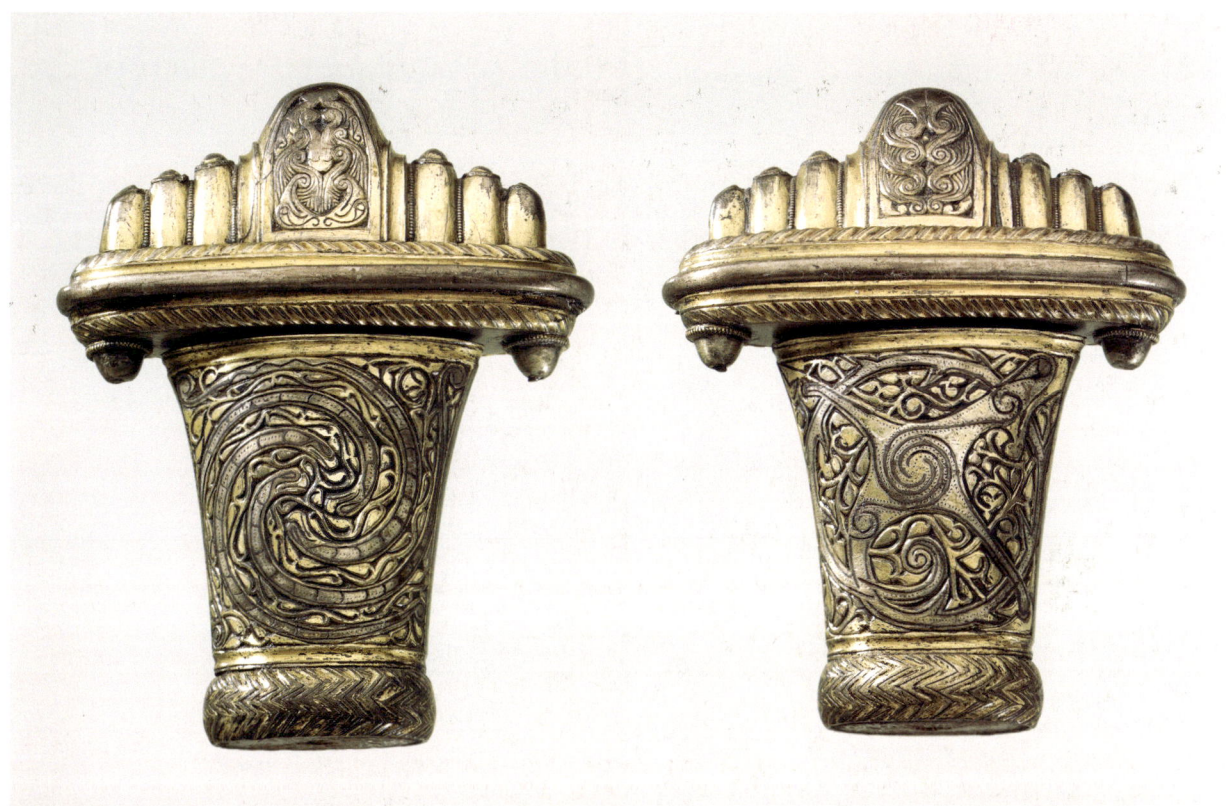

107. Silver-gilt sword-hilt (both sides) with whirling snake and spread-eagled beast. Fetter Lane, City of London, late 8th century. L. 8.7 cm (British Museum)

This mobility may, for instance, explain the presence of weapon fittings of Mercian type – two scabbard chapes and a sword pommel – in a large hoard of silver objects from St Ninian's Isle in Shetland. The distinctive speckled interlacing animals on the pommel, with their shovel-shaped muzzles and extremely extended bodies, have close parallels in Mercian metalwork.[24] More beasts with these distinctive muzzles appear on the two chapes, where the most prominent ones entrap their own tongues or a small fish in their fiercely fanged jaws (fig. 105). Shovel snouts and gaping heads very similar to these appear on silver-gilt sword-hilts and other weapon fittings from London (Fetter Lane and the Thames at Battersea; figs 107 and 108) and from near Newbury in Berkshire.[25] They can also be seen in the surreal decoration of the silver-gilt sword pommel from near Woodeaton, Oxfordshire, where other animal ornament, including beasts with dramatically extended bodies, and a schematic inhabited vine scroll, exhibits motifs echoed in Pictish sculpture as well as metalwork (fig. 17). One of the St Ninian's chapes also bears a protective prayer, a feature seen elsewhere on weapon fittings and armour from the Mercian sphere of influence (fig. 105). Whether the St Ninian's Isle weapon fittings – like other metal objects in that hoard – were made in Pictland, copying Anglo-Saxon originals, or perhaps more plausibly, came from an

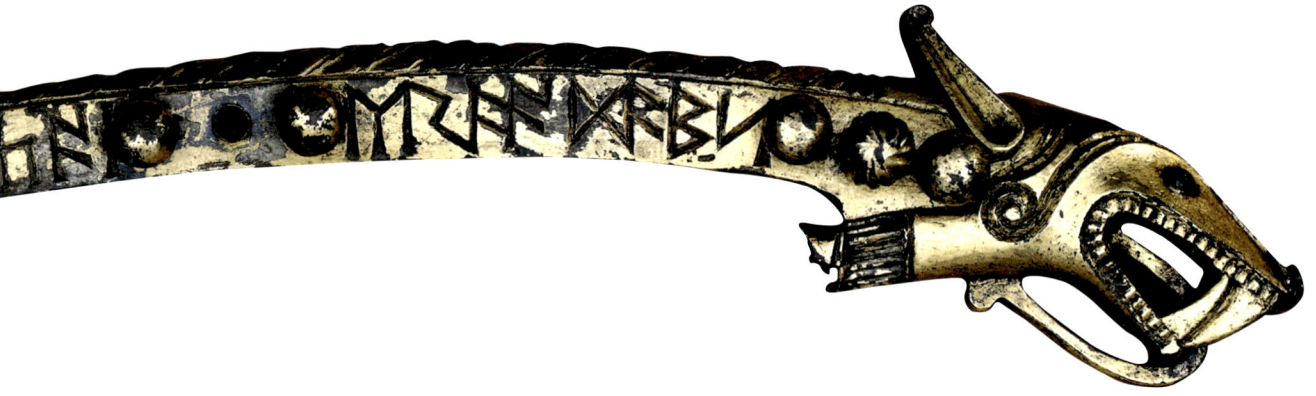

Anglo-Saxon weapon suite which made its way to the extreme north, they undeniably reflect productive contacts between Pictland and Mercia in the eighth century.

The troubled ninth century and the rise of the Trewhiddle style

The later eighth and early ninth centuries saw the heyday of Mercian art; but after Coenwulf's death in 821, the Mercian supremacy began to disintegrate, and throughout England stability was increasingly threatened by Viking attacks. These had begun towards the end of the eighth century, initially picking on easy coastal targets, but gradually moving inland with greater forces. The looting and burning of the monastery of Lindisfarne on 8 June 793 had come out of the blue, generating ripples of shock across the wealthy courts and ecclesiastical institutions of western Europe; this new external threat heralded an age of turmoil and disruption. Shortly after the raid, the Anglo-Saxon scholar Alcuin summed up the fears in a letter written from Charlemagne's court to Æthelred of Northumbria: 'never before has such terror appeared in Britain as we have suffered from a pagan race, nor was it thought such an inroad from the sea could be made.'

The attacks increased steadily, with Kent and southern England targeted in the 840s and large Viking war-bands regularly over-wintering in England from the 850s. From these bases, such as Sheppey and the Mercian royal centre at Repton, they could extend their attention to prosperous inland towns and monasteries. It is largely due to these repeated attacks that so little in the way of decorated manuscripts, ecclesiastical metalwork and fine sculpture survives from the ninth century; as Alfred wrote, 'before it was all ravaged and burnt, I had seen how the churches throughout England stood filled with treasures and books'.[26] The *Codex Aureus* is an exceptional example of an ecclesiastical treasure to have been purchased back from the Vikings and returned to its monastic home. But the attacks not only robbed monasteries of their

108 (*above*). Silver-gilt mount (detail) from a seax scabbard, with fierce animal head and inscribed runic charm. River Thames at Battersea, London, late 8th century. L. 18.8 cm (British Museum)

109 (*opposite*). The Royal (or Canterbury) Bible: purple-stained page with the symbol and portrait of St Luke. Second quarter of the 9th century. 46.7 x 34.5 cm (British Library, Royal MS 1.E.vi, fol. 43r)

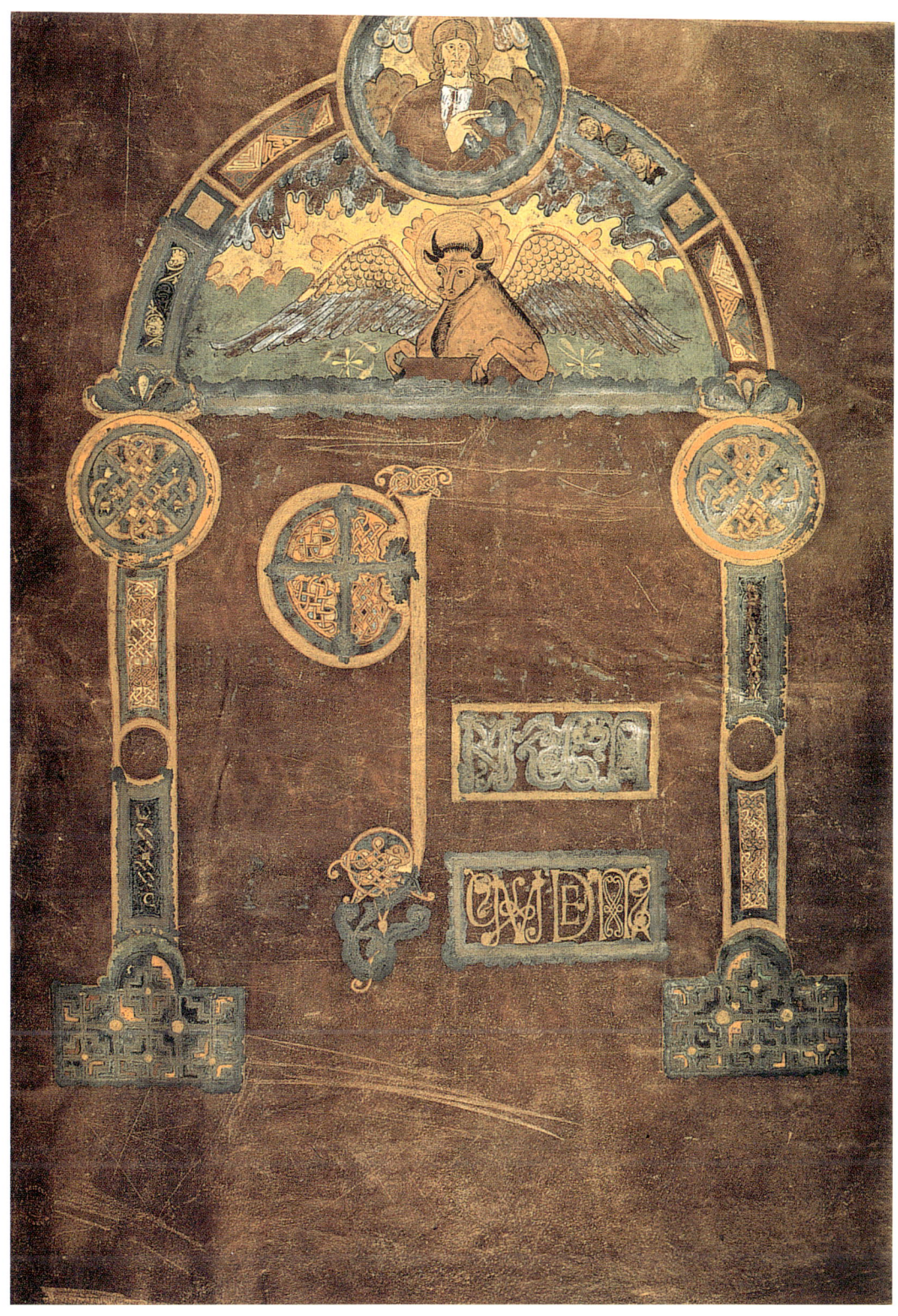

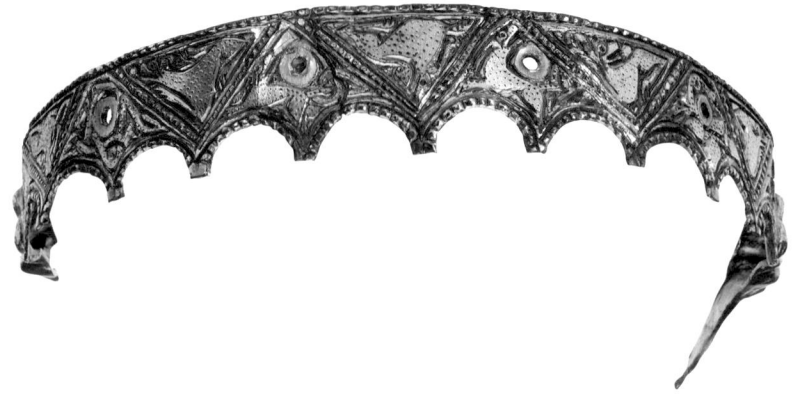

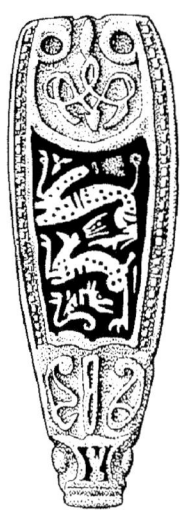

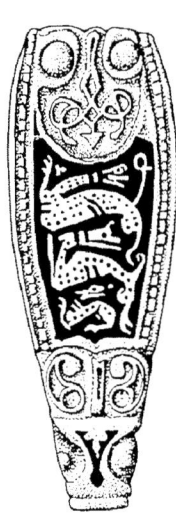

treasures; the widespread destruction and disruption that they caused were inimical to the production of artworks of all kinds, and indeed to religious life and learning itself.

Nevertheless, it was during this period that the fortunes of the Wessex dynasty began to rise, filling the power vacuum left by the collapse of Mercia. Æthelwulf (r. 839–58), father of Alfred the Great, seems to have had control of Essex and with it London, Kent and much of the south-west. Like the powerful Mercian kings before him, he had a close relationship with Carolingian contemporaries – something which is reflected, as we shall see, in artefacts associated with Wessex's rise to power. The cult of kingship promoted by the Carolingian emperors – still grandly visible today in Charlemagne's imperial chapel at Aachen, Germany – deliberately revived a new version of imperial Rome, in architecture, manuscripts, ivory carving and metalwork.

The manuscripts made for the emperors and the great monasteries of the realm abound in exalted visual tributes to their Carolingian patrons. Their pages are stained with an imperial purple and encrusted with gold, while classical motifs, such as acanthus ornament, and new iconographies inspired by late Antique and Byzantine sources are prominent. A few glimpses of Anglo-Saxon emulation of the court art of their wealthy Carolingian neighbours can be seen in some manuscripts of the Tiberius group. The Barberini Gospels (*c.* 800) already demonstrates an acquaintance with early Carolingian figure style (see fig. 74). The fragmentary Royal Bible, made at Canterbury in the second quarter of the ninth century, hints at access to even grander Carolingian models (fig. 109). The purple-stained opening to the Gospel of Luke, with its gold and silver script, and illusionistic representations of Christ and the clouds of revelation surrounding the ox (the symbol of St Luke), represents an ambitious new dimension in the decoration of the book in Anglo-Saxon England. Its grandiose decoration is far removed from the much simpler late sixth-century St Augustine Gospels (fig. 47), which was at Canterbury and may have provided the model for the evangelist symbol. The only surviving

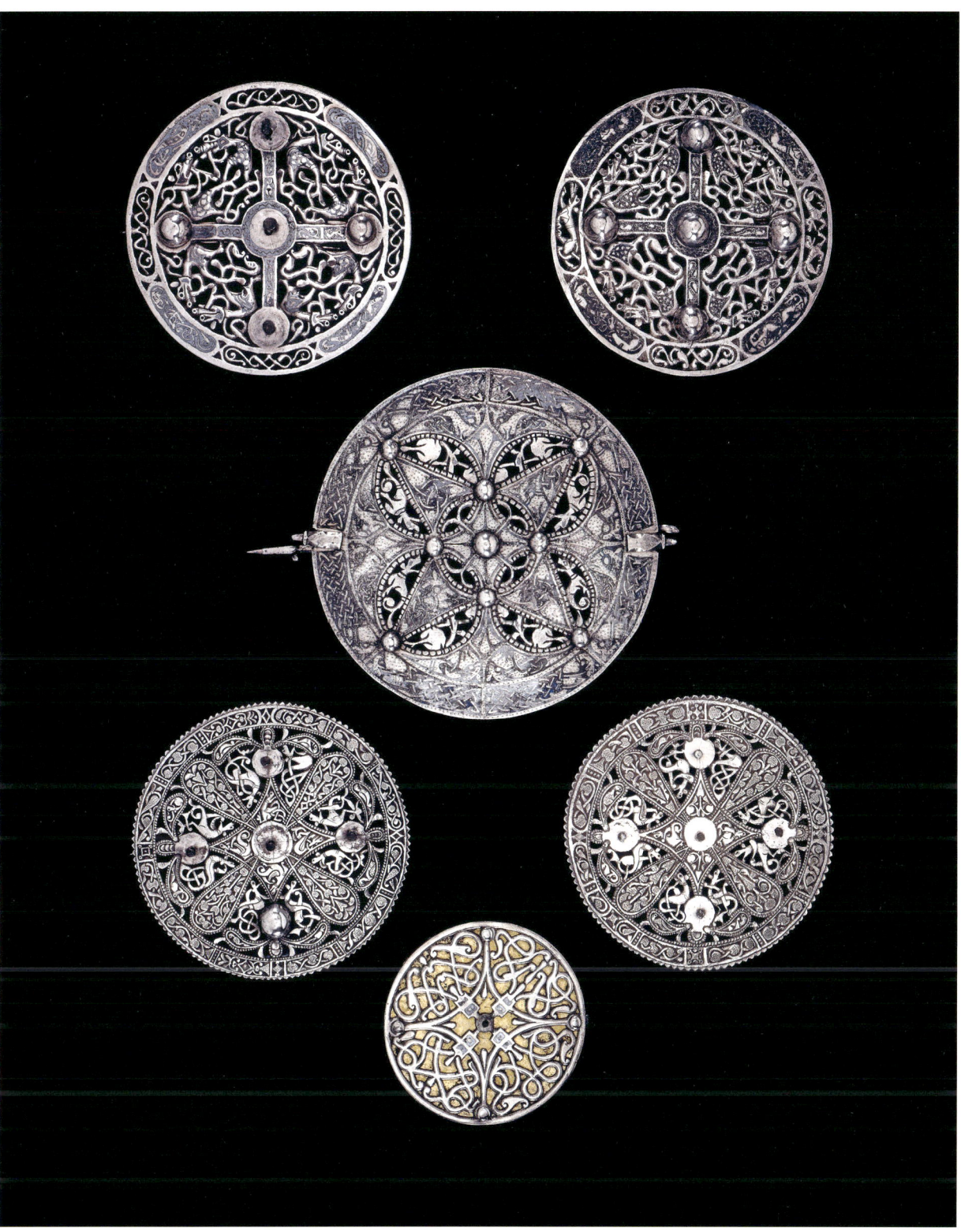

example of the increasing influence of Carolingian manuscript art in the first half of the ninth century, this late representative of the Tiberius group has nevertheless kept a strong connection with the vigorous animal art of the past. Unlike their ninth-century Continental counterparts, the tall arcades of its surviving canon tables teem with creatures drawn from the Insular tradition, evident descendants of Mercian creatures in their questing heads and sprightly poses.[27] In the Royal Bible many of them appear in white, starkly set against a black background. This is a direct reference to a new metalwork version of animal ornament, and as clear an indication of the interaction between manuscript artists and goldsmiths as the similarities between the symbols of St Matthew in the Book of Cerne and St John on the Brandon gold plaque.

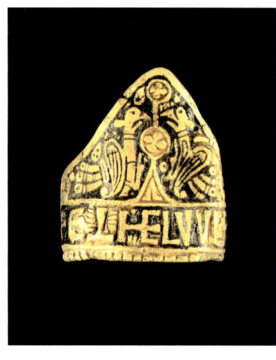

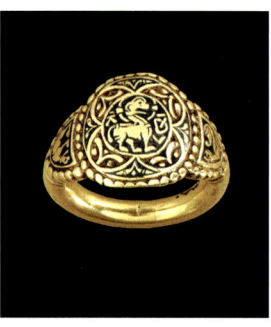

113. Gold and niello rings: (*above*) Ring of King Æthelwulf of Wessex. Laverstock, Wiltshire, mid-9th century. Diam. (hoop) 2.8 cm; (*below*) Ring of Æthelwulf's daughter, Queen Æthelswith of Mercia. Sherburn in Elmet, Yorkshire, mid-9th century. Diam. (hoop) 2.6 cm (both British Museum)

The new style has acquired the suitably quirky name of the 'Trewhiddle style', after a hoard of silver and copper alloy artefacts found at Trewhiddle, near St Austell, Cornwall, together with coins dating the hoard to about 868. Along with a chalice and an ecclesiastical scourge, the hoard contains a number of secular prestige objects including fittings from a seax and perhaps from riding-gear, decorated with typical elements of the style (fig. 110). This is characterized by small fields or cartouches, usually with beaded frames, containing lively, often speckled, animals, foliage and geometric motifs, the background often inlaid with niello. At this time the use of gold in metalwork, whether secular or ecclesiastical, was rare, except for small prestige objects such as finger-rings. Trewhiddle-style decoration occurs mainly on silver items, where the bright metal motifs stand out in sharp contrast against the smooth black niello inlay (fig. 111). It is this contrast that we see echoed in the black and white motifs of the canon tables in the Royal Bible.

This exuberant style was tremendously popular, spreading throughout Anglo-Saxon England from Cornwall to Northumbria, and beyond; from its earliest appearances, around the 820s, its advance was irresistible. The Pentney (Norfolk) hoard of Anglo-Saxon disc brooches, buried around this time, gives a snapshot of the style as it began to take off. Probably a jeweller's hoard, it contains five splendid disc brooches in the latest fashion (fig. 112). The smallest brooch has plant ornament, with no zoomorphic decoration; it is the earliest of the five, and the only one to show any sign of wear. One pair of brooches displays classic examples of heraldic Mercian beasts, with restrained niello detailing, while another pair has lively openwork creatures in an early version of the Trewhiddle style. The fifth brooch is the largest and most accomplished, with fully developed Trewhiddle-style creatures, characteristically frisking in small fields bordered by beaded frames, and accompanied by small foliate and geometric motifs, all with extensive use of niello inlay. All but the smallest brooch are crisp and unworn, suggesting that they were made at much the same time, and in a workshop where craftsmen were beginning to move from one decorative tradition to another – to the new fad for large silver disc brooches, and the Trewhiddle style that embellished them, and other fine secular metalwork of the ninth century.

This new style grew out of the earlier Mercian animal style, but it was soon favoured by Wessex royalty. Two fine gold rings inlaid with niello are directly associated by their inscriptions with Æthelwulf and his daughter Æthelswith (r. 853/4–88), sister of Alfred the Great; she was married to the Mercian king Burgred, who was deposed by the Vikings in 874 (fig. 113). Because they can be closely dated, they are key pieces for the dating and localization of this influential style. The rings are not the personal rings of the two royal figures, but would probably have been given to loyal supporters, as a reward or a badge of rank, or to diplomatic messengers as a means of authentication. Both also exhibit – on a very small scale – something of the new artistic ideas absorbed from Carolingian sources. Above its prominent inscription, ÆTHELWULF REX, the ring of Æthelwulf has a design of peacocks drinking from the Fountain of Life, a shorthand image drawn from more elaborate versions, examples of which can be seen in two surviving Carolingian manuscripts from the time of Charlemagne. In early Christian and Carolingian art, the image of peacocks, deer and other creatures drinking at the fountain is associated with ideas of baptism and spiritual rebirth. The ring of Queen Æthelswith carries an image of the Agnus Dei – in Christian thought, both the Lamb of God that brings Judgement in the Book of Revelation, and the sacrificial Paschal Lamb that takes away the sins of the world, a symbol of the risen Christ. The image was, at that period, rare in Anglo-Saxon England, but again appears in Carolingian manuscripts; a Continental source may have inspired it. The appearance of such succinct iconographies, even in the restricted scope of a finger-ring, harks back to the use of equally resonant motifs in earlier Anglo-Saxon metalwork. This reminds us once again of the importance of the image to everyday life and thought, in a society in which literacy was confined to the privileged few, and oral and visual traditions retained their power.

The two royal associations date the decoration of both rings to the middle years of the ninth century. Their perky animals – peacocks, the lamb and its attendant creatures – and foliage are classic examples of the Trewhiddle style. The style is Anglo-Saxon but, as we have seen, the influences are Frankish. Æthelwulf cultivated a close connection with the Frankish king, later emperor, Charles the Bald, making an extended visit to him on his way to Rome in 855, and marrying his daughter Judith (his second wife) on the way back in 856. The Anglo-Saxon king made generous gifts to the king's favoured shrine at St Denis, near Paris, and no doubt also to Charles the Bald himself, though those are not described. Reciprocal Carolingian gifts of metalwork, ivories and manuscripts would certainly have made their way back to England with the royal party. Some hint of this gift exchange between rulers and their entourages may perhaps be visible in a ninth-century Carolingian-style purse reliquary with acanthus ornament, which was excavated in the royal centre of Winchester.[28] As a young boy, Æthelwulf's son and eventual successor, Alfred, had already been sent on his own to Rome, in 853, and accompanied his father on Æthelwulf's journey to Francia and Rome in 855/6. On the latter occasion, the king presented important gifts of Anglo-Saxon metalwork to the Pope – a golden crown weighing four pounds, two gold beakers, a sword bound with gold, four silver-gilt bowls of Saxon workmanship, and various decorated garments. Such travels were certainly not unique; documentary sources tell of increasing numbers of Anglo-Saxon lay travellers, as well as ecclesiastics, who – like Æthelric from Deerhurst – made the pilgrimage to Rome. Indeed, when expelled from his kingdom, Burgred of Mercia retired to Rome and his queen, Æthelswith, who died at Pavia in 888, may have gone with him at that time. Another Anglo-Saxon traveller somehow parted with an imposing Trewhiddle-style gold ring in Bologna.[29] Despite (or perhaps also because of) the disruptions caused by the raids at home, the travels of church-men and wealthy laity from England to the Continent had never been greater, reinforcing and expanding artistic influences and contacts with the cultural inheritance of the post-classical world. Certainly, the impact on the young Alfred of his extended visits to Francia and Italy was profound, as was to become clear when he eventually succeeded to the kingdom of Wessex in 871.

Change and innovation: art in the reign of Alfred

Alfred (r. 871–99), raised to the status of national hero in Victorian times, remains today the best known of all Anglo-Saxon kings, famous in popular memory for candle-clocks, cake-burning, defeating the Danes and founding the royal navy. But as well as a creative thinker, military leader and powerful ruler, he was also a learned reformer of the English Church, who drove forward an ambitious and successful programme of spiritual regeneration and education, hand in hand with his radical governmental reforms. In both these capacities, a new

114. The Alfred Jewel: gold handle for a manuscript pointer, with enamel and rock-crystal setting. Athelney, Somerset, late 9th century. L. 6.2 cm (Ashmolean Museum, University of Oxford)

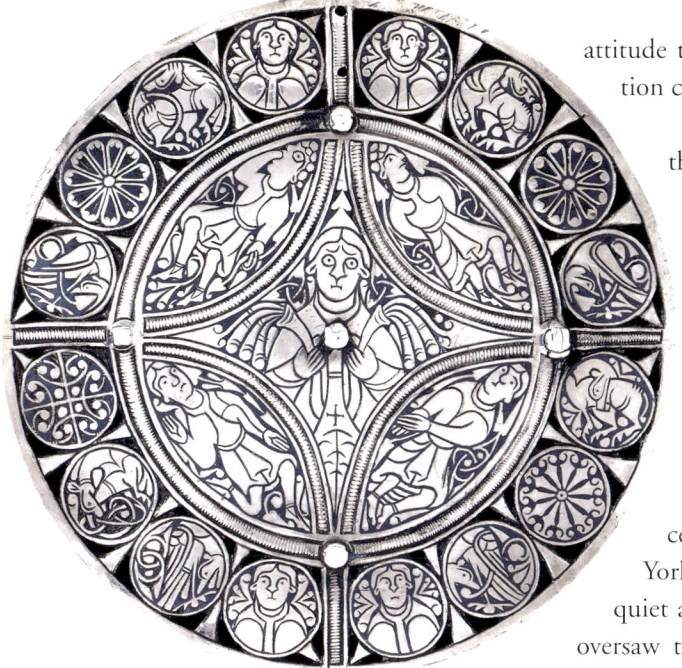

attitude to both secular and ecclesiastical artistic production can be traced.

Alfred came to the throne after the death of the last of his three brothers, Æthelred (r. 865–71), at a time when England was under continuous fierce attack from Danish Vikings in the east and south. His successful campaigns recaptured London in 886, and established Wessex as the dominant power south of what, by stages, became the Danelaw. This was an area under Scandinavian control extending north of the Thames through East Anglia and the eastern midlands up into Northumbria, with its northern centre at the former Anglo-Saxon trading centre of York. The decade that followed was comparatively quiet and it seems to have been in this lull that Alfred oversaw the translation of texts that were central to his thought and his programme of education and renewal.

Alfred's biographer, the Welsh churchman Asser (quoted at the beginning of this chapter), writes in glowing detail of his achievements. Even allowing for an understandable degree of hyperbole, it is evident that Alfred had a radical impact on the religious, intellectual and artistic life of England, as much as on its military and urban structures. The translation of a number of exemplary texts into Old English from Latin originals is ascribed to him. Although most of these were probably commissioned, or works of collaboration rather than undertaken personally, there can be no doubt that these texts, chosen by him, were central to his concerns about the attainment of spiritual wisdom through learning and reading. He saw this as an essential occupation for a Christian ruler, for his bishops and priests, his officials such as ealdormen and reeves, and for 'all the free-born young men now in England who have the means to apply themselves'.[30] Successful secular authority had to be grounded in religious understanding, and the church could not perform its task of education without itself being re-educated. One of the key texts in Alfred's revival of learning was an English translation of Gregory the Great's *Regula Pastoralis*, the *Pastoral Care*, a manual for bishops and clergy on how to do their job (see fig. 121). In his preface to the text, Alfred declared his intention to revive learning among the clergy, since standards:

had declined so thoroughly in England that there were very few men on this side of the Humber who could understand their divine services in English, or even translate a single letter from

115 (*above*). The Fuller Brooch: silver disc brooch with niello-inlaid design centred on the Five Senses. Late 9th century. Diam. 11.4 cm (British Museum)

116 (*below*). Gold handle for a manuscript pointer, with a central blue glass setting. Bowleaze Cove, Dorset, late 9th century. L. 2.8 cm (British Museum)

Latin into English: and I suppose that there were not many beyond the Humber either.

The manifesto was sent out to all the bishops of his kingdom and with each copy, as Alfred's preface also states, went an *æstel* worth fifty *mancuses*. Much ink has been expended in debating the exact meaning of the Old English word *æstel*, but it is generally agreed that it was a pointer used to follow the text along the page in a way that would be helpful in a context of teaching and learning. Astonishingly, it seems that a number of handles from such manuscript pointers still survive, some of them very splendid indeed. The most famous is the Alfred Jewel, found near a monastery founded by Alfred at Athelney, Somerset, and so named because an inscription around its edges reads ÆLFRED MEC HEHT GEWYRCAN, 'Alfred commanded me to be made' (fig. 114).[31] This is a remarkable piece of goldsmith's work. It consists of a large polished tear-shaped rock crystal set over an enamelled image and held by an elaborate gold frame with the openwork inscription. At the pointed end of the setting, an animal's head, encrusted with fine filigree decoration, holds a short tube in its mouth, designed to hold the bone or ivory rod which was the pointer. The back is flat and engraved with a Tree of Life motif. The enamelled figure is half-length and appears to hold foliate stems in its hands; its eyes are very prominent. Its identity has been much debated, but it is best understood as an image intimately connected with Alfred's concerns about the attainment of wisdom, notably, the way in which it is acquired by both the physical and the mind's eye.[32] This would explain the prominent eyes, suggesting that it may be a personification of Sight or of Wisdom itself. This may seem an elaborate argument, but another spectacular piece of metalwork dated to Alfred's time has a similar theme. The Fuller Brooch (named for a former owner) is a great silver disc brooch inlaid with niello in a very late version of the Trewhiddle style, and dates to the end of the ninth century (fig. 115). It is decorated with skilfully executed personifications of the Five Senses, with Sight, the largest image, at the centre holding leafy stems, surrounded by Touch, Taste, Hearing and Smell, all in lively attitudes suggesting their nature. These in turn are surrounded by roundels containing human, plant geometric and animal images, perhaps representing the diversity of Creation. The brooch is a superb piece of craftsmanship, so fine, indeed, that it was for many years thought to be a forgery. We can now see more clearly that, through its subtle iconography, it too proclaims a very Alfredian emphasis on the primacy of Sight as a pathway to the gaining of spiritual wisdom. Perhaps this magnificently didactic brooch was designed to be worn prominently by a nobleman or official at Alfred's court, or even a high-ranking churchman.

The other surviving *æstels* are less sumptuous than the Alfred Jewel, though all have similar sockets and a flat base, suitable for sliding smoothly

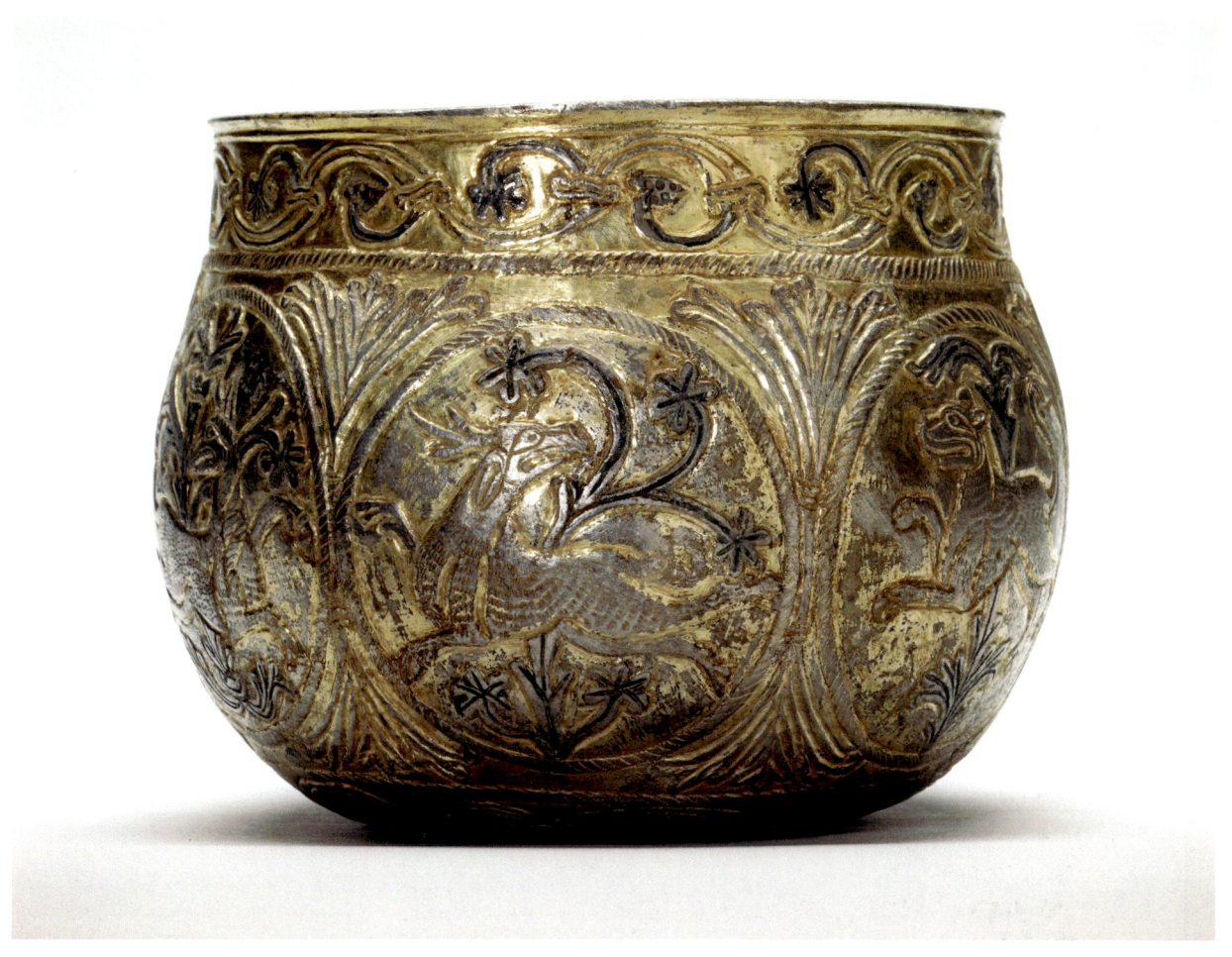

117. Silver-gilt Carolingian bowl, possibly from a set of altar vessels. From the Vale of York Hoard, buried *c.* 927 near Harrogate, North Yorkshire. Mid-9th century. H. 9.2 cm (British Museum/Yorkshire Museum)

across the surface of a page (fig. 116). Stylistically they seem to be of the same date, and most share at least one other similarity with the Jewel – a rock crystal, blue enamel or glass inlays, or a filigree animal head. Yet none comes near it in complexity, or reflects a value of fifty *mancuses* mentioned in Alfred's preface to the *Pastoral Care*. Some may even have been made for other contexts. One comes from a lord's hall at Borg in northern Norway – perhaps Viking loot, or the lost property of a wandering missionary. And although they were circulated for use in an ecclesiastical context, they also delivered another message, about the king's authority. As a manuscript pointer, the Alfred Jewel honours and emphasizes the power of the Word of God, and the wisdom to be gained from it; but through its explicit inscription – 'Alfred commanded me to be made' – its craftsmanship and its opulence, it would have also acted as a vivid and daily reminder of the king's command to his clergy to put their house in order. Secular and religious power once again combine in an object of supreme artistry.

As well as the scholars and churchmen from France and Germany whom Alfred attracted to work in his programme of religious renewal, Asser refers to the 'foreign craftsman from many races' that he imported to make the many treasures that furnished his churches and palaces. Alfred's earlier experiences at the Frankish court and in Rome must have supplied him with many new ideas about how these precious objects should look. The Alfred Jewel, for instance, uses rock crystal and enamel in ways not seen before in Anglo-Saxon England. Perhaps Alfred drew inspiration for this from seeing rock crystals and other precious stones deployed on some of the magnificent objects at the shrine of St Denis, which he might have visited with his father. A few of these treasures survive to this day, and drawings of others were made before their destruction during the French Revolution – enough to hint at possible sources of inspiration, or the involvement of Continental craftsmen. One or two other traces of the influence of Carolingian art survive in Alfred's circle. These include a fine silver sword belt fitting with Carolingian acanthus ornament from Wareham, one of Alfred's new fortified towns or *burhs*; and a fragment of a wall-painting from Winchester, with rows of serious saintly faces, in style very similar to surviving Carolingian wall-painting (fig. 10). It is even possible that the two fine matching silver-gilt Carolingian bowls which were found in two separate Viking hoards, one in the Vale of York, the other at Halton Moor, Lancashire, may have come to England not as Viking loot from raids in northern France, but as part of a set of grand altar vessels brought here in the reign of Alfred or his father (fig. 117).

But perhaps the most distinctive hallmark of the surviving art of Alfred's reign is a new emphasis on Christian iconography. It was already present in the Carolingian-inspired motifs on the royal rings of his father and sister, but in Alfred's reign it becomes much more marked. It is there in the Alfred Jewel and the Fuller Brooch, and we see it again in the ingeniously worked evangelist symbols on a sword-hilt from Abingdon, Berkshire, a suitable set of images for a Christian warrior in Alfred's mode (fig. 119). It also appears on a strap-end from Cranbourne, Dorset, which is linked both in style and theme to the Fuller Brooch, through its image of a figure cutting a bunch of grapes from a fruiting vine, perhaps representing the sense of Taste (fig. 118). Could this have been part of a belt-set comprising a buckle with the image of Sight, and four other strap-ends with images of the subsidiary senses?

There is little sculpture that can be confidently ascribed to Alfred's reign, but one piece that might date to the later ninth century is an unusual stone cross shaft from Codford St Peter, Wiltshire, with a dancing male figure. With one hand he grasps a fruiting vine branch, and in the other he holds a flask, presumably of wine (fig. 122). The dress and posture of the figure appear quite similar to the little silver strap-end described above. This suggests an alternative interpretation of the image, a eucharistic image of the faithful,

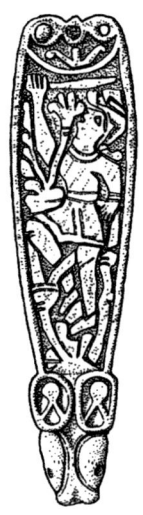

118. Silver strap-end with man cutting grapes. Cranborne, Wiltshire, late 9th century (Drawing, N. Griffiths)

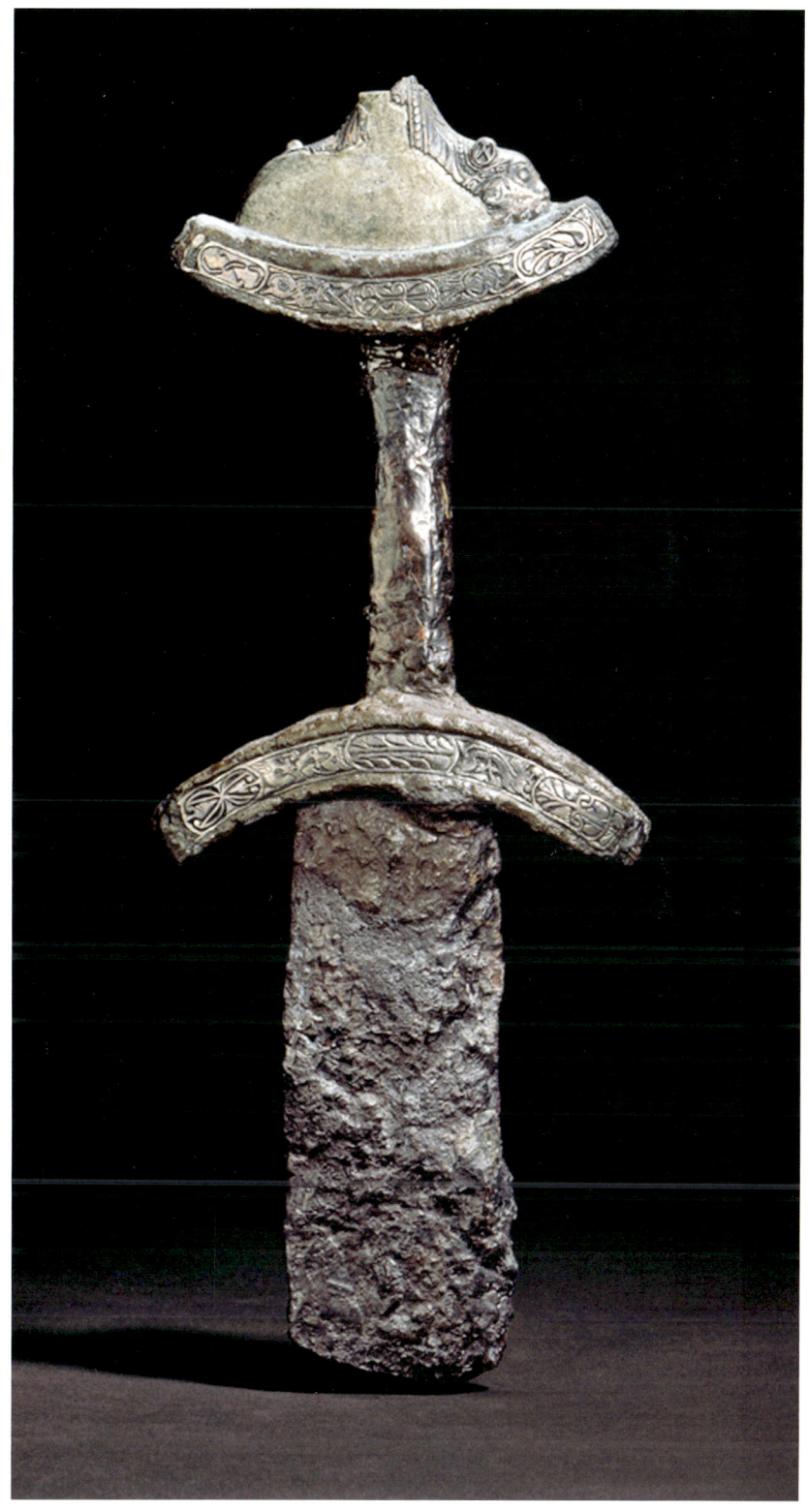

119. Sword-hilt with silver and niello-inlaid mounts, with evangelist symbols. Abingdon, Berkshire, late 9th century, L. (max) 31.5 cm (Ashmolean Museum, University of Oxford)

120. Antler fitting
with animal and
plant decoration.
c. 900. L. 12 cm
(British Museum)

feeding on the vine
that is Christ.

Although Viking attacks were
renewed towards the end of Alfred's reign, there
was one area in which Scandinavian contacts brought
about innovation, which was to have important artistic conse-
quences in the succeeding centuries. Among the texts which Alfred had
translated was Orosius's *Universal History against the Pagans*, to which he
made certain additions. One of these describes the arrival at his court of travellers from the north, including the Norse trader, Ohthere (Ottar), who gave
an account of his travels in the Arctic seas off Russia, and the walruses he
encountered there.[33] He presented the king with specimens of their tusks,
which were described as being very good for carving. This is the first account
of the appearance of walrus ivory in western Europe, which was quickly to
become the principal vehicle for ivory carving, since the traditional African
sources of elephant ivory had dried up. It is typical of Alfred's intellectual
curiosity that he gives prominence to this account of a new commodity, and
the strange world from which it came, but all the more frustrating that no
such carving survives from his reign. The only decorative carving to survive
from this period is a small antler fitting of about 900, carved with birds, beasts
and acanthus foliage in a style seen also in the surviving manuscripts of Alfred's
reign (fig. 120).

Visually, these are something of a disappointment; in fact, no manuscripts of much artistic consequence survive from this period. This may well
be an accident of survival; given the grand quality of the Alfred Jewel and
some of the secular metalwork that survives from his reign, it would be surprising if Alfred had not included illuminated Bibles, gospel-books and
psalters among his gifts to his own and other favoured foundations, though if
he did, they have not come down to us. But there may be another factor here:
Alfred's driving interest was in the intellectual and spiritual message of his
texts, to which perhaps other considerations, such as decoration and fine
bindings, came second. The copy of the *Pastoral Care* that was sent to Worcester, the only surviving example of Alfred's original texts (fig. 121), and a late
ninth-century manuscript of Aldhelm's *De virginitate*,[34] made for his old tutor,
Bishop Werferth of Worcester, give a flavour of the modest decoration of the

manuscripts associated with Alfred and his circle. They are sprinkled with small initials formed from creatures and plants which have clearly grown out of the Trewhiddle-style tradition, with here and there a human face, or a geometric motif; frilled foliage now and again sprouts into acanthus leaves of Carolingian ancestry. But in general, the seriousness of their purpose puts content above artistry.

Nevertheless, the few surviving products which can be associated with the time of Alfred – the *æstels* and other intellectually conceived metalwork, the wall-painting and sculpture – all indicate a desire to foster the making of ambitious and complex artefacts, some with visible Carolingian influence. They fully confirm the account of Alfred's great projects given by his biographer – the employment of foreign craftsmen and scholars, and the imaginative and innovative treasures in gold and silver with which he adorned his royal and ecclesiastical institutions. There clearly was an Alfredian court art, even if we can hardly glimpse it today. Through his programmes of renewal and reorganization, the king had put his own unique stamp upon Anglo-Saxon art and culture, in ways which were ultimately to feed into the remarkable artistic developments of the next century, and which culminated in the products associated with the great reform movement in Benedictine monasticism, discussed in the next chapter.

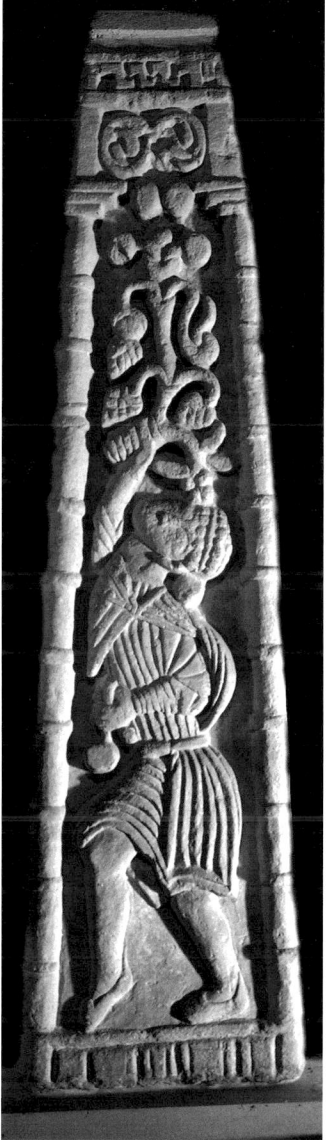

121 (*below*). Alfred's translation of Gregory the Great's *Pastoral Care*: detail of initial with animal decoration. Late 9th century. Whole page 27 x 22 cm (Bodleian Library, University of Oxford, MS Hatton 20, fol. 93v)

122 (*right*). Cross shaft with man harvesting grapes. Late 9th century. H. 125 cm (Codford St Peter parish church, Wiltshire)

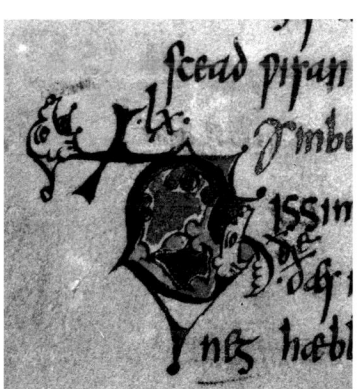

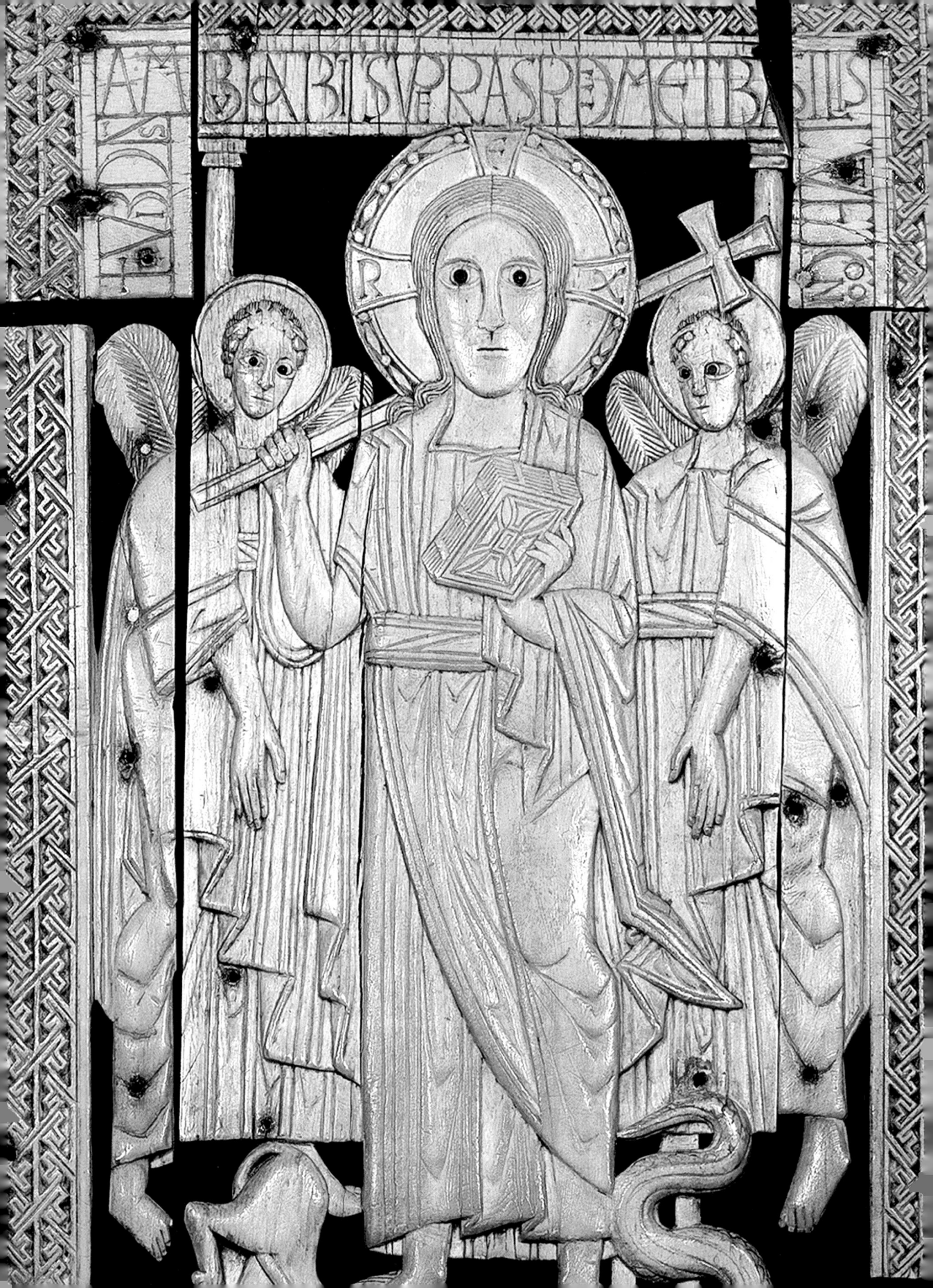

CHAPTER 6

In your goodness you have often comforted my sadness
both with the solace of books and assistance with clothing.
So now I pray you to add to what you have, namely to write
for me in gold the epistles of my lord, St Peter the Apostle,
to secure honour and reverence for the Holy Scriptures when
they are preached from before the eyes of the heathen;
and because I particularly wish to have always with me the
words of him who guided me to this course.

Letter from Boniface to Abbess Eadburg
of Minster in Thanet, 735/6[1]

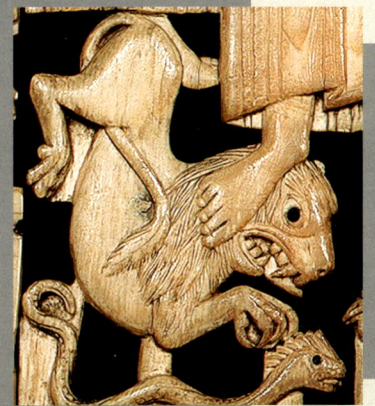

MISSION AND REFORM

EIGHTH TO ELEVENTH CENTURIES

Details from the Genoels-
Elderen ivory diptych
(see fig. 127).

The drive to conversion

In previous chapters we have seen how Anglo-Saxon art regularly and enthusiastically adapted to new influences from the Continent, introduced through both ecclesiastical and secular connections. This is a pattern that continues throughout the entire period. But in this chapter, we begin by considering the reverse process, reflected in the activities of seventh- and eighth-century Anglo-Saxon missionaries and scholars working abroad, and in the artistic influence that the books and other artefacts that accompanied them exerted on their new converts.

For Christians in the early medieval period, the conversion of unbelievers was a central concern. As Gregory the Great put it in a letter to King Æthelbert in 601, the conversion of the pagan Anglo-Saxons was a matter of urgency, because:

we would wish your majesty to know that the end of the world
is at hand, as we learn from the words of Almighty God in the

holy scriptures; and the kingdom of the saints which knows no end is near.

In Christian theology Doomsday (literally the Day of Judgement), which marked the end of the world and the fulfilment of mankind's personal and collective destiny, would occur only after the word of the gospel had been spread to all parts of the earth. It was this necessity to convert that had inspired the Roman and Celtic missions to the Anglo-Saxons, and it was not long before Anglo-Saxon Christian missionaries were in turn venturing to Frisia, and to Hesse, Franconia, Thuringia and Bavaria in Germany, even – fruitlessly at the time – to Denmark, to bring the new religion to those pagan peoples, and to consolidate the faith where standards of Christianity were not high. As Willibald, St Boniface's biographer, recorded:

> an exceedingly large number of holy men from Britain came to his aid, among them readers, writers, and learned men trained in the other arts.. . . By their help the heathen population . . . was recalled from the errors and profane rites of their heathen gods.[2]

Some of these missions ended in failure, most notably for St Boniface himself, who, after a lifetime dedicated to missionary work in Germany and Frisia, was eventually killed in 754 at Dokkum in Frisia, along with fifty-two of his monks. A book that he owned, which is still kept at the monastery of Fulda where he was buried, bears hefty cut marks said to have resulted from being used to protect the saint from the swords of his pagan attackers. But Boniface's earlier missions, and many others afterwards, were successful, and led to the foundation or revival of scores of monasteries and bishoprics, such as Echternach in modern Luxembourg, Fulda in Hesse, Eichstätt in Bavaria and Salzburg in what is now Austria. Alongside a number of earlier Irish foundations, centres such as these introduced and fostered Insular artistic traditions across much of western Europe. Other monks and nuns also went abroad to pursue the Christian life through exile and pilgrimage, ending their days in Continental foundations. Many lay people also made the pilgrimage to Rome, though not without peril – as Boniface wrote in 745:

> a great many of them [women pilgrims] perish and few keep their virtue. There are many towns in Lombardy and Gaul where there is not a courtesan or harlot but is of English stock.

The letters of Boniface carry many references to the demanding nature of his work, as well as to essential gifts of religious books, clothing and money received from his friends and colleagues back in England. In his letter, quoted at the beginning of this chapter, to Eadburg, Abbess of Minster in Thanet (a regular correspondent and herself a teacher of considerable influence), he asks for a copy of the Epistles of St Peter written in gold. This is a revealing document on several counts. First, it shows how important the business of exporting and copying manuscripts was in this period, for the missionaries themselves, of course, but also for the new foundations they set up on the Continent. Second, it is one of several sources showing that educated nuns, both in England and on the Continent, were themselves making fine copies of books for missionary use, as well as sending other gifts, such as church textiles, garments and gold. Finally, it reveals how Boniface intended to use the golden text itself to impress the Word of God, as revealed through His apostle Peter, on his pagan audience. This text was to be in itself an icon, just as much as the images that Benedict Biscop had hung around his churches at Wearmouth and Jarrow (see p. 80).

Missionary art: icons of faith in the eighth century

Such books, some with fine decorated covers, and many other kinds of Anglo-Saxon religious artefacts – altar crosses, reliquaries, chrismatories, textiles such as the Maaseik embroideries and other church furnishings – all formed part of the missionary equipment taken to the Continent. Some manuscripts, such as the early eighth-century Insular-style gospel-book possibly made at the Northumbrian St Willibrord's foundation at Echternach, and the Cutbercht Gospels, written by an Anglo-Saxon scribe in southern Germany in the late eighth century, remind us that texts and artefacts were also produced abroad by Anglo-Saxon craftsmen working in monasteries founded or re-established by the pioneer missionaries.[3] Other objects arrived as prestige gifts, like those given by King Æthelwulf to Pope Benedict III (see p. 152 above); Anglo-Saxon bowls decorated with lions, griffins and serpents are listed among the possessions of other late eighth- and early ninth-century popes.[4] The impact of such Anglo-Saxon liturgical and devotional objects led to a Continental production of manuscripts, ivories and metalwork influenced by Insular style. In northern Francia, for instance, a Franco-Saxon manuscript style developed, in which elements of Insular decoration – interlace and animal ornament – were grafted onto a spare geometric framework. Anglo-Saxon influence is also visible in some other prestigious artefacts: the splendid gilded chalice commissioned by Duke Tassilo of Bavaria (748–88), with its animal decoration inspired by chip-carved Mercian animal ornament; and the lower cover of the Lindau Gospels, a sumptuous piece of metalwork from the southern Rhine area, decorated in an Anglo-Carolingian style which owes a clear debt to early ninth-century Anglo-Saxon animal ornament.[5]

A number of the Anglo-Saxon exports carry iconographies explicitly related to the themes of Christ's sacrifice, and of personal salvation through

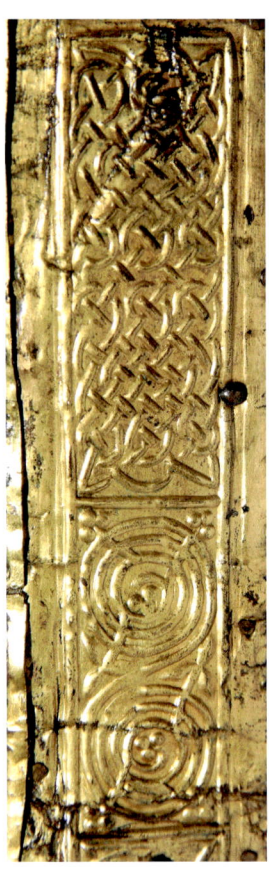

the sacraments of the Eucharist and baptism – key messages in the conversion of new peoples. The mighty (nearly 160 cm tall) late eighth-century ceremonial cross from the church at Bischofshofen, near Salzburg (now in the Salzburg Diocesan Treasury) is a fine example (see Chapter 4, p. 106; fig. 71). It was probably made for the abbey cathedral of St Peter at Salzburg, which had come under Boniface's jurisdiction as Archbishop of Mainz, and was a centre of Anglo-Saxon influence in spite of Boniface's quarrel with its Irish bishop, Vergilius (Fergal). It is impossible to say whether the cross was brought to Salzburg from England, or made there by an Anglo-Saxon monastic craftsman, but it is clearly of Anglo-Saxon workmanship, as three distinctive stylistic elements show. Its lively Southumbrian animal ornament is close in style to that seen on the Ormside bowl (fig. 93); its inlaid glass mounts with running spirals reflect the Celtic thread in the Insular tradition; and finally, the distinctive interlace and hairspring coils of the vine scroll along its narrow sides have close parallels in contemporary Mercian stone sculpture and metalwork (fig. 123). The burgeoning foliage in which birds and animals clamber and feed, and which covers the surviving metal sheeting on the back of the cross, is well known in Anglo-Saxon religious art of this period. The image represents at once another version of the familiar eucharistic vine scroll – Christ as the vine on which the faithful feed – and, in the specific context of a grand altar cross, the Cross as the living tree on which Christ was crucified. In the great Anglo-Saxon poetic meditation on the sacrifice of the Crucifixion, the *Dream of the Rood*, the cross that addresses the poet is a living tree that was cut down from the forest's edge. Yet it is also covered with gold and (like the Staffordshire Hoard cross) set with five gems representing the five wounds of Christ – this is a *crux gemmata*, the jewelled cross of early Christian tradition. The Bischofshofen cross is a majestic visual counterpart to this poetic version, its five large glass insets and many other smaller ones placing it clearly in the *crux gemmata* tradition. A rare reminder of the theatrical quality of Anglo-Saxon church furnishings, this magnificent icon of salvation was designed for contemplation as well as ostentation – a powerful embodiment of the Christian message, just as the gold-lettered Epistles of St Peter were for the mission of Boniface.

123 (*left*). The Bischofshofen cross (see fig. 71): detail of Insular-type interlace and tightly scrolled vine ornament. Bischofshofen, near Salzburg, mid- to late 8th century. H. (whole cross) 158 cm (Cathedral Treasury, Salzburg)

124 (*below*). Gilt-copper and wood chrismatory (see figs 125 and 126): detail of side panel with winged griffins. Later 8th century. W. of panel approx. 5.8 cm (Private owner)

125 (*opposite, top*). Gilt-copper and wood house-shaped chrismatory: front view with the risen Christ, vine scrolls and evangelists. Later 8th century. H. 15.6 cm (Private owner)

126 (*opposite, bottom*). Gilt-copper and wood house-shaped chrismatory: back view with chalice and inhabited vine-scroll ornament. Later 8th century. H. 15.6 cm (Private owner)

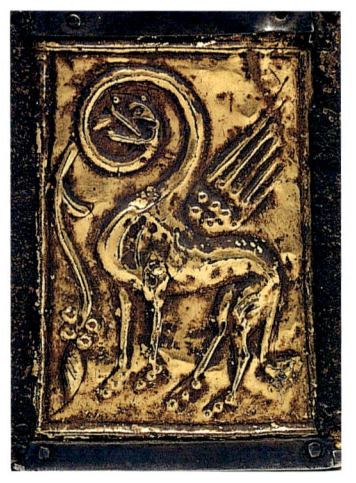

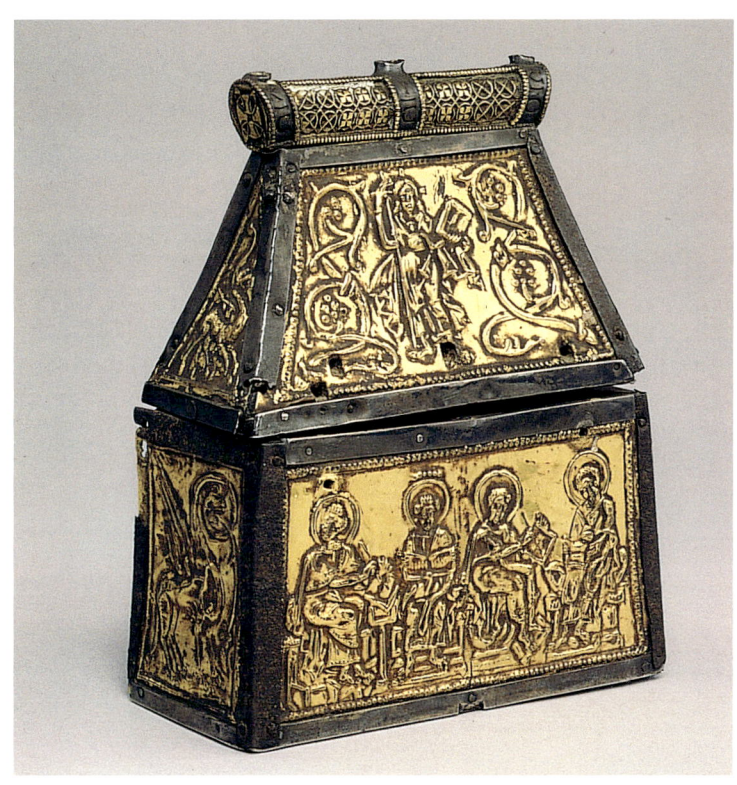

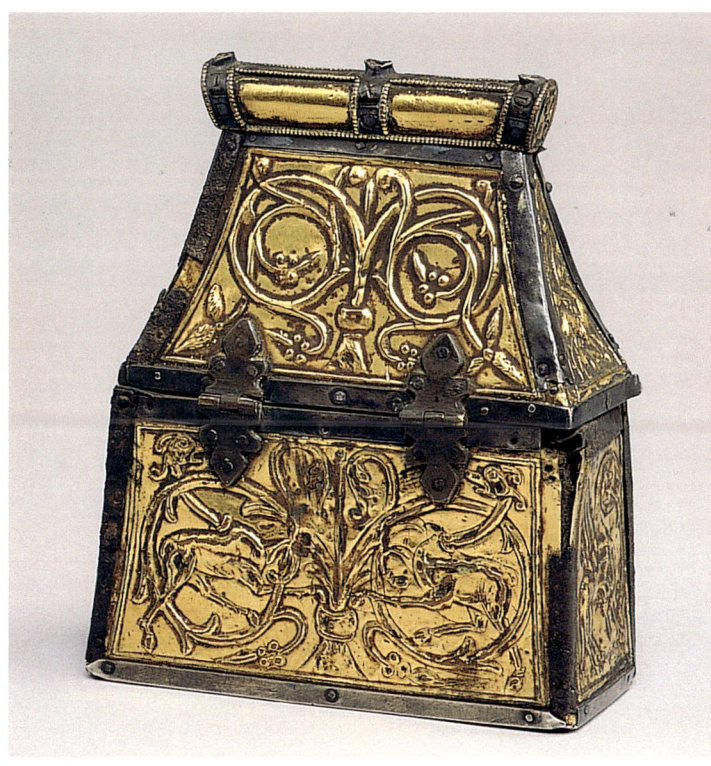

A few other remarkable survivals of metalwork and ivories from Continental church treasuries testify to the activities of Anglo-Saxon ecclesiastics on the Continent in the eighth century. Closely related in style to the Bischofshofen cross is a recently discovered Anglo-Saxon *chrismal*, or chrismatory (figs 124–6).[6] It seems to have been in Moissac, south-western France, in the early nineteenth century, and, like the Franks Casket, was probably removed from a church treasury during the despoliation of churches at the time of the French Revolution. Like the whale-bone Gandersheim Casket, it was a small portable house-shaped container designed to hold oils and sometimes the reserved host, which were required for sacramental rites such as baptism, the Eucharist and the administration of the last rites. Its house shape – constructed from gilded copper-alloy sheets covering an oak core, with a hinged lid and locking mechanism – is characteristically Insular, as is the principal decoration. On the front are the four evangelists, all seated and without their symbols; above them, on the lid, is the risen Christ holding the Cross and book, flanked by berried vine scrolls; on the back, two deer flank a chalice from which springs a fruiting vine (a similar chalice without the animals appears on the lid); and the end panels display images of sprightly winged griffins. The exaggerated necks and playful poses of the animals, and the fruiting vine motifs, are extremely close in style to those on the Bischofshofen cross and the Ormside bowl, pointing clearly to an Insular craftsman. But the figure style also shows a clear acquaintance with Carolingian models which could suggest that it was produced in a Continental, possibly Frankish, centre – or simply that, as with some late eighth-century Mercian manuscripts, the maker was influenced

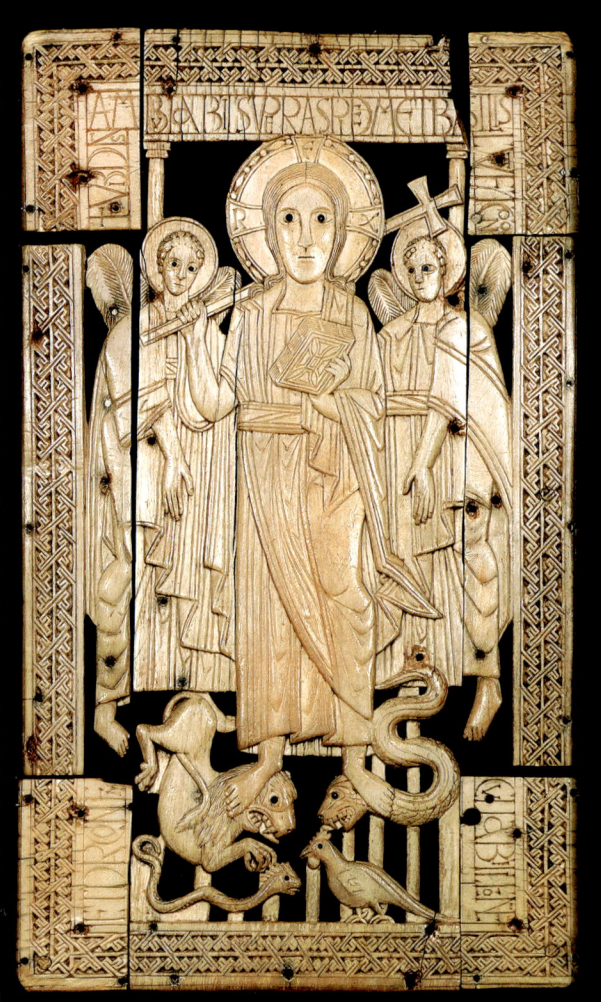

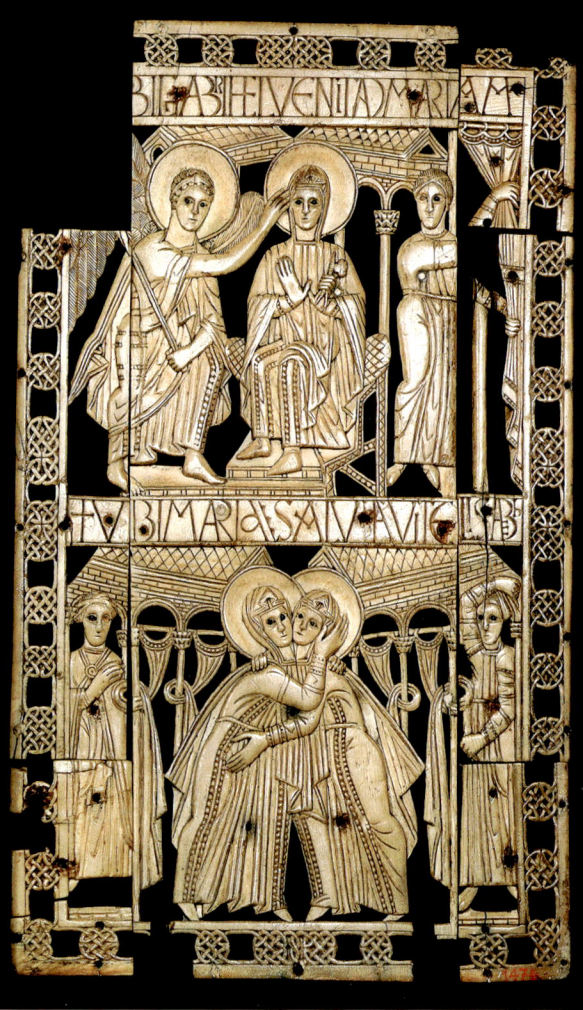

by such models. Later, probably in the ninth century, the ridge-pole on the lid was replaced; its decoration and inscription suggest that this probably took place in northern Francia. But the striking iconography of this *chrismal* also sits comfortably within the Anglo-Saxon tradition.

On the lid of the chrismatory the risen Christ, flanked by Insular-type vine scrolls evoking Christ as the true vine, the well-known symbol both of Christ nourishing his church and of the Eucharist itself (fig. 125). This is emphasized by the image of St John below, distinguished from the rest of the evangelists by his more elaborate halo, and by Christ's Cross, which points to him. It is in St John's Gospel that Christ declares that he is 'the true vine', and in which great emphasis is laid upon the triumph of the risen Christ. On the back panels the deer feed on the Tree of Life; here the eucharistic symbolism is reinforced by the chalice from which the fruiting vine springs (fig. 126).

127. Ivory diptych with Christ Triumphant and scenes of the Incarnation. St Martin's church, Genoels-Elderen, Belgium, later 8th century. H. 30 cm (Musées Royaux d'Art et d'Histoire, Brussels)

The winged griffins in Anglo-Saxon style on the end panels were understood as symbols of Christ's human and divine nature, and so, also, of salvation (fig. 124). The tradition of close reading that we have tracked from the earliest Anglo-Saxon artefacts is seen once more in this subtle iconography, which reflects the function of the container as a vehicle for the sacraments. And this function can be in no doubt – the inscription in a mixture of Greek and Latin on the later ridge-pole invokes Christ as Saviour, and describes the chrismatory itself as a 'baptismal casket', making very clear its sacramental role. Chrismatories such as this would have formed a regular part of the equipment of travelling ecclesiastics, especially appropriate to missionaries who took the Christian message to the heathen, and through the sacramental act of baptism, converted them.

Ivory and bone carvings were also among the artefacts exported and copied abroad. The eighth-century whale-bone Gandersheim Casket, already encountered in Chapters 4 and 5, is another chrismatory which encapsulates a rich eucharistic and cosmological iconography (figs 72 and 100). Made at much the same time as the one discussed above, its very different appearance hints at the wide range of artefacts available to the Anglo-Saxon ecclesiastics who took to the road at this time. Hints of other contemporary carvings which must have made a similar journey can be seen in some early Carolingian ivories that display interlace and vine scrolls with animal heads, which evidently derive from Southumbrian models. An ivory in the Victoria and Albert Museum, and a closely related piece showing the Ascension now in Munich, were probably made in southern Germany around the year 800, within a zone of Anglo-Saxon missionary activity.[7]

A somewhat earlier case, showing the influence of models disseminated from Northumbria – perhaps via Willibrord's important foundation at Echternach – is a delicate pair of openwork ivory panels from St Martin's church at Genoels-Elderen, in what is now Belgium (fig. 127). These were probably originally fitted to a book cover. Like many other Continental ivories of this period, these exquisitely carved panels have been cannibalized from a late Antique ivory diptych; the use of several separate plates in their construction suggests that the precious material was eked out, and is a testimony to its scarcity in the eighth century. It also suggests that they were made outside England, where whale-bone and antler were used instead for fine carving at this time. The primary panel shows the risen Christ triumphant over sin and death, and flanked by angels; the other illustrates two scenes, the Annunciation and the Visitation of the Virgin Mary to her cousin Elizabeth. Stylistically, the lettering of the accompanying inscriptions, the elongated faces, the linear zig-zags and flattened folds of the draperies, and the interlace and key-patterning of the borders all point to Northumbrian exemplars, themselves drawing on earlier north Italian iconographic sources. The iconography of the book covers, which juxtapose Christ's redemptive victory over sin and death with two depictions of his Incarnation, carries an over-riding message of salvation, powerfully rendered in these bold images.

Alcuin: Anglo-Saxon influence at the Carolingian court

The influence of Anglo-Saxon churchmen was felt abroad in other ways. Copies of works by Aldhelm, Bede and Boniface were already circulating on the Continent in the eighth century. But the scholar who had the greatest influence on the development of Carolingian culture was Alcuin of York (*c.* 735–804). This exceptionally learned teacher and writer, a native of Northumbria, was established at York Minster when he was invited by Charlemagne to join other scholars at his court in the early 780s. There he became a key figure in the creation of the Carolingian Renaissance – a revival of classical learning and culture in the Frankish kingdom which was in turn to be immensely influential throughout western and central Europe, including England. He ended his days as abbot of Tours in western France, which, under his guidance, became an important centre of Bible production in France, and a training ground for many of the Continental churchmen of the next generation.

It was on foundations laid by Alcuin that the scholarship, learning and artistic output of the courts of Charlemagne and his successors such as Charles the Bald and Lothair were built. These in turn became a source of renewal and inspiration for Alfred's less grandiose, but innovative and scholarly reforms, with their emphasis on new icons of wisdom and Christian learning (see p. 156, and figs 114 and 115). Indirectly, through its contributions to the Carolingian Renaissance, the Continental legacy of Anglo-Saxon missionaries and scholars was also to influence the creation of a new Anglo-Saxon art in the tenth and eleventh centuries.

New images of devotion: art in Æthelstan's reign

Alfred's son and grandson, Edward the Elder (r. 899–924) and Æthelstan (r. 924/5–39), continued the push towards reconquest of the Danelaw. Under Edward, all England south of the Humber was brought under the control of the Wessex kings and, subsequently, Æthelstan extended this power-base. In 927 he received the submission of the Northumbrians, Scots, Welsh and Strathclyde Britons, enabling him to proclaim himself (somewhat misleadingly) king of all Britain, and to celebrate the event and the title in a coin issue of 927–8.

Alongside his military campaigns, Æthelstan maintained and extended the Wessex dynasty's connections with Continental scholars from many lands, as well as engineering diplomatic marriages for four of his half-sisters into Continental noble and royal families, relationships which he continued to foster. Some Carolingian manuscripts known to have been in the king's possession have survived, including the splendid Coronation Gospels.[8] This was given to Æthelstan by the German king (later emperor) Otto the Great (912–73), who was married to Æthelstan's sister, Eadgyth. Æthelstan in turn gave it to Christ Church, Canterbury, and, as its name implies, it was considered important enough to be used in later centuries as an oath-book in the coronation rites of English kings. It is a fine example of the kind of Continental manuscripts that were now entering England in the first half of the tenth century, and that were to be so influential in laying the foundations of the art of the 'Winchester' school (see pp. 174–5). No doubt many other

128. Bede's *Lives of St Cuthbert*: dedication page with King Æthelstan presenting the book to the shrine of St Cuthbert. Winchester, before 937. 29.3 x 19.1 cm (Corpus Christi College, Cambridge, MS 183, fol. 1v)

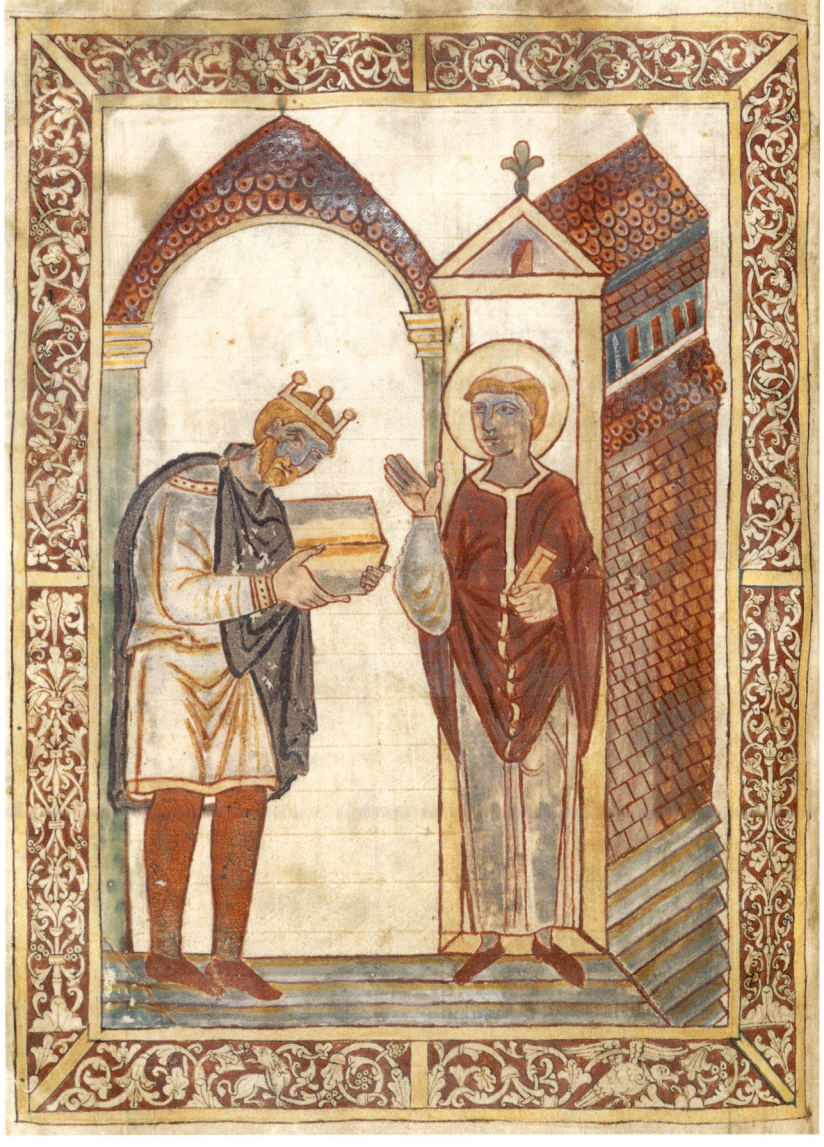

such manuscripts, ivories and pieces of fine metalwork entered England during Æthelstan's reign through the close links he had established with his Continental peers, scholars and churchmen.

The king's political ascendancy was also marked by many royal gifts and acts of patronage. Æthelstan was an avid patron of books and collector of relics, and gave generously to religious houses throughout the land – around the year 932, for example, he gave some 150 relics to the minster at Exeter. Two years later, in 934, while on his way to attack Scotland with a great army and fleet, he presented a great many gifts of relics, church furnishings, books and estates to the shrine of St Cuthbert, which in 883 had come to rest at Chester-le-Street (County Durham), following years of wanderings after the Viking raids on Lindisfarne. (In this, he followed a Wessex precedent: shortly before his death, Alfred had sent two gold arm-rings and a gold censer to the shrine.) The list of these gifts is formidable and includes, among its many treasures, two copies of the gospels ornamented in gold and silver, church vestments and furnishings, gold- and silver-mounted horns, two silver candelabra, a gold and ivory crucifix, a silver chalice and two patens, one of Byzantine workmanship. The giving of such treasures to the foremost saint of Northumbria was, of course, as much a political demonstration of Wessex's overlordship of Northumbria as an act of piety (as well as a bid for St Cuthbert's blessing and protection for his expedition, which naturally ended in a resounding victory). But the nature of the gifts shows the king as a patron of religious art as well as of relics.

Among Æthelstan's gifts was a copy of Bede's prose and verse *Lives of St Cuthbert*; its full-page frontispiece shows the king reverentially presenting the book to the saint, whose hand is raised in blessing (fig. 128). A border of delicate acanthus-leaved vines, with birds and the occasional beast feeding on the berries that hang from the foliage sprays, provides an animated contrast to the static quality of the figures it frames. This is the first of several presentation images known from Anglo-Saxon England, and the first surviving non-numismatic image of a reigning king (another, showing Æthelstan kneeling at the feet of St Cuthbert, perished in the great conflagration of Sir Robert Cotton's library at Ashburnham House in 1731). It introduces a new iconography of Anglo-Saxon kingship, portrayed in an act of Christian reverence and dedication, in which the sub-text is that temporal success comes through religious devotion and observance. Such images of kingship were to become increasingly popular among Æthelstan's successors. This is an image of the Good King in a very Alfredian manner, but seen through Carolingian spectacles. The concept, as well as the appearance of the image itself, owes much to Carolingian models, but a certain robust linearity in the figure style and, especially, the lively scrolls and sprigs of inhabited acanthus show that this painting is fully grounded in the Anglo-Saxon tradition.

129. The Æthelstan Psalter: the risen Christ with martyrs, confessors and virgins. Old Minster, Winchester, second quarter of the 10th century. 12.8 x 8.8 cm (British Library, Cotton MS Galba A.xviii, fol. 21r)

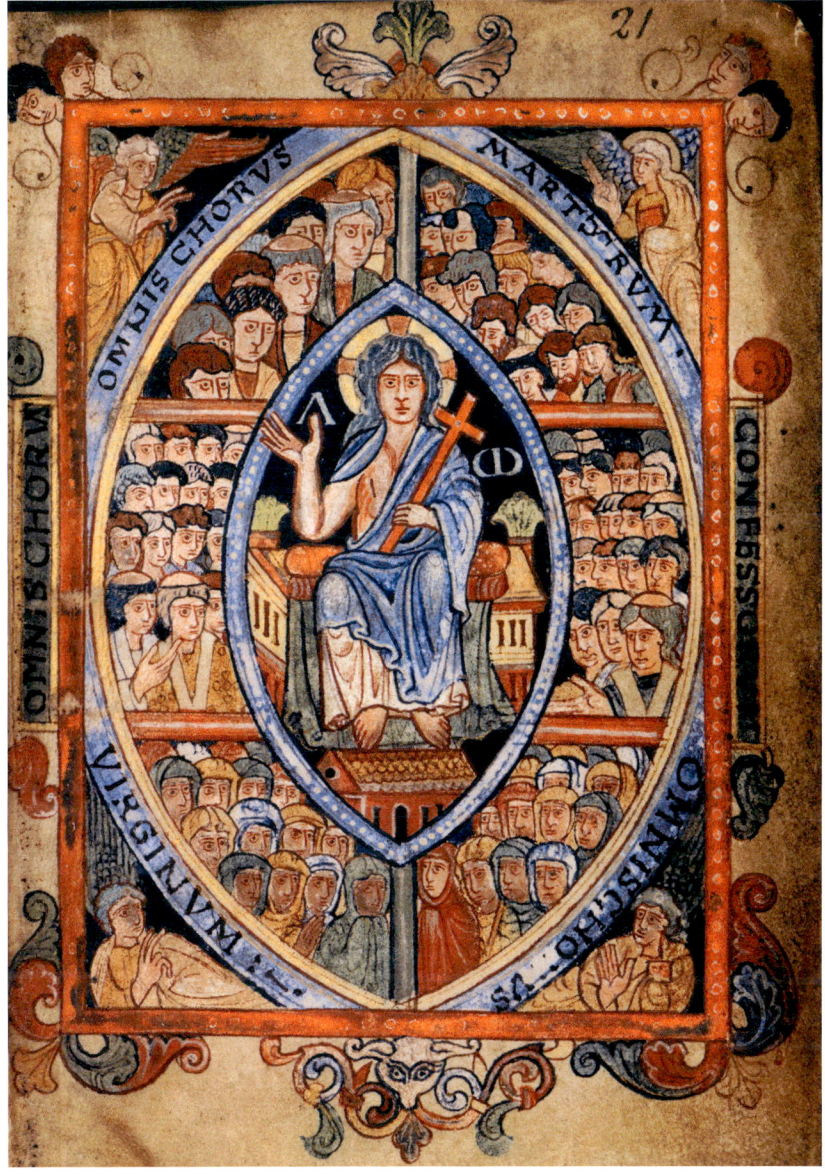

Among other decorated manuscripts that survive from Æthelstan's reign, the Æthelstan Psalter is a small ninth-century Carolingian psalter from Liège, Belgium, to which a number of Anglo-Saxon miniatures were added in Winchester in the early tenth century (fig. 129). It was at Winchester throughout the medieval period, and by tradition is said to have been given to the Old Minster by Æthelstan himself. This was, however, a book intended for private prayer and meditation, not public display in church services, and the painted images have an intimate quality. Scaled down from grander models, the small gesturing figures in the four surviving images are delicately coloured in subdued pinks, blues, greens and yellows; they are a stylistic bridge between the solemn gazing figures of the late ninth-century Winchester wall-painting fragment (fig. 10) and the animated figures of the fully-fledged 'Winchester' style which was to become the hallmark of the monastic reforms later in the tenth century. It may indeed originally have been adapted for use by the king himself – two images in the psalter refer to the spear with which Christ was pierced at the Crucifixion, a relic Æthelstan is known to have acquired.

The psalter's image of Christ in Majesty in mandorla (a pointed oval frame signifying divine glory), surrounded by crowds of martyrs, confessors and virgins, also has an interesting parallel in a contemporary ivory panel from a book cover.[9] This shows a seated figure of Christ in Majesty surrounded by the four evangelist symbols, and framed by delicate twisting scrolls of lush acanthus foliage. Formerly in Continental collections, it has been argued to be of later tenth-century date and Continental manufacture; but the close resemblance between the two Christ figures suggests a possible Anglo-Saxon origin. Their poses and gently rippled garments, and the striking similarity of the foliage ornament in the ivory panel to that in the frontispiece of Æthelstan's presentation copy of the *Lives of St Cuthbert*, suggest that this prestigious ivory may also have originated in an early tenth-century southern English context, closely associated with the production of royal manuscripts. Certainly it would not have appeared unusual among the ivory, gold and silver treasures offered by the king to his favoured institutions; and if it was taken abroad in Æthelstan's reign, it could have been as a mount on one of the fine book covers or reliquaries presented by the king to his Continental associates.

One other set of items presented by the king to St Cuthbert's shrine has survived: a magnificent embroidered silk stole, maniple and girdle (ecclesiastical vestments), with decoration worked in gold and coloured silks on a pale silk ground (fig. 130). An embroidered text records that they were made for Bishop Frithestan of Winchester (909–31) at the behest of Ælfflæd, the wife of Edward the Elder. The queen died in 916, so the date of the embroideries is narrowed down to the years between 909 and 916, and their likely origin to the royal and ecclesiastical centre of Winchester. Outstanding examples of the skill of Anglo-Saxon embroiderers, the stole and maniple are decorated with images of evangelists, prophets, saints and deacons of the church, accompanied by lush frills of dark green acanthus leaves. The gravely monumental figure style of these embroideries closely resembles the figures in the slightly later Æthelstan manuscripts; that the king must have held them in the highest regard is clearly revealed by his gift of them to Cuthbert's shrine. We can see here the beginnings of the art style which came to be so closely associated with the name of Winchester.

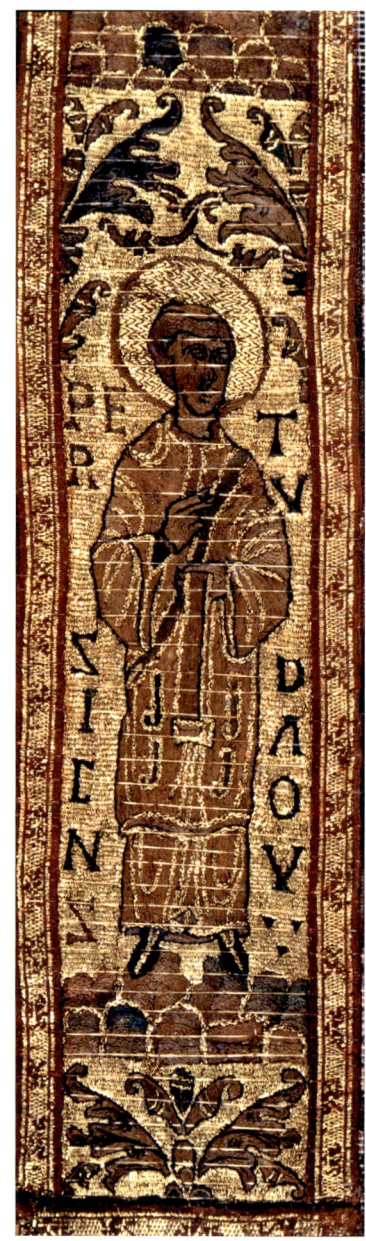

130. Detail of Peter the Deacon on a gold-embroidered silk stole from the shrine of St Cuthbert. 909–16. Whole stole L. 82 cm (Durham Cathedral Treasury)

Art and reform in the tenth century

Among Æthelstan's royal household in the 930s were two young clerics, Dunstan and Æthelwold, who were to be prime movers in the ecclesiastical reforms of the middle and later years of the tenth century. They introduced the strict observance of the Rule of St Benedict – guidance on how to conduct the monastic life – into Anglo-Saxon monasteries from the Continent. After Æthelstan's death in 939 they retreated to Glastonbury, where Dunstan had been educated, and spent some years in further study of, among other texts, the Benedictine Rule and commentaries on it by Continental scholars.

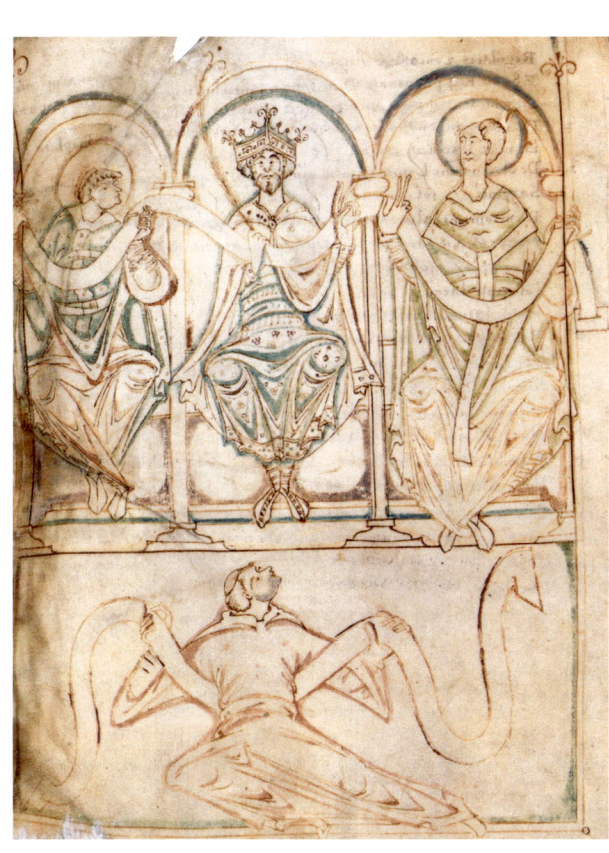

131. The *Regularis concordia*: prefatory page showing King Edgar seated between Dunstan and Æthelwold. Christ Church, Canterbury, *c.* 1050. 24 x 17.7 cm (British Library, Cotton MS Tiberius A.iii, fol. 2v)

Dunstan became abbot of Glastonbury in the early 940s, but had to seek exile in Ghent between 956 and 958, after he had condemned King Eadwig (r. 955–9) for immorality. There he studied at the reformed monastery of St Peter's, and saw at first hand the benefits of the application of a universal set of rules to the organization of monastic life, in contrast to the rather unstructured and haphazard way in which individual houses had become accustomed to regulate their way of life in England. He was recalled to England in 958 by King Edgar (r. 959–75), who was at that time in control of England north of the Thames, and appointed to the bishoprics of London and Worcester. When Edgar, who had been Æthelwold's pupil, succeeded to the English throne in 959, he made Dunstan Archbishop of Canterbury, an office he held until he died in 988. With the king's committed support, Dunstan and his colleagues energetically pursued the reform of the monasteries.

Æthelwold, in the meantime, had become abbot of the monastery of Abingdon in about 954, which he briskly renovated and reformed. He was appointed Bishop of Winchester by Edgar in 963, where he remained hugely influential until his death in 984, translating the Benedictine Rule into Old English, and composing the major document known as the *Regularis Concordia* (fig. 131). This set out a uniform code of monastic observance and, in its prologue and epilogue, confirmed the beneficial concordat between the monarchy and the reformed Church. He introduced Benedictine monks from his reformed monastery at Abingdon to the Old Minster at Winchester and, with Dunstan, was active in promulgating the new code.

The third principal figure in the reform movement was Oswald, who studied and was ordained a monk at the influential reformed house of Fleury in the French Loire valley. He later became Bishop of Worcester (961–92) and

Archbishop of York (971–92), and also founded a number of important monasteries across England.

This brief introduction to the Benedictine reform movement highlights the active network of relationships, within England and abroad, which brought about the reforms of the mid- to late tenth century, and engendered the extraordinary flourishing of art in all media which accompanied it. The reform of existing monasteries, and the foundation of new ones, gave a great impetus to the Church, as well as to its royal and secular patrons, to commission splendid new illuminated books, often lavishly decorated with gold, and other prestige ecclesiastical items to aid study and glorify worship. Indeed, the considerable number of important and richly decorated manuscripts which survive from this period can scarcely be adequately dealt with in a study of this short length, so this overview will inevitably be very selective.[10] By contrast, the survival of fine ecclesiastical metalwork from this period is severely limited, though there are a number of documentary sources, of varying reliability, which give vivid accounts of the church treasures that once existed.[11] Ivory carving – specifically, carving in walrus ivory – however, comes into its own during this period, particularly as a medium associated with personal devotion.

The characteristic art of the reform movement is often rather misleadingly referred to as the 'Winchester' school or style, even though versions of it were certainly practised at many other reformed monastic centres. Nor is it a uniform style; there is a world of difference between the solemn monumental line drawing of Christ in St Dunstan's Classbook and the febrile flutterings and agitated gestures of the Harley Psalter, or between the dense acanthus vegetation and ornate gold of the pages of the Benedictional of St Æthelwold and the spare angularity of the Tiberius Psalter (see figs 134, 138, 142, and 149). In other media, different forms and emphases are apparent. Nevertheless, they are all united by the common factor of inspiration from a number of Continental sources, accelerated by the close contacts with reformed monasteries in northern France and elsewhere abroad – though, as before, this influence is tempered and modified by Anglo-Saxon tradition.

The Winchester style was immensely powerful and its influence was felt widely, not only in England but also abroad, especially in northern France and Normandy, where centres with close links to English monasteries also produced manuscripts and other artefacts in the style. In its broadest sense, it endured for over a hundred years, so it is hardly surprising that it took many different forms during its currency between the mid-tenth and mid-eleventh-centuries, and even beyond the Norman Conquest. One of its notable features is its use of pure and elegant line drawing – often in several colours – in contrast to more elaborate painted images seen in some manuscripts, where the figures are naturalistically modelled and, in the grandest manuscripts, framed by lush acanthus borders and lavishly embellished with gold leaf. Also striking

132 (*opposite, top*). The Junius Psalter: detail of initial with human and animal elements. Winchester, second quarter of the 10th century. Whole page 24.2 x 17.2 cm (Bodleian Library, University of Oxford, MS Junius 27, fol. 135v)

133 (*opposite, bottom*). Bede's *Lives of St Cuthbert*: detail of initial D with eagle and lion heads. Christ Church, Canterbury, second half of the 10th century. Whole page 25.5 x 17.5 cm (British Library, Harley MS 1117, fol. 45r)

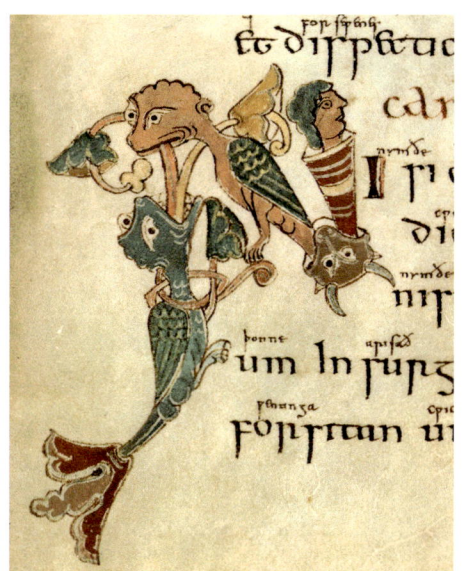

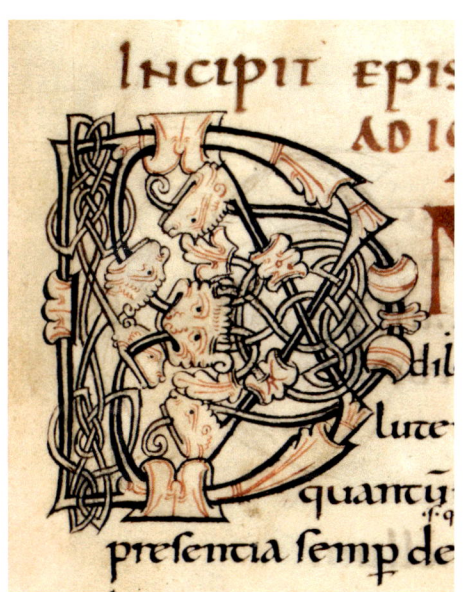

is the use of inventive and elaborately ornamented initials, in several guises. The sheer variety of techniques and level of inventiveness which makes the art in this final phase of Anglo-Saxon England so remarkable and powerful is scarcely equalled among the surviving decorated manuscripts of previous Anglo-Saxon generations (although as we have noted, this probably reflects the extent of losses, rather than the true state of affairs).

Images of devotion: manuscripts of the tenth to eleventh centuries

An examination of the art of the reform movement has to begin with the magnificent and extremely varied array of decorated manuscripts which have become the defining images of this period, and the many influences that went into their creation. We saw in the last chapter how the manuscripts of Alfred's reign and of the early tenth century were distinguished by a use of lively animal and human motifs in the initials of key parts of the texts; these were mostly in monochrome, and in manuscripts which were designed for teaching and study, rather than the grand manuscripts associated with church offices.

Decorated initials continue to be an important feature in manuscripts associated with the Winchester style, where they take two main forms.[12] In the first group, particularly but not exclusively associated with the beginnings of the style, initials are formed from robustly drawn birds, beasts and snakes which munch on one another and the occasional sprout of foliage, sometimes with acrobatic men clambering perilously among the animals and leaf tendrils to form the letters. Some of these are brightly coloured in shades of pink, brown, blue, ochre and yellow, adding to their corporeal presence. Characteristic examples are nicely illustrated in two manuscripts of the first half of the tenth century, the Junius Psalter and a Bede manuscript (figs 132 and 19). The use of human figures as well as beasts in these initials is noteworthy because there are no obvious or immediate precedents for this in either Anglo-Saxon or Carolingian manuscripts; they may perhaps look back to earlier Continental and Anglo-Saxon sources for inspiration, such as late eighth- and ninth-century Anglo-Saxon manuscripts and sculpture, where combinations of animals, plants, and occasionally humans, also appear.

In the second group, and overlapping chronologically with the earlier type, there is a series of more delicate initials, composed of fine interlace and acanthus foliage, in which a riot of disembodied eagle and lion heads emerges from intricately interlaced foliate strands to snap at each other and the engulfing interlace and plant life, as in a copy of Bede's *Lives of St Cuthbert* from Christ Church, Canterbury (fig. 133). These are elegant pieces of

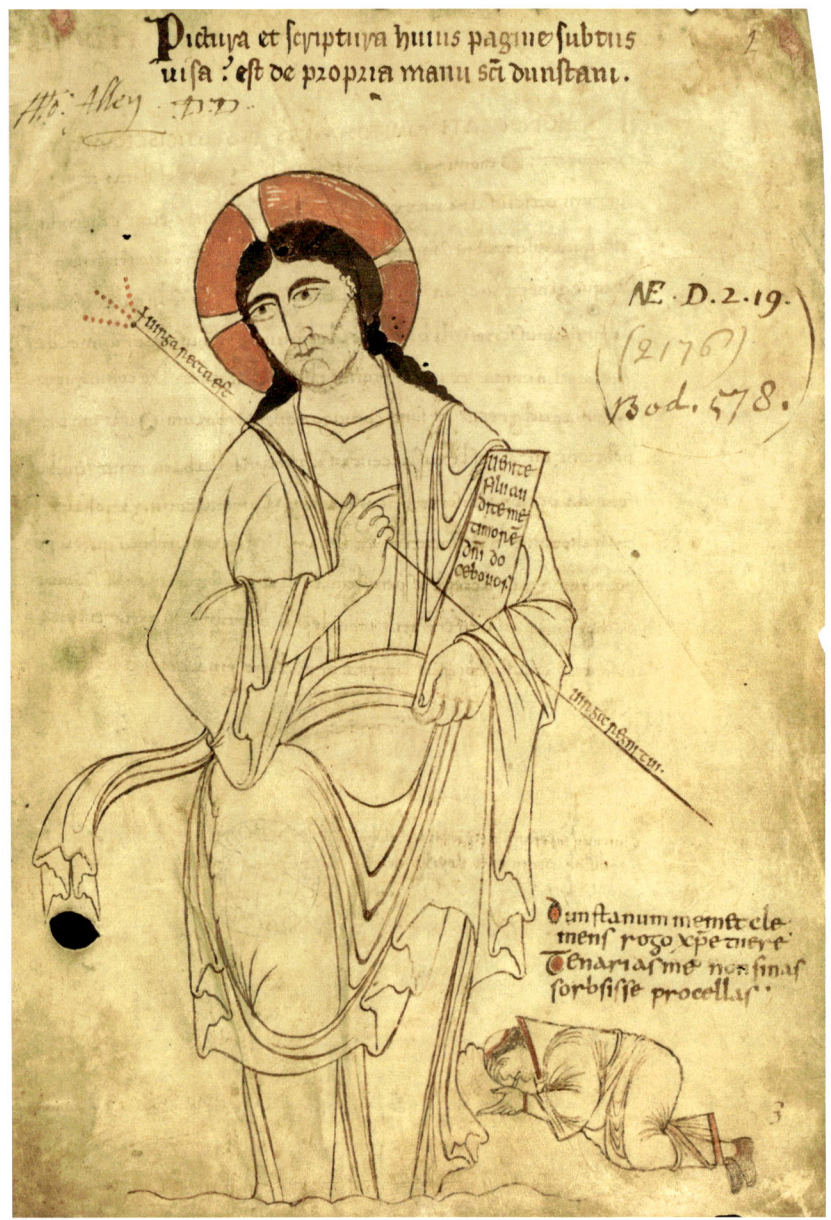

Pictura et scriptura huius pagine subtus
visa : est de propria manu sci dunstani.

AE·D·2·19·

(2176)

Bod. 578.

134. St Dunstan's
Classbook: St Dunstan at
the feet of the risen
Christ. Glastonbury,
mid-10th century. 24.5 x
17.9 cm (Bodleian Library,
University of Oxford,
MS Auct.F.4.32, fol. 1r)

penmanship, mostly in monochrome, though some have touches of colour. Many of the manuscripts with this decoration were produced at Canterbury, and date to the later tenth and early eleventh centuries. These highly distinctive initials, like the first type, have their origins firmly in that long Anglo-Saxon tradition of ornamenting text with animated animals, stretching back into the eighth century.

Finally, a number of very large and colourful initials, mostly associated with psalters and gospel-books, show another facet of the Winchester

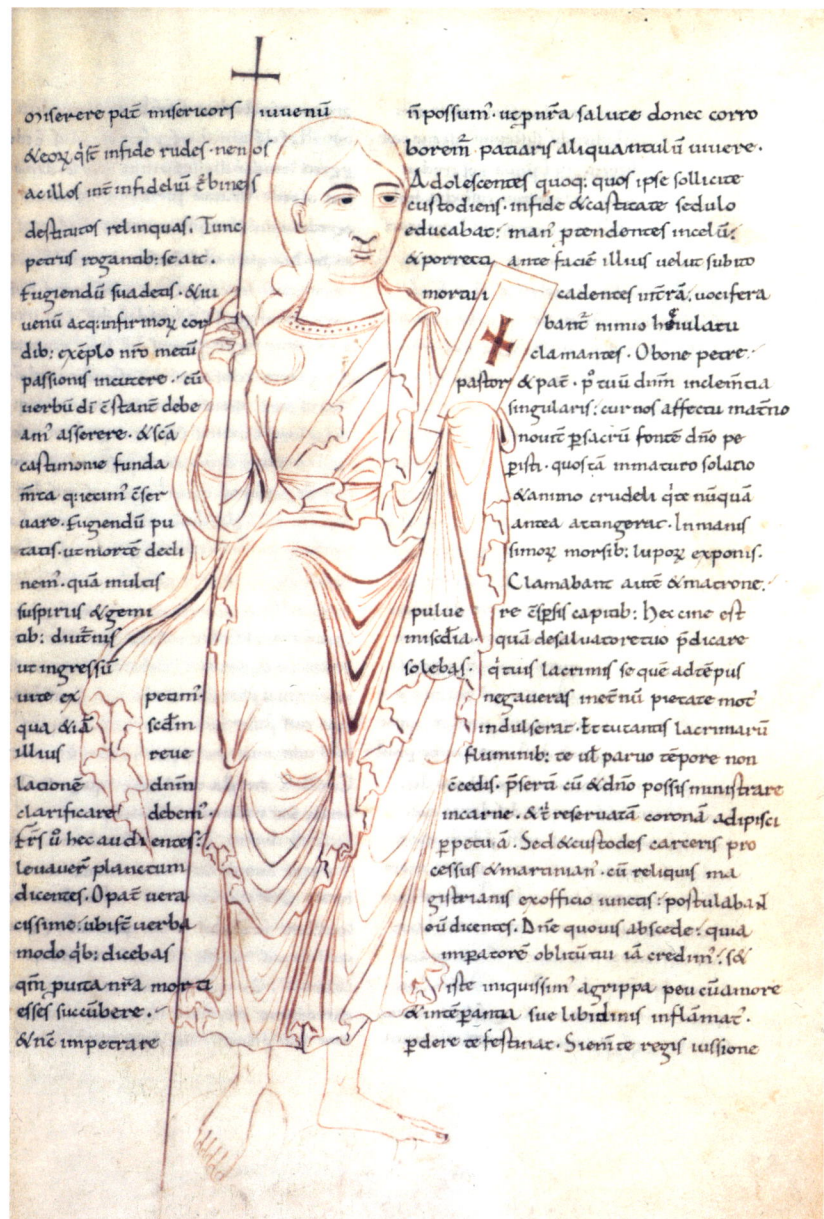

135. Gregory the Great, *Pastoral Care*: figure of Christ. ?Canterbury, mid-10th century. 32.8 x 23.7 cm (St John's College, Oxford, MS 28, fol. 2)

style; in particular, a growing focus of ornate decoration on the initial B, which heralded the opening words of Psalm 1, '*Beatus vir*', 'Blessed is the man'. By the end of the tenth century this had become an important vehicle for ornament involving interlace and lush foliage sprouting from a leonine head; a late tenth-century psalter manuscript, sometimes known as the Ramsey Psalter,[13] is a key piece here, setting the trend for many similar initials in later centuries (see fig. 6).

    An outstanding characteristic of the Winchester school, as mentioned above, is its sophisticated and elegant tradition of line drawing, which had its heyday in the later tenth and early eleventh centuries. It is influenced by a variety of Carolingian schools, which must have been represented in the books, ivory carvings and other artefacts that had travelled to England in earlier years. These included, in particular, products of the court schools of Charlemagne and Charles the Bald, and the schools of Metz and Reims. But with the exception of the Reims manuscripts, there is less emphasis on pure line drawing in the Carolingian models favoured by the Anglo-Saxon artists. The supremely confident use of the flowing, expressive line that characterizes Winchester-style drawing owes more to long-standing Anglo-Saxon traditions of depiction, in which bold, linear treatments of the human form, and a delight in dense patterning of surfaces, is such a persistent theme.

Two main drawing styles are apparent: one earlier and more static, owing much to the court schools of Charlemagne and Charles the Bald; the other, more impressionistic and animated, deriving largely from the art of the manuscripts and ivories of ninth-century Reims – although there is an overlap between the two. Both styles are equally apparent in the more elaborate, painted, images, discussed later in this section. The earliest surviving example of the first style is a drawing added to the manuscript known as

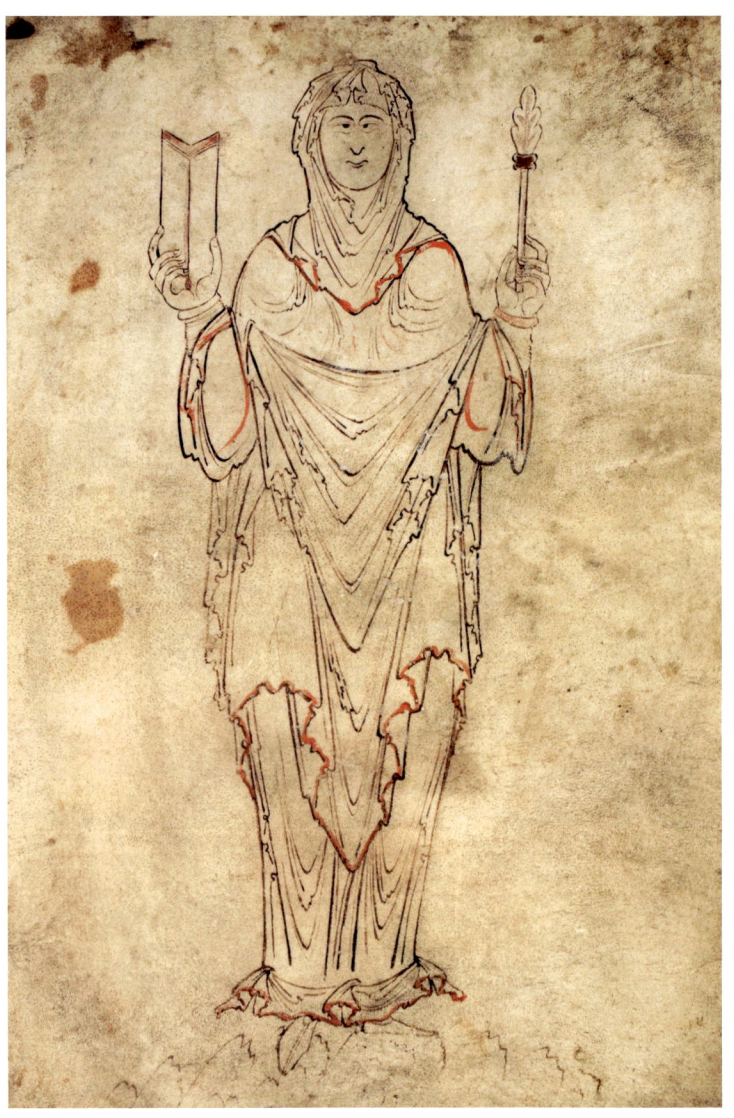

136. Boethius, *The Consolation of Philosophy*: figure of Philosophy. St Augustine's, Canterbury, c. 970. 29.2 x 22.7 cm (Trinity College, Cambridge, MS O.3.7, fol. 1)

St Dunstan's Classbook, which was made at Dunstan's monastery of Glastonbury in the middle of the tenth century, and presumably dates to the years before Dunstan's exile in 956 (fig. 134). On its opening page is a gravely monumental three-quarter figure of Christ with book and staff, depicted as the Wisdom of God. At his feet, the small kneeling figure of Dunstan kisses the ground in reverence; an accompanying prayer identifies the figure, and being written in the first person, implies that both drawing and inscription are in the hand of Dunstan himself. The saint's renown as an artist and scribe, as well as a skilful craftsman in metal, lends support to this attribution. The drawing is executed in a brown ink, the only colour being the red infill of Christ's halo. The head of Christ is powerfully emphasized, with a piercing, distant gaze, strongly delineated features and dark flowing hair. His garments descend in linear V-shaped patterns, terminating in cascades of rippling folds which are a hallmark of the style, as is also the flying drapery of his girdle which flutters out from the side of his garment. The disparity of scale between the awe-inspiring divine presence and the small human figure of Dunstan emphasizes the devotional nature of the image, and adds a dynamic tension to the drawing. The image itself owes something to the art of the court school of Charlemagne, but the austere pleasure taken in patterning the garments is very different from its richly painted or modelled Continental exemplars; this supremely controlled and beautiful drawing encapsulates many of the traits we shall observe elsewhere in the art of the reform movement.

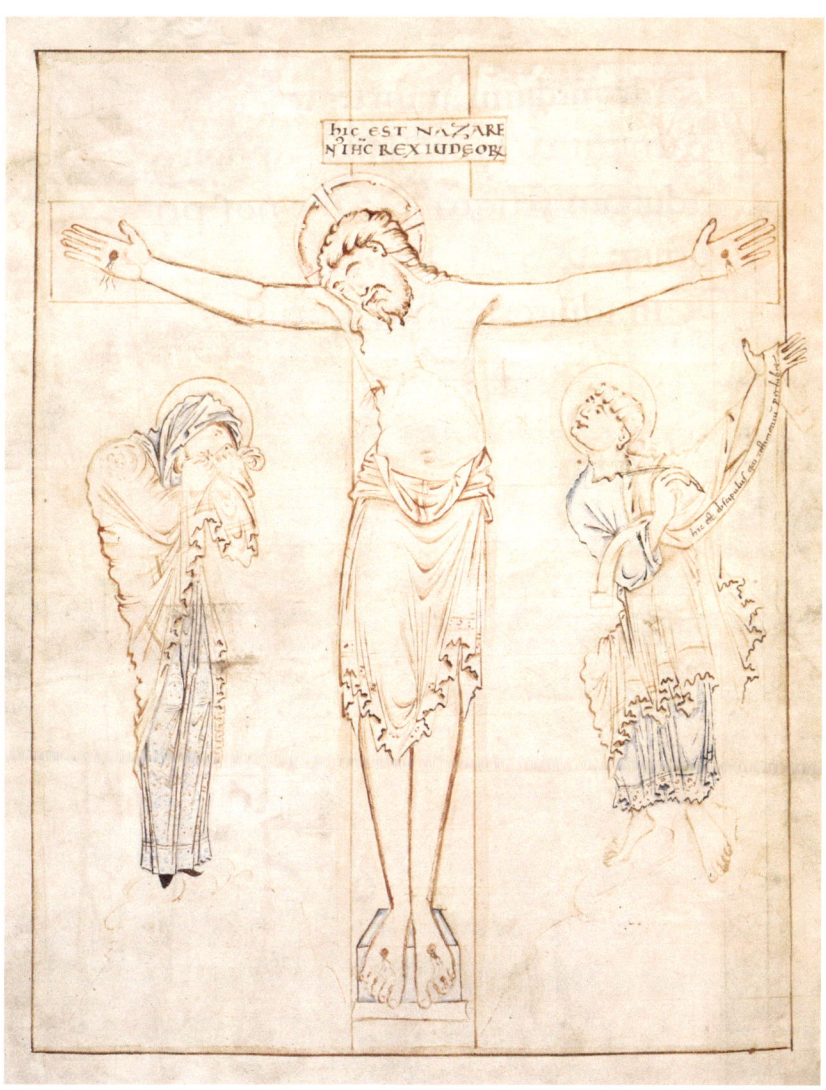

137. The Ramsey Psalter: Christ on the Cross with the Virgin and St John. Winchester, *c.* 1000. 28.5 x 24.2 cm (British Library, Harley MS 2904, fol. 3v)

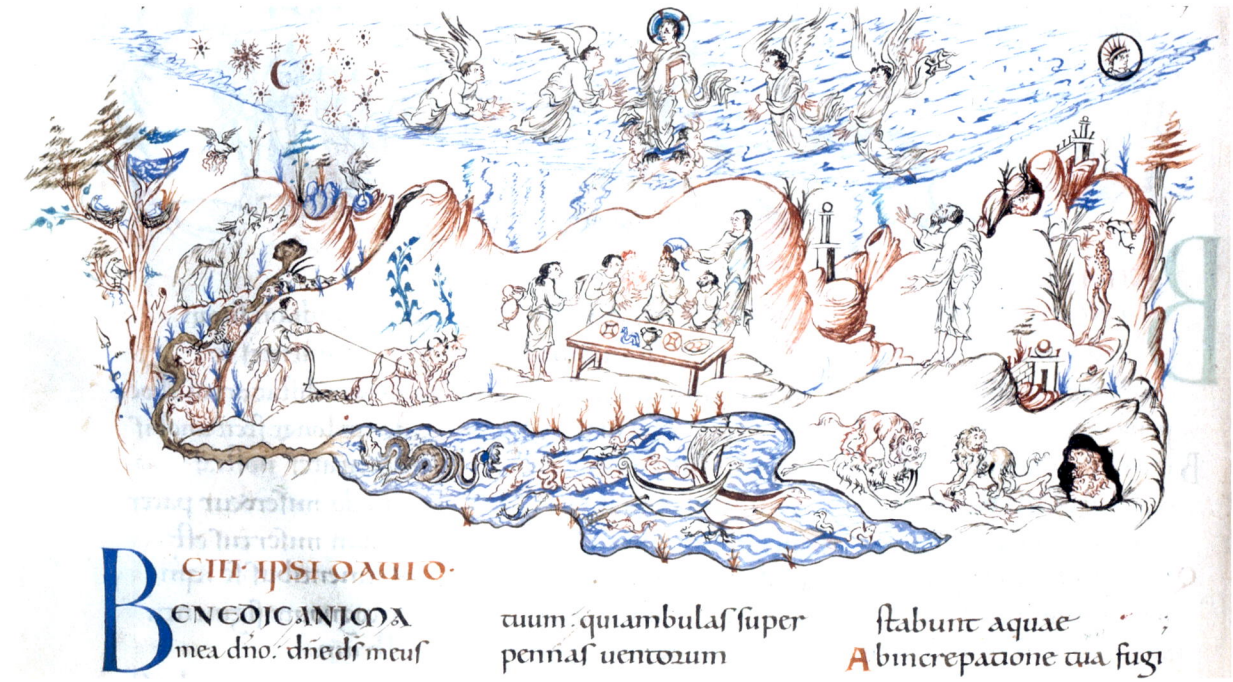

CIII IPSI DAUID
BENEDICANIMA
mea dno. dne ds meus
tuum quiambulas super
pennas uentorum
stabunt aquae
A bincrepatione tua fugi

138. The Harley Psalter: illustration to Psalm 103 (detail). Christ Church, Canterbury, c. 1020. Whole page 38 x 30.9 cm (British Library, Harley MS 603, fol. 51v)

Other full-page drawings which relate to this show something of the range and development of this first style over the years. A drawing of the youthful Christ on the fly-leaf of a manuscript now in St John's College, Oxford, is clearly related to the Christ image in St Dunstan's Classbook, and so may also come from Glastonbury, though its script suggests that Canterbury may be a more likely origin (fig. 135). It probably dates to the third quarter of the tenth century. The Christ here is shown full-length, and while his garments are evidently of the same order as those worn by Christ in the earlier manuscript, their folds zigzag and flutter in greater animation, and with a more evident sense of agitation. In the depiction of the personification of Philosophy in a manuscript of Boethius's *Consolation of Philosophy*, written at St Augustine's Canterbury, and dated to around 970 (fig. 136), this nervous, fluttering line is greatly emphasized by the contrast of light and heavy penstrokes, drawn in brown ink with touches of red. This female figure, front-facing, and holding her book and a sceptre to signify her authority in surprisingly large and capable hands, is otherwise incorporeal, her whole being subsumed in a torrential cascade of frills that have replaced her physical body. It may have been the artist's deliberate choice to portray a personified concept not as an embodied human, but as a metaphysical entity – as real, but physically insubstantial. The style continued into the early years of the eleventh century, as seen in the illustrations to a gospel-book which was at Barking Abbey, near London, in the twelfth century.[14] Here the angel of St John, his garments fluttering in a heavenly breeze, has a visible form beneath the agitations of the draperies; but their animated flying folds suggest that he floats, rather than stands, upon the cloud beneath his feet. The greater use of a heavy line to accentuate the folds of his garment is also apparent, a foretaste of the hardening of line which is increasingly evident in manuscripts of the eleventh century.

The second style, sometimes rather confusingly known as the 'Utrecht' style for reasons explained below, shows a strong influence from the art of the Reims school. It displays a lightness of touch and a capacity for depicting emotional interaction, reflected in the animated gestures and active postures of its figures, which often seem frozen in motion. A supreme illustration of this is seen in the Crucifixion scene in a prestige psalter made at Winchester towards the year 1000 (fig. 137). This represents something completely new. Christ on the Cross is portrayed as a realistic image of suffering and compassion, delicately drawn in brown ink, highlighted in red. On either side, the Virgin and St John express their grief in gestures which seem to be echoed in the agitated ripples of their garments, drawn with a light and flickering touch which gives dynamic tension to the whole image. The work of the artist (and scribe) who conceived this startling image is traceable in other manuscripts, including two at least which were produced abroad, at the French monasteries of St Bertin and Fleury – perhaps a sign of the esteem in which this consummate draughtsman must have been held.

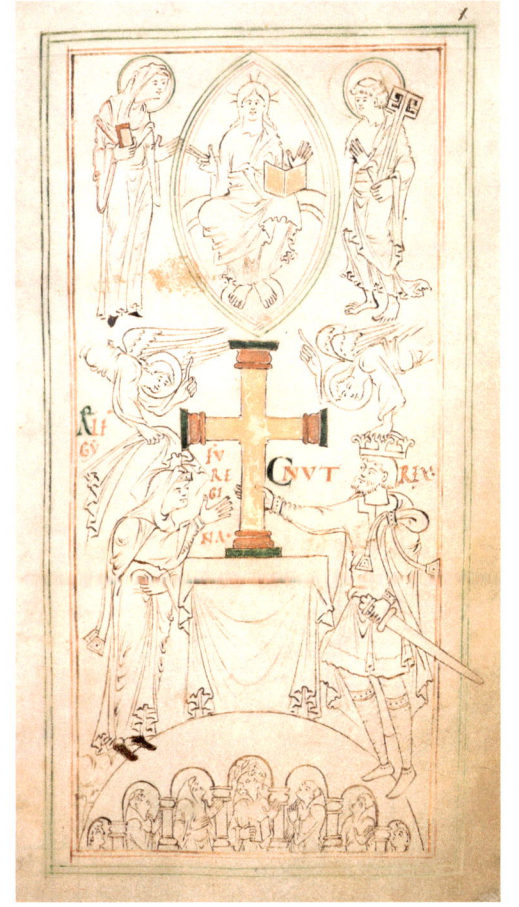

139. The New Minster *Liber Vitae*: dedication page showing King Cnut and Queen Emma presenting a golden altar cross to the New Minster, Winchester. 1031. 25.5 x 15 cm (British Library, Stowe MS 944, fol. 6r)

The technique of the flickering line, highlighted with hints of colour, and the agitated gestures and dynamic postures of the figures drawn in this second style occur in many manuscripts of the later tenth and early eleventh centuries. But the other key manuscript for this style is the Harley Psalter (fig. 138), copied from an illustrated Carolingian psalter now in Utrecht, which was made at Hautvilliers near Reims in the 830s – hence the 'Utrecht' designation sometimes used for the Anglo-Saxon style. This manuscript came to Christ Church, Canterbury, around the end of the tenth century, and the English copy was made there in the years around 1020, since a well-known and prolific scribe, Eadui Basan (Fat Eadui), who was active between about 1010 and 1030, is one of several hands that can be traced in it. The Utrecht Psalter is an extraordinary manuscript; its illusionistic illustrations teem with movement, the heavens and landscape alike seem invested with energy, and the lively small figures within this world are sketched in short dashing pen-strokes which add to the sense of perpetual motion. During its years in England, the psalter had a distinct and wide-reaching influence on Anglo-Saxon (and later) artists, who adapted it in their own manner. Though a faithful copy of its original, the Anglo-Saxon Harley Psalter is interestingly different

– not only in its use of coloured inks instead of monochrome, but in its less frenetic style; its figures and landscapes are lively and vigorous, captured in busy activity, but they are less impressionistic, easier to read and understand.

Another fine example of this second style can be seen in the prefatory pages of the *Liber Vitae* (The Book of Life) of the New Minster and Hyde Abbey at Winchester, which dates to 1031 (figs 139 and 140). The book records the names of monks and benefactors of a community, both living and dead, who were prayed for on feast days throughout the year, in anticipation of Doomsday when all would be judged by their deeds written in the eternal Book of Life. This manuscript is important not just for its elegant Utrecht-style drawing, but for its significance as an image of the alliance of ecclesiastical and royal interests. The first of these pages shows King Cnut (r. 1016–35) and his wife Emma/Ælfgyfu presenting a great golden altar cross to the New Minster; above them is Christ in Majesty, flanked by the Minster's patron saints – the Virgin in her role as intercessor for the souls of the dead, and St Peter carrying the key which signifies his role as gatekeeper of Heaven (fig. 139). Cnut, carrying his sword, is crowned by a descending angel who points to Christ, while another angel, also pointing heavenwards, bestows a headdress on his queen. Below, an audience of monks – presumably those of the community commemorated in the Book – gaze up at the scene.

The image is exceptional, not least because of the most unusual presence of an image of the queen, in an age when queens were rarely prominent in the exercise or depiction of power. Ælfgyfu (her Anglo-Saxon name) was, however, an exception; born Emma, sister of the Duke of Normandy, she was of Danish descent, and was married first to the Anglo-Saxon king Æthelred II (r. 978–1016). Her subsequent marriage to the Danish Viking conqueror, Cnut, in 1017 was clearly important in legitimizing him as an acceptable occupant of the English throne, and her personal status is reflected in the public role she had as a witness of charters and a prominent patron. (She later went on to play a significant part in the power-games after Cnut's death, and commissioned an *apologia*, or vindication, of her career as queen, the *Encomium Emmæ Reginæ*.) Her presence in this image signifies this importance, her role as queen shown as divinely ordered by the angel veiling her head, a parallel to the crown which is placed on the head of Cnut. For queen as well as king, this is an image of royal power reinforced by royal patronage of the church.

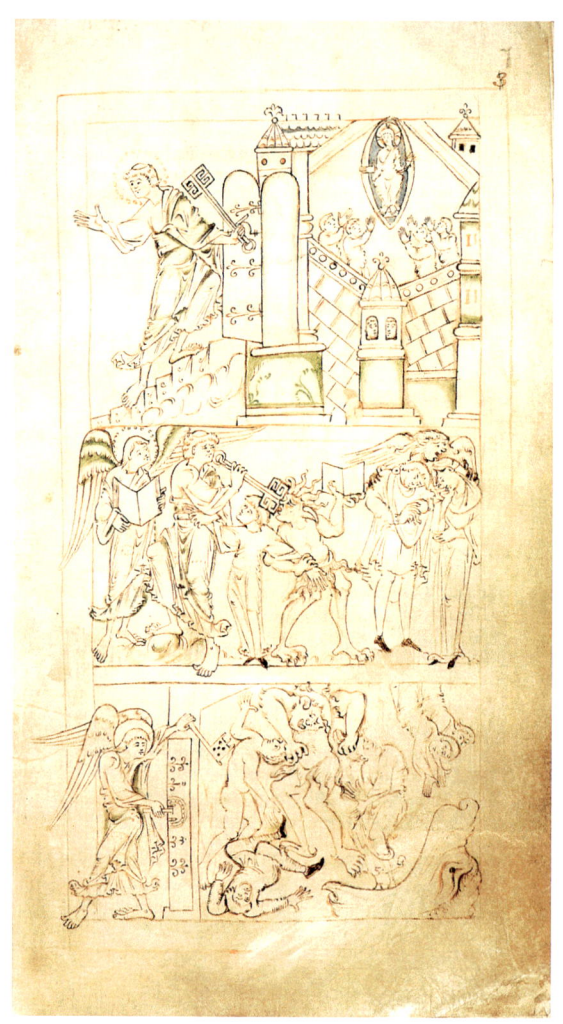

140. The New Minster *Liber Vitae*: scenes from the Last Judgement. Winchester, 1031. 25.5 x 15 cm (British Library, Stowe MS 944, fol. 7r)

The equally remarkable opening which follows (appropriately for a *Liber Vitae*, which memorializes those worthies for whom the Book of Life would account at Doomsday) shows an image of the Last Judgement spread across the two pages. On the left page, saints and archangels escort the Blessed to the gates of Heaven. On the right are three tiers of activity: St Peter welcoming the Blessed into Heaven, where Christ is adored by his saints; below, an archangel holding the Book of Life as St Peter rescues a young soul from the Devil; while the lowermost tier shows an archangel locking the gates of Hell as the Devil throws the damned into the gaping mouth of Hell (fig. 140). Unsurprisingly more animated than the preceding presentation image, this

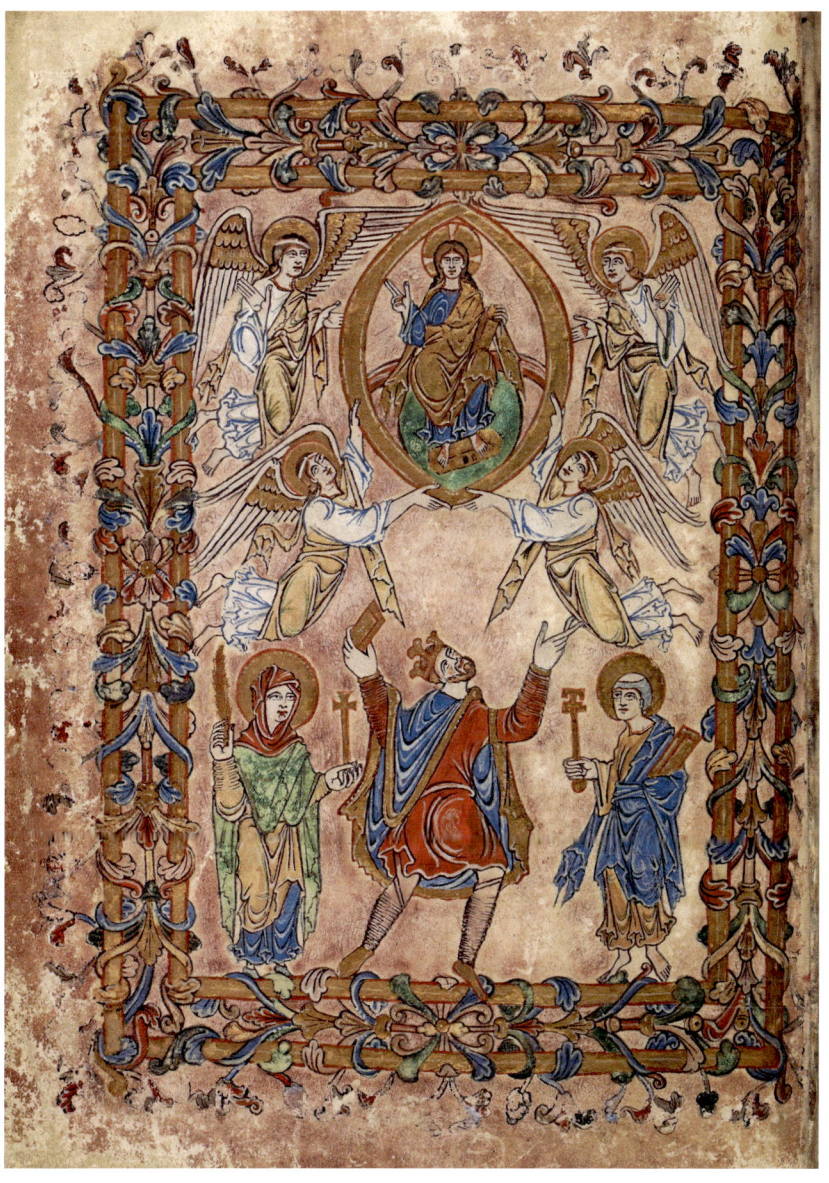

141. The New Minster Charter: dedication page with King Edgar. Winchester, *c.* 966. 28.8 x 16.2 cm (British Library, Cotton MS Vespasian A.viii, fol. 2v)

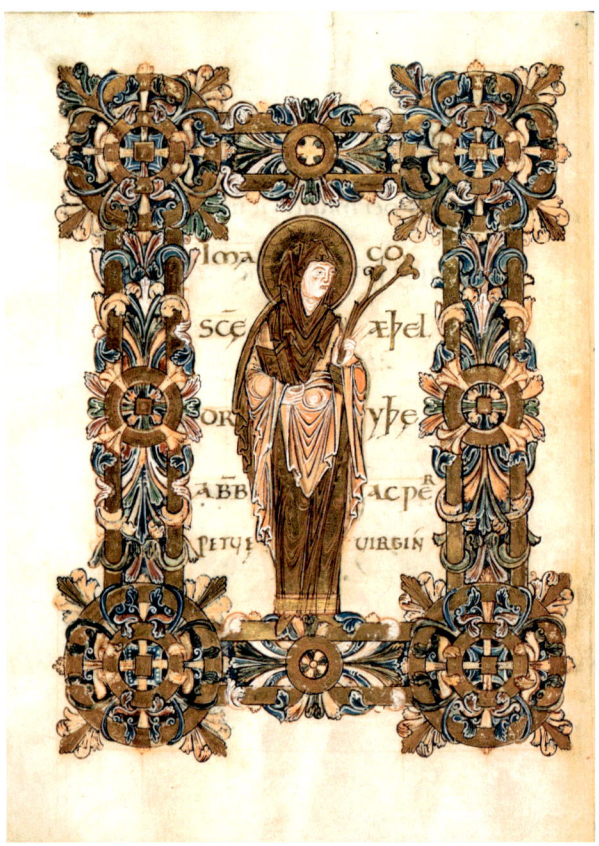 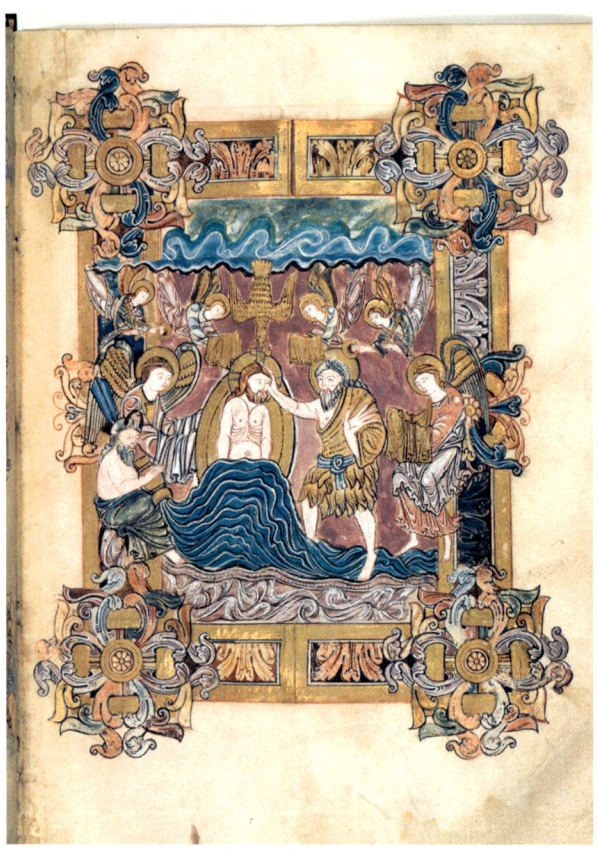

lively drawing in brown ink, with flashes of green, blue and red, epitomizes the second style in its energy and vivid characterization, its gestures and postures.

It is, however, elaborate painted miniatures for which the 'Winchester' school is most famous; richly painted in dense but subtle colours, framed by trellises of tumultuous acanthus leaves and often liberally spiked with gold, these paintings are among the most sophisticated of the early medieval world. The earliest datable painting in the series is the preface to the New Minster Charter, dated to around 966. In this year King Edgar granted a charter to the New Minster at Winchester, commemorating the introduction of Benedictine monks into the house and its adoption of the reformed monastic code (fig. 141). The whole page is painted on a background stained with imperial purple, and the lettering on the introductory pages of the charter is in gold. This, like the *Liber Vitae*, is a royal presentation image. At its centre the king, crowned, and brightly clad in red, blue and gold, presents the charter to Christ in Majesty, who is robed in gold and blue, and seated in a golden mandorla supported by four angels. The Virgin and St Peter stand on either side of the king, and the whole image is framed by a golden trellis in which acanthus

142 (*above, left*). The Benedictional of St Æthelwold: St Æthelthryth (Etheldreda), an Anglo-Saxon royal saint who founded the monastery at Ely. Winchester, 971–84. 29.3 x 22.5 cm (British Library, Add. MS 49598, fol. 90v)

143 (*above, right*). The Benedictional of St Æthelwold: Baptism of Christ. Winchester, 971–84. 29.3 x 22.5 cm (British Library, Add. MS 49598, fol. 25r)

sprays twist and entwine. The king's attitude is one of reverence – his back is turned to the viewer, his knee is bent, his head raised up towards Christ and his hands raised in adoration. This lively icon of devout kingship is far removed from the static image of Æthelstan at St Cuthbert's shrine, though the two representations have a similar purpose. This is an expressive and rather more animated version of the first style as we saw it in drawings; while the sources of the rich acanthus-filled frames foliage so characteristic of this and other prestige Winchester-style painting are to be found in Carolingian manuscripts and ivories, particularly those of the Metz school.

Only a little later, the Benedictional of St Æthelwold reveals the heights to which this art aspired (figs 142 and 143). A benedictional, a rather rare kind of manuscript, is a book of blessings for a bishop to offer on feast days throughout the year. This example was made for Æthelwold at the New Minster, Winchester, while he was Bishop of Winchester from 963 to 984, although internal evidence suggests that it probably dates to 971 or later. It is a sumptuous manuscript, the undoubted masterpiece of the Winchester school, containing twenty-eight surviving full-page miniatures, and two

144. Carolingian ivory casket with the Baptism of Christ. Metz, late 9th or early 10th century. H. 15 cm (Herzog Anton Ulrich-Museum, Braunschweig)

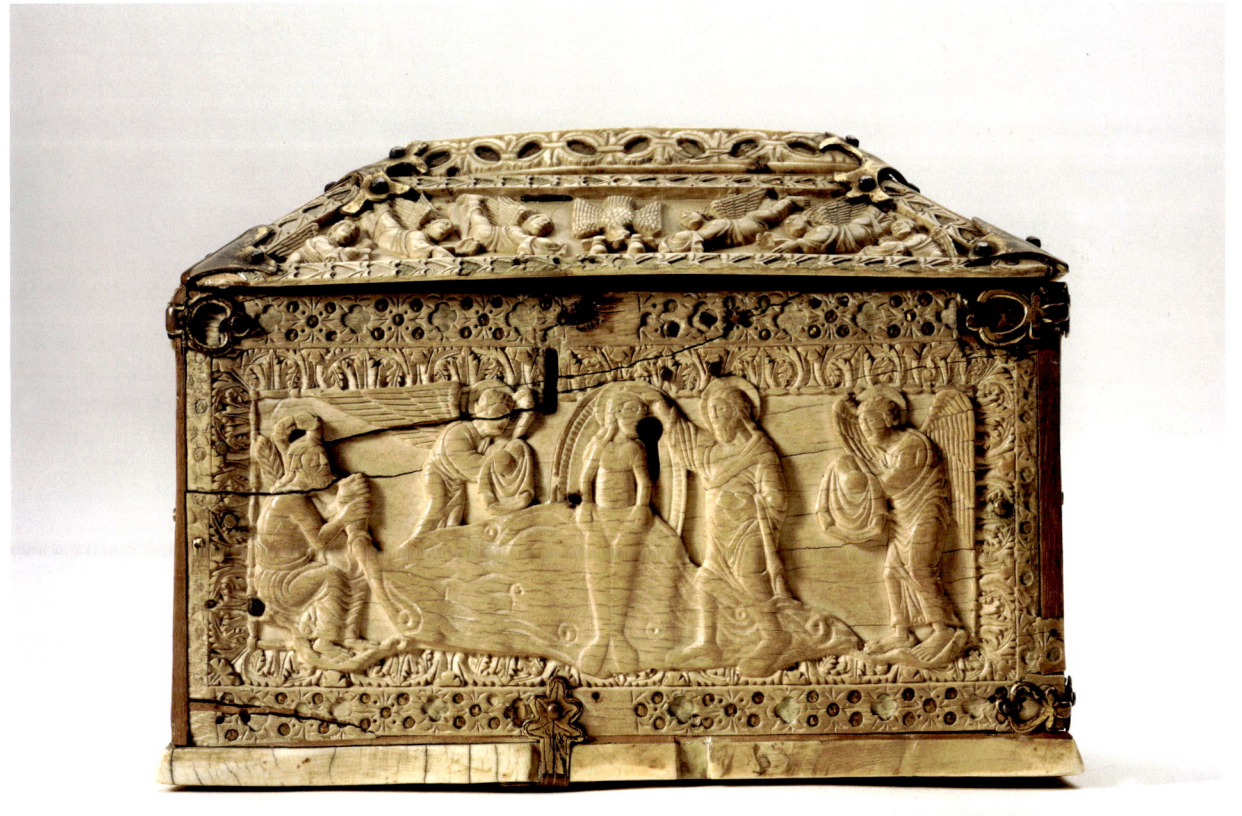

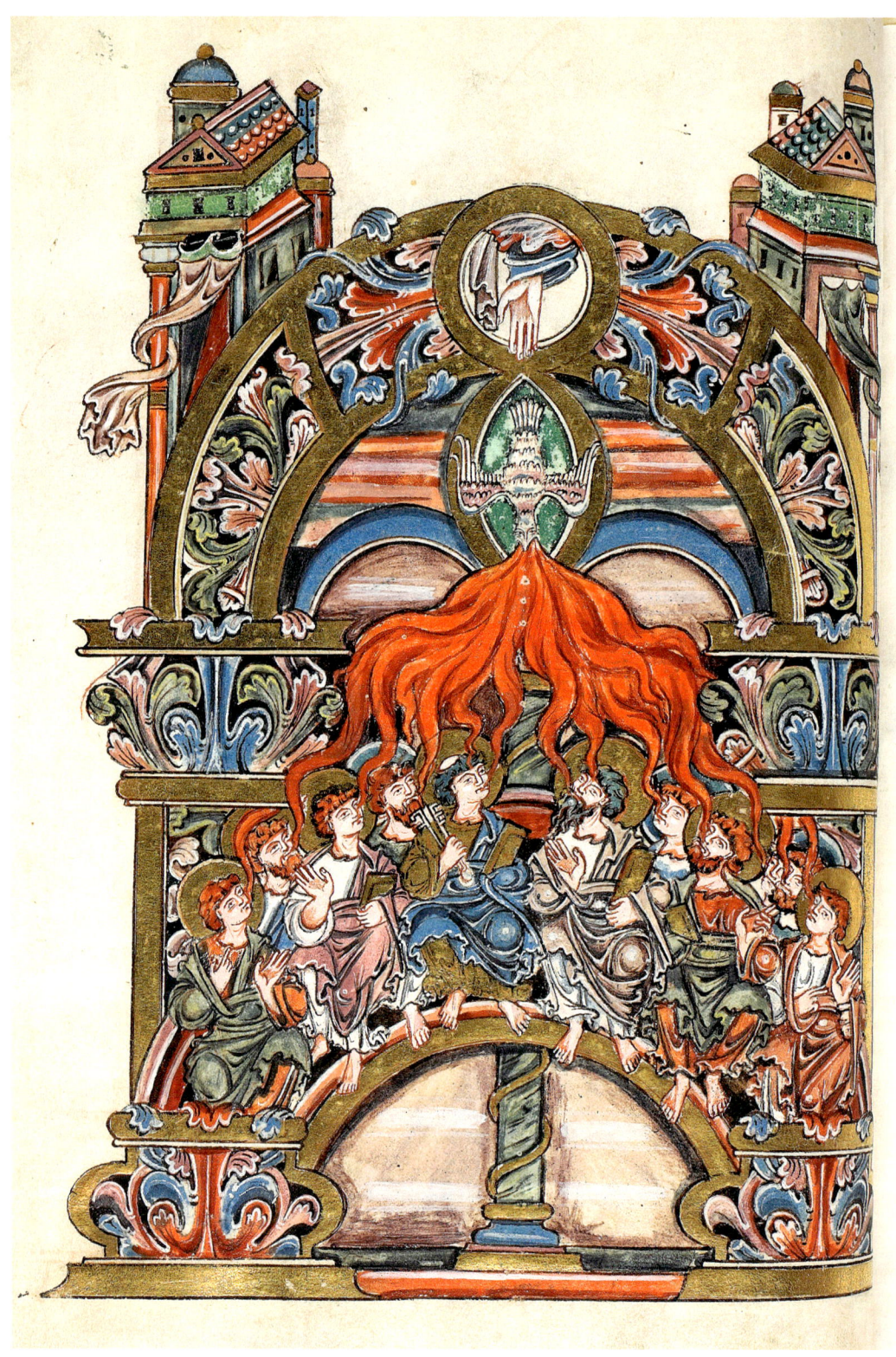

elaborate full-page initials with figures of Christ. It was a book intended to be displayed, as its scribe Godeman implies in a poem written in gold, which tells how Æthelwold commanded that the book should be decorated with 'well-adorned frames' and figures 'with many beautiful colours and gold'. The palette is certainly rich and subtle, with distinctive greenish blues, purples and pinks, along with orange, brown, deep red and bright green, characteristically highlighted with a chalky white, and lavishly adorned with gold. The painting is expertly modelled and the figure style throughout is fairly static, with strongly defined cascading draperies in the manner of the first style – for example, in the figure of St Æthelthryth in her gold and pink robes, framed in a golden trellis of luscious acanthus furls (fig. 142). Many images show a very clear debt to Continental exemplars, particularly, as with the acanthus decoration, to late ninth- and early tenth-century products of the Metz school. The

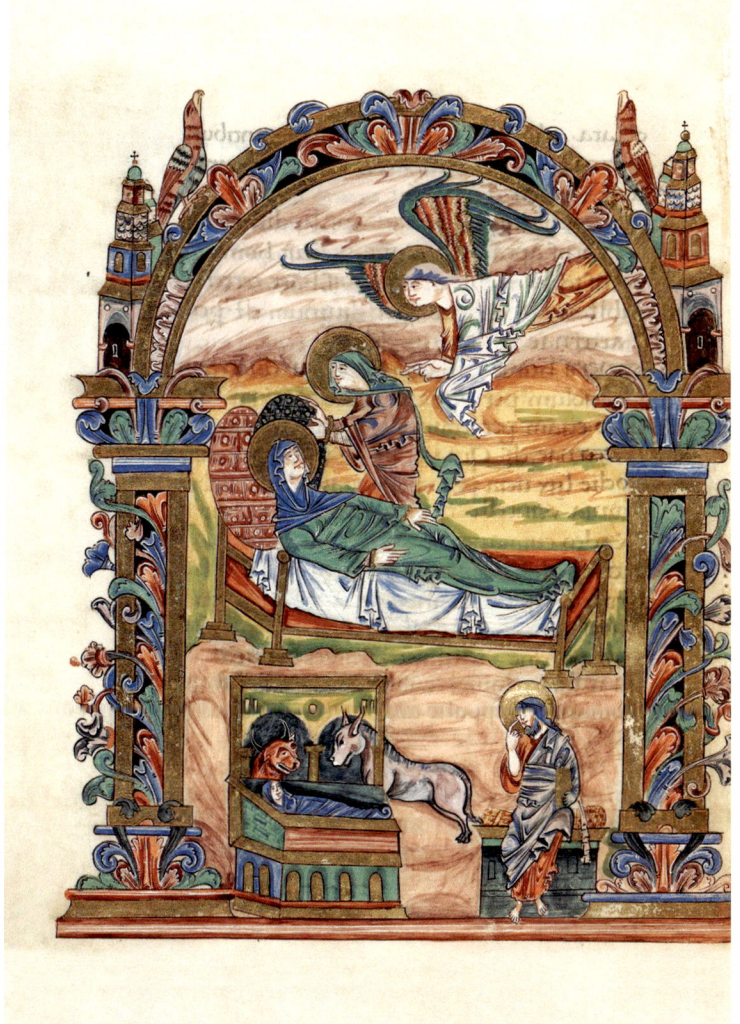

145 (*opposite*). The Benedictional of Archbishop Robert: Pentecost. New Minster, Winchester, *c.* 980. 32.3 x 24.5 cm (Bibliothèque Municipale de Rouen, MS Y.7(369), fol. 29v)

146 (*below*). The Missal of Robert of Jumièges: the Nativity. Winchester, *c.* 1020. 34.2 x 22 cm (Bibliothèque Municipale de Rouen, MS Y.6(274), fol. 32v)

Baptism of Christ (fig. 143), as noted in Chapter 1, clearly shares a model with a similar scene on a Carolingian ivory casket, now in Braunschweig, Germany (fig. 144). The monumentality of the Christ figure and the Baptist reflects something of the style of the Carolingian source, but their busy surroundings – tumultuous clouds of heavenly glory, the turbulence of the River Jordan and its rugged shore, and the frilled and folded draperies of the attendant angels – all combine with the lush acanthus frame to create a dense overall pattern of textures which is much more in tune with Anglo-Saxon taste and tradition. This delight in rich patterning is particularly marked in the miniatures in the Benedictional of St Æthelwold.

Slightly later than the Æthelwold manuscript – perhaps from around 980 – is another benedictional known as the Benedictional of Archbishop Robert (fig. 145). Only three of its original illustrations survive, but these are more than enough to show that this, too, is a splendid product of the New Minster in Winchester, possibly also made for Æthelwold himself. Its palette is rather heavier and bolder than the Æthelwold Benedictional, with lots of rich brown, red, blue and orange, as well as subtler

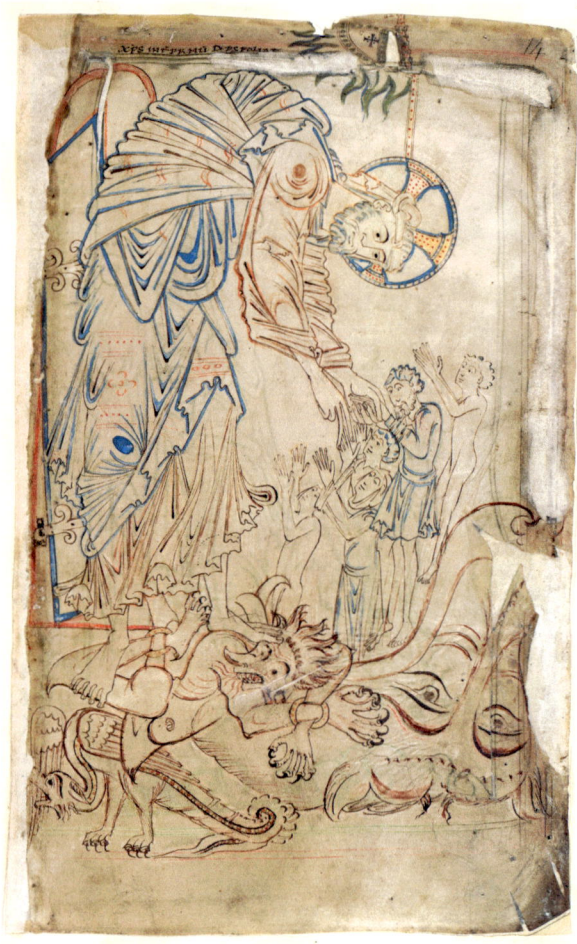

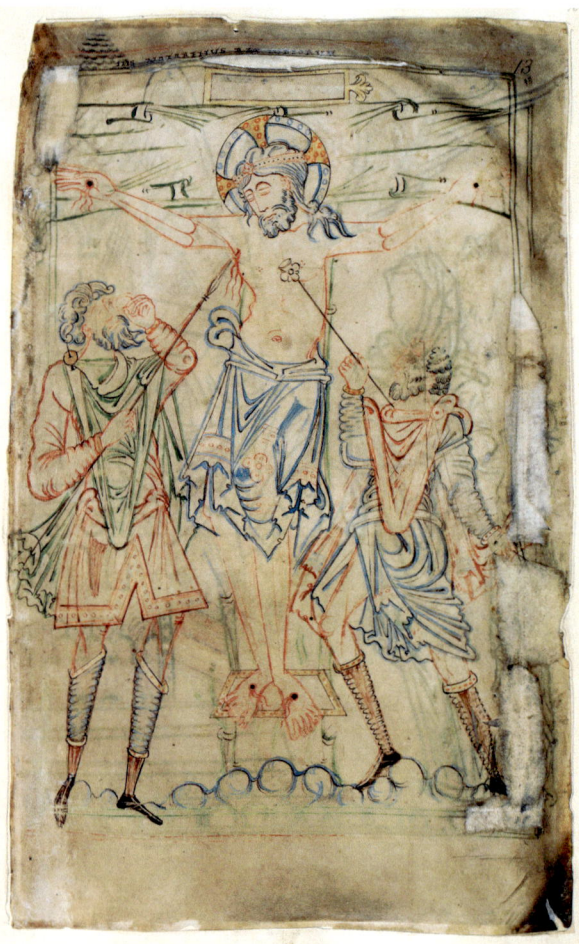

blue-greys and mauve, and white highlighting is again prominent along with plenty of gold. The style is heavier, too, but also less busy, so that there is space around the central figures to allow the eye to rest on them and reflect.

There are many other lavishly ornamented gospel-books and church service books from the late tenth and early eleventh centuries which come close to these examples in ambition and grandeur, among them the Copenhagen Gospels, the silver-decorated Grimbald Gospels, the York Gospels, and the Trinity Gospels.[15] From the early eleventh century, the influence of the Reims style becomes more apparent in these grand painted service books and gospels; supreme among these is the Missal of Robert of Jumièges dating to around 1020 (fig. 146). Its impressionistic, dashing lines, scribbled backgrounds, flickering draperies and long tendrils of acanthus seem to vibrate in sympathy with one another, producing an overall effect which has been rightly described as disturbing. But by the second quarter of the eleventh century a new, harder edge begins to appear in figure drawing. In the Bury Psalter,[16] for

147 (*above, left*). The Tiberius Psalter: the Harrowing of Hell. Winchester, *c.* 1050. 24.8 x 14.6 cm (British Library, Cotton MS Tiberius C.vi, fol. 14r)

148 (*above, right*). The Tiberius Psalter: the Crucifixion. Winchester, *c.* 1050. 24.8 x 14.6 cm (British Library, Cotton MS Tiberius C.vi, fol. 13r)

149. The 'Hereford' Troper:
St Peter's release from
prison. ?Canterbury,
c. 1050. 21.6 x 15.5 cm
(British Library, Cotton MS
Caligula A.xiv, fol. 22r)

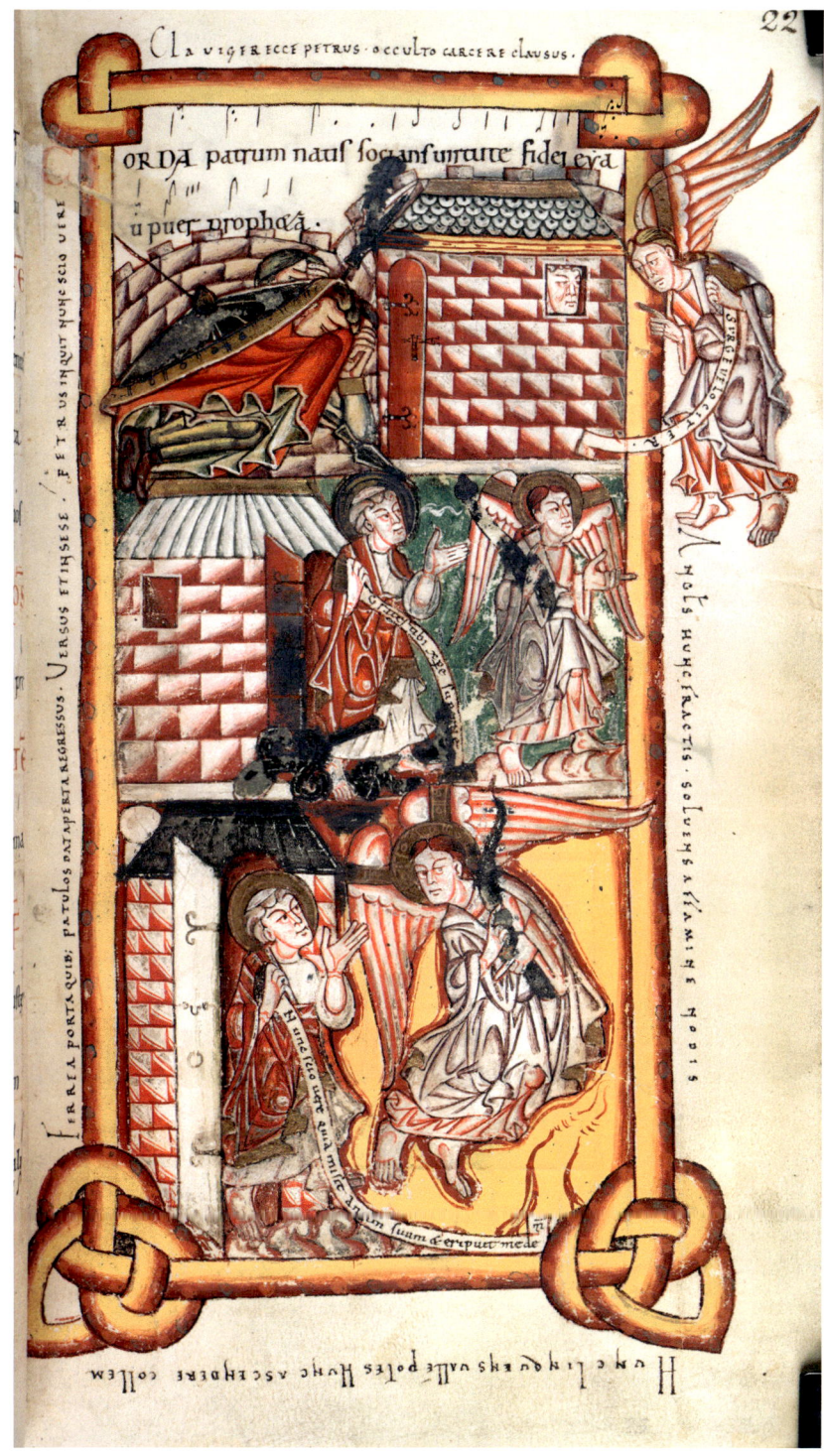

example, which was made at Christ Church, Canterbury, around 1030–35, the margins of the pages are crammed with a riot of line drawings illustrating the text, mostly based on illustrations in the Utrecht Psalter and its copy, the Harley Psalter, and adapted to the marginal format. The expressive gestures and sense of turmoil that we can see in the earlier psalter figures are here enlarged with sweeping lines. Some images are linked down the margins by long scrolls or extended arms, creating a sense of vertical rhythm and movement. The style is impressionistic, with a delicate use of line, but also with a tendency to elongate the figures to a point where long curving or straight lines start to become dominant. A slightly later version of this – arguably as late as 1051 – can be seen in the Crucifixion image in the Judith of Flanders Gospels, where the long, straight folds of the Virgin's garments are stiffened, echoing the lines of the hewn tree of the Cross on which the exhausted figure of Christ is portrayed with great intensity.[17] At much the same time, towards 1050, the Tiberius Psalter takes this hard-edged style a little further, in a dramatic series of illustrations depicting the lives of David and Christ. In the Harrowing of Hell (fig. 147) Christ descends into Hell to rescue the souls of virtuous pre-Christians who had died before the gospel message could reach them. The towering figure of Christ, wrapped in corrugated swathes of draperies, bends over to gently pick up the tiny imploring figures who stand in Hell's mouth. The Crucifixion image (fig. 148) and the two-page opening depicting the tale of David and Goliath (fols 8v and 9)[18] are studies in angularity, full of harsh straight lines which accentuate the violence of both scenes. Though the Tiberius Psalter is entirely illustrated with line drawings, their brown and red outline is emphasized throughout in bright blues, greens, reds and oranges which adds to the dynamic effect. A very different contemporary version of this hard, linear style can be seen in the Crucifixion image in the Arundel Psalter, made at the New Minster around 1060, one of the latest surviving illuminated manuscripts from before the Norman Conquest of England in 1066 (fig. 150). Here, the thickened line is frozen into rigidity, and Christ has become a hieratic figure who stands erect on the Cross, while the flatly linear, static figures of the Virgin and St John express their grief in nothing more than a gesture of the

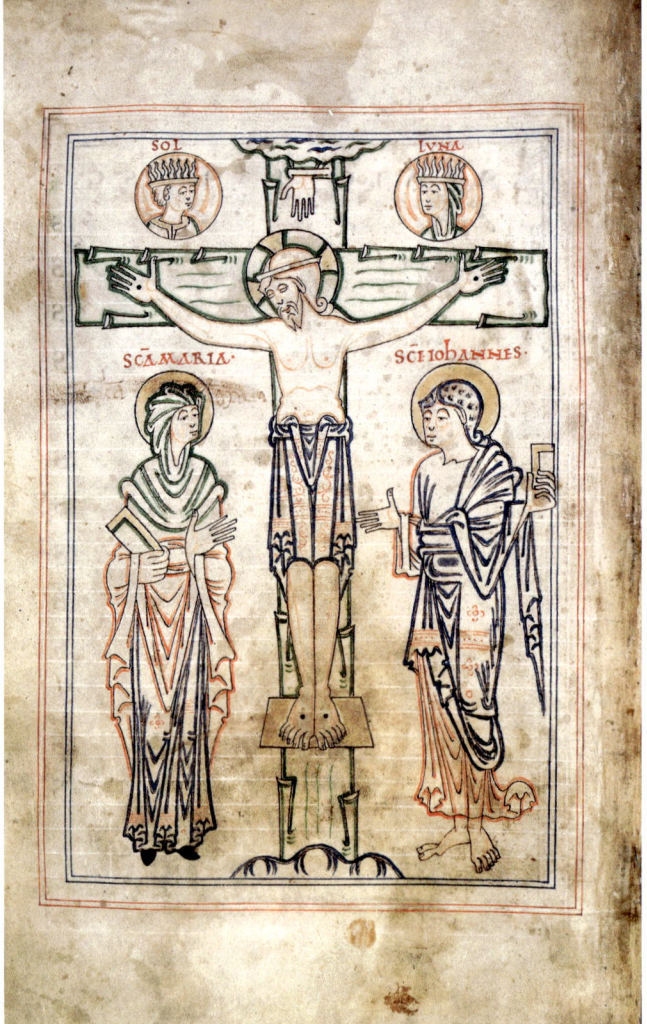

150. The Arundel Psalter: the Crucifixion. New Minster, Winchester, c. 1060. 30.6 x 19.2 cm (British Library, Arundel MS 60, fol. 12v)

hand. It is a far cry from the emotion of Crucifixion scenes in the Ramsey Psalter (fig. 137) or, indeed, the near-contemporary Judith of Flanders Gospels and the Tiberius Psalter.

Towards the end of the Anglo-Saxon period, new influences appear. Two painted manuscripts from around 1050 seem to indicate the beginning of another direction in English art: the Hereford Gospels[19] and the Hereford Troper, a collection of musical chants inserted into the mass (fig. 149). In fact, neither was produced at Hereford, and both have been tentatively ascribed to Canterbury. Their very different style of figure drawing is immediately striking; although both manuscripts share something of the hard-edged trend seen in the Tiberius and Arundel Psalters, and show a typical Anglo-Saxon interest in all-over patterning, their distinctive use of bright colours, harsh, corrugated surfaces and a subtle use of shading reflects new Continental influences from Germany and Flanders, prefiguring the Romanesque style.

151. The Anglo-Saxon Hexateuch: Joseph's brothers at the court of Pharaoh (above), and feasting scene (below). Canterbury, 1040s. Whole page 32.8 x 21.7 cm (British Library, Cotton MS Claudius B.iv, fol. 63r)

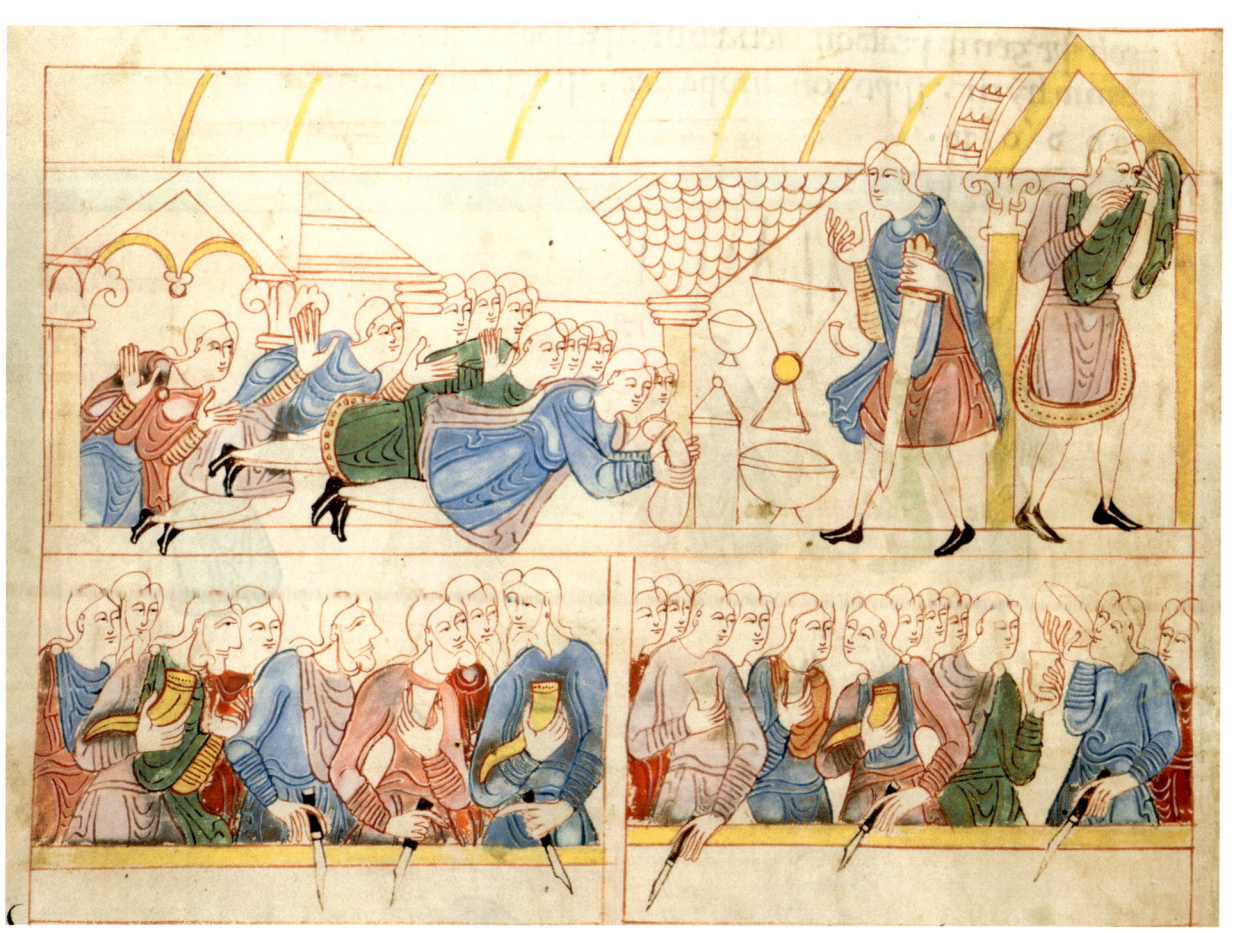

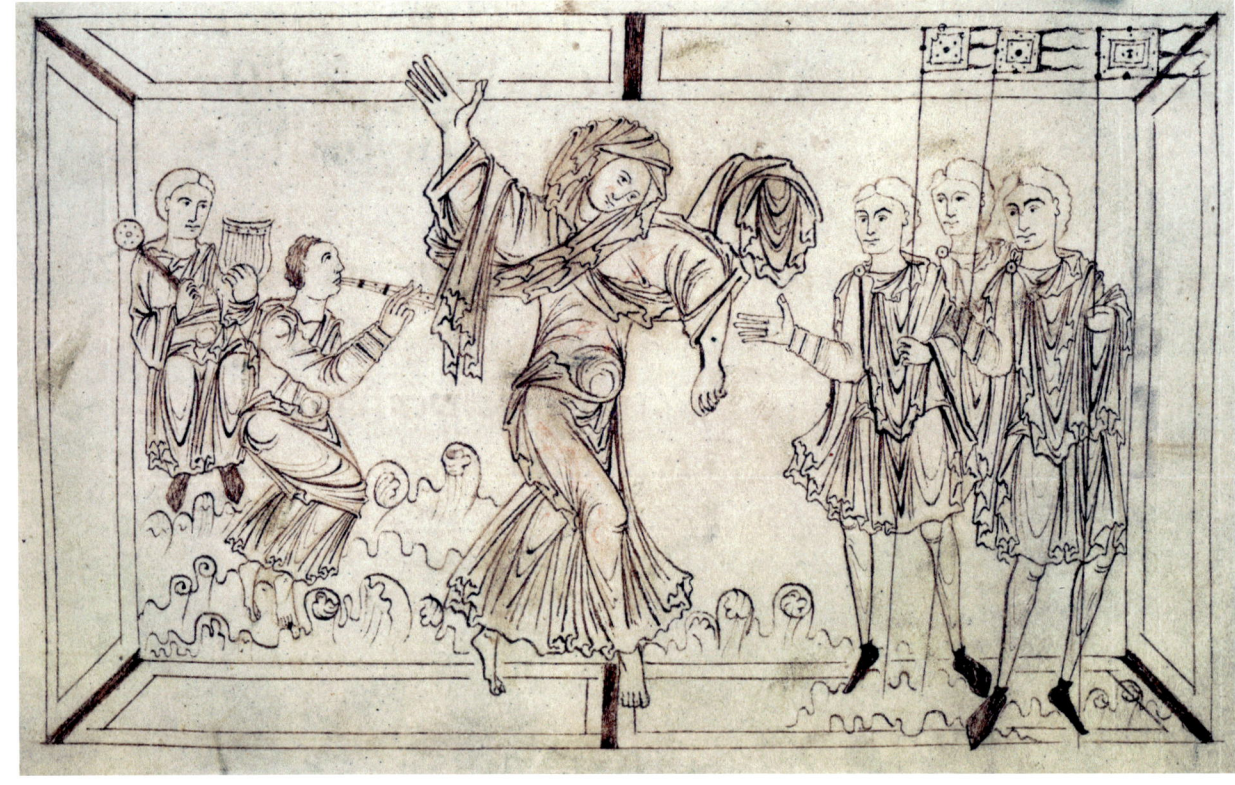

Narrative illustration: manuscripts of the tenth and eleventh centuries

Most of the manuscripts examined so far have been gospels and service books of one sort or another, or documents commemorating royal patronage of the church. But there are many other kinds of decorated Anglo-Saxon manuscripts from this period, which bear witness to a vigorous tradition of narrative art. Most of these have survived because they have religious themes or an educative function, and many are based on Continental models. But the exuberance and accomplishment of some of them testify to the existence of a parallel secular tradition of Anglo-Saxon narrative art, exemplified back in the eighth century by the Franks Casket, and later, by the Bayeux Tapestry. Some of them certainly delight in depictions which, despite a biblical theme, record vivid snatches of contemporary life. For instance, an illustration in the manuscript known as the Old English Hexateuch (the first six books of the Old Testament) shows Joseph's brothers in contemporary Anglo-Saxon dress presenting gifts for the pharaoh, and the ensuing entertainment (fig. 151). The gifts include recognizable Anglo-Saxon vessels and the entertainment is presented as an Anglo-Saxon feast, with the (all-male) company each grasping a drinking horn, and a characteristically Anglo-Saxon angle-backed knife, as they await the food. This is a Canterbury manuscript of the 1040s, in which

152. Prudentius's *Psychomachia*: men abandoning themselves to Luxuria (detail). Late 10th century. Whole page 26 x 18 cm (British Library, Add. MS 24199, fol. 18r)

a cycle of over four hundred lively, idiosyncratic, mostly coloured, drawings bring the Old Testament to life in a totally confident fusion of Anglo-Saxon contemporary culture with the biblical story. Somewhat similar touches are seen in another set of narratives, the Old English Genesis, or Junius manuscript, made at Christ Church, Canterbury, around the year 1000 (see fig. 194).[20] It contains four poems in Old English drawn from the first book of the Bible, with thirty-eight line drawings in the Winchester style. One of its two artists, who has a quirky, rather crude style, displays an eye for vernacular detail, for example in the building of Noah's Ark, in which Noah uses an Anglo-Saxon T-shaped carpenter's axe to produce a craft with a fine North Sea animal-headed prow.

Apart from these Bible-based narratives, there are also works from the period which have themes derived from classical sources, such as Prudentius's *Psychomachia*. This is a Latin poem on the battle of the Vices and Virtues

153 (*right*). Anglo-Saxon Scientific Miscellany: Marvels of the East, detail of an elephant and a two-headed man. ?Winchester, mid-11th century. Whole page 26 x 21.8 cm (British Library, Cotton MS Tiberius B.v, fol. 81r)

154 (*below*). Anglo-Saxon Scientific Miscellany: Calendar, January, detail of a ploughing scene. ?Winchester, mid-11th century. Whole page 26 x 21.8 cm (British Library, Cotton MS Tiberius B.v, fol. 3r)

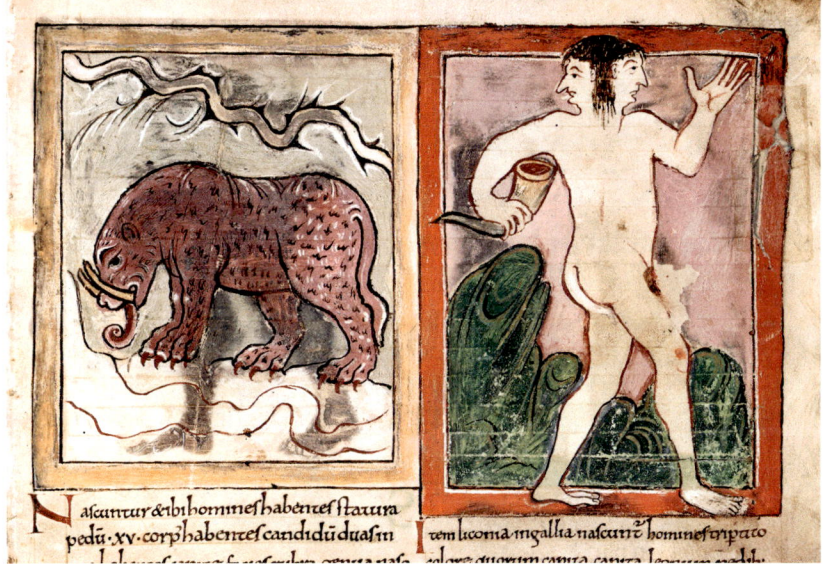

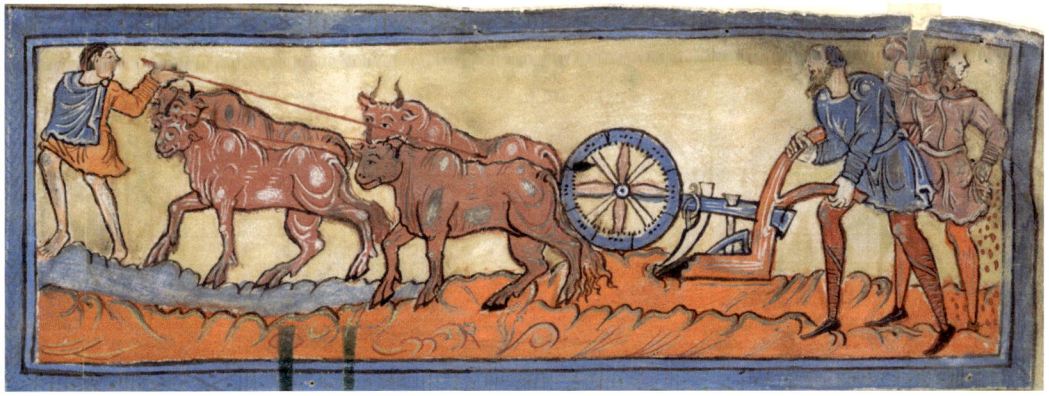

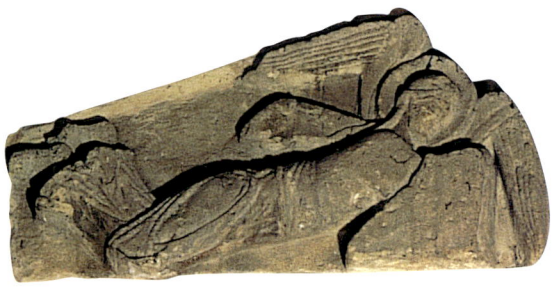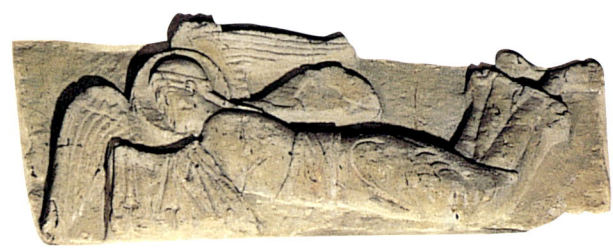

which was evidently much enjoyed in Anglo-Saxon ecclesiastical circles at this time, as no fewer than four copies survive (fig. 152). Although based on a common late Antique model, all four Prudentius manuscripts have touches – drinking horns, some dress styles, tableware and so on – that link the images to contemporary life.

A different kind of manuscript is represented by the reference book known as the Anglo-Saxon Scientific Miscellany, a mid-eleventh-century compilation of geographical, scientific, calendrical and astronomical texts taken from a variety of sources. One of them, the 'Marvels of the East', is a late Roman account (ultimately of Greek origin) of the outlandish people and monsters that inhabit the earth, vividly illustrated with images that include – among many other marvels – an elephant, a two-headed man, men with their heads beneath their shoulders, men who generously give their wives to strangers, a centaur and, to set the scene, a splendid *mappa mundi*, the medieval imagining of the world (fig. 153). The bilingual Latin and Old English text also employs different scripts for the two different languages used to describe these strange mythological beings, underlining its learned nature. The Scientific Miscellany also contains one of the two surviving illustrated Anglo-Saxon calendars, essential works of reference for saints' days and other feasts of the church. This example is brightly painted with busy illustrations of the labours of the months (fig. 154). Although derived from Continental models, they give a lively, if somewhat stereotyped, month-by-month impression of late Saxon activities such as ploughing, haymaking, carting timber and threshing grain.

Images of devotion: sculpture and wall-painting of the tenth and eleventh centuries

Many of the grand ecclesiastical manuscripts would have found their place on altars, destined to be displayed and used in church services and ceremonies. Anglo-Saxon church buildings were in effect the stage on which such rituals were enacted, and indeed there is evidence to suggest that some form of religious dramas,

155 (*above*). Two angels, possibly from a Crucifixion scene. Early 11th century. L. (each) 152 cm (St Lawrence's chapel, Bradford on Avon, Wiltshire)

156 (*below*). Gravestone with hanging lamp. Winchester, late 10th century. H. 62 cm (Winchester City Museums)

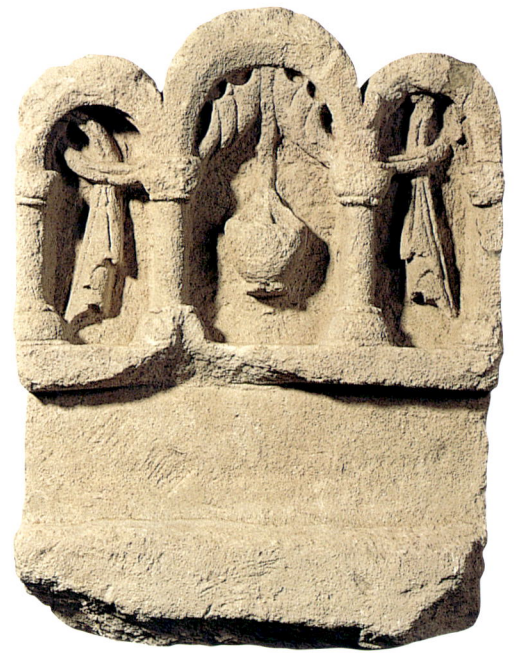

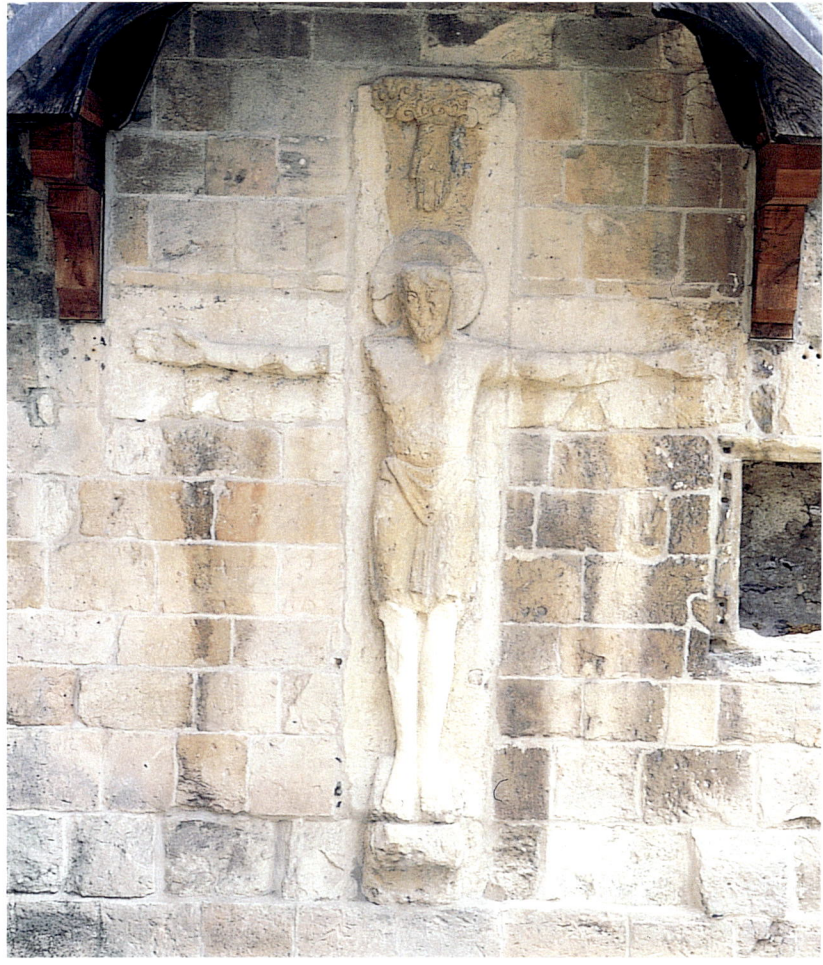

157. Christ on the Cross, set in an outer wall of the church. Mid-11th century (Romsey Abbey, Hampshire)

as well as music, were performed in churches across the land. Certainly the interiors, with their wall-paintings and architectural sculpture, and sometimes upper galleries, would have provided a suitable setting for theatrical forms of worship. With gold-embellished Bibles glittering on candle-lit gold and silver altars, sumptuously decorated shrines, rich vestments, altar cloths and wall-hangings, and the glowing colours of the wall-paintings and internal sculpture, the wealthier Anglo-Saxon churches must have made a dramatic impression.

As noted in the Introduction, wall-paintings are exceptionally rare in Anglo-Saxon England, though descriptions of a few, such as those at Wilton, do survive. The best preserved, still in their original position, are those at Nether Wallop in Hampshire.[21] Here, in images familiar from manuscripts, ivories and architectural sculpture, angels fly upwards to adore the figure of Christ in Majesty (largely destroyed by the insertion of a later chancel arch). The painting of the angels is in a delicate and accomplished version of the Winchester style, with outline drawing in red-brown. A pair of very similar

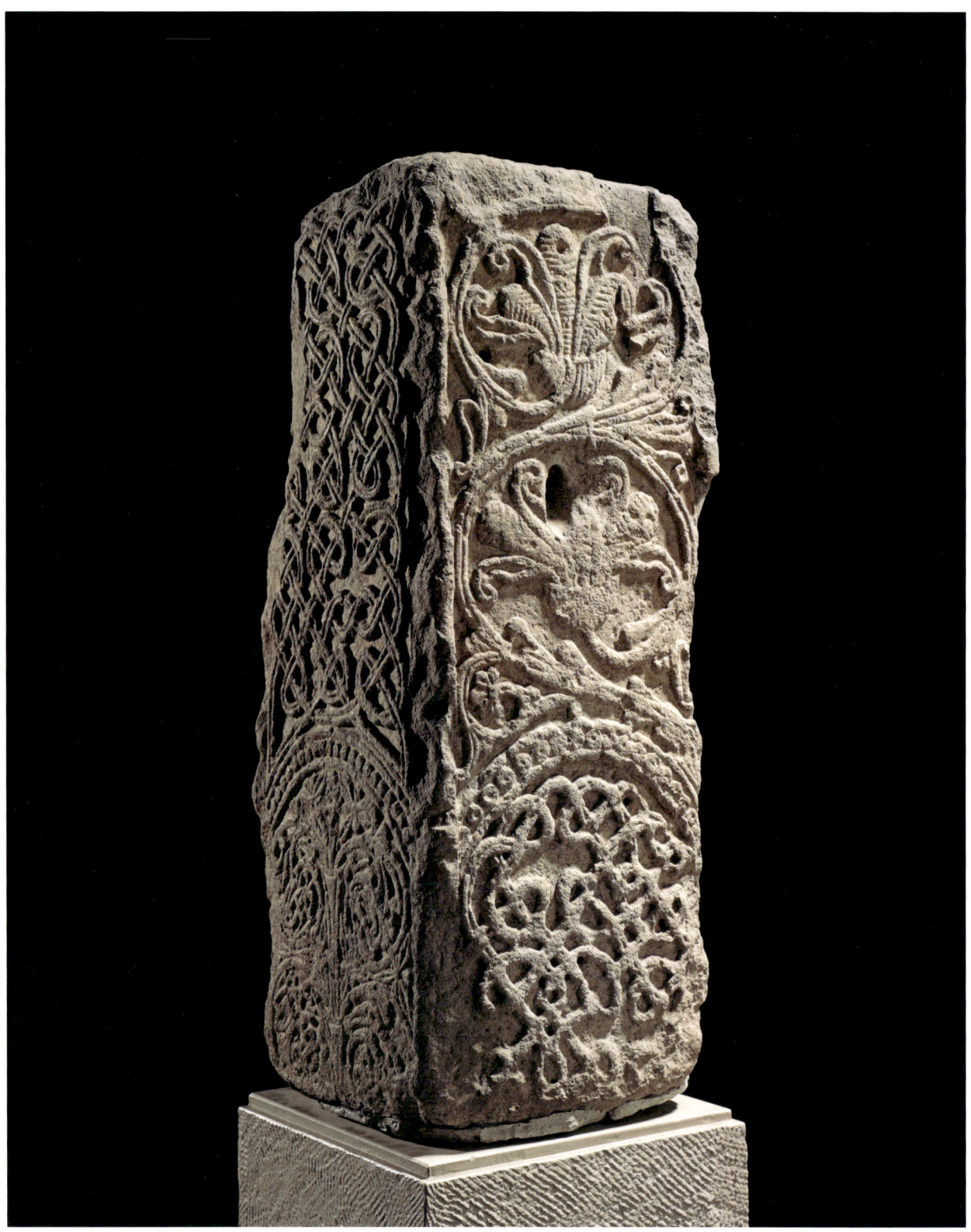

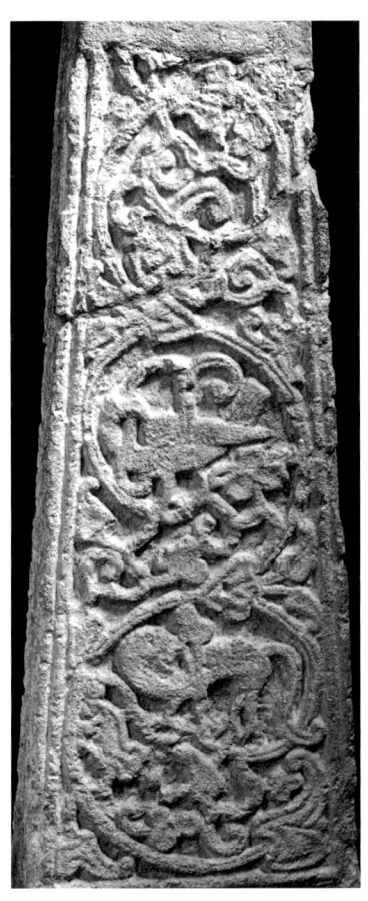

158 (*opposite*). Limestone cross shaft with elaborate plant and interlace ornament. East Stour, Dorset, early 10th century. H. 67 cm (British Museum)

159 (*below*). Cross shaft with early Winchester-style inhabited vine scroll (detail). Early 10th century. H. (whole) 226 cm (St Andrew's church, Colyton, Devon)

sculptured angels, now inserted high up on the walls at the chapel of St Lawrence at Bradford on Avon, Wiltshire, must have accompanied a similar wall-painting or sculpture, possibly of the Crucifixion (fig. 155). There are a number of other interior church sculptures from this period, which hint at similar large-scale compositions. The grievously mutilated Crucifixion group at Breamore church, Hampshire, was once one such; here the faint outlines of Christ, the Virgin and St John, accompanied by personifications of the Sun and Moon, can be traced.[22] Images like these, moving in themselves, would also have made a suitable backdrop for the enactment of religious dramas at Easter and other major feasts of the church.

The exteriors of churches could also be adorned with large sculptures, such as the imposing Crucifixions set into the walls at Langford (Oxfordshire) and Romsey (Hampshire), which would have been a focus for ceremonies (fig. 157). Even some grave-markers have a certain theatrical quality, as exemplified by one from the Old Minster at Winchester, in which a lamp, hanging from the central arch of three, is revealed by curtains which have been looped back on either side (fig. 156) – perhaps a reference to Isaiah 9:2: 'they that dwell in the land of the shadow of death, upon them hath the light shined'.

Alongside these innovative and dramatic large-scale images, other more traditional forms of sculpture occur in southern England, albeit sparsely, adapting to the new styles of the age. An early tenth-century cross shaft from Colyton, Devon, displays the traditional vine scroll as inhabited acanthus foliage, and a near-contemporary cross-shaft fragment from East Stour, Dorset, also follows the tradition with a particularly elaborate scheme of delicate interlace and blossoming acanthus scrolls (figs 158 and 159). Symmetrical plant decoration branching from a central stem also remains popular, as, for example, on a grave-cover fragment from St Oswald's, Gloucester, and on a panel set into the Anglo-Saxon church tower at Barnack, Northamptonshire.[23] Much further north, at Durham, where St Cuthbert's relics had found their final resting-place in 995, a series of linked cross-head fragments, probably dating to the early eleventh century, displays an interest in the Lamb of God of the Day of Judgement.[24] This apocalyptic iconography must have reached Northumbria from the south where, as we shall see, it had become rather prominent in this period.

Images of devotion: ivory carving and metalwork of the tenth and eleventh centuries

We know from documents that many great Anglo-Saxon churches were filled with magnificently decorated altars, crucifixes, altar vessels, candlesticks and candelabra, statues, shrines and reliquaries.[25] Æthelwold's gifts to Abingdon, for instance, were lavish, and of a great variety. Descriptions of the reformed monastery at Ely mention an eleventh-century altar frontal there which was encrusted with gold, silver and jewels, and had an image of Christ in Majesty, with personifications of the Sun and Moon, and four ivory angels. There was also a statue of the enthroned Virgin and Child, from around the year 1000, 'the height of a man' and made of gold, silver and gems. Such large effigies, made in metal-sheeted wood, of Christ, the Virgin and saints, were not uncommon, and some attracted gifts of jewellery – gold rings and necklaces – which were hung upon them (see fig. 190). Handsomely bound books, their covers enriched with gold and silver, studded with gems, and carrying images of Christ in Majesty or the Crucifixion, also appear in the inventories. Almost all of this tremendous metalwork perished, as the fate of the great gold Virgin at Ely, broken up by the Conqueror's men, suggests. Only a few lesser pieces which survived in Continental churches hint at the nature and quality of these vanished church treasures, along with less evidently valuable items such as ivory carvings.

While it is the manuscripts of the tenth and eleventh centuries that first impress themselves on the imagination through their beauty and virtuosity, there are also many ivory carvings of the late Anglo-Saxon period that are their equal in subtlety and power of expression. They are made not of elephant ivory, but from walrus tusks brought back from Arctic waters – one of the more beneficial results of Viking contacts, described in Alfred's additions to his translation of Orosius (see p. 158). Disassociated from their original contexts, it is often difficult to be sure of the original functions of these delicate carvings. Their small scale may reflect not only the constraints of scale imposed by the diameter of the walrus tusk, but sometimes also their use in contexts of personal, rather than public, devotion. Many small ivory panels were probably mounted on the covers of gospels, psalters and prayer books, others perhaps set into reliquaries or crosses.

Ivory carvings derive, of course, from the same sources that influenced manuscripts, and so we can trace in them the early and later styles associated with the Winchester school. Some are particularly close to images in manuscripts, such as the beautiful ivory panel with a Nativity scene, which probably shares a model with the same scene in the contemporary Benedictional of St Æthelwold (fol. 15v), down to the ox and ass peeping over the manger in which the infant Christ lies (fig. 160). Its restrained style links it to the Metz school ivories, such as the Carolingian casket mentioned earlier (see p. 187,

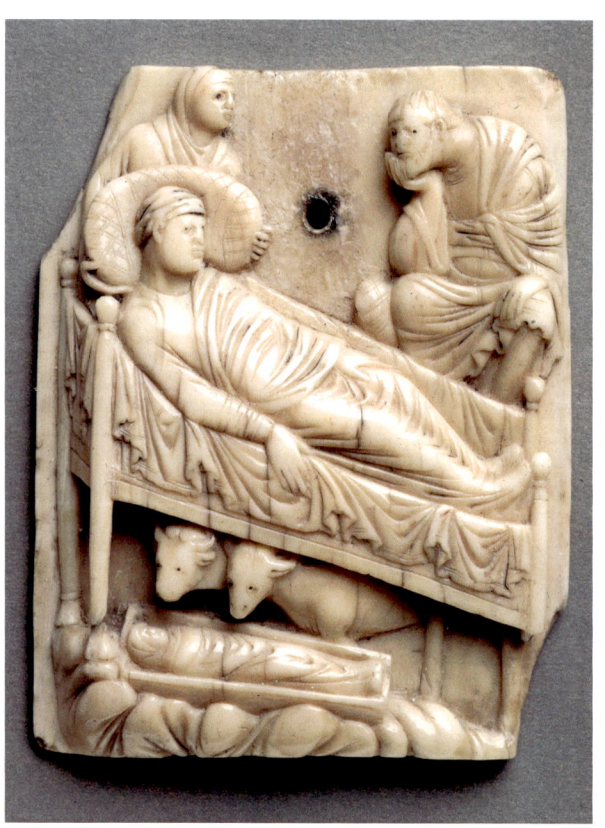

160. Walrus ivory of the Nativity. Late 10th century. H. 8 cm (World Museum, Liverpool)

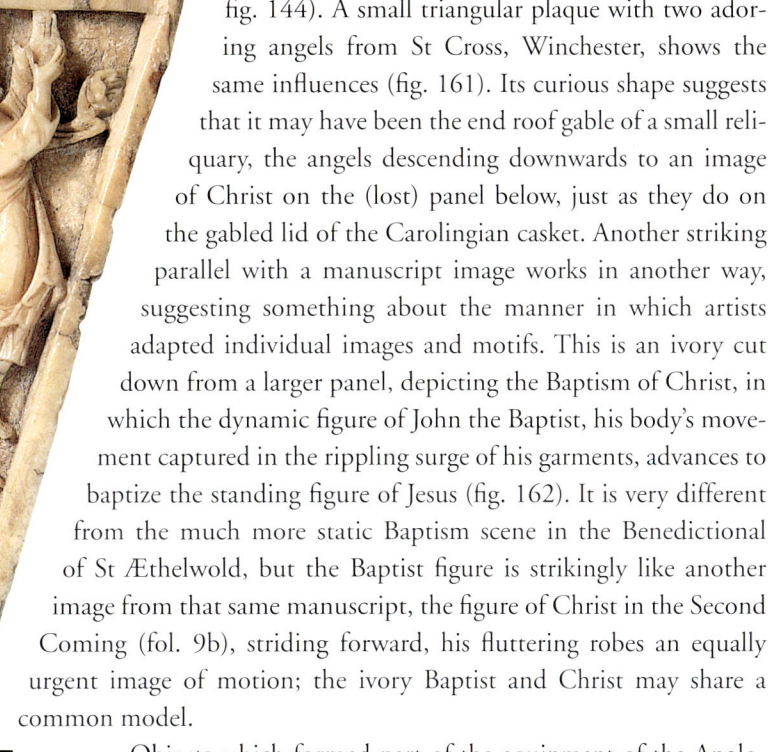

161 (*right*). Walrus ivory with angels. St Cross, Winchester, late 10th century. H. 7.6 cm (Winchester City Museums)

162 (*below*). Walrus ivory depicting the Baptism of Christ. Late 10th century. H. 9.3 cm (British Museum)

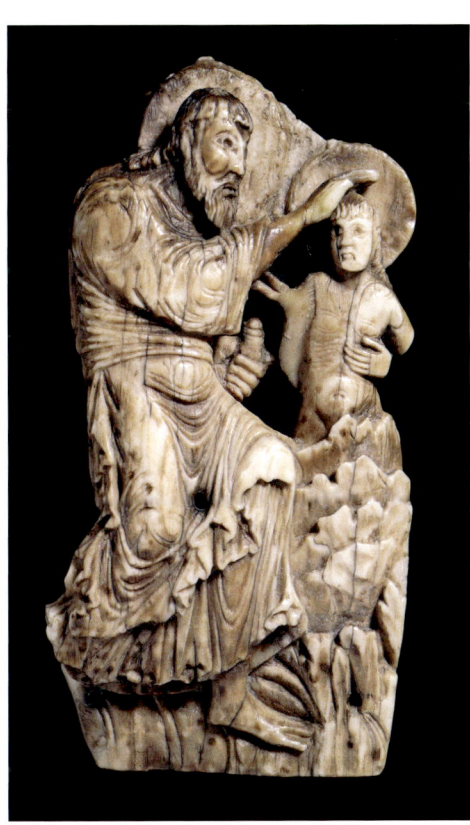

fig. 144). A small triangular plaque with two adoring angels from St Cross, Winchester, shows the same influences (fig. 161). Its curious shape suggests that it may have been the end roof gable of a small reliquary, the angels descending downwards to an image of Christ on the (lost) panel below, just as they do on the gabled lid of the Carolingian casket. Another striking parallel with a manuscript image works in another way, suggesting something about the manner in which artists adapted individual images and motifs. This is an ivory cut down from a larger panel, depicting the Baptism of Christ, in which the dynamic figure of John the Baptist, his body's movement captured in the rippling surge of his garments, advances to baptize the standing figure of Jesus (fig. 162). It is very different from the much more static Baptism scene in the Benedictional of St Æthelwold, but the Baptist figure is strikingly like another image from that same manuscript, the figure of Christ in the Second Coming (fol. 9b), striding forward, his fluttering robes an equally urgent image of motion; the ivory Baptist and Christ may share a common model.

Objects which formed part of the equipment of the Anglo-Saxon altar, or which were formerly attached to reliquaries, croziers or books, are naturally prominent among this material. A magnificent reliquary cross in the Victoria and Albert Museum (fig. 163) consists of an ivory figure of Christ attached to a filigree decorated gold cross, set with enamelled roundels with evangelist symbols and a *titulus* (the panel with the name of Jesus in Latin). The metalwork and enamelling is of late tenth- or early eleventh-century Continental origin, but the moving figure of the suffering Christ is close in style and sensitivity of execution to the great Crucifixion image in the Ramsey Psalter (fig. 137). The cross has an original suspension loop, but is probably too heavy to have been worn regularly; it may have been suspended above an altar. In its superb quality and its fine gold setting, it is a unique witness to those lost crosses described in documentary sources, such as the gold and ivory cross which Æthelstan donated to the shrine of St Cuthbert.

The figure of Christ is usually accompanied, as in the psalter image, by the two mourning figures of the Virgin and St John. A pair of such figures survives from an ivory Crucifixion group, from the Abbey of St Bertin at St Omer in northern France – a monastery with close ties to England and where Anglo-Saxon scribes are known to have worked (fig. 164). These consummately beautiful carvings, made towards the end of the tenth century, were certainly the work of an Anglo-Saxon artist well acquainted with the style of the grandest Winchester manuscripts, whether he was active in England or at St Bertin. Exquisitely carved in the round and, like many of these ivories, with dark glass inlays for their eyes, the slender figures express their grief in gesture and facial expression. Emotion is transferred into the cascades of shivering drapery which descend from the Virgin's head and hand, raised to her weeping face, while the more robust figure of St John suggests a physical embodiment of grief, in contrast to the Virgin's spiritual anguish.

Two rare survivals of Anglo-Saxon church equipment from the first half of the eleventh century – a reliquary cross in Brussels Cathedral and a portable altar now in the Cluny Museum in Paris – are among the few objects of precious metalwork associated with worship in this period, both preserved because they went abroad. Only the back and sides of the cross survive, the presumably more valuable front having been stripped off (fig. 165). It would originally have carried a Crucifixion scene. What remains are engraved, partly gilded, silver sheets with, at the centre of the cross, an image of the Lamb of God of the Book of Revelation, holding the Cross and Book of Judgement, and surrounded by symbols of the four evangelists, one on each terminal. This is an unusually literate object.

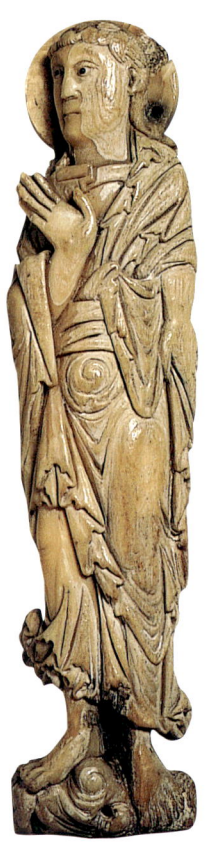

A prominent inscription names its maker as Drahmal, and round the sides, interspersed with Anglo-Scandinavian Ringerike-style decoration, are two longer texts in Old English. The first consists of two lines from a version of the poem known as the *Dream of the Rood*, which we have encountered before (see p. 88), on the great eighth-century stone cross at Ruthwell: 'Cross is my name; once, trembling and drenched with blood, I bore the mighty king'. The second inscription records that two brothers, Æthelmær and Æthelwold, had the cross made for the glory of Christ and the soul of their brother, Ælfric. Here the salvation which comes through Christ's sacrifice

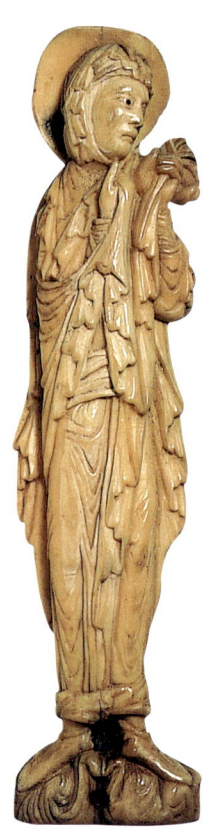

163 (*above*). Gold reliquary cross with enamels, and walrus ivory figure of the crucified Christ (cross, Ottonian workmanship; ivory figure of Christ, Anglo-Saxon), *c.* 1000. H. of cross 18.5 cm (Victoria and Albert Museum, London)

164 (*left*). Walrus ivory figures from a Crucifixion group: the Virgin Mary (left) and St John (right). St Bertin, northern France. Anglo-Saxon, *c.* 1000. H. of each 12.5 cm (Musée Sandelin, St Omer)

on the Cross is combined with images associated with the Last Judgement that awaits everyone, an iconography which becomes common in this period, and which, of course, is directly relevant to the fate of the dead brother's soul.

The powerful and long-standing idea of the Cross as a living tree, which is inherent in the poem, and often visually depicted in manuscripts of this period, is also presented on the portable altar, in a small image of the Crucifixion on the upper edge (fig. 166). The altar is made of the stone porphyry, prized since Roman times for its imperial deep purple colour, and often used in portable altars because of its symbolic colour and rarity. It is fixed on an oak base and partly encased by a border of silver plates. These are decorated with evangelist symbols, the Virgin and St John with the archangels Raphael and Gabriel, symbolizing heaven and earth united in grief, and on the lower edge, directly below the Crucifixion, the Agnus Dei. Latin inscriptions around the sides describe these images. Like the Brussels cross, it links the redemptive message of the Crucifixion with the Doomsday image of the Lamb, but both images are also connected here with the celebration of the mass. At the heart of that is Christ, the Lamb of God that takes away the sins of the world; so the imagery reflects the purpose of the altar on which the mass is celebrated. Like many other Anglo-Saxon liturgical objects, the seemingly straightforward cross and portable altar in fact carry quite complex layers of meaning in their iconography and their inscriptions, to be understood and meditated on.

Some more enigmatic items which may also represent church equipment are three openwork cast

165 (*above*). Silver-sheeted oak cross with Old English inscriptions, the Agnus Dei and evangelist symbols. Second quarter of the 11th century. H. 54.9 cm (Cathedral of St Michel and St Gudule, Brussels)

166 (*right*). Porphyry portable altar with silver-gilt casing, with Agnus Dei, the Crucifixion, evangelist symbols and angels. Second quarter of the 11th century. L. 26.1 cm (Musée de Cluny, Paris)

bronze objects from the later tenth and eleventh centuries, which have been described as censer covers.[26] Most are about 11 cm high, but more recently three much smaller ones have been found, which could not have had the same function. All take the form of a gabled structure rather like a church tower. On the most elaborate, from Pershore in Worcestershire, the gables are represented as shingled, and the roof sits on arcades below (fig. 167). An inscription proclaims that it was made by Godric, perhaps the same goldsmith as one who around 1050 is recorded as having made a gold and silver gem-studded shrine at the nearby abbey of Evesham. If these distinctive objects, the larger of which have attachment lugs at the base, were indeed the upper parts of censers, it seems odd that no matching lower parts survive. Such definite Anglo-Saxon censers as do survive are all bowl-shaped and not designed to carry a cover. In addition, contemporary manuscript depictions of censers show them as lidded, but round in shape and, of course, suspended on chains, which these objects cannot have been.[27] All of this suggests that these singular fittings probably had some other function – perhaps, given their openwork construction, as components of lamps or candelabra, or as decorative finials from furniture.

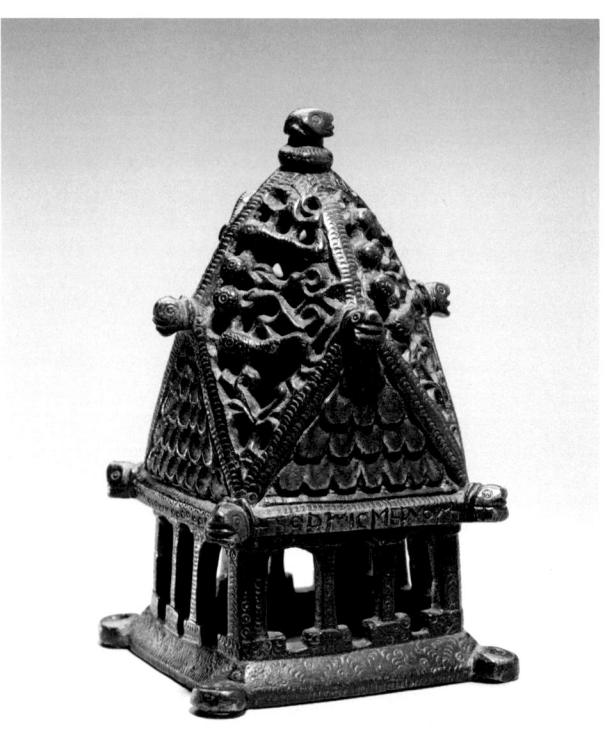

167. Copper-alloy house-shaped cover, inscribed 'Godric made me'. Pershore, Worcestershire, mid-11th century. H. 9.7 cm (British Museum)

Another puzzling item is a small Winchester-style oval ivory box with miracle scenes (fig. 168). Its unusual iconography has not been fully explained, though it seems to refer to a miracle connected with the recovery of a lost chalice.[28] The prominent scene of celebration of a mass suggests that it may have functioned as a pyx, in which the host (the bread reserved for the mass) was kept. More easily recognizable are a number of late tenth- and eleventh-century fine walrus-ivory croziers, both the T-shaped type common in the early medieval period, and the more familiar scroll of a shepherd's crook. Some, like the one found in the rectory garden at Alcester in Warwickshire (fig. 169), were originally very grand, decorated with gemstones and pearls, and sheets of gold, tiny traces of which still survive. It reminds us that a number of these ivories would have been richly embellished, not only with precious metal and gems, but also, like sculpture, through painting.

Smaller ivory panels, including a number of Crucifixion scenes, and images of the Virgin and Child, and Christ in Majesty, were probably set into book covers, or may have adorned portable altars or reliquaries. A powerful Christ in Majesty originally had a blue-painted background, and traces of gold leaf are present over the clothing, throne, hair and crown (fig. 172).[29] Other

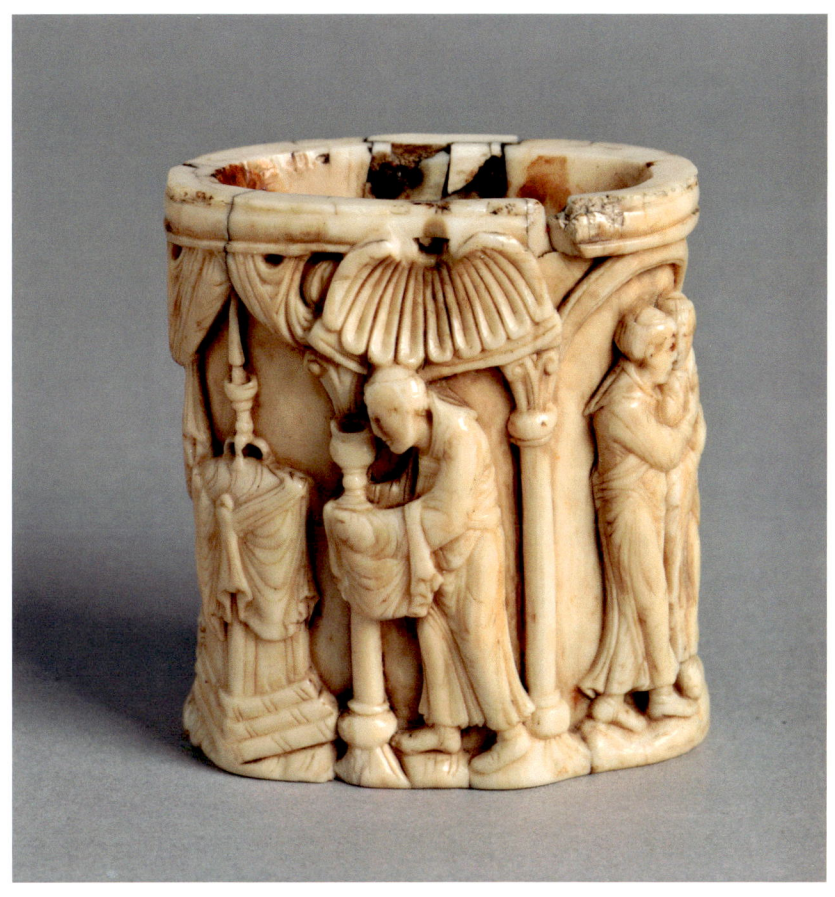

168. Walrus ivory oval container with miracle scenes. Second quarter of the 11th century. H. 10 cm (Victoria and Albert Museum, London)

169. Walrus ivory crozier head, with the risen Christ in a mandorla; originally inlaid with gold. Alcester, Warwickshire, *c.* 1000. L. 14 cm (British Museum)

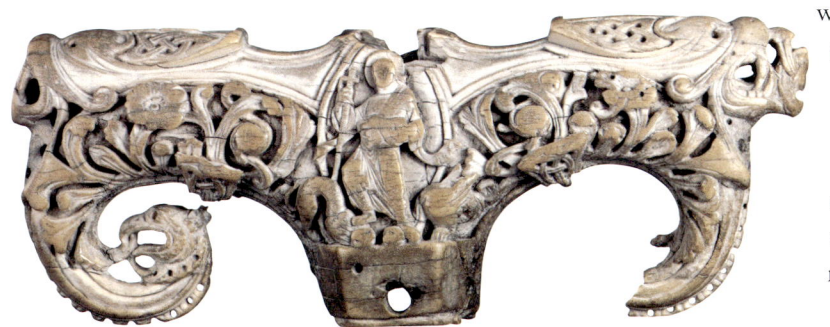

pieces may have been made to be worn. An imposing double-sided carving, which is evidently from a large quatrefoil-shaped cross (the lateral arms are missing, but their attachment dowels survive) also has a suspension hole at the top (fig. 171). This, and the marked wear on its back, suggest that it was worn as a pectoral cross. The principal side depicts Christ in Majesty and the back, the Agnus Dei with evangelist symbols; its St Omer provenance suggests that it may have been produced by one of the Anglo-Saxons based at the monastery of St Bertin, in the first third of the eleventh century. Fragments of gilded metal attached to the background indicate that its original appearance was even grander. Another possible pectoral cross is a remarkable openwork reliquary cross of the mid-eleventh century, with a decorative suspension loop at the top (fig. 170). It has a hinged lid at the front; this, and the openwork construction was evidently designed to reveal a gold or silver reliquary within.

The elegant decoration is constructed around an iconography of the inhabited Tree of Life, which contains within it the archer as a symbol of the Word of God, and the image of the Agnus Dei surrounded by evangelist symbols.

An equally extraordinary object belongs to the same mid-eleventh-century horizon, an almost unique surviving example of wood carving from this period; it is a small house-shaped boxwood casket carved with scenes from the life of Christ (fig. 173). Its function is uncertain, though its iconography and hinged, lockable, lid suggest that it most probably served as a container for the sacraments, rather than as a reliquary. Stylistically, its rather squat and angular figures embody hints of the Romanesque style, already beginning to take shape on the eve of the Conquest, recalling the German and Flemish influences seen in the miniatures in the 'Hereford' Troper and Hereford Gospels (see p. 191, and fig. 149).

From much the same period, though more mainstream in its style, an intricately carved ivory pen case offers a rather different set of images (fig. 174). Although it was evidently made for a literate, probably ecclesiastical owner, its exuberant decoration shows a relish for strange creatures and men in vigorous activities – archery, hunting, delving – that recall the vernacular style of some of the illustrated narratives; stylistically, it resembles some manuscripts from the monastery of St Bertin, where Anglo-Saxon influence was strong.[30] Dragons swallowing smaller beasts decorate both ends, not unlike manuscript depictions of Hell's mouth, but a little less threatening. Perhaps these images are intended to recall the wording of some of the Psalms, and so might suggest a contemplative theme – it is hard to be sure in a period where

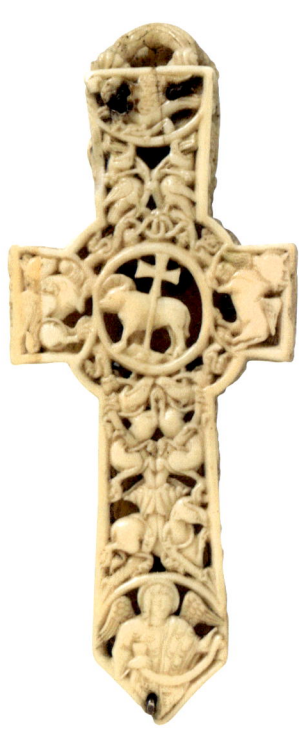

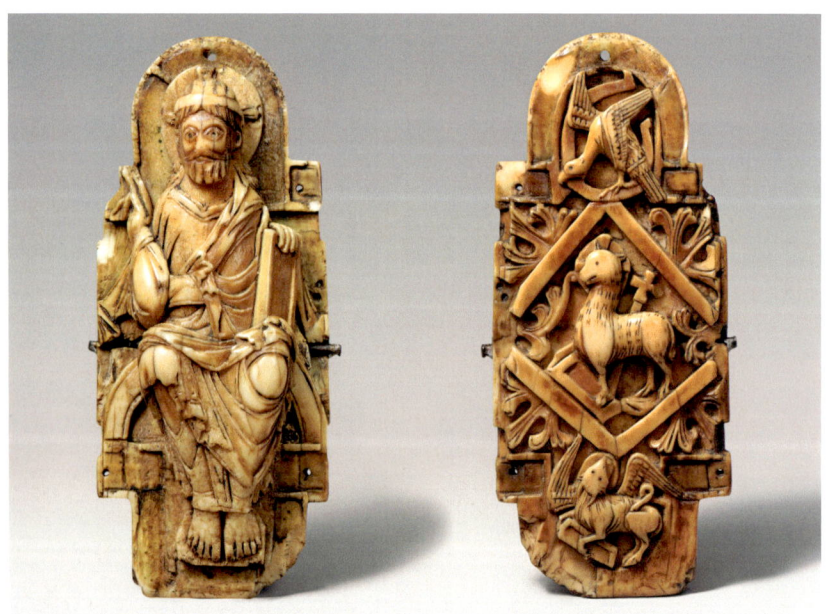

170 (*above*). Walrus ivory openwork crucifix reliquary, with Agnus Dei and evangelist symbols. Mid-11th century. L. 11.6 cm (Victoria and Albert Museum, London)

171 (*left*). Double-sided walrus ivory of Christ in Majesty, with Agnus Dei on the reverse. Early 11th century. H. 14.9 cm (Metropolitan Museum of Art, New York)

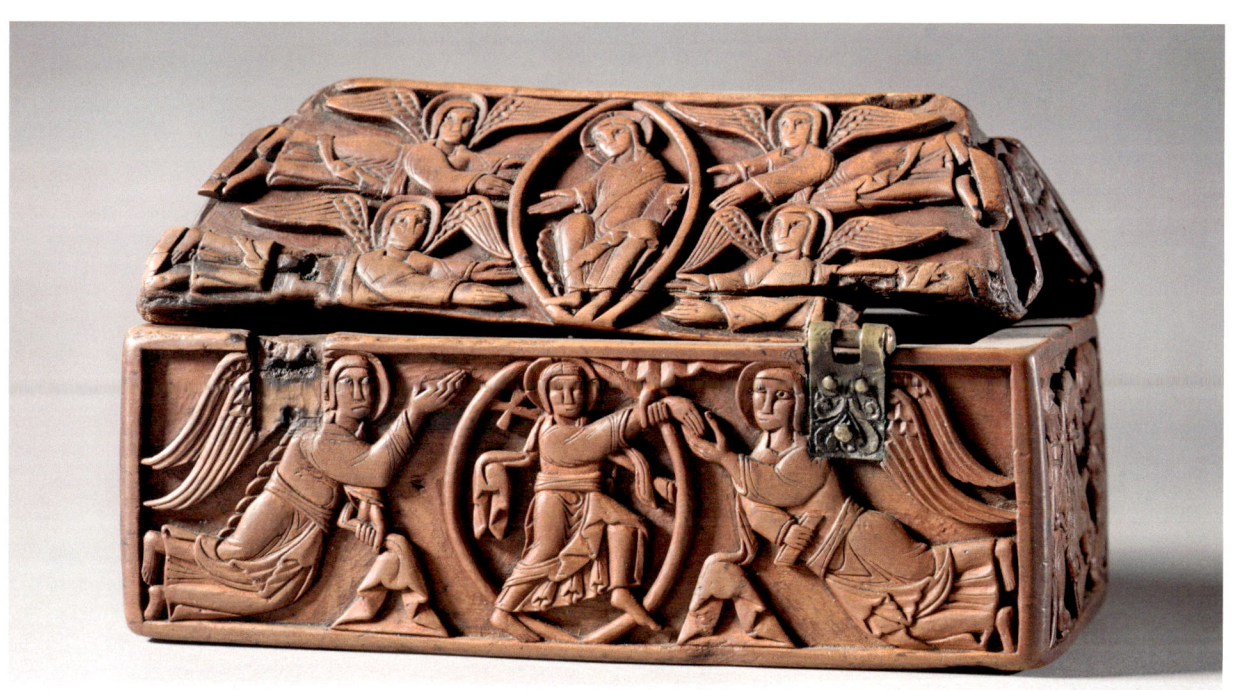

the imagery of the sacred and the secular worlds interpenetrated each other to such a degree. The flourishing inhabited Tree of Life on the lid certainly not only recalls the borders of illustrations in religious manuscripts, but also the pervasive acanthus decoration, peopled by birds and beasts, which decorates purely secular bone and bronze items of dress, such as belt fittings (fig. 175).

A handsome openwork panel in the Cluny Museum in Paris, probably from a casket, and ornamented with dense Winchester-style foliage crawling with birds and beasts, is as likely to be from a secular container as from one made for church purposes.[31] Other fine ivory and metal objects with a more practical purpose include seal-dies, both of monarchs – as in the surviving battered wax impression of Edward the Confessor's seal – and noblemen and high-status ecclesiastics, such as that of Godwin, decribed as a minister, or *thegn*, who shares a double die with a nun 'given to God', Godgytha (fig. 176). There is a close affinity between the images used on coins and those used on some of these seal-dies, not only in the use of an inscription surrounding the image, but in the posture and attributes of the image itself: both are images of power and authority. Indeed, it is quite possible that the same craftsmen were responsible for cutting both coin- and seal-dies.

172 (*above*). Walrus ivory (originally painted) with Christ in Majesty, perhaps from a book cover. *c.* 1000–20. W. (max) 5.8 cm (Victoria and Albert Museum, London)

173 (*below*). Boxwood casket with scenes from the Life of Christ (back view). Mid-11th century. L. 15.7 cm (Cleveland Museum of Art)

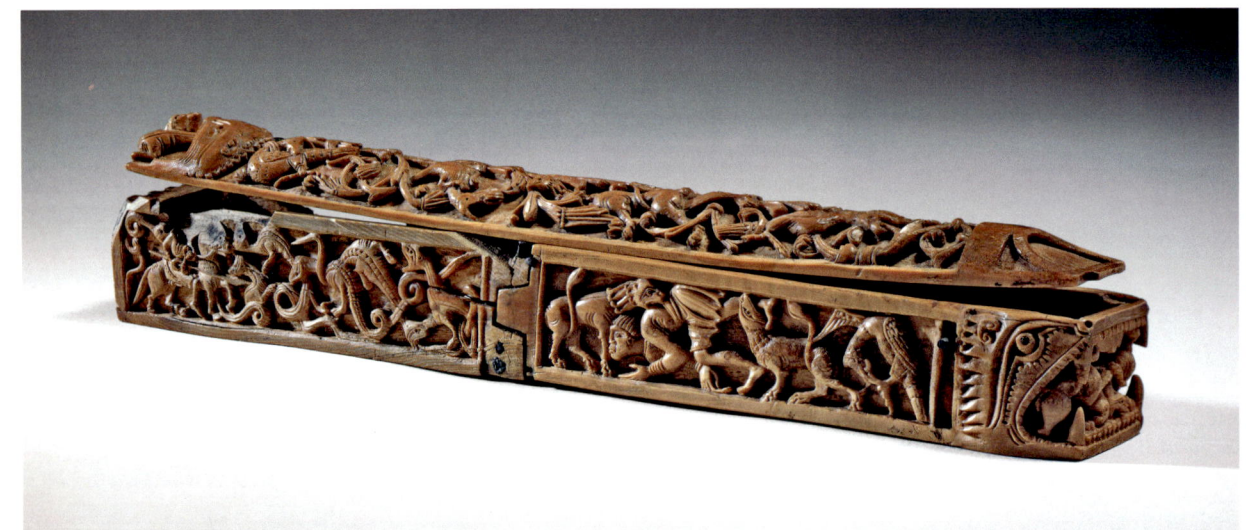

This connection between coins and items which express a personal identity or belief is seen in another very striking way, in a group of items associated with one of the most troubling episodes of Æthelred II's troubled reign, in the year 1009.[32] The potentially significant year 1000 had passed, but since only God can know the day and the hour of Judgement, anxieties about the end of the world had not departed. As early as the 980s, as the second wave of Viking attacks and their increasingly harsh tribute payments intensified, poems such as the Old English 'Doomsday' were beginning to dwell on this topic. Sombre homilies and sermons on the theme were delivered by senior churchmen such as Abbot Ælfric of Eynsham. As the devastations continued, they seemed to some to herald the Last Days before the Second Coming, when the Antichrist would be unleashed and heresy, omen and terror would reign, as described in the Book of Revelation. In a number of homilies in the first decades of the eleventh century, Archbishop Wulfstan of York forcefully hammered home the point: 'now are Satan's fetters completely dissolved, and the time of the Antichrist is well at hand'. This heightened perception of the imminence of Doomsday in the decades surrounding the year 1000 suggests that it is no coincidence that iconography associated with the Last Judgement features on so many of the late tenth- and early eleventh-century ivories and metalwork discussed in this chapter. The Agnus Dei with Christ's Cross and Book of Judgement is the clearest example – the image of both Doomsday and Christ's ultimate redemption of mankind expressed in the sacrificial Lamb that takes away sin (figs 170 and 171).

One final vivid and revealing illustration of the anxieties of the age is seen in the actions of the church and king in the year 1009, following the arrival of Thorkell the Tall's army in August that year and the widespread

174 (*above*). Walrus ivory pen case with animal and plant decoration and human figures engaged in various activities. Mid-11th century. L. 23.2 cm (British Museum)

175 (*below*). Copper-alloy strap-end with inhabited plant decoration. Winchester, mid- to late 10th century. L. 6.9 cm (Winchester City Museums)

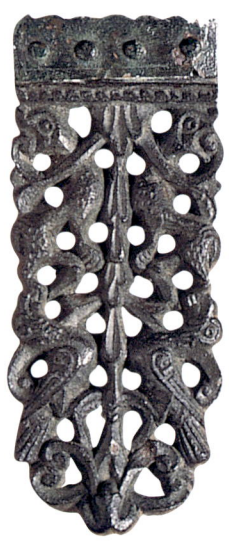

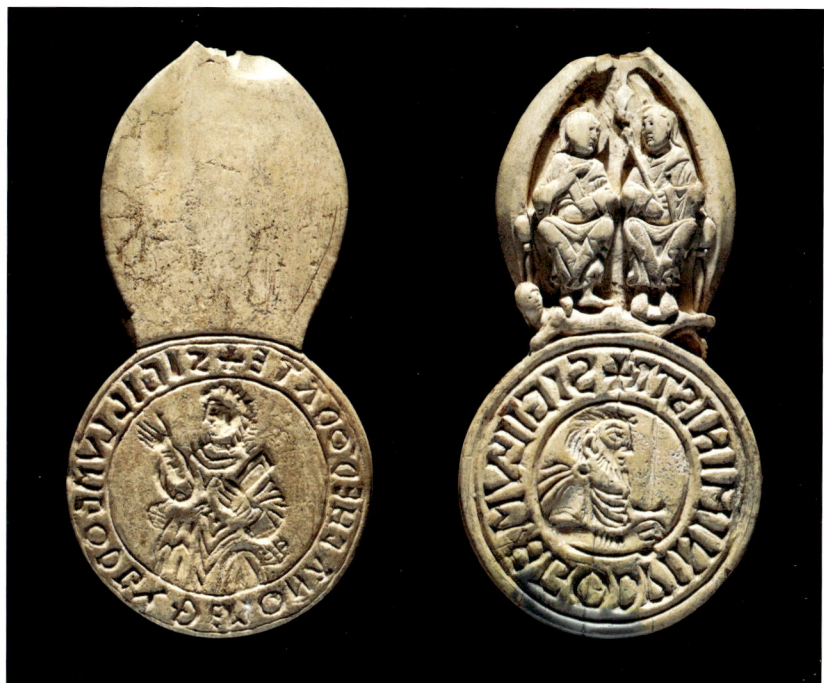

176. Walrus ivory double-sided seal-die of Godwin, a *thegn*, and Godgytha, a nun (a later addition). Wallingford, Berkshire, early 11th century. L. 8.6 cm (British Museum)

devastation that followed. The king issued an edict headed 'This was decreed when the Great Army came to the country', urging a general public fasting and penance, confession, and the daily saying of the Mass against the heathen, along with barefoot processions with relics, at which the litany with the Agnus Dei refrain was chanted. At the same time, Æthelred issued a most unusual new coinage, depicting on the obverse the Lamb of God, and on the reverse the Holy Spirit as a dove.[33] Almost immediately a series of cheap bronze brooches were made with very similar images, clearly based – if not very expertly – on the new coins. These were talismans, images of devotion which were designed to proclaim both the true faith of the wearer in what seemed quite possibly the prelude to the final Judgement Day, and to invoke God's mercy and protection against the calamity of yet more Viking attacks. They were, of course, ineffective: in 1013 Swein Forkbeard seized the throne, eventually followed in 1016 by his son Cnut, acts which were to shape the political and artistic future of England.

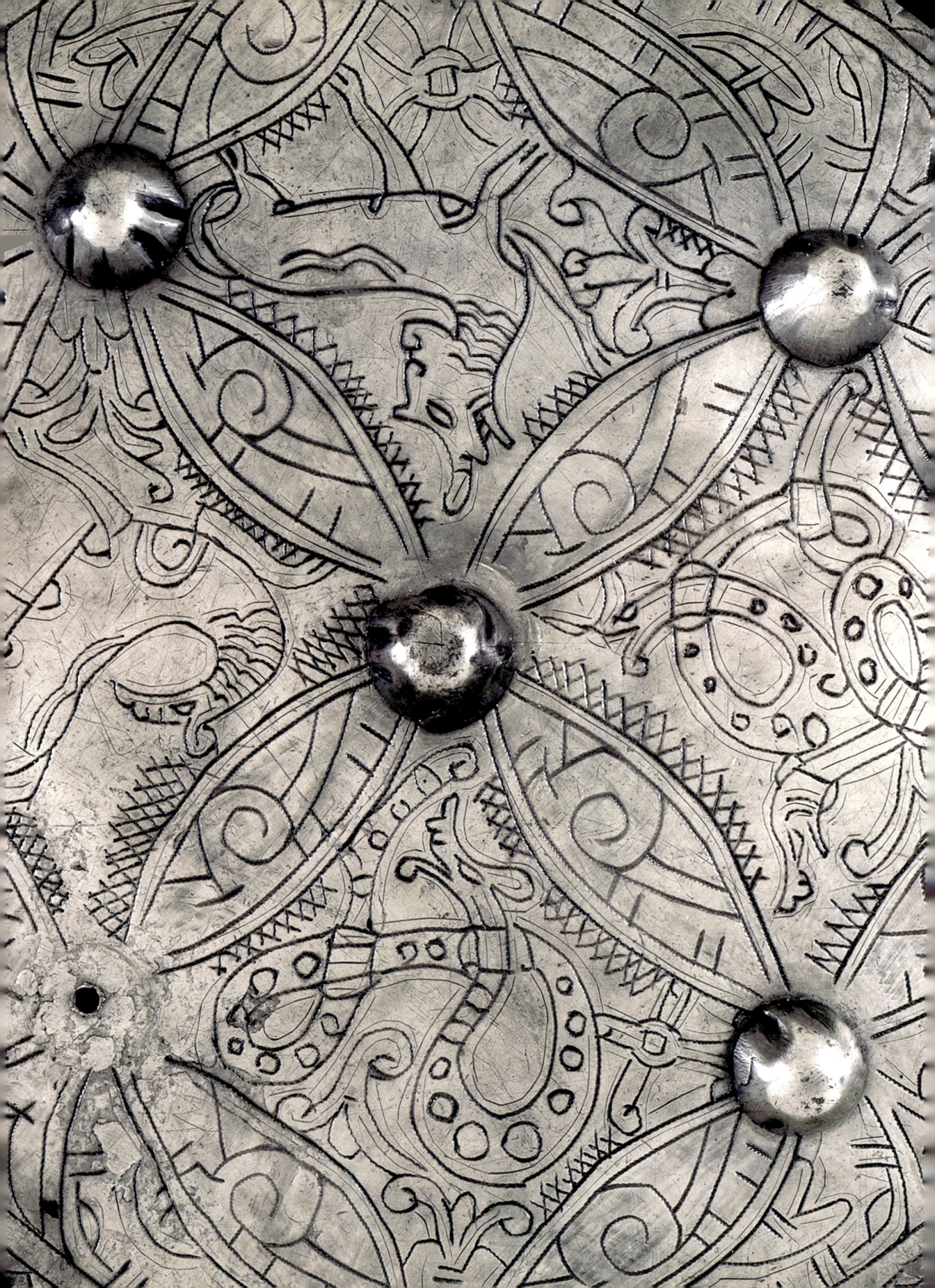

CHAPTER 7

On one side lions moulded in gold were to be seen
on the ships, on the other, birds on the tops of the
masts indicated by their movements the winds as they
blew, or dragons of various kinds poured fire from
their nostrils. Here there were glittering men of solid
gold and silver nearly comparable to live ones, there
bulls with necks raised high and legs outstretched
were fashioned leaping and roaring like live ones. One
might see dolphins moulded in electrum, and centaurs
in the same metal.

From the description of Swein Forkbeard's
fleet in 1013, *Encomium Emmæ Reginæ*[1]

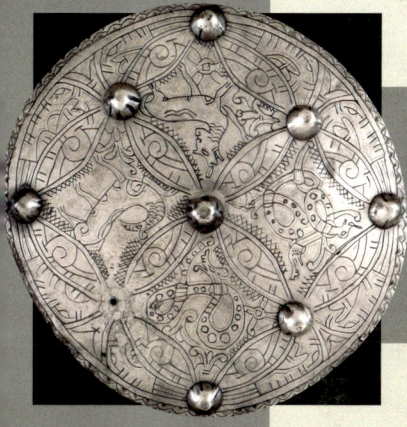

Brooch from Sutton, Isle
of Ely (see fig 195)

THE NORTH ASCENDANT: THE VIKING IMPACT

The Viking settlements: new influences

From the first raids of the late eighth century up to the Norman Conquest and
even beyond, the sight of Viking ships off the English coast was bad news:
they presaged looting and devastation, widespread slaughter, the capture of
slaves and, from the 990s until 1018, the payment of massive tributes in silver,
the Danegeld. Contemporary accounts give a grim picture of the scale and
ferocity of the attacks: in 1011, the Anglo-Saxon Chronicle bleakly reported
that the foreigners had overrun:

> East Anglia, Essex, Middlesex, Oxfordshire, Cambridgeshire,
> Hertfordshire, Buckinghamshire, Bedfordshire, half Huntingdon-
> shire, much of Northamptonshire; and south of the Thames, all
> Kent, Sussex, Hastings, Surrey, Berkshire, Hampshire and much of
> Wiltshire.

It added that, for all that truces had been made and tributes paid, the Viking
bands continued to plunder, harry and kill. The year after, Vikings seized the

Archbishop of Canterbury and, when he refused to pay a ransom, they got very drunk on 'wine from the south', and pelted him with bones and ox-heads until one of them killed him with a blow to the head with the butt-end of an axe.

This image of the Vikings as an uncontrollable force of evil, drunken pagans who leached England of its riches and failed to play by the rules, is undoubtedly true in part, though it is arguable that they were scarcely worse than their adversaries, who could behave just as badly, given the chance. But it is also only one side of the coin. For one thing, from the later ninth century many Vikings had become Christian. Some who settled in the Danelaw had adopted the local religion and, like the last owner of the Ormside bowl, were buried with some possessions in Anglo-Saxon churchyards. Others, like Alfred's adversary, Guthrum (d. 890), were baptized in England or abroad, usually as part of a peace settlement. Denmark itself had officially adopted Christianity by about 960, when the Danish king Harald Bluetooth (d. 985/6) recorded on his great rune-stone at Jelling that he had 'made the Danes Christian'. His grandson, Cnut, was irreproachably Christian, a king who made himself almost more Anglo-Saxon than the Anglo-Saxons themselves.

In addition, many Viking raiders had integrated into a new life in England. In the course of the later ninth and early tenth centuries, Viking freebooters-turned-farmers had settled across northern England, many marrying Anglo-Saxons and creating their own hybridized culture. In Northumbria the Scandinavian takeover of York (Old English *Eoferwic*) created the northern Viking power-base, *Jorvík*, an important trading and manufacturing centre on the East–West trading chain between Viking Dublin and Scandinavia, and beyond, to Russia, Constantinople and Baghdad. The thriving Anglo-Scandinavian culture of the Danelaw in the north and east of the country, despite recurrent unrest, had a productive relationship with the Anglo-Saxon kingdom to the south. The voyages in distant northern waters which were recounted to King Alfred by the Norwegian magnate Ottar (Ohthere in Old English) and the presumably Anglo-Saxon merchant Wulfstan confirm what is also revealed through archaeology – a network of contacts between Scandinavians, Anglo-Saxons and other, remoter, northern European peoples, such as Lapps and Finns.[2] Walrus ivory and furs arrived by these northern routes; and from Viking voyages to the East came Arabic silver and exotic imports such as Central Asian silks and other goods, Byzantine textiles and the occasional peacock. These were beneficial connections, which fed new contacts into the Anglo-Saxon economy, alongside its own established network of merchants and traders, with their own links to the Baltic, the Low Countries, Germany, France, down to Italy and the Mediterranean.

At the same time the history of the Viking settlements in Britain and Ireland was complicated: before the settlement of Danelaw in the late 870s, Norwegian Vikings had travelled west and southwards around northern

Scotland from much earlier in the ninth century. This was initially to raid the soft targets of Irish monasteries, but they soon began to establish themselves in Orkney and Shetland, in Caithness and in the Hebrides, as well as in Ireland and, by the end of the century, in the strategically placed Isle of Man. From these bases on the Irish Sea they installed themselves in coastal Cumbria and touched on other points of the western seaboard of England and Wales. The bases established in Ireland from the mid-ninth century, notably Dublin, developed close links with the Viking kingdom of York, and after their temporary expulsion from Dublin in 902, Irish Viking exiles also sought refuge on the Isle of Man, in north-west England and in parts of northern Yorkshire. Their particular Irish-Norse culture is not part of this story, except for their spectacular large silver cloak brooches, which, with their distinctive compartmentalized animal ornament separated by silver bosses, clearly reveal the influence of the ninth-century Trewhiddle style (see pp. 146–52). The raiders who settled in eastern Yorkshire and the Danelaw region from the 870s seem to have been predominantly Danes, although even from the beginning Norwegians and Swedes were numbered among them, as they certainly also were among the attackers of the tenth and eleventh centuries. This is supported by the fact that, alongside Irish shrine mounts and horse gear, Anglo-Saxon ecclesiastical metalwork, coins and trinkets occur in Norwegian graves, and in Swedish as well as Danish hoards and burials. These new immigrants to England brought their own language and traditions with them, which were to have a lasting effect on the cultural fabric of the country – its place-names, its language, its standing monuments and portable art – in the form of a distinctive and vigorous Anglo-Scandinavian style.

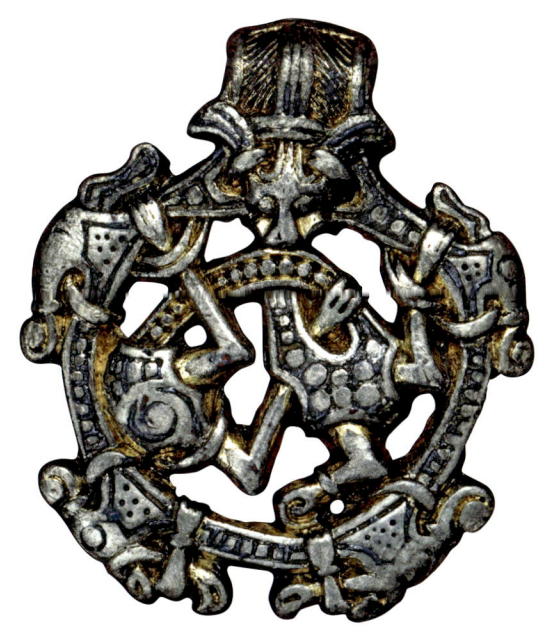

177. Silver-gilt pendant with 'Gripping Beast', found at Little Snoring, Norfolk. Scandinavian, late 9th or early 10th century. H. 4.2 cm (British Museum)

Viking art: background and styles

The traditions of decoration which the Viking settlers brought with them took root all the more successfully in an Anglo-Saxon setting because they had grown out of the same artistic and mythic tradition of complex zoomorphic decoration that the Anglo-Saxons had brought with them from southern Scandinavia and northern Germany when they first colonized England in the fifth century. Even allowing for a certain degree of exaggeration, the thrilling description of the magnificently decorated ships of the Danish king Swein Forkbeard's fleet quoted at the beginning of this chapter makes it graphically clear that they were decorated with animal ornament – from the gilded weathervanes with dragons and serpents which adorned the masts, down to the lion-like creatures and other prancing beasts which adorned the prows and sides of the ships. We know these ships and their bold animal ornament from many other sources – from the beautiful surviving ships from the Gokstad and Oseberg burials in Norway, and the carved wooden objects that were buried with them, from finds of gilded ships' weathervanes and, not least, from depictions in Anglo-Saxon manuscripts and the Bayeux Tapestry. This was an art in which animal ornament still reigned supreme – as with early Anglo-Saxon art, the human image was largely elusive, mostly surviving in religious or amuletic contexts depicting the afterlife in Valhalla.

The pervasive animal decoration had, however, developed in rather different directions in Scandinavia, though always remaining faithful to the original concept of covering a surface with dense and complex animal patterns. Unlike Anglo-Saxon zoomorphic art, it had not needed at that stage to absorb and adapt to Christian convention and usage; there were no church manuscripts to decorate or shrines to ornament. Yet it was not immune to external influences, particularly from Carolingian, Anglo-Saxon and Irish metalwork; as already noted, the Irish-Norse Vikings developed distinctive styles which drew on both the latter traditions (see p. 211). From the Carolingian metalwork that they acquired through their trading and raiding, Vikings took the unfamiliar image of the lion, and created their own version, the so-called 'Gripping Beast', a rather endearing creature with a cat-like face, which tenaciously fastens its paws onto the tangled bodies of its fellow beasts (fig. 177). This motif first appears towards the end of the eighth century and continues as an element in decorative styles for over a hundred years. Later on, other transformations of Carolingian lions begin to appear on the beautiful gilded weathervanes of ships, on walrus-ivory caskets, and in the great heraldic creatures seen on tenth- and eleventh-century memorial stones such as those at Jelling in Denmark and Vang in Norway.[3] The acanthus decoration which dominates fine Carolingian sword belt fittings and other prized metalwork, such as the silver bowls from the hoards found at Halton Moor and the Vale of York, was, along with the equally influential Anglo-Saxon Winchester-style foliage, transformed into the fleshy leaves and tendrils of Viking ornament (see p. 156, and fig. 117).

Thus, over time, Viking art developed its own succession of flamboyant decorative styles, which have come down to us in metalwork, bone and ivory carving, and in wood and stone sculpture. The main styles which characterize Viking art in the years between the end of the eighth and the eleventh centuries have been named by art historians after particular areas or find-places associated with typical objects: the Borre, Jellinge, Mammen, Ringerike and Urnes styles. These are labels of convenience, for in fact there is chronological and stylistic overlap between all of these styles; and once they were exported beyond their Scandinavian homelands, they quickly developed local variations wherever they migrated – in Ireland, in the Isle of Man, in Scotland and in England. However, before discussing the particular manifestations of

178. Copper-alloy sword chape with Borre-style decoration. Possibly from Suffolk, early 10th century. H. 5.6 cm (British Museum)

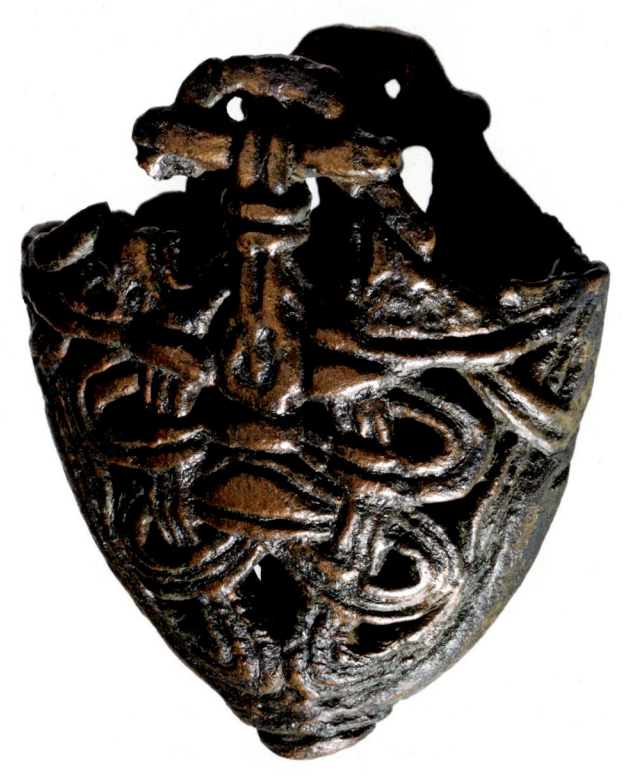

Anglo-Scandinavian art in England, it will be helpful to describe the main forms of each of these styles, since – as with the early Anglo-Saxon zoomorphic styles – the conventional characterizations and terminology offer a simple way into the subject.

The Borre style is named after the findspot of a Norwegian ship burial in which strap and harness mounts in this style were found. Dendrochronological and coin dating has confirmed that the style can be dated to the late ninth and tenth century. It has two principal components: interlacing creatures of the Gripping Beast kind, either entire or as individual elements of clutching paws and triangular face-masks; and a form of stranded angular interlace in which usually diamond-shaped elements are linked by rings and bars, known as ring-chain (fig. 178). Masks and paws of this type frequently appear with stranded interlace in Danelaw metalwork. A subtler, 'vertebral' variant of the ring-chain also occurs in sculpture of the Isle of Man and in northern England; it substitutes a sub-triangular element for the diamond, and joins it up to the rings, so that they articulate one with another (see fig. 182). Another version of the style, dating to the same period, has closed knot patterns related to ring-chain. It appeared initially as filigree motifs on gold and silver jewellery, but was rapidly copied in cheaper products, particularly small copper-alloy metal brooches, which proved popular in England.

The Jellinge style is named after the Danish royal site of Jelling, and is more or less contemporary with the Borre style, with which it shares some features, such as the occasional gripping paw. A small silver cup and other objects from burials at the site, which date to the middle years of the tenth century, exemplify the style.[4] Elongated, intertwining ribbon animals, with double-contoured and ribbed bodies, and spiral hips dominate the decoration. Their profiled heads, round eyes and interlacing pigtails are also distinctive. In England the style became especially popular on sculpture in northern and eastern Yorkshire, though it can appear on metalwork as well (see figs 187 and 189).

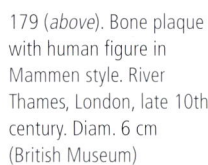

The Mammen style is named after the location of a rich grave in Denmark which contained a fine inlaid axe-head decorated with a classic version of the style.[5] Closely related to the Jellinge style, it is dominated by large creatures, some of which, while retaining the body contouring and spiral hips of the Jellinge beasts, show a descent from classical lions; they are dynamic animals, often with pelleted bodies, and enmeshed in asymmetrical foliage tendrils (fig. 186). Curling fronds on the creatures' lips or noses, known as lappets, also occur. Occasionally human elements appear, as on a bone belt-slide from the Thames at London (fig. 179). It is a relatively uncommon style, though it appears across Europe; in England, it was current between the mid- to late tenth century.

The Ringerike style takes its name from the Norwegian source of a reddish sandstone used for some rune-stones in the style. The great beast with spiral hips which first appears in the Mammen style is here often found in combination or combat with a snake-like animal; and, most distinctively, they are characteristically accompanied by entanglements of long, curling tendrils, which clearly owe much to Anglo-Saxon Winchester-style (and perhaps also, Ottonian) versions of acanthus foliage (fig. 180). The style dates to the late tenth and first half of the eleventh centuries and, as we shall see, became especially popular in southern England after the accession of Cnut in 1016.

179 (*above*). Bone plaque with human figure in Mammen style. River Thames, London, late 10th century. Diam. 6 cm (British Museum)

180 (*below*). Gilded copper-alloy strip (drawing), with a spread-eagled Ringerike-style great beast. Winchester, early 11th century. L. 29 cm (Strip, Winchester Cathedral Treasury; drawing after Kjølbye Biddle)

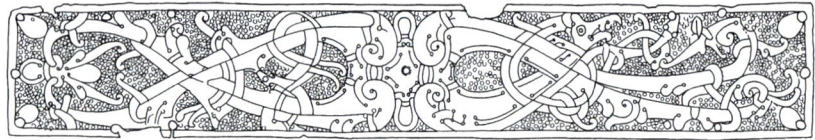

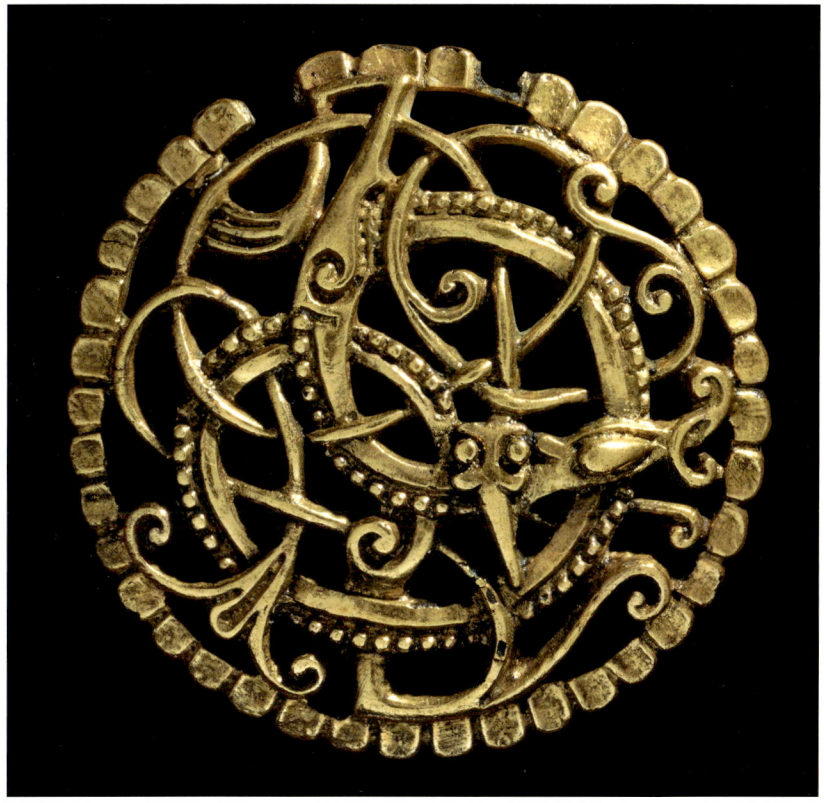

181. Gilded copper-alloy openwork brooch in the Urnes style. Pitney, Somerset, late 11th century. Diam. 3.9 cm (British Museum)

The final Viking style which was current in England is the Urnes style, named after the remarkable carvings on the exterior of the wooden stave-church at Urnes, western Norway.[6] The church dates to the early twelfth century, but the carvings were probably made for an earlier, eleventh-century church on the same site. The style features elegant creatures with tear-shaped eyes and distinctive tendrils on their muzzles; they are usually depicted in biting combat with a slender, snake-like animal, but the overall effect is rhythmical and strangely delicate. Versions of the style were particularly current in Ireland, where they occur in several media, and are particularly prominent on ecclesiastical artefacts; but in England the style as it survives is largely confined to fine metalwork (fig. 181) and post-Conquest sculpture. As this implies, the latest of the Viking styles dates to the mid-eleventh to early twelfth centuries.

Viking art: the north and the Danelaw

As this brief review has indicated, Viking art in England, and its interconnection with Anglo-Saxon material culture, has its own individual story. This is partly a tale of north and south, and of early settlements versus later incomers. In the north, Vikings settled on both sides of the Pennine hills that form the high watershed between east and west, from the Scottish border down to the northern midlands. West of this, they mainly occupied the flatter coastal plains, from the Carlisle region down to the Wirral in Cheshire, along with some Pennine high pasture sites. Culturally, the Cumbrian and Pennine settlements mostly looked westward, to the Isle of Man and beyond, to Ireland. East of the Pennines, from Durham down to the Danelaw borders, the land was more forgiving and the population denser. Stone was very plentiful throughout much of this zone, and one of the most ubiquitous signs of the Scandinavian presence in the northern Danelaw (apart from place-names) is a rich body of sculpture in naturalized versions of Viking styles.[7]

The Viking incomers had brought their own animal ornament with them, in the form of jewellery, sword fittings and amulets (see fig. 180), and though there was almost no tradition of stone carving in relief in Viking Scandinavia before the later tenth century (except on the Baltic island of Gotland), they came with a long tradition of wood carving; all this interacted fruitfully with the indigenous Anglo-Saxon tradition. Within a generation of their arrival in England, many settlers had intermarried with the Anglo-Saxon population, and were at least nominally Christian. Their own stylistic and iconographic traditions were quickly adapted to the production of Christian monuments of Anglo-Saxon type, such as crosses and grave monuments.

One of the most imposing of these is the great red sandstone cross which still dominates the churchyard at Gosforth on the Cumbrian coastal plain (fig. 182). It dates to the first half of the tenth century. Standing nearly four and a half metres high, it is unusually slender by comparison with Anglo-Saxon stone crosses; this, together with its construction – a cylindrical lower shaft which metamorphoses into a square-sectioned upper shaft – reflects wood-carving techniques and traditions, implying the parallel existence of wooden crosses. The cross is magnificently decorated in relief with various kinds of interlace, a Crucifixion scene and an extensive series of images drawn from the tale of the overthrow and destruction of the Norse gods in the Viking version of the end of the world, Ragnarök. But these scenes drawn from pagan mythology are not, on this cross, pagan in purpose; the traditional tales are used to illustrate the Christian theme of Doomsday – just as, in a similar context of religious assimilation, the Franks Casket juxtaposed Christian and pagan tradition two centuries earlier (see p. 92). Also prominent in the decoration of the Gosforth Cross is the vertebral version of the Borre-style ring-chain; this is particularly common on Viking stone cross slabs on the Isle of Man, which lies opposite the Cumbrian shore, and is easily visible from the churchyard. It is quite possible that the sculptor knew this material and adapted the style to his own fashion.

Many other sculptures across the north adapted Scandinavian mythology to Christian purposes. There is a fragment from another sculpture at Gosforth with an image of the god Thor fishing to catch the Midgard

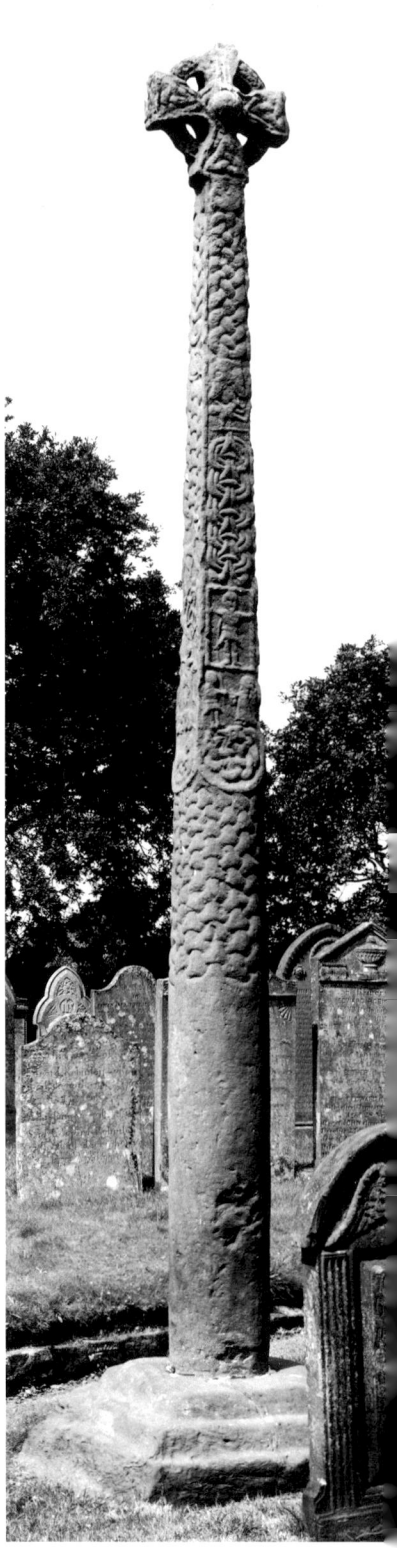

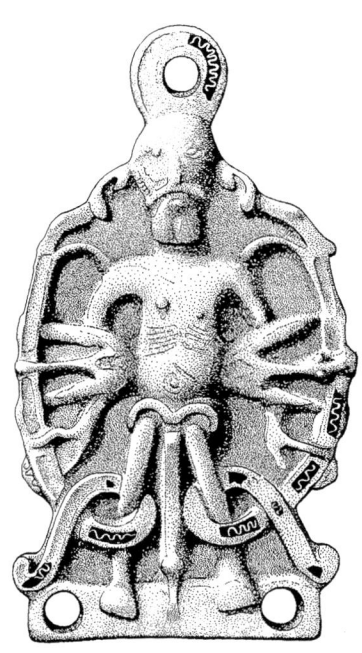

(Middle-earth) serpent – perhaps a parallel to the biblical sea-creature Leviathan. Scenes from the legends of the heroes Weland and Sigurd also occur on several crosses in the region, such as those at Halton (Lancashire) and Leeds.[8] A number of images found across England, both in sculpture and on small personal items of metalwork, such as stirrup mounts, are more ambiguous (fig. 183). Some seem to conflate the image of Christ crucified with that of the god Odin bound, smaller versions of the great Crucifixion image of the bound Christ seen on the rune-stone at Jelling that Harald Bluetooth set up around 865 in honour of his parents, proclaiming that he had united Denmark and Norway, and made the Danes Christian. A fragment of a cross shaft from Kirkby Stephen (Cumbria) depicts a figure whose body and limbs are similarly encircled by ribbony loops (fig. 184). Are the curling ribbons extending from his head hair or yet more loops? Or should they be read as horns, suggesting the Devil bound in Hell or the Viking trickster god, Loki, who was also bound until his release at Ragnarök, the Viking Doomsday? This seems to be another image which is meant to be read in more than one way.

One particularly distinctive form of sculpture exclusive to Viking areas of Britain is the so-called 'hogback' monument. These are gravestones in the shape of a contemporary boat-shaped long-house, with curving walls and a curving ridged, sometimes shingled, roof; some have powerful, muzzled bear-like beasts at each end (fig. 185). Variants occur across North Yorkshire and Cumbria, and into western Scotland, their distribution strongly suggesting a correlation with Irish Viking and Norwegian settlers who entered this region in the early years of the tenth century. This is a monument type unknown in Scandinavia, and may derive from Northumbrian stone shrine monuments, similar in type to the 'Hedda' stone at Peterborough[9] – another example of the interaction of the two cultures.

A little further south, in Yorkshire, notable schools of Anglo-Scandinavian sculpture, centred on York and Ryedale, developed their own native versions of the Jellinge and Mammen styles, with varying degrees of competence. In the

182 (*opposite*). Standing cross with Crucifixion scene and images drawn from Ragnarök, the Viking version of the end of the world. First half of the 10th century. H. 440 cm (Gosforth, Cumbria)

183 (*above*). Stirrup mount with an image of a bound male figure. Sherburne St John, Hampshire, first half of the 11th century (Drawing after Williams 1997)

184 (*right*). Stone fragment with a bound male figure. Late 10th century. H. 65 cm (Kirkby Stephen parish church, Cumbria)

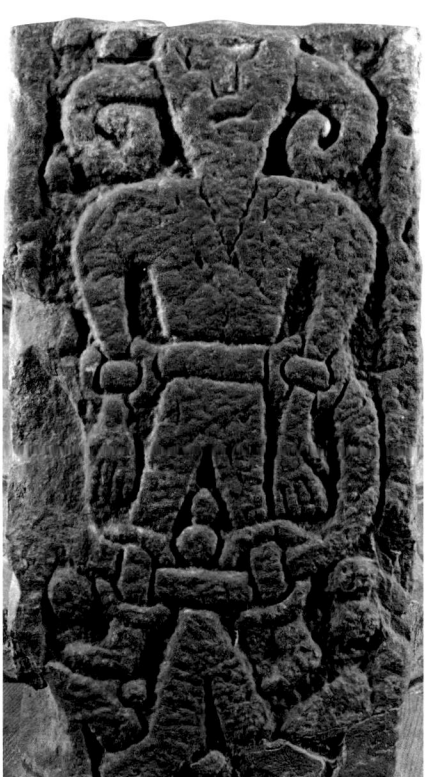

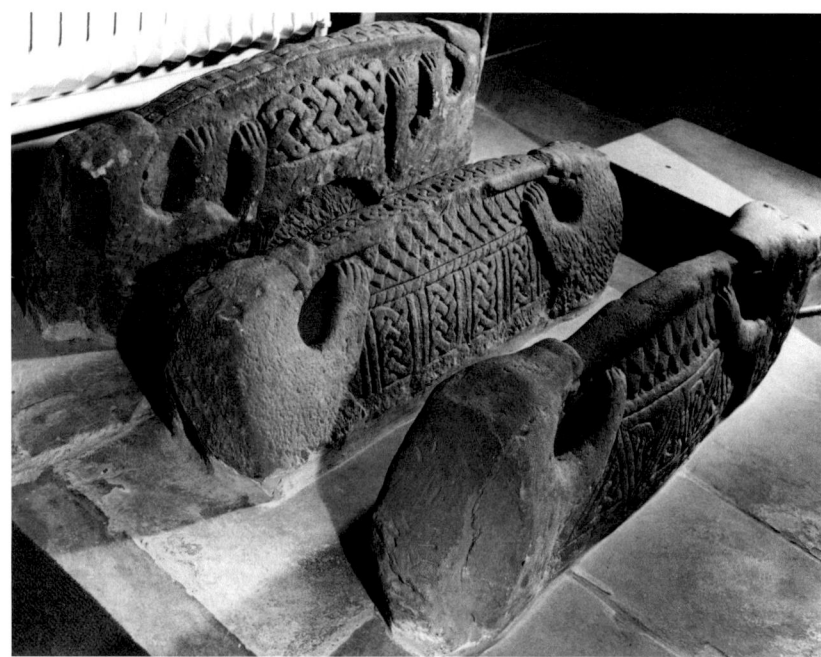

185. Stone hogback
monuments. 10th century.
Average L. 120 cm
(Brompton parish church,
North Yorkshire)

Ryedale group, the naive and coarse Jellinge ornament seen on crosses from
Sinnington and Middleton, North Yorkshire,[10] is rarely matched by more
accomplished sculpture, such as the splendid beast on the Mammen-style
grave slab at Levisham, North Yorkshire (fig. 186). From York itself a number
of cross fragments and grave-covers, with typical Anglo-Scandinavian versions
of intertwining Jellinge animals, testify to a busy workshop serving the anglicized tastes of this wealthy urban community. The fine-grained local stone
lent itself well to finely detailed sculpture; in some of the surviving pieces,
such as a cross-shaft fragment from Newgate, marking-out lines can be seen
– one of the several indications that sculptors were using markers and perhaps
templates to scale up their designs sketched on parchment or bone (fig. 187).
Some of the excavated pieces from York also show clear signs of plaster coating
and painting, reminding us once more of the colourful decoration of churches
during this period.

     Along with Lincoln, and no doubt other Danelaw towns, Anglo-
Scandinavian York was also a centre for metalwork production, as finds of
dies, moulds and crucibles from excavation in these Viking towns have shown.
All kinds of relatively cheap, locally made personal equipment – strap-ends,
strap distributors, scabbard fittings, small brooches and the like – was circulating throughout the Danelaw, adapting Scandinavian styles to local taste. Some
local products were made on a more ambitious scale, such as the large silver
and niello disc brooch with Jellinge-style animals from Canterbury,[11] and
some rather crude silver shrine fittings in the same style (fig. 188). Part of the

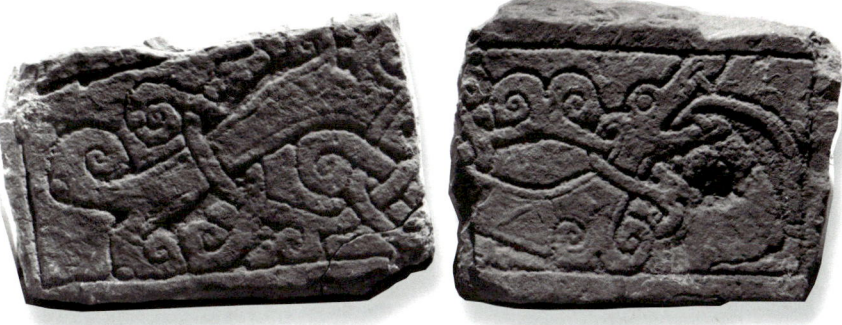

186. Fragments from a grave slab with Mammen-style animal. Late 10th century. L. 124 cm (Levisham parish church, North Yorkshire)

187. Fragment from a cross shaft with Jellinge-style animals. Newgate, York, mid- to late 10th century. H. 65 cm (Yorkshire Museum)

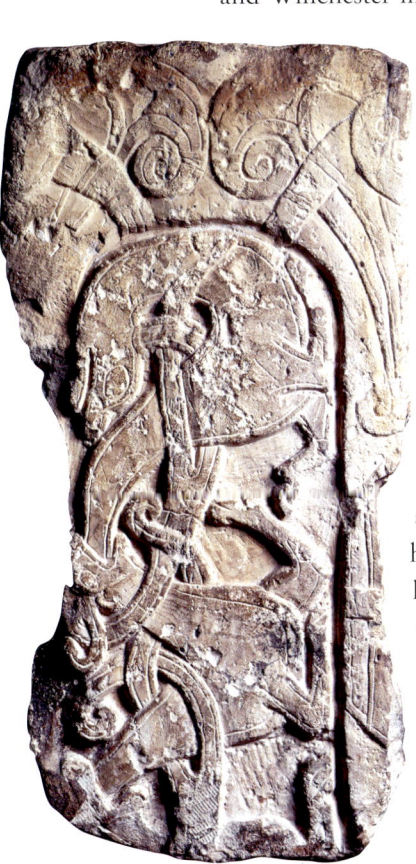

success of Anglo-Scandinavian metalwork was undoubtedly the visible affinity that Viking styles had with Anglo-Saxon traditions of animal ornament, and its easy adaptation to Anglo-Saxon object types. For instance, the coarse Viking-style interlace and animal head on a strap-end from York follows the characteristic template of an Anglo-Saxon ninth-century strap-end (fig. 189). But though produced within the region of the Danelaw, Viking-style objects also travelled beyond it, as a number of finds from southern England show: Anglo-Scandinavian Jellinge and Mammen-style pieces were reaching London and Winchester in the later tenth century. And it was, of course, the south of England that became a new focus of Viking artistic influence, after Cnut of Denmark took control of the Anglo-Saxon kingdom in 1016.

Viking art: new rulers, new styles

As we saw in the previous chapter, the great wealth of the Anglo-Saxon ecclesiastical establishment is mirrored in the manuscripts and ivories which survive, rather than in its lost church treasures. But as tenth- and eleventh-century Anglo-Saxon wills show, despite the renewed depredations of the Viking raids from the 980s onwards, high-status individuals of secular or ecclesiastical standing were able to bequeath substantial quantities of gold and silver, as well as richly mounted swords, luxurious household goods and other possessions, such as slaves and horses. The will of Wulfwaru, for example, a Somerset woman who died in 1016, lists heavy gold arm-rings, brooches and bowls of precious metal, two gold crucifixes and hall tapestries, among much else.[12] A few personal items, such as gilded silver belt fittings, gold-inlaid silver disc brooches and gold finger-rings, survive to testify to this considerable secular wealth (fig. 190).

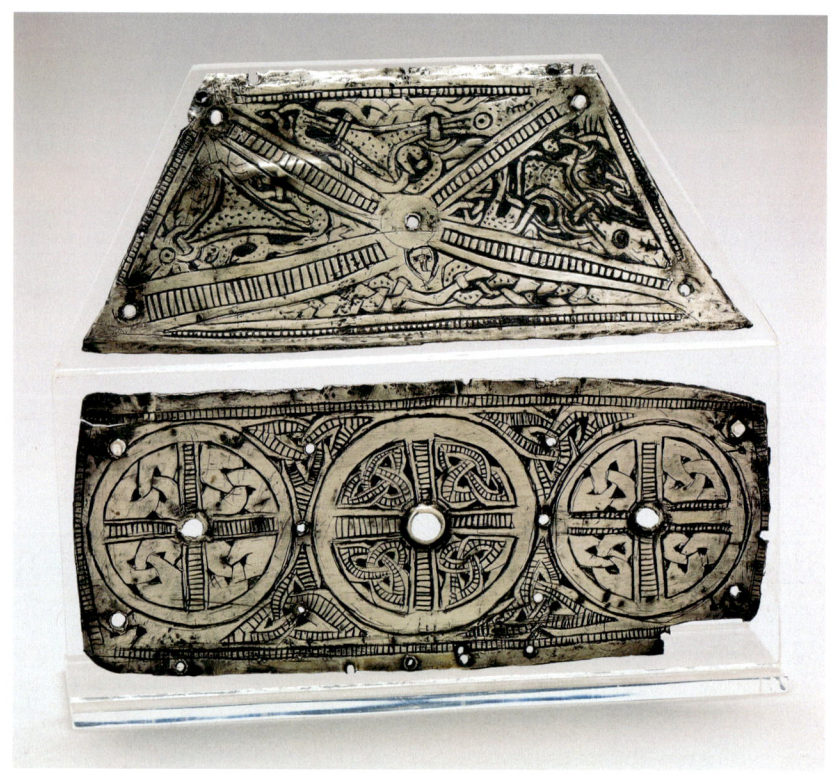

188 (*left*). Silver shrine plates with niello-inlaid interlace designs and animals in the Jellinge style. Mid-10th century. L. 12.1 and 12.6 cm (British Museum)

189 (*below*). Copper-alloy strap-end with Viking-type interlace. York, 10th century (after Hall 1984)

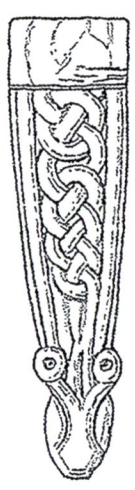

Despite all the troubles and depredations of Æthelred's reign, at its upper levels this was still a rich society with a sophisticated culture. The new Danish king, Cnut, was quick to adapt to it, making himself the very model of an Anglo-Saxon Christian ruler. Having undermined rival claims to the throne from Æthelred's offspring by marrying Æthelred's wife, Emma, he secured the support of the church by acts of atonement for various Viking misdeeds (including the murder of the unfortunate Archbishop of Canterbury, described above), and by his many generous donations. The presentation page in the Winchester *Liber Vitae*, showing Cnut and Emma/Ælfgyfu presenting a huge golden cross to the New Minster, is a contemporary snapshot of effective royal patronage in action (fig. 139). His pilgrimage to Rome in 1027, when he attended the coronation of the German emperor, Conrad II, and exchanged many precious gifts with the emperor and the Pope, gave further public confirmation both of his piety, and his considerable standing among European rulers.

But although Cnut became as Anglo-Saxon as his subjects, and was closely advised by leading churchmen such as Archbishop Wulfstan of York, he also depended on loyal Viking followers through whom he imposed his authority. After the Battle of Ashingdon in 1016, when he took over the throne, the Anglo-Saxon Chronicle recorded that 'all the nobility of England was there destroyed'. To control his English kingdom, with its regional factions and potential for rebellion, Cnut appointed Scandinavians to positions of power in the regions, and he continued to maintain a personal elite force of loyal Danes and Norwegians. After 1028, when he added the kingdom of Norway to his existing rule in Denmark and southern Sweden, the regular traffic between Scandinavia and England must have increased, a perfect vehicle for ensuring that the latest Viking tastes and fashions were introduced into southern England – and that Anglo-Saxon influences also travelled in the opposite direction.

Paramount among these new fashions, the Ringerike style, as it appears in England, is to some extent a reflection of Cnut's accommodation with the Anglo-Saxon establishment. This was a well-connected art, with a particular affinity to late Anglo-Saxon artistic tradition. It already owed something to Ottonian and Winchester-style acanthus ornament, and perhaps partly for that reason it was especially popular in southern England, where its influence can be traced in metalwork, sculpture and – unlike the art of earlier Viking styles in the north – even manuscripts. A well-known eleventh-century gravestone from St Paul's churchyard in London is emblematic of the new style and the people through whom it was introduced to England (fig. 191). It is probably the end slab from a sarcophagus, and depicts a flamboyant great beast with typical Ringerike tendrils streaming from its head and tail, in combat with a similarly fronded snake-like creature. Paint traces show that the two animals were originally coloured in a blueish black with white spots, and their fronds and the frame were coloured red – all against a whitened

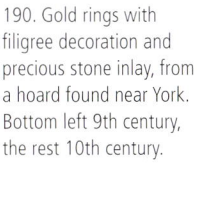

190. Gold rings with filigree decoration and precious stone inlay, from a hoard found near York. Bottom left 9th century, the rest 10th century.

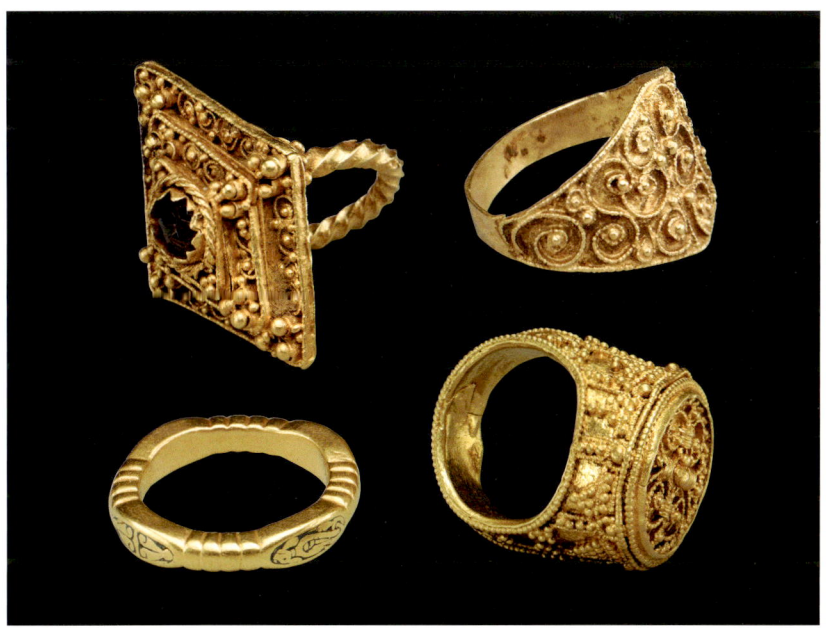

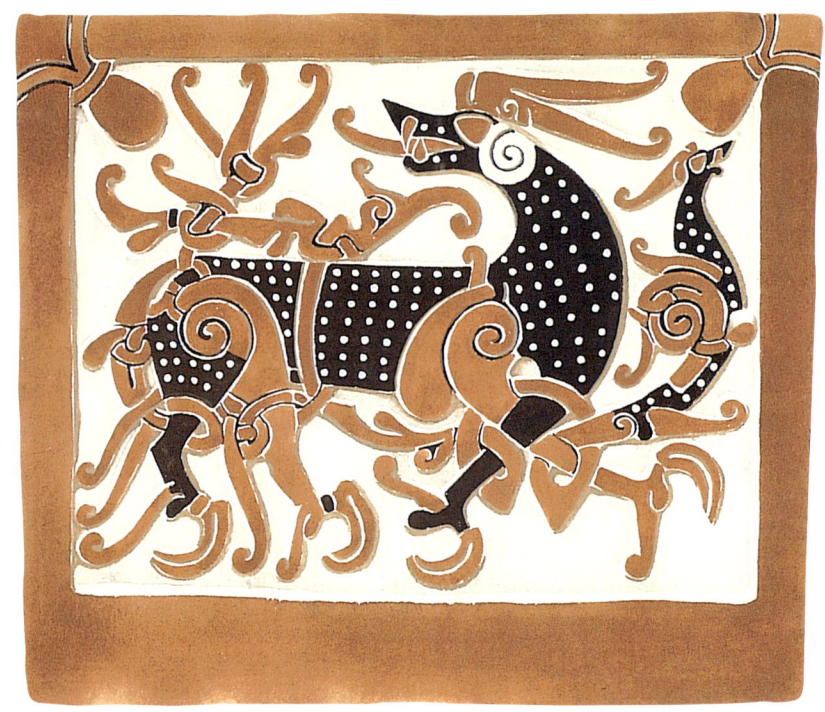

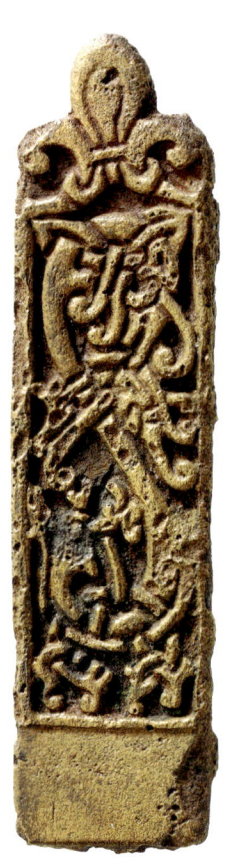

background. An incomplete inscription in Scandinavian runes which runs along its edge records that 'Ginna and Toki had this stone set up'. These were evidently well-to-do Scandinavians who may have been members of Cnut's entourage. The considerable comings and goings between southern England and Scandinavia in the reign of Cnut is well evidenced by other memorials; there is another Ringerike-style gravestone from the vicinity of St Paul's, also with possible Scandinavian runes; a painted Ringerike fragment from Rochester, Kent; and a grave-cover from Winchester which commemorates a man with the Scandinavian name of Gunni, described as 'the earl's companion' – presumably one of Cnut's men.[13] Contemporary Swedish memorial stones commemorate other travellers who died in London, or on their way to England.

The reverse aspect of this constant traffic is seen in a few prestige Viking objects from Scandinavia which reflect Anglo-Saxon influence, such as the early eleventh-century gilded-silver fittings from two swords from the Swedish province of Skåne, then under Danish rule.[14] They display interlaced bird and foliage ornament which clearly copies Winchester-style inhabited plant work. These were perhaps made for homecoming warriors after their campaigns in the early 1000s, or possibly used by Vikings in Swein's or Cnut's entourages.

Many kinds of objects testify to the new popularity of the Ringerike style. Fine Ringerike metalwork and bone carvings have been found in London, Winchester and elsewhere in the south, some confirming manufacture of objects decorated in the style – for example, bone trial pieces from London and a bronze die for making decorative foils, found at Hammersmith (fig. 192). A gilded bronze strip from Winchester, which may have been mounted on a casket, has a particularly fine version of a great Ringerike beast embattled with snakes among foliage, and reflects Anglo-Saxon influence in its symmetry and its lobed quatrefoils and other foliate details, suggesting that it, too, was probably made here (see fig. 180).

Hints of the style enter manuscript art as well. The thin, rather leggy tendrils of the acanthus border in the Winchcombe Psalter (fol. 5) – all pulling away with a diagonal motion – and a number of plumed and fronded beast initials in the same manuscript, show a clear feedback from Ringerike-style tendrils and animal heads into the later Winchester style (fig. 193).[15] The Junius poetical manuscript is another place where this Scandinavian style makes its presence felt. Here some inserted sketches, perhaps for an arm-ring and leather bindings, show a very competent understanding of complex Ringerike ornament, adapted to Anglo-Saxon taste (see fols 225 and 230); in the main body of the manuscript, other, more dishevelled, versions break out (fig. 194).[16] But these occurrences are relatively rare in manuscripts, at least in those that have survived.

Elements of Ringerike-style decoration may, however, have been more common in those manuscripts where greater emphasis was placed on depictions based on secular life. This is suggested by the case of the Old English Hexateuch, in which elements of the style are seamlessly integrated into the narrative programme. The various illustrations of Noah's Ark in the manuscript all depict the mighty vessel with haughty Ringerike-style animal heads atop their prows and stern-posts, fully equipped with crests, curling nose-lappets, tendrils and snakes looping around their necks (fig. 195). They are beautifully painted in blues, reds, yellows and greens, much as actual carved wood prows would have looked.[17] This is a vessel which clearly proclaims a Viking ancestry, and which (its unusual cargo and construction apart) would not have looked out of place among the handsomely decorated warships of Swein Forkbeard's fleet.

Less competent, hybrid versions of the style also began to appear, as it was increasingly absorbed by Anglo-Saxon craftsmen in other media. Two large silver disc brooches from the first half of the eleventh century, one from Barsham in Suffolk,[18] the other from a hoard buried around the time of the Conquest at Sutton, Isle of Ely, have Ringerike-inspired elements in their decoration which recall the shell-like spirals, snarling serpents and great beasts of the style. But here the style is poorly understood and is inexpertly grafted

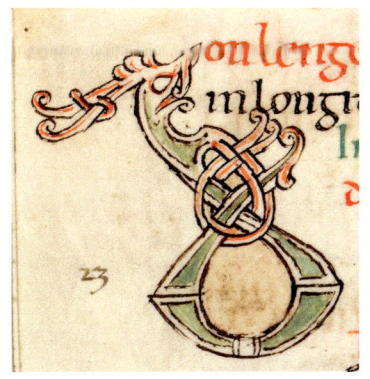

193. The Winchcombe Psalter: detail of initial with Ringerike-style animal. Winchcombe, Gloucestershire, *c.* 1030–50. Whole page 27 x 16 cm (University Library, Cambridge, MS Ff.I.23, fol. 37v)

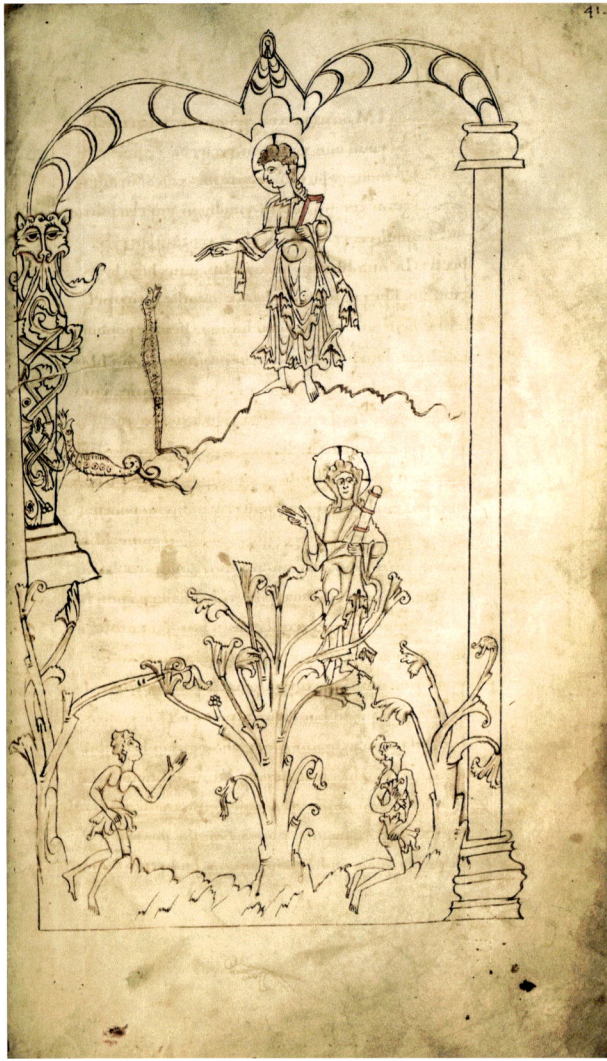

194 (*left*). The Junius Poetical Manuscript: God condemning the serpent, and Adam and Eve. Christ Church, Canterbury, first quarter of the 11th century. 31.8 x 19.5 cm (Bodleian Library, University of Oxford, MS Junius 11, fol. 41r)

195 (*opposite*). The Anglo-Saxon Hexateuch: Noah's Ark. Canterbury, 1040s. 34.2 x 21.7 cm (British Library, Cotton MS Claudius B.iv, fol. 14r)

onto bossed brooches of purely Anglo-Saxon type, to suit local taste (fig. 196). The Sutton brooch was certainly intended for an Anglo-Saxon clientele – an inscription on its reverse tells how it was made for an Anglo-Saxon woman, Ædwen, and piously calls on God to curse anyone who takes it from her against her will. A grave-cover fragment from Bibury, Gloucestershire, displays a slightly more competent, if eccentric, hybrid style, in which two moustached lion heads peer out from the looping bodies of two beasts entangled with acanthus sprays (fig. 199).

After the death of Cnut in 1035 the English throne eventually passed in 1042 to Edward (r. 1042–66), a grandson of Æthelred, who had spent most of his life abroad in Normandy. Manuscripts from the middle years of the

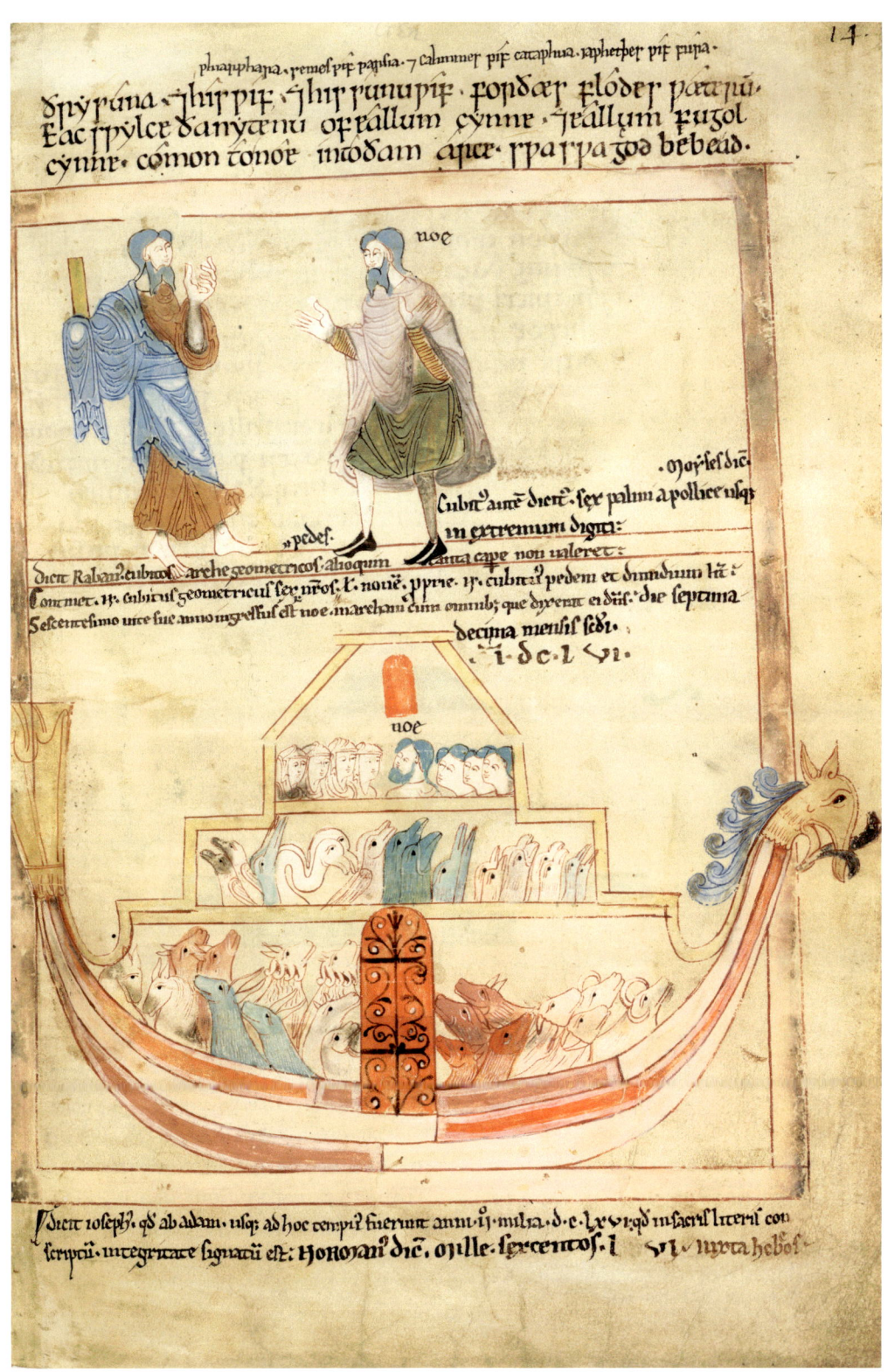

eleven century, and what remains of other religious art from his reign, have been discussed in the previous chapter. However, what little we know of other art in this period shows that Viking influences continued to be important, especially native versions of the Urnes style, which emerged in the middle years of the eleventh century. This style continued to be influential for a good fifty years or more after the Conquest, as the silver-plated iron crozier found in the grave of a Norman bishop, possibly Ranulph Flambard, at Durham Cathedral demonstrates.[19] Flambard died in 1128, but the crozier has impeccably elegant Urnes-style decoration inlaid in niello – a rare English survival of this type of decoration on an ecclesiastical object. A series of fine openwork bronze mounts, mainly from belts and horse gear, and almost all from the former Danelaw region, attests to the popularity of the Urnes style on objects of secular use, and suggests the existence of one or more active workshops, perhaps based in Lincoln and other former Danelaw towns (fig. 198). Much further south, from Pitney in Somerset, an elegant gilded bronze openwork brooch gives a version of the Urnes beast and snake combat which is fully Romanesque, and must belong to the late eleventh, if not early twelfth century (see fig. 181).

A small amount of sculpture in the Urnes style also exists, with a wide distribution, from East Yorkshire down to Sussex – where, at Jevington, a fine carving of the risen Christ with Urnes-style beasts at his feet is all that remains of what must have been an ambitious sculptural programme (fig. 197). As with the metalwork, the Urnes style continued to appear in sculpture for some considerable time after the Conquest, for instance on panels above doorways (tympani) at Ipswich (Suffolk) and Southwell Minster (Nottinghamshire), and on capitals at Norwich Cathedral.[20]

The dynamics by which this late Viking style gained such apparent currency before the Conquest, let alone afterwards, are less clearly understood. Certainly there was a continuing strand of Scandinavian culture in England, especially in the north, although the style's presence in the south may be harder to explain. Perhaps, as has been suggested,[21] the rhythmically flowing lines and delicate interlacings of the Urnes style had a particular appeal for Anglo-Saxons, with their long-standing taste for such mannerisms.

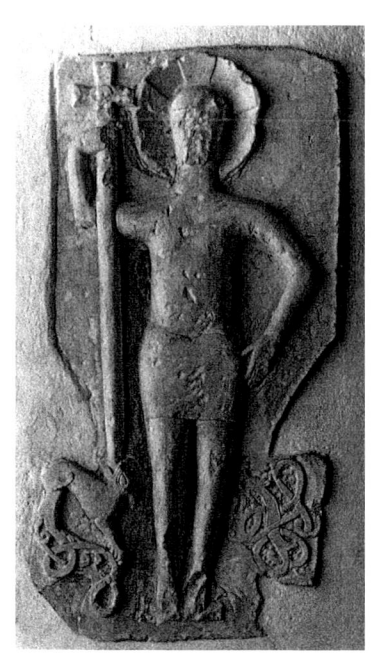

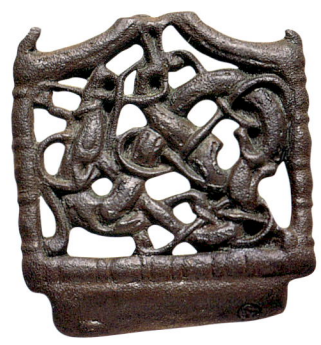

The Norman Conquest and after

As we have just seen, Anglo-Saxon art and its Anglo-Scandinavian versions did not come to an end with the Conquest. The illuminations in manuscripts such as the Wadham Gospels show that Anglo-Saxon manuscripts continued to be copied and emulated for a long time afterwards.[22] Lively animal ornament, initials with figures clambering in foliage, versions of acanthus ornament and interlace, densely framed borders and, above all, the great tradition of line drawing all fed into the manuscripts, sculpture and metalwork of the Romanesque period and beyond.

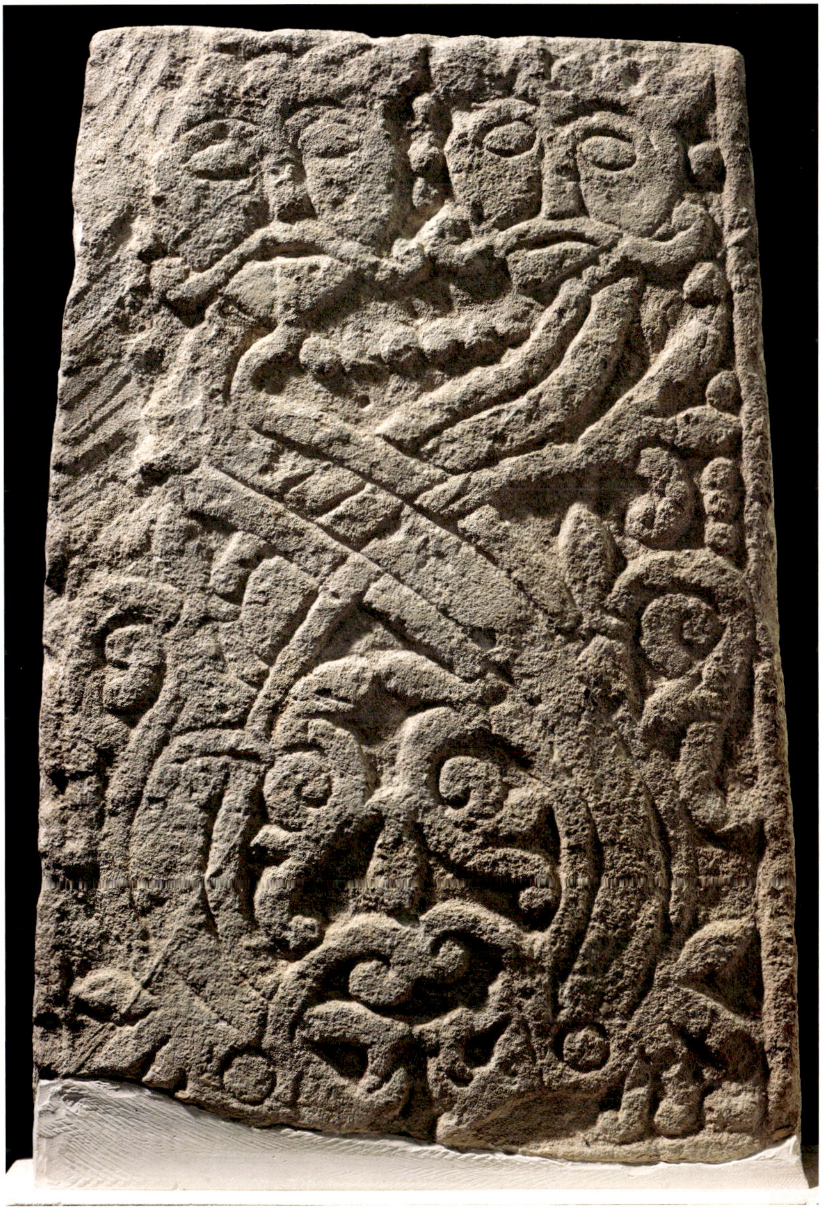

196 (*opposite, top*). Silver brooch with hybridized Anglo-Scandinavian ornament, from a hoard buried shortly after the Conquest. Sutton, Isle of Ely, Cambridgeshire, mid-11th century. Diam. approx. 15.5 cm (British Museum)

197 (*opposite, below*). Sculpture of the risen Christ with Urnes-style beasts at his feet. Late 11th century. H. approx. 100 cm (St Andrew's church, Jevington, Sussex)

198 (*above*). Copper alloy mount, with openwork animals in the Urnes style. Hemel Hempstead, Hertfordshire, mid-11th century. L. 4.5 cm (Verulamium Museum, St Albans)

199 (*right*).Grave-slab fragment with Anglo-Scandinavian ornament. Bibury, Gloucestershire, first half of the 11th century. H. 63.5 cm (British Museum)

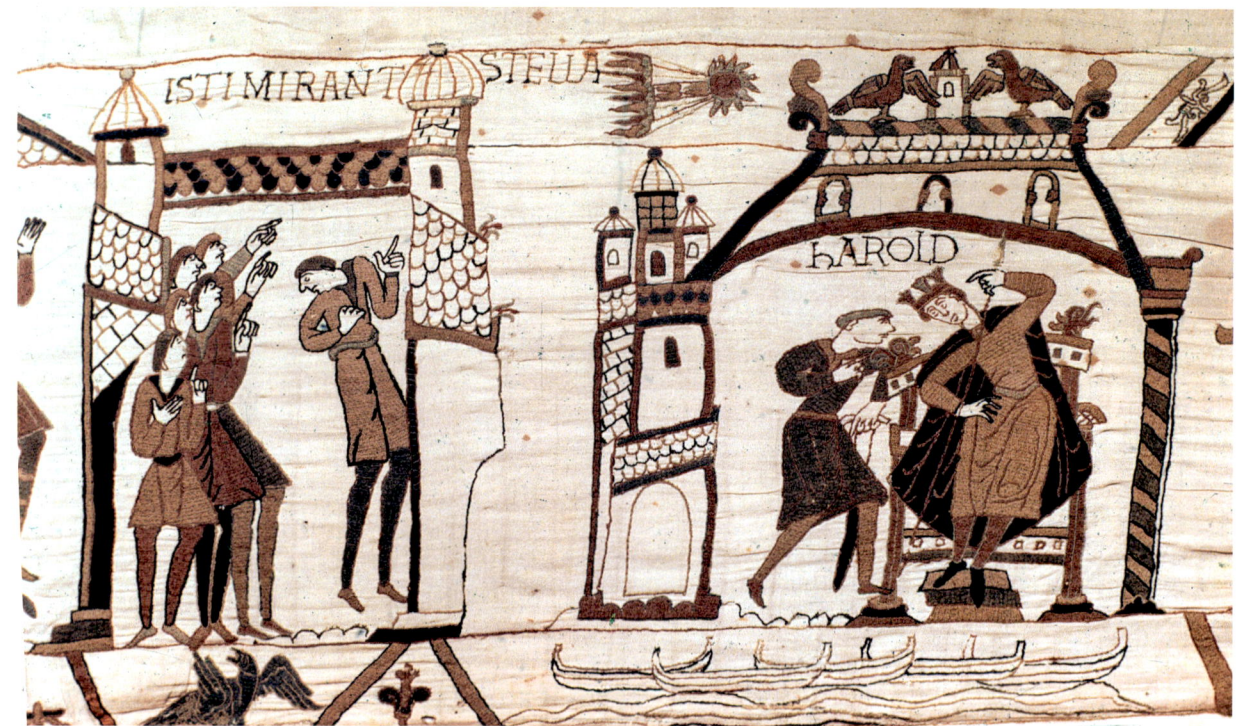

200. The Bayeux Tapestry (detail): Halley's comet is seen, and messengers announce to Harold the launch of William's war-fleet. *c.* 1066–82. H. 50 cm (Musée de la Tapisserie de Bayeux)

Unquestionably, the outstanding witness to the prestige in which Anglo-Saxon art was held after the Conquest, and its influence on the Norman successors, is the Bayeux Tapestry (fig. 200).[23] This 68.4-metre-long embroidery, in wool on a linen ground, was made in England by Anglo-Saxon women, perhaps for Bishop Odo of Bayeux, half-brother of the Conqueror, before his imprisonment by William in 1082, and was designed to hang on the walls of a large hall. It gives an almost cinematically conceived account of the events leading up to the Norman invasion of 1066, and the fateful battle at Hastings, at which King Harold of England was killed, and Duke William of Normandy (1035–87) was the victor. The end of the embroidery is missing, but it no doubt culminated in the coronation of William as king of all England. Although the visual narrative is supported by brief texts, there is a general agreement that this vindication of the Norman victory was also intended as a backdrop to sung or recited poems celebrating the theme and praising the Norman protagonists.

A few fragments of other embroidered wall-hangings exist from elsewhere in northern Europe, enough at least to suggest their appearance and competence. Some of them had perhaps hung in halls like Heorot in *Beowulf*, where adventures and ancestries were praised in song. We know of others from written sources: the embroidery celebrating the deeds of the ealdorman Byrhtnoth, which his widow gave to Ely, was mentioned earlier (see p. 127).

Also relevant is an intriguing fragment of a stone architectural frieze from Winchester, which, from its archaeological context, must have been destroyed before 1093 and probably dates on stylistic grounds to the middle years of the eleventh century (fig. 201). It depicts an armed warrior and a bound man with a wolf bending over his face. It is unclear whether this enigmatic scene is part of a cycle of Scandinavian mythological subjects celebrating Cnut's ancestry, or whether it depicts some Anglo-Saxon scene of martyrdom.[24] Whichever the case, as part of a much larger narrative frieze, it suggests a possible context of recitation.

However, the Bayeux embroidery remains unique in its heroic scale and its artistry. A remarkable piece of art by any standards, it visualizes events in frames that flow smoothly from one to the next, like a newsreel, with a narrative that is driven on by gesture and attitude, in subtly managed forward

201. Fragment from a narrative frieze, with figures of a warrior, a bound man and a wolf. Winchester, mid-11th century. H. 69.5 cm (Winchester City Museums)

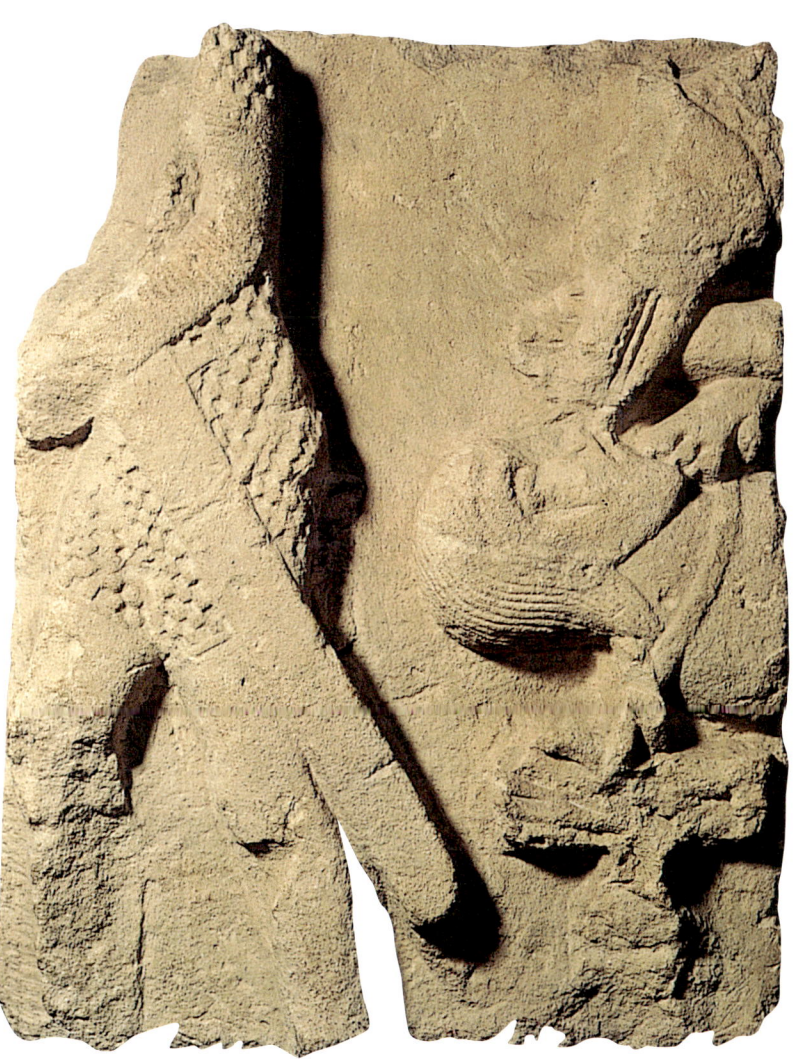

motion that impels even static scenes such as Harold's oath-swearing and the death of Edward the Confessor. The tremendous energy of the whole, from its beginning at King Edward's court to the turmoil and chaos of the ultimate battlefield, is combined with succinct characterization, all plotted in a meticulous and aesthetically satisfying overall design.

Accompanying and framing the embroidery are visual subtexts. Much of the main narrative sequence is punctuated by stylized trees, with urgent, writhing branches which often reveal a Ringerike-style ancestry. Some are there to separate events or indicate a wood; but others seem to mimic the action, such as the tree with a chain-mail panel which bends toward mail-coated William as he addresses his army, or the unique and dismal pollard that divides the Norman pursuers from the Anglo-Saxon fugitives in the final surviving scene. Most of the tapestry is also framed by two borders that occasionally provide a visual commentary on the action. In them, birds and beasts of every description disport themselves – among them, peacocks, lions, griffins, centaurs, camels and dragons – and genre scenes of various kinds appear. These include not only hunting and agricultural scenes familiar from illustrated calendars and ivory carving, but other images which only rarely find a place in Anglo-Saxon art. There is bear-baiting, for instance, and a considerable number of scenes involving gesticulating naked figures, both male and female, in a variety of postures and contexts which for the most part do not suggest the biblical Adam and Eve. They recall the lively naked men that feature on a few Anglo-Saxon strap-ends, who may have been luck-bringers, meant to turn away evil. But some more subtle reference may be intended here. Some of these figures seem to offer a comment on the main-frame action; for instance, a naked man mimics the gestures of the cleric above him, who, in an unexplained scene, reaches through an enclosing arch to touch a woman, presumably suggesting a sexual impropriety.[25] When messengers hurry to announce to Harold that William's fleet is on its way to England, the grave portent of Halley's comet flares above; and ominously, in the border below, warships glide through the sea (fig. 200). Most poignantly among these framing images, the terrible violence of the battle itself is accompanied by a long sequence in the lower border in which the bodies of the dead and dying lie amid their broken weapons in the jumbled postures of death, as archers advance and men strip the dead of their chain mail. Nowhere else in Anglo-Saxon art do we see a contemporary narrative portrayed so graphically, or so powerfully – and yet, such a fully realized and accomplished piece of contemporary myth-making is unlikely to have been unique.

In this respect, the Bayeux Tapestry reminds us – once again – of just how skewed is the sample of Anglo-Saxon art that has survived the centuries, and how much more significant are the losses than the survivals. The early grave deposits are only partial records of a partly understood society, as the many enigmas of the Staffordshire Hoard have recently shown. Until the tenth and eleventh centuries, the survival rate of prestige manuscripts and ecclesiastical metalwork is poor, and in the ninth century, minimal. The manuscripts of the late Anglo-Saxon period show that complex and aesthetically sophisticated narrative schemes were produced, but the Tapestry apart, there is no comparably ambitious secular art to balance this ecclesiastical output. Without wood carving, textiles and secular wall-paintings, our perception is limited.

Yet, despite these lacunae, one can speak of a distinctive tradition of Anglo-Saxon art in much the same way that one can speak of a distinctive tradition of Anglo-Saxon poetry; they share several characteristics, including a taste for riddles and complicated modes of expression. In art the same tastes can be traced through the entire Anglo-Saxon period. The dense surfaces of the Chessell Down brooch that we encountered in Chapter 1, with their complex visual metaphors, their busyness and their delight in contrast and complication, share many characteristics with the Ruthwell Cross, the Benedictional of St Æthelwold and the Bayeux embroidery. All require the onlooker to 'listen with the eyes'.[26] The continuing Anglo-Saxon fascination with the expressive, mobile line can also be traced down the centuries; in the symmetries of Style II animal ornament and the interlacing beasts in the Lindisfarne Gospels, in the emotive line drawings of the Winchester school, in the English versions of the Urnes style, and in the writhings of the Bayeux trees. And throughout, the enduring presence of animals in decoration, and the importance of their symbolism in both pagan and Christian contexts, tells us something of a world view in which man's place in nature was part of a greater unity. The Bayeux Tapestry is wholly in this tradition. And although it celebrates an end to Anglo-Saxon England, it also looks forward to the contribution that Anglo-Saxon art made not only to the Romanesque style of the new, Norman, order, but as an enduring strand in the English artistic tradition.

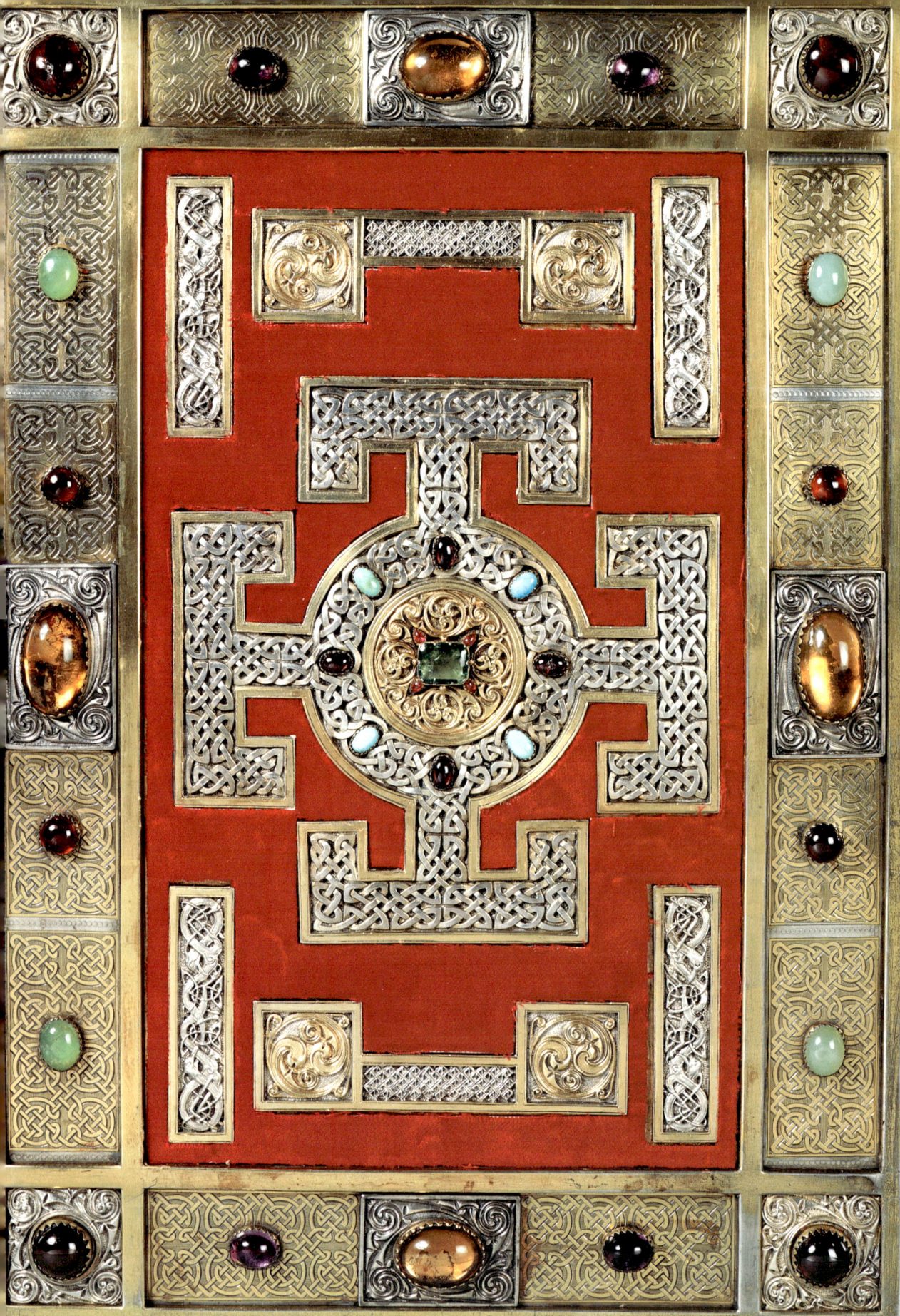

Alice . . . was still looking intently along the road,
shading her eyes with one hand. 'I see somebody
now!' she exclaimed at last, 'But he's coming very
slowly – and what curious attitudes he goes into!'
(For the Messenger kept skipping up and down, and
wriggling his hands like an eel, as he came along with
his great hands spread out like fans on each side.)
'Not at all', said the King. 'He's an Anglo-Saxon
Messenger – and those are Anglo-Saxon attitudes.
He only does them when he's happy.'
Through the Looking Glass, and what Alice found There,
Lewis Carroll (Charles Lutwidge Dodgson), 1871

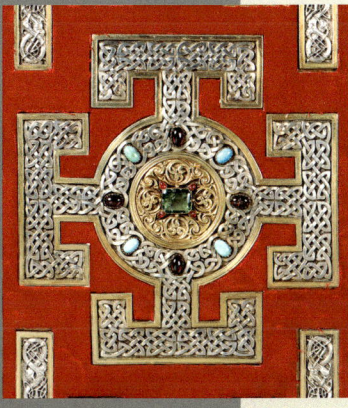

Detail from a cover made
for the Lindisfarne Gospels
in the 19th century
(see fig. 204).

AFTERWORD

Anglo-Saxon art did not die a heroic death after Hastings. The previous chapter pointed to some of the ways in which Anglo-Saxon art made its own particular contributions to the Romanesque style that flourished under Norman rule. Arguably, the stiff, linear style which developed in England in the middle years of the eleventh century was Romanesque already, influenced by the harder-edged modes of German, Flemish and Norman art that were reaching England through royal and ecclesiastical contacts during the reigns of Cnut and Edward the Confessor. Anglo-Saxon influences had also been absorbed into Norman manuscript illumination before the Conquest, ensuring that Anglo-Saxon traditions of animal and foliate ornament, of initials with spirited human input, and the fascination with outline drawing, remained a significant strand in Romanesque manuscript decoration. Anglo-Saxon craftsmanship was greatly admired by Norman commentators,[1] and the continuing influence of Anglo-Saxon and Anglo-Scandinavian animal ornament, and a distinctively Anglo-Saxon treatment of the human figure, can be traced in metalwork, ivories and stone sculpture.[2]

But this is only the beginning of the more complicated, and in some ways surprising, story of how Anglo-Saxon art has continued to exert a long and lively influence, right down to the present day. The great art historian Nikolaus Pevsner saw something in the Anglo-Saxon fascination with the flow of line and surface patterning which seemed to speak to English sensibilities, persisting down the ages from the Romanesque to the 'flaming line' of William Blake's drawings and beyond;[3] he famously defined it as part of the 'Englishness of English art'. This character can be traced in the work of William Morris and the Arts and Crafts movement, and is a very visible thread in English neo-Romanticism. The visionary landscapes of Samuel Palmer and, in the twentieth century, of Paul Nash and Eric Ravilious, the busy, driven patterns of John Minton's drawings and paintings, and the insistent swirls and grooves of David Hockney's swimming pools and Yorkshire fieldscapes all reflect this taste for fluid line and insistent pattern. Kendrick, who saw the Winchester style as 'the first really English thing in English art', suggested that these qualities were transmitted, not just as a reflection of a general English sensibility towards line and rhythm, but as a direct and discernible legacy from the great illuminated books and other works of Anglo-Saxon art that have survived, keeping knowledge of the Anglo-Saxon tradition alive.[4]

Certainly, a great deal of Anglo-Saxon art, including outstanding icons such as the Lindisfarne Gospels, the Benedictional of St Æthelwold and the Ruthwell Cross, continued to be accessible treasures after the Conquest, a source of potential inspiration throughout the Middle Ages. Manuscripts, sculpture, wall-paintings and other religious artefacts remained in ecclesiastical care – not just seen, but actively used, as later comments and doodles on the pages of some manuscripts show. But with the sixteenth-century Protestant Reformation in England, following Henry VIII's definitive break with the Church of Rome, the treasures of the great churches and monasteries were dispersed and broken up. Some manuscripts passed into secular hands; but others were destroyed, or survive only as leaves, while some church sculpture, as we have seen, was defaced by iconoclasts.

Among the manuscripts that passed at this time into private ownership was the Lindisfarne Gospels. As part of the possessions of the Community of St Cuthbert, this had travelled with the saint's shrine and its treasures throughout the period of Viking unrest, until it came finally to rest at Durham Cathedral at the end of the tenth century. It was seized by Henry's commissioners and sent south, subsequently entering the library of Sir Robert Cotton (1571–1631). This was an unrivalled treasure-house of Anglo-Saxon and medieval manuscripts which eventually passed into the collection of the British Museum, and in 1973, the British Library. The other outstanding collection of Anglo-Saxon manuscripts is that assembled by Matthew Parker (1504–75), Archbishop of Canterbury under Elizabeth I, which he left to

Corpus Christi College, Cambridge. Parker was one of the leading architects of the Anglican Church, and his interest in preserving Anglo-Saxon manuscripts was in large measure connected with the securing of evidence to support the ancient origins of this newly independent Church of England, directly descended from Augustine's mission, and 'freed', in his words, from the 'tortures and the toys of Rome'. For the sixteenth-century reformers, the Anglo-Saxon Church, and with it Anglo-Saxon art and culture, had become political.

A new scholarly interest in the study of Old English – an essential tool to understanding – and Anglo-Saxon literature began. Parker encouraged the publication of texts, and even commissioned a special printing type, copying Anglo-Saxon letter forms, to print these editions. The increased accessibility of so many key texts and illuminated manuscripts in the Parker and Cotton libraries greatly enabled this work, resulting not only in the transcription and publication of major Anglo-Saxon literary, administrative and documentary texts, but in a growing appreciation of Anglo-Saxon script and ornament, recorded through careful copying. Throughout the seventeenth and eighteenth centuries many notable scholars, such as Elizabeth Elstob, Humphrey Wanley and George Hickes, brought this material into the public domain and, increasingly, that included publication of Anglo-Saxon antiquities. The Ruthwell Cross, the brooch from Sutton, Isle of Ely, and the Alfred Jewel were some of the well-known items which first gained public attention during this period.

In the nineteenth century, interest in the art of the Anglo-Saxon period was fuelled by new factors. Excavation of Anglo-Saxon cemeteries – following on from the pioneering work of James Douglas and Bryan Faussett in the late eighteenth century – became an increasingly popular antiquarian diversion, especially in Kent, where graves were often richly furnished, and where the chalk bedrock into which they had been cut made excavation easy. Picnic outings, at which a few graves would be opened by way of an afternoon's diversion, were quite popular, and ditties were sometimes composed on the occasion. More serious antiquarian studies of this material were also beginning to be published, for the first time bringing the study of the earliest Anglo-Saxon metalwork into discussions about the origins of Anglo-Saxon England and its art.

At the same time, Anglo-Saxon art and antiquities were beginning to play a role in articulating the broader history of England. At the British Museum, Augustus Franks was eagerly collecting Anglo-Saxon archaeological material as part of a drive to create a national collection of British antiquities; during his long career, he built up an unrivalled collection of Anglo-Saxon artefacts, matching the Museum's superb holdings of Anglo-Saxon manuscripts, which are now in the British Library. One of his greatest gifts to the Museum, the Franks Casket, was perceived by some as an icon of the

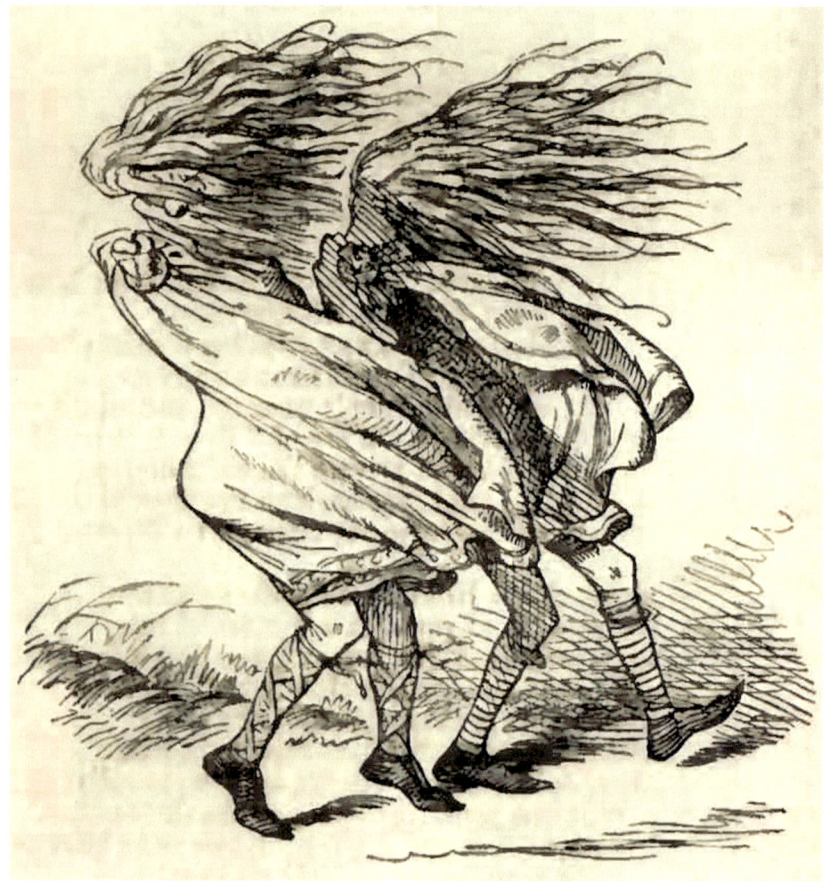

independent character of Englishness, with its combinations of runic inscriptions and Latinity, and Germanic heroic legend with Christian tradition (see p. 92). This sense that Anglo-Saxons had a distinctive, independent culture chimed with other new readings of the Anglo-Saxon past that fed into a Victorian notion of Britain – and England within it – as the sturdy and industrious moral heart of the British Empire. This was a period when it could seem entirely natural that a statue of Queen Victoria and her German consort, Albert, attired in a romantic idea of Anglo-Saxon dress, should grace the royal mausoleum at Frogmore, Berkshire – a sentimentalized evocation at once of the shared cultural origins of the Germans and English, and of those domestic and political values which were through to reflect that Anglo-Saxon heritage.[5] At the same time, the Anglican Church (and especially its Anglo-Catholic Tractarian wing) once again looked to Anglo-Saxon Christianity to validate its customs and beliefs. St Cuthbert and St Augustine of Canterbury became popular church dedications for new, urban Anglo-Catholic churches, and the Great Exhibition of 1851 even included what must have been a remarkable photograph entitled 'The Venerable Bede blessing an Anglo-Saxon child (after nature)'.

The English legal system was also seen as deriving from equivalent Anglo-Saxon institutions, and certain historic Anglo-Saxon figures were accorded almost mythic status. King Alfred (now dubbed 'The Great') was promoted as the model of a heroic Englishman: pious, learned, moral and victorious. The radical popular historian Frederic Harrison described him as representing 'at once the ancient Monarchy, the army, the navy, the law, the literature, the poetry, the art, the enterprise, the industry, the religion of our race' – all emblems of the Victorian ideal. The cult of Alfred in fact has a very long history, which fascinatingly reflects the changing political temper in England from the sixteenth century onwards;[6] it reached its High Victorian peak in 1901, the millenary of his death, with a great celebration at Winchester and an exhibition at the British Museum commemorating Alfred and his times. At the unveiling of yet another Alfred statue at the Winchester celebrations, Lord Rosebery described him as:

> without fear, without stain, and without reproach. In him, indeed, we venerate not so much a striking actor in our history, but the ideal Englishman, the perfect sovereign, the pioneer of England's greatness.

Alfred's popularity was reflected in the many replicas of the Alfred Jewel, both official and opportunistic, that were produced in the early 1900s by several

203. 'The Anglo-Saxon messenger Haigha hands a sandwich to the Red King'; illustration by John Tenniel from Lewis Carroll's *Through the Looking Glass* (1871).

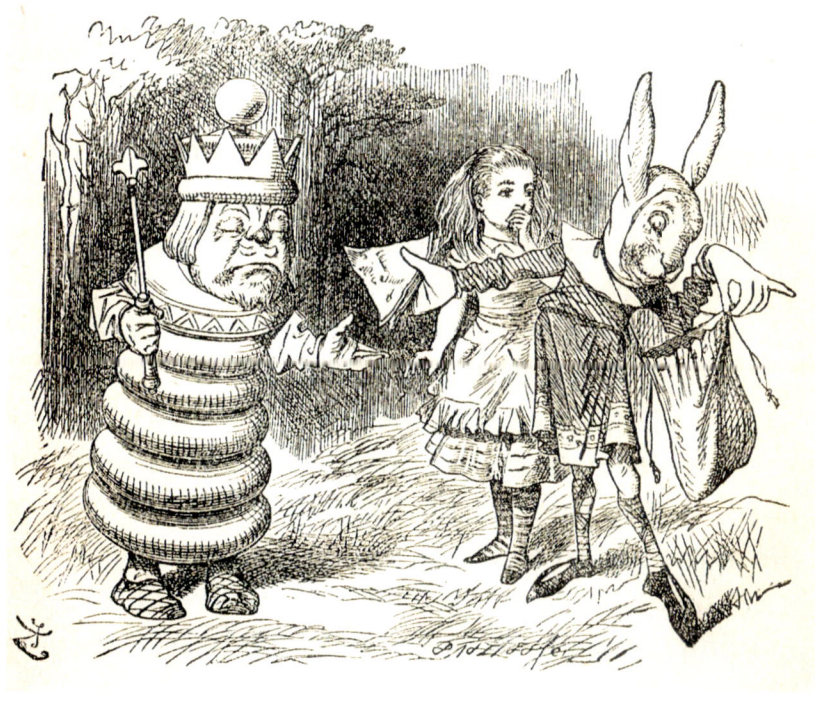

manufacturers and eagerly snapped up; all indications of the growing awareness not just of Alfred, but of all things Anglo-Saxon.

But already by the 1860s some knowledge of Anglo-Saxon art was percolating down to popular levels. In early 1860 the weekly journal *Punch* ran a series of humorous articles, 'Punch's Book of British Costumes', which included four chapters on Anglo-Saxon costume (fig. 202). These were illustrated by an anonymous artist who clearly had some acquaintance with late Anglo-Saxon manuscript art, perhaps picked up from J.O. Westwood's book of medieval biblical illustrations, in which hand-drawn copies of a number of Anglo-Saxon manuscripts appear.[7] The style of some of these *Punch* drawings is remarkably similar to that of John Tenniel, *Punch*'s chief cartoonist of the era, who also memorably illustrated Lewis Carroll's *Alice's Adventures in Wonderland* (1865) and *Through the Looking Glass, and what Alice found There* (1871). Certainly, Tenniel's immortal illustrations of 'Anglo-Saxon' characters in *Through the Looking Glass* look very similar to the *Punch* sketches, and display, like them, an approximate knowledge of the Winchester style (fig. 203).

The shy Oxford mathematics don Carroll also knew something about late Anglo-Saxon art. The famous description of the messenger Haigha, with which this chapter opens, is evidently meant to evoke the exaggerated gestures and tripping gait of figures in late Anglo-Saxon manuscripts, such as the image of King Edgar in the New Minster Charter (see fig. 141). But Carroll's acquaintance with Anglo-Saxon culture went rather deeper than that. The two messengers – and their names, Haigha and Hatta – are Anglo-Saxon versions of the March Hare and the Mad Hatter, who first appear in *Alice's Adventures in Wonderland*. Carroll's much-loved mock-heroic poem, *The Jabberwocky*, which plays on the weird word-forms and monster-battling of *Beowulf* and other Germanic epics, shows that he also had some acquaintance with Anglo-Saxon poetry. Both Carroll's surreal imaginings and Tenniel's playful visualizations of them illustrate a growing popular interest in things Anglo-Saxon; but less frivolous versions of Anglo-Saxon art were also current.

In 1852 the Bishop of Durham paid for a London goldsmith to make a new cover of decorated silver inlaid with precious stones for the Lindisfarne Gospels (by then in the collection of the British Museum). This was intended to recall the lost jewelled cover of gold that Billfrith the anchorite had made for the original, restoring it to its former magnificence (fig. 204). The replacement is in a style which reflects the decoration of the manuscript, one of a few ambitious pieces of metalwork which sought to emulate Anglo-Saxon ornament in the furnishings of the church. Another is an extraordinary 1880s lectern at St Cuthbert's church in Earl's Court, London, mischievously described by John Betjeman as 'neo-Viking'.

However, a more subtle impact made by Anglo-Saxon art in the later nineteenth century is seen in the contributions it made to the Arts and Crafts

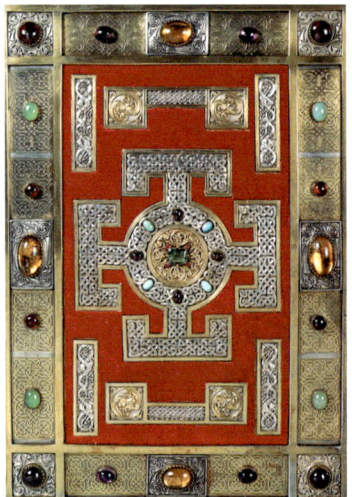

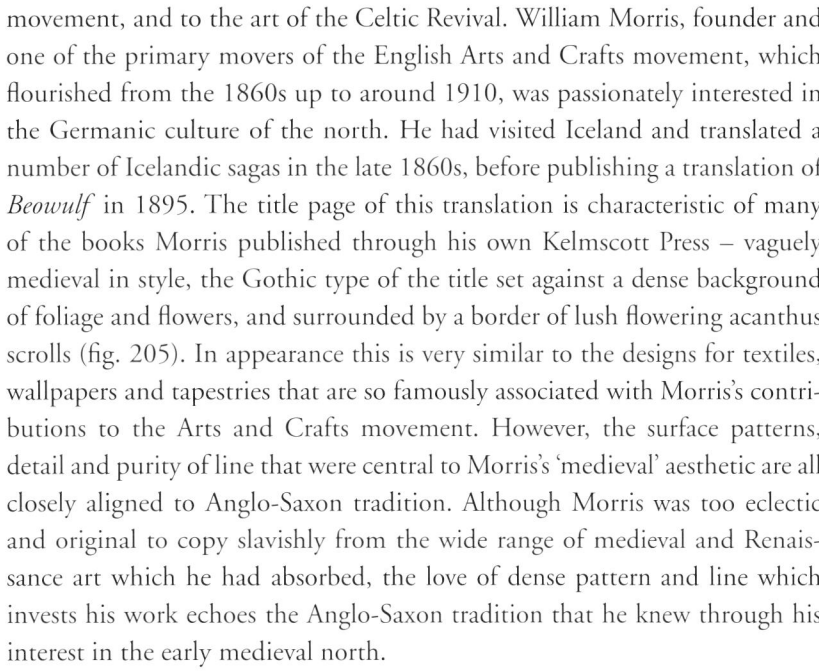

movement, and to the art of the Celtic Revival. William Morris, founder and one of the primary movers of the English Arts and Crafts movement, which flourished from the 1860s up to around 1910, was passionately interested in the Germanic culture of the north. He had visited Iceland and translated a number of Icelandic sagas in the late 1860s, before publishing a translation of *Beowulf* in 1895. The title page of this translation is characteristic of many of the books Morris published through his own Kelmscott Press – vaguely medieval in style, the Gothic type of the title set against a dense background of foliage and flowers, and surrounded by a border of lush flowering acanthus scrolls (fig. 205). In appearance this is very similar to the designs for textiles, wallpapers and tapestries that are so famously associated with Morris's contributions to the Arts and Crafts movement. However, the surface patterns, detail and purity of line that were central to Morris's 'medieval' aesthetic are all closely aligned to Anglo-Saxon tradition. Although Morris was too eclectic and original to copy slavishly from the wide range of medieval and Renaissance art which he had absorbed, the love of dense pattern and line which invests his work echoes the Anglo-Saxon tradition that he knew through his interest in the early medieval north.

More immediately visible are the Anglo-Saxon influences that went

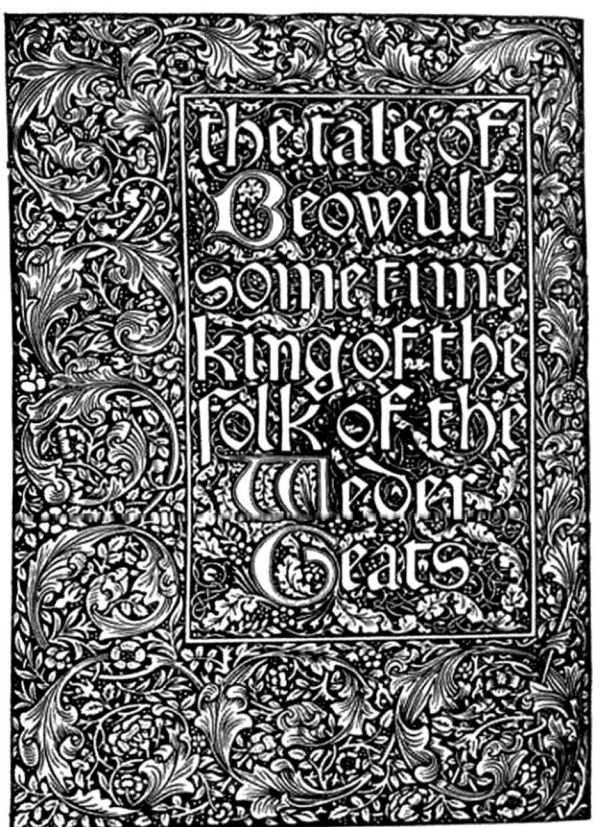

into the making of the art of the Celtic Revival, and its many descendants which still flourish today – from the finest tapestries and metalwork down to tourist memorabilia such as tea towels and, latterly, inventive body tattoos. Although its origins lie chiefly in the Irish Celtic Revival, in which icons of medieval and earlier Irish art, such as the Book of Kells, played a major part in establishing an idea of a national Irish (and Scottish) style and identity, this Celtic style also subsumes motifs taken from the Lindisfarne Gospels and other Insular manuscripts, and interlace of a typically Anglo-Saxon kind. We can see a rather similar phenomenon in the Norwegian *Dragestil* (*c.* 1880–1910), which, like Celtic Revival art, is also closely linked to the Art Nouveau movement; it is based on elements of late Viking ornament, and at the time it was conceived, it too reflected a strong sense of national identity.

The twentieth and twenty-first centuries have brought major new Anglo-Saxon discoveries, and with them, a huge increase in research and publication. As the Bibliography in this book shows, there is a very wide range of publications on the subject. Increasingly, publications and raw data, such as manuscript facsimiles and

204 (*opposite*). Silver book cover, inlaid with precious stones, made for the Lindisfarne Gospels in 1852. 34 x 24 cm (British Library, Cotton MS Nero D.iv, binding)

205 (*below*). Title page to William Morris's translation of *Beowulf*, Kelmscott Press, London, 1895

major archaeological finds, are also available online. All this activity has gradually extended the awareness of Anglo-Saxon art and archaeology to a wider audience. However public perception of the subject really began to change in earnest with the discovery of the Sutton Hoo ship burial in 1939, and its full unveiling to the public in the 1950s and 1960s, once conservation and research had been completed. Indeed, several novels have taken inspiration from the find and its circumstances, including Angus Wilson's *Anglo-Saxon Attitudes* (1956), which incidentally gave a new lease of life to Lewis Carroll's original phrase. The Sutton Hoo helmet (see fig. 16), with its powerful and enigmatic mask that seems to speak to us from the past, has become, like the Lindisfarne Gospels, an icon of Anglo-Saxon England in the popular imagination. But the critical factor in bringing the astonishing wealth and artistry not just of Sutton Hoo, but of Anglo-Saxon art in general, into public awareness and enthusiasm has undoubtedly been television, through a steady stream of programmes from the 1960s to the present day. A widening popular interest has also been engaged by the growing hobby of metal detecting. Recent spectacular finds made by detectorists have stirred the fascination not only for Anglo-Saxon metalwork but for Anglo-Saxon art and culture as a whole. Re-enactment groups have become enormously popular, and with the need to dress up in character has come a whole new industry devoted to copying Anglo-Saxon jewellery, buckle and belt fittings, swords, decorated drinking horns and so on – a quick trawl of the web produces hundreds of images of every kind of accoutrement imaginable. The wish to participate in some way in Anglo-Saxon culture, or at least celebrate it through ownership of such things, has been important for museums, too; the sale of Anglo-Saxon replicas and souvenirs in Anglo-Saxon style, from copies of Queen Æthelswith's ring to scarves and ties with Lindisfarne Gospel beasts, has burgeoned.

But there have been other, less innocent, emulations. Forgeries of Anglo-Saxon artefacts, unsurprisingly, go back to Anglo-Saxon and medieval times. Counterfeit Anglo-Saxon coins and lead rings posing as silver were produced, as well as dubious charters. More learned, antiquarian, Anglo-Saxon forgeries followed after the Reformation, some made to support a particular cause, others simply to deceive wealthy collectors. The recent notorious trial of members of the Greenhalgh family of Bolton, Lancashire, has drawn attention to how readily fake antiquities, including Roman and Anglo-Saxon creations, can be introduced into the art and antiquities market. The astonishingly varied and prolific forgeries produced by Shaun Greenhalgh include three Anglo-Saxon reliquaries, one loosely based on the Alfred Jewel (fig. 206) and another, enamelled and gilded, purporting to be a relic of King Harold, which allegedly came from the collections of Battle Abbey, near the fateful engagement of 1066. A ninth-century-type silver and niello ring, and a seventh-century-style helmet were among several other Anglo-Saxon fakes

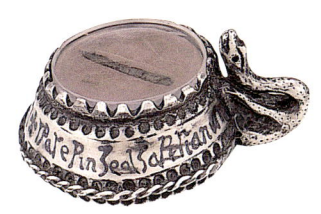

206. 'Reliquary' in Anglo-Saxon style, made by Shaun Greenhalgh, c.1989, and loosely based on the Alfred Jewel.

which were dangled before the eyes of museum curators and sale-rooms, all supported by elaborately concocted pedigrees of varying degrees of plausibility. The Greenhalgh fakes are by no means alone; other even more ambitious forgeries of Anglo-Saxon fine metalwork are in circulation at the time of writing, and will doubtless continue to be so long as the fascination for Anglo-Saxon art and artefacts continues.

A particular effect of the heightened appreciation of Anglo-Saxon objects of art in the last fifty years has been the rise in popular pressure to retain or reclaim major items for their perceived place of origin – often identified with one of the seven kingdoms of the so-called Anglo-Saxon Heptarchy. Calls for the return of the Lindisfarne Gospels to Northumbria, even to Lindisfarne itself, have not been placated by the presentation of facsimiles to both Durham Cathedral and to the Heritage Centre at Lindisfarne, or by the accessibility of a complete online digitized version. Most recently, the public campaign to keep the Staffordshire Hoard within ancient Mercia has seen thousands of people contributing towards its acquisition by the two regional museums. Public interest in, and identification with, these supreme achievements of Anglo-Saxon art tell us a great deal about its power to engage and move us to this day.

And as the Staffordshire Hoard has vividly reminded us, this is not a static body of material. New finds, whether as a result of metal detecting, archaeological excavation or chance discovery, continue to expand our understanding of the subject. As well as objects uncovered from the earth, recent discoveries include Anglo-Saxon sculptures concealed in the walls of churches or, like the Lichfield Angel, under their floors. Other treasures have emerged from French and English attics, such as the gilt-bronze Anglo-Saxon chrismatory (see figs 124–6) and a number of Anglo-Saxon ivories which have come to light in recent years. Even fragments of Anglo-Saxon manuscripts, and occasional later copies of them, surface from time to time – though it is sadly unlikely that we shall ever see an Anglo-Saxon equivalent to the Irish late eighth-century psalter from Faddan More, County Tipperary, recovered intact in 2006 from the Irish bog where it had lain for over 1,200 years.

Such enthralling new finds continually enhance – and sometimes complicate – our understanding of the art of this period, in all its ingenuity, beauty, imagination and daring. But the sense that this is not in any way a closed book is perhaps the supreme fascination of a field in which new discoveries and insights continue to challenge our ideas, and increase our wonder at this extraordinary phenomenon.

GLOSSARY

acanthus Plant decoration with crisply modelled fronded and furled leaves, of classical derivation.

bead and reel ornament A decorative border in which beadlike elements alternate with cylindrical ones.

beaded wire Gold wire with a beaded appearance.

Benedictine Rule Book of precepts for the governance of monasteries, written by St Benedict (480–547).

bracteates Gold repoussé single-sided disc pendants with Style I decoration, originally based on Roman gold coins and medallions.

cabochon Polished gemstone or glass inlay of convex shape, usually set singly.

Carolingian Term used to describe both the dynasty of Frankish rulers descended from Charles Martel (686–741), and the artistic culture that was associated with them *c.* 780–900, especially during the reigns of Charlemagne (747–814) and Charles the Bald (823–77).

carpet page Manuscript page consisting purely of decoration (sometimes incorporating a cross into its design), reminiscent of an Eastern carpet.

chape Protective metal fitting from the end of a scabbard.

Chi-Rho XP monogram denoting the first two letters of Christ's name in Greek, often used as a Christian symbol.

chip-carving Originally a wood-carving technique adapted (by way of carved models) to cast metalwork, in which sharply angled cuts produce a glittering faceted surface on the finished product.

***chrismal*, chrismatory** Small portable container for holy oils used in administering the sacraments, and sometimes the host; in Insular contexts, usually shaped like a gabled house, and decorated.

cloisonné Inlay, normally gemstones, glass or enamel, set in a metal framework of individual cells, or cloisons.

consular diptych Late Roman de luxe commemorative object, consisting of a pair of linked ivory panels, distributed by a new consul to his supporters. They show the consul presiding over the games held in his honour, accompanied by signals and symbols of his office, including the sceptre, the *mappa*, and the dispensing of gold coins (*largitio*).

Coptic Term used to denote the Christian church in Egypt/North Africa.

cruciform brooch, florid cruciform brooch Fifth- and sixth-century copper-alloy bow-brooch type of cruciform shape, mainly current in the Anglian areas of Anglo-Saxon settlement. Its early forms are plain, with an animal head at the foot; later types may be gilded, with silver plating, and carry florid Style I animal ornament.

Diatessaron Gospel harmony, combining the four gospels into a single narrative.

display script Decorative script, generally incorporating higher-grade letter-forms, and used (along with an enlarged initial) to emphasize textual openings.

Dragestil (lit. 'dragon style') Norwegian late nineteenth-century style, incorporating animal motifs based on late Viking styles; especially used in wooden architecture and in metalwork. A parallel development to the British Arts and Crafts movement, and the Irish Celtic revival, in a newly independent Norway it carried strong nationalistic overtones.

emporium (pl. **emporia**) The Latin word for a large trading centre, or market-place. The Old English term is *wic*.

evangelist symbols The evangelists, in their symbolic guise, derived from the biblical vision of Ezekiel: Matthew, represented as a man, Mark as a lion, Luke as a bull, and John as an eagle.

filigree Delicate applied decoration, in which shaped gold wire (often beaded) and granules are soldered onto a gold base.

folio Sheet of vellum, one half of a bifolium.

hairspring coils Very tightly coiled roundels of decoration, resembling the hairspring or balance spring of mechanical timepieces.

hanging-bowls Beaten copper-alloy bowls with soldered attachments enabling them to be suspended; the more elaborate have openwork or enamelled decoration on these mounts, and may have additional internal and external decoration mounts.

heptarchy Term denoting the seven predominant Anglo-Saxon kingdoms of the sixth to ninth centuries: Kent, Essex (East Saxons), Sussex (South Saxons), Wessex (West Saxons), Mercia, East Anglia and Northumbria (various Anglian groups).

Hiberno-Saxon Term used to signify the cultural overlap between Ireland and England, of particular relevance to Northumbria.

historiated initial Initial letter containing a scene or figure germane to the text of the manuscript.

Incipit The opening of a (gospel) text.

Insular Term used to signify the close cultural interaction of Great Britain and Ireland during the period *c*. 550–900, which sometimes avoids the need to differentiate between areas.

lapidary work The shaping, polishing and setting of gem stones.

largitio, **largesse** Formal distribution of gold coins or treasure by emperors, consuls, and other rulers.

lidded cell technique An adaptation of cloisonné work in which the cell framework is concealed by gold lidding, giving the impression that the garnets are inlaid directly into a solid gold base.

mancus Generally signifies a unit of around 4.25 g of gold, but also used as a unit of value and account equivalent to thirty silver pennies; it occasionally took the form of an actual gold coin.

mandorla A pointed oval frame signifying divine glory.

mappa The folded ceremonial cloth with which a consul signals the opening of the games.

mappa mundi A medieval map of the world.

Merovingian The dynasty of the Frankish kings, *c*. 450–752; named after their supposed founder, Merovech.

millefiori Literally 'thousand flowers': decorative glass inlays produced by cutting transverse slices from thin bundles of multi-coloured glass rods.

niello A soft black sulphide inlay, usually of silver or copper, occasionally a mix of both.

Old English The language of the Anglo-Saxons.

opus signinum Pink-coloured flooring in the Roman tradition, made of crushed tile or brick in a mortar base.

Ottonian Term used to describe the culture and dynasty of the German kings (919–1024), named after Otto I and his successors.

palmette Stylized symmetrical palm-frond motif derived from late Roman art.

pelta Decorative motif with one convex and two concave sides, named after a classical shield which it resembles.

porticus Porch-like structure or side-chapel attached to the main body of a church.

repoussé Technique of decorating sheet metal by impressing it into a matrix from the back.

runes An alphabet used by Germanic peoples, including the Anglo-Saxons and Vikings; originally designed for carving on hard surfaces such as wood, stone or metal, its letters are essentially angular in their construction.

saucer brooch Fifth- and sixth-century copper-alloy (or, rarely, silver) round brooch with a saucer-shaped profile, usually associated with areas of Saxon settlement. It is gilded and decorated, and exists in two forms: a cast version, and a so-called 'applied' version, in which an upper, decorative sheet is soldered to a plain base, and a separate rim is fixed to it.

sceat (pl. **sceattas**) Term used since the seventeenth century to denote the small coins which were the earliest Anglo-Saxon silver pennies.

Scots, Scottish In the early medieval period, refers to people of Irish stock, including those who settled in the Argyll area of Scotland, creating the Scottish kingdom of Dál Riata.

scriptorium Writing office, generally (but not exclusively) of a church or monastery.

seax Old English word for a single-edged weapon.

square-headed brooch Late fifth- and sixth-century copper-alloy or silver bow-brooch type with a square head-plate; usually with Style I animal ornament and gilded, and sometimes with garnet inlays. A variant has a decorated disc on the bow. Initially a Kentish type, it became more widely popular.

solidus Standard late Roman and Byzantine gold coin weighing around 4–5 grams; a lighter series weighing around 4–25 grams issued in Italy was copied by Germanic rulers in the West.

tesserae Small coloured glass cubes used in late Antique mosaics; often cannibalized for melting into glass in northern Europe.

trial piece Piece of bone, wood or stone on which designs are tried out.

trumpet scroll A curl which widens into a broad curve ending in an oval motif like a trumpet mouth.

vellum Term often used generically to denote animal skin prepared to receive writing, although it is more correctly applied to calf-skin, and the term parchment to sheep or goat-skin.

Vulgate The Latin translation of the Bible mainly made by St Jerome in the late fourth century.

wic The Old English word for a trading centre, or emporium.

zoomorphic Composed of animal forms.

ANGLO-SAXON ENGLAND IN THE FIRST HALF OF THE EIGHTH CENTURY

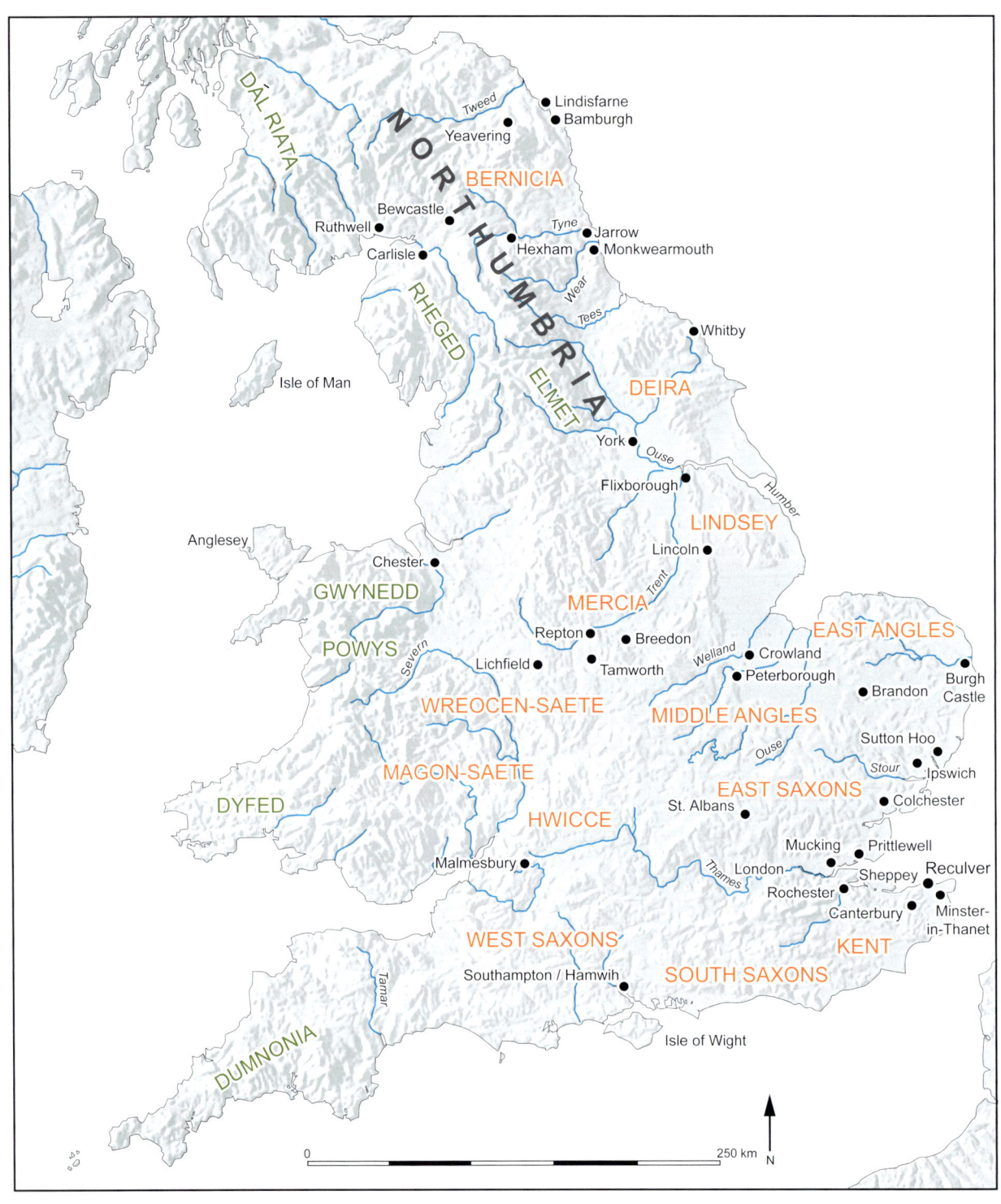

DÁL RIATA

NORTHUMBRIA

Tweed
Lindisfarne
Bamburgh
Yeavering

BERNICIA

Bewcastle
Ruthwell
Tyne
Jarrow
Carlisle
Hexham
Monkwearmouth

RHEGED

Wear
Tees

Whitby

Isle of Man

ELMET

DEIRA

York
Ouse
Flixborough
Humber

Anglesey

LINDSEY

Lincoln

Chester

GWYNEDD

MERCIA

Trent

Repton
Breedon
EAST ANGLES

POWYS

Lichfield
Tamworth
Welland
Crowland
Peterborough
Brandon
Burgh
Castle

WREOCEN-SAETE

Severn

MIDDLE ANGLES

Ouse

Sutton Hoo
Stour
Ipswich

MAGON-SAETE

EAST SAXONS

DYFED

HWICCE

St. Albans
Colchester

Malmesbury

Mucking
Prittlewell

Thames
London
Sheppey
Reculver
Rochester
Canterbury
Minster-
in-Thanet

Tamar

WEST SAXONS

Southampton / Hamwih

SOUTH SAXONS

KENT

DUMNONIA

Isle of Wight

0   250 km
N

ANGLO-SAXON ENGLAND IN THE FIRST HALF OF THE TENTH CENTURY

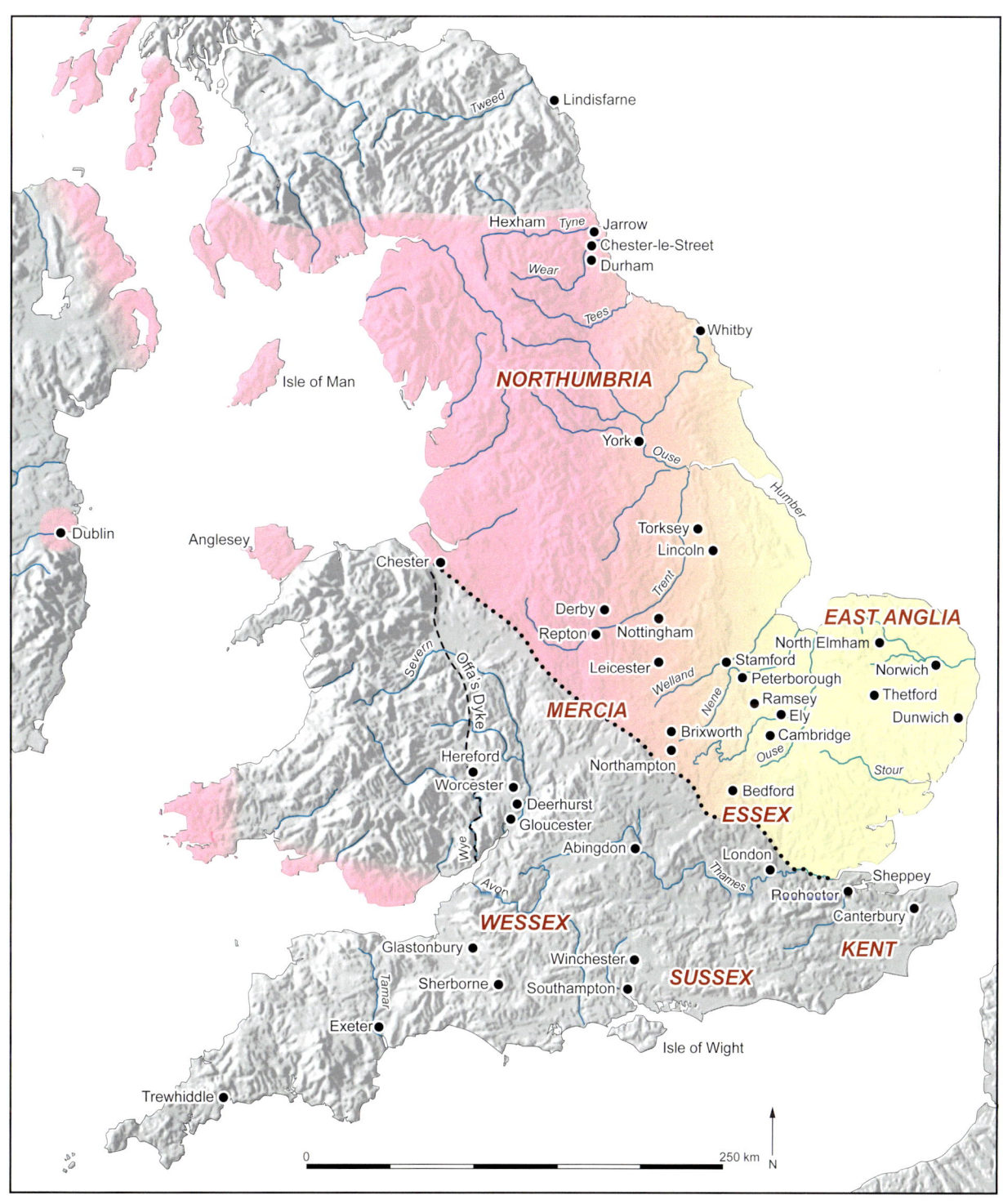

Tweed

Lindisfarne

Hexham *Tyne* Jarrow
Chester-le-Street
Wear Durham

Tees Whitby

Isle of Man

NORTHUMBRIA

York *Ouse*

Humber

Dublin

Anglesey Chester

Torksey
Lincoln

Trent

EAST ANGLIA

Derby Repton Nottingham

North Elmham Norwich
Stamford Thetford
Leicester *Welland* Peterborough Dunwich
Ramsey
Ely
Brixworth Cambridge

Severn Offa's Dyke

MERCIA

Hereford
Worcester
Deerhurst *Wye*
Gloucester

Northampton *Nene* *Ouse*

Bedford *Stour*

ESSEX

Abingdon *Avon* *Thames* London Sheppey

Rochester
Canterbury

WESSEX

Glastonbury *Tamar*
Sherborne Winchester
Southampton

KENT

SUSSEX

Exeter

Isle of Wight

Trewhiddle

0   250 km
N

NOTES

Introduction

1. Translated by S.J. Bradley, adapted by the author.
2. Though excavations have revealed traces in the ground of great halls of this period in Denmark, Sweden and Norway, and at some sites in England, including at the Northumbrian royal palace site at Yeavering, Northumberland, nothing physical remains of these grand structures and their decoration.

Chapter 1: Reading the Image, Seeing the Text

1. Translation by the author.
2. Kendrick 1938, 2.
3. British Library, MS Cotton Nero D.iv; Alexander 1978, cat. 9.
4. Alexander 1978, figs 50, 76.
5. K. O'Brien O'Keeffe, *Visible Song: Transitional Literacy in Old English Verse*, Cambridge 1990.
6. Bede: ed. Colgrave and Mynors 1969, Book II, chapter 13.
7. Florence, Biblioteca Medicea Laurenziana, MS Amiatino 1; Alexander 1978, cat. 7.
8. For the Rochester stone, see D. Tweddle, M. Biddle and B. Kjølbye-Biddle, *South-East England*, CASSS vol. 4, Oxford 1995.
9. Rodwell, Hawkes, Howe and Cramp 2008.
10. E.g. A.G. Holder (transl.), *Bede: On the Tabernacle*, Liverpool 1994, Books 2 and 3.
11. Gem, Howe and Bryant 2008.
12. Gem and Tudor Craig 1981.
13. Axboe 2007 gives a good overview of the subject.
14. Dickinson 2005.
15. Pratt 2003.
16. Haseloff 1981, 118, 450–54; Leigh 1984; Webster 2005.
17. Webster 2003a.
18. J.H. Pitman (ed. and transl.), *The Riddles of Aldhelm*, New Haven and London 1925, riddle no. 55.
19. Schön 1999.
20. A. Blackett, 'An Anglo-Saxon figure-decorated plaque from Ayton (Scottish Borders)', *Medieval Archaeology* 51 (2007), 165–71.
21. Kendrick 1938, 1; see also Pächt 1986, 66, for a similar view.

Chapter 2: Rome Reinvented: the early inheritance

1. Translated by S.J. Bradley.
2. See, e.g., Jørgensen, Storgaard and Thomsen 2003.
3. See, e.g., C. Johns, *The Hoxne Late Roman Treasure: Gold Jewellery and Silver Plate*, London 2010.
4. S. Hirst and D. Clark, *Excavations at Mucking*, vol. 3: *The Anglo-Saxon Cemeteries, part ii; Analysis and discussion*, London 2009, 441–2.
5. For general background, see Hamerow, Hinton and Crawford 2011.
6. Translated by S.J. Bradley.
7. Inker 2006.
8. Schön 1999.
9. Inker 2006.
10. Suzuki 2000.
11. S.C. Hawkes and G.M. Dunning, 'Soldiers and settlers in Britain', *Medieval Archaeology* 5 (1961), 1–70.
12. Salin 1904 has been the foundation of all subsequent studies. The most recent overview, excellently illustrated, is Haseloff 1981; see also Haseloff 1974 for a brief English summary.
13. Jørgensen, Storgaard and Thomsen 2003.

14. Haseloff, cited in Dickinson 2002, 163.
15. Hines 1997.
16. Speake 1980; Høilund Nielsen 1999a; Høilund Nielsen 1999b.
17. E.g. Haseloff 1981, 246–59.
18. See illustrations in Speake 1980.

Chapter 3: Rome Reinvented: the impact of Christianity

1. Translation by J.F. Webb.
2. Bruce-Mitford 1969.
3. Wilson 1984, 116.
4. See Youngs 1989.
5. Henderson and Henderson 2010.
6. Durham Cathedral Library, MSS A.II.10 and A.II.17; Alexander 1978, cats 5, 10.
7. Paris, Bibliothèque Nationale, MS Lat.9389.
8. A. Campbell (ed. and transl.), *Æthelwulf: De Abbatibus*, Oxford 1967.
9. Durham Cathedral Library, MS B.II.30; Alexander 1978, cat. 17.
10. Bailey 2009.
11. Durham Cathedral Library, MS A.II.17; Alexander 1978, cat. 10.
12. Alexander 1978, cat. 21, figs 82 and 80.
13. Wilson 1984, fig. 187.
14. J. Hawkes, 'The Rothbury cross: an iconographic bricolage', *Gesta* 35/1 (1996), 77–94.
15. Hawkes 2009.
16. Webster 1999; Webster 2011.
17. Webster 2011, fig. p. 34.

Chapter 4: Celtic connections, Eastern influences

1. A. Campbell (ed. and transl.) *Æthelwulf: De Abbatibus*, Oxford 1967.
2. Bruce-Mitford with Raven 2005.
3. Youngs 2009b.
4. Youngs 2009a, 52.
5. Alexander 1978, cats 4, 2, 3.
6. Durham Cathedral Library, MS A.II.10.
7. Youngs 2009a, 53–5.
8. See, for instance, C. Farr, 'The Sign at the Cross-Roads', in Crawford and Hamerow 2009, 79–88; J. O'Reilly, 'Patristic and Insular traditions of the evangelists: exegesis and iconography', in A.M. Luiselli Fadda and É. Ó Carragáin, *Le Isole Britanniche e Roma in Età*, Rome 1998, 49–94.
9. British Library, MS Royal 1 E vi; Alexander 1978, cat. 32.
10. Bailey 2002, 14–21.
11. See M. Swanton, 'Ælfric's Colloquy', in *Anglo-Saxon Prose*, London 1975, 107–15.
12. Nordenfalk 1977, 24–5.
13. Webster and Backhouse 1991, cat. 68.
14. Rodwell, Hawkes, Howe and Cramp 2008, 74–5.
15. Bailey 2002, 7–11.
16. Gem 2008, 21–5.

Chapter 5: Art and Power, from Sutton Hoo to Alfred

1. Keynes and Lapidge 1983.
2. finds.org.uk/staffshoardsymposium.
3. Høilund Nielsen 2011.
4. Durham Cathedral Library, MS A.II.10; Alexander 1978, cat. 5.
5. Høilund Nielsen 2011.
6. L. Webster, 'Image, Identity and the Staffordshire Hoard', in Niles, Klein and Wilcox forthcoming.
7. Ganz 2011; Okasha 2011.
8. See Webster and Backhouse 1991, cat. 46.
9. J. Story, 'Charlemagne's black marble: the origins of the Epitaph of

Pope Hadrian I', *Papers of the British School at Rome* 73 (2005), 157–90.
10. R. Gem, *Architecture, Liturgy and Romanitas at All Saints' Church, Brixworth*, Leicester 2011.
11. See Cramp in Rodwell, Hawkes, Howe and Cramp 2008.
12. E.g. Gannon 2003, fig. 2.10.
13. Mitchell 2010, 266.
14. Gem 2008, 26.
15. Mitchell 2010, 262–3.
16. Webster and Backhouse 1991, cat. 210.
17. Wilson 1984, fig. 90.
18. Webster 2001a; Webster 2001b.
19. Webster and Backhouse 1991, fig. 25; Wilson 1984, fig. 180.
20. Bailey 2000, 46–7.
21. Webster 2001b; for new finds, consult the Portable Antiquities website, finds.org.uk/database.
22. E.g. Plunkett 1998.
23. G. Henderson and I. Henderson, *The Art of the Picts, Sculpture and Metalwork in Early Medieval Scotland*, London 2004.
24. Webster and Backhouse 1991, cats 177–8.
25. *Export of Objects of Cultural Interest*, DCMS report, London 2007, 73–4, pl. 20.
26. Alfred, *Preface* to his translation of Gregory the Great's *Pastoral Care*: Keynes and Lapidge 1983, 125.
27. Wilson 1984, figs 103–4.
28. D.A. Hinton, D. Keene and K. Qualmann, 'The Winchester reliquary', *Medieval Archaeology* 25 (1981), 45–77.
29. Webster and Backhouse 1991, cat. 201.
30. Keynes and Lapidge 1983, 126.
31. Hinton 2008.
32. Pratt 2003; Webster 2003b.
33. C. Fell and N. Lund, *Ohthere and Wulfstan: Two Voyagers at the Court of King Alfred*, York 1984.
34. British Library, MS Royal 5.F.iii; Temple 1976, cat. 2.

Chapter 6: Mission and Reform, eighth to eleventh centuries

1. Translation by D. Whitelock.
2. Willibald, *Life of St Boniface*, in C.H. Talbot, *The Anglo-Saxon Missionaries in Germany, Being the Lives of SS. Willibrord, Boniface, Leoba and Lebuin together with the Hodoepericon of St Willibald and a selection from the correspondence of St Boniface*, London and New York 1954.
3. Paris, Bibliothèque Nationale, MS Lat.9389; Alexander 1978, cats 11, 37.
4. See Dodwell 1982, 205–7.
5. Webster and Backhouse 1991, cats 131, 132.
6. I am indebted to Richard Camber, Jane Hawkes and Lawrence Nees, some of whose ideas are reflected in this brief discussion.
7. Williamson 2010, cat. 37.
8. British Library, MS Cotton Tiberius A.ii.
9. Backhouse, Turner and Webster 1984, cat. 21.
10. See esp. Temple 1976.
11. See esp. Dodwell 1982.
12. Wormald 1945.
13. British Library, MS Harley 2904.
14. Oxford, Bodleian Library, MS Bodley 155, fol. 146v; Temple 1976, cat. 59.
15. See Temple 1976, cats 47, 68, 61 and 65.
16. Vatican City, Biblioteca Apostolica Vaticana, MS Reg. Lat.12; Temple 1976, cat. 84.
17. New York, Pierpont Morgan Library, MS 709, fol. 1v; Temple 1976, cat. 93.
18. Temple 1976, cat. 98, figs 307–8.
19. Cambridge, Pembroke College, MS 302; Temple 1976, cat. 96.
20. Oxford, Bodleian Library, MS Junius 11; Temple 1976, cat. 87.
21. See Gem and Tudor-Craig 1981.
22. Kendrick 1949, pl. 40(i).
23. Wilson 1984, fig. 250.
24. Backhouse, Turner and Webster 1984, cat. 139.
25. For a useful account, see Dodwell 1982, esp. ch. 7.
26. Wilson 1964, cats 9, 44 and 56.
27. See, for example, the Anglo-Saxon Hexateuch, fols 120–21.
28. Williamson 2010, cat. 67.
29. Williamson 2010, cat. 61.
30. See, e.g., Pächt 1986, fig. 117.
31. See Backhouse, Turner and Webster 1984, cat. 131.
32. Webster 2008; Keynes 2008.
33. Keynes 2008, 190–201, pl. 3a and b.

Chapter 7: The North Ascendant: the Viking impact

1. A. Campbell (ed. and transl.), *Encomium Emmæ Reginæ*, London 1949, Book 1, 4.
2. C. Fell and N. Lund, *Ohthere and Wulfstan: Two Voyagers at the Court of King Alfred*, York 1984.
3. Wilson and Klindt-Jensen 1966, pls 49, 57.
4. Wilson and Klindt-Jensen 1966, pl. 34a.
5. Wilson and Klindt-Jensen 1966, pls 52–3.
6. Wilson and Klindt-Jensen 1966, pl. 69.
7. Bailey 1980.
8. Bailey 1980, fig. 15, pl. 29.
9. Wilson 1984, fig. 93.
10. Bailey 1980, pls 14, 15.
11. Wilson 1964, cat. 10.
12. Whitelock 1979, no. 116.
13. D. Tweddle, M. Biddle and B. Kjølbye-Biddle, *South-East England*, CASSS vol. 4, Oxford 1995.
14. Backhouse, Turner and Webster 1984, cat. 96.
15. Temple 1976, cat. 80.
16. Temple 1976, cat. 58.
17. Temple 1976, cat. 86; British Library Digitised Manuscripts website. See esp. fols 14r–15v.
18. S. West, 'A Corpus of Anglo-Saxon Material from Suffolk', *East Anglian Archaeology* 84 (1998), fig. 8:4.
19. See Backhouse, Turner and Webster 1984, cat. 270.
20. Kendrick 1949, pls 86, 87.
21. Kendrick 1949, 126.
22. Oxford, Wadham College, MS A.10.22; Backhouse, Turner and Webster 1984, cat. 263.
23. Wilson 1985.
24. See Biddle in Backhouse, Turner and Webster 1984, cat. 140.
25. Wilson 1985, 170, pl. 17.
26. J. Alexander, preface to Pächt 1986, 8.

Afterword

1. Dodwell 1982, 193, citing William of Poitiers.
2. G. Zarnecki, 'General Introduction', in Zarnecki, Holt and Holland 1983, 15–26.
3. Pevsner 1956, 119–20.
4. Kendrick 1949.
5. The statue is by William Theed (1804–91); a copy of it can be seen in the National Portrait Gallery, London.
6. Keynes 2000.
7. J.O. Westwood, *Palaeographica Sacra Pictoria*, London 1843–5; see also his later book *Facsimiles of the Miniatures and Ornaments of Anglo-Saxon and Irish Manuscipts*, London 1868.

BIBLIOGRAPHY AND WEB RESOURCES

The books, articles and websites listed below are intended as a guide to further exploration.

General studies

Alexander, J.J.G. 1978. *Insular Manuscripts, Sixth to the Ninth Century. A Survey of Manuscripts Illuminated in the British Isles*, vol. 1, London.

Backhouse, J., Turner, D.H., and Webster, L. (eds) 1984. *The Golden Age of Anglo-Saxon Art 966–1066*, London.

Bede: see Colgrave, B., and Mynors, R.A.B. (transl. and eds) 1969. *Bede's Ecclesiastical History of the English People*, Oxford.

Bradley, S.A.J. (transl. and ed.) 1995. *Anglo-Saxon Poetry* (Everyman), London.

Brown, M.P. 2007. *Manuscripts from the Anglo Saxon Age*, London.

Cather, S., Parks, D., and Williamson, P. (eds) 1990. *Early Medieval Wall Painting and Painted Sculpture* (British Archaeological Reports British Series, 216), Oxford.

CASSS 1984–. *Corpus of Anglo-Saxon Stone Sculpture*, regional volumes, Oxford. See http://www.dur.ac.uk/corpus/index.php3.

Crawford, S., and Hamerow, H., with Webster, L. 2009. *Form and Order in the Anglo-Saxon World, AD 600–1100* (Anglo-Saxon Studies in Archaeology and History, 16), Oxford.

Dodwell, C.R. 1982. *Anglo-Saxon Art: a new perspective*, Manchester.

Hamerow, H., Hinton, D.A., and Crawford, S. (eds) 2011. *The Oxford Handbook of Anglo-Saxon Archaeology*, Oxford.

Hills, C. 2003. *Origins of the English*, London.

Hinton, D.A. 2005. *Gold and Gilt, Pots and Pins: Possessions and People in Medieval Britain*, Oxford.

Karkov, C.E. 2011. *The Art of Anglo-Saxon England*, Woodbridge.

Kauffman, C.M. 1975. *Romanesque Manuscripts, 1066–1190: A Survey of Manuscripts Illuminated in the British Isles*, vol. 3, London.

Kendrick, T.D. 1938. *Anglo-Saxon Art to AD 900*, London.

Lapidge, M., Blair, J., Keynes, S.D., and Scragg, D. (eds) 1999. *The Blackwell Encyclopaedia of Anglo-Saxon England*, Oxford.

Nees, L. 2002. *Early Medieval Art* (Oxford History of Art), Oxford.

Niles, J.D., Klein, S.S., and Wilcox, J. (eds) forthcoming. *Anglo-Saxon England and the Visual Imagination* (Essays in Anglo-Saxon Studies, 6), Tempe.

Pächt, O. 1986. *Book Illumination in the Middle Ages*, London and Oxford.

Temple, E. 1976. *Anglo-Saxon Manuscripts 900–1066. A Survey of Manuscripts Illuminated in the British Isles*, vol. 2, London.

Webster, L. 2011. 'Style: influences, chronology, and meaning', in Hamerow, Hinton and Crawford 2011, 460–502.

Webster, L., and Backhouse, J. (eds) 1991. *The Making of England: Anglo-Saxon Art and Culture AD 600–900*, London.

Whitelock, D. (ed.) 1979. *English Historical Documents*, vol. 1, Oxford (2nd edn).

Wilson, D.M. 1984. *Anglo-Saxon Art*, London.

Chapter 1: Reading the Image, Seeing the Text

Bailey, R.N. 2009. 'Anglo-Saxon art: some forms, orderings, and their meanings', in Crawford and Hamerow 2009, 18–30.

Leigh, D. 1984. 'Ambiguity in Anglo-Saxon Style 1', *Antiquaries Journal* 64, 34–42.

Webster, L. 2003a. 'Encrypted visions: style and sense in the Anglo-Saxon minor arts, A.D. 400–900', in C.E. Karkov and G.H. Brown (eds), *Anglo-Saxon Styles*, Albany, 11–30.

Webster, L. 2005. 'Visual literacy in a protoliterate age', in P. Hermann (ed.), *Literacy in Medieval and Early Modern Scandinavian Culture* (Studies in Northern Civilization 16), Viborg, 21–46.

Chapter 2: Rome Reinvented: the early inheritance

Axboe, M. 2007. *Brakteatenstudier*, Copenhagen. This has a useful English summary.

Dickinson, T.M. 2002. 'Translating animal art: Salin's Style 1 and Anglo-Saxon cast saucer brooches', *Hikuin* 29, 163–86.

Dickinson, T.M. 2005. 'Symbols of protection: the significance of animal-ornamented shields in early Anglo-Saxon England', *Medieval Archaeology* 49, 109–63.

Haseloff, G. 1974. 'Salin's Style I', *Medieval Archaeology* 18, 1–15. A very brief summary of the subject in English.

Haseloff, G. 1981. *Die Germanische Tierornamentik der Volkerwanderungszeit*, vols 1–3, Berlin. The most recent study, with very helpful analytical illustrations.

Hedeager, L. 1999. 'Myth and art: a passport to political authority in Scandinavia during the Migration Period', *Anglo-Saxon Studies in Archaeology and History* 10, 151–6.

Hines, J. 1997. *A new Corpus of Anglo-Saxon great square-headed Brooches* (Reports of the Research Committee of the Society of Antiquaries, 51), London.

Høilund Nielsen, K. 1999a. 'Style II and the Anglo-Saxon elite', *Anglo-Saxon Studies in Archaeology and History* 10, 185–202.

Høilund Nielsen, K. 1999b. 'Animal style, a symbol of might and myth: Salin's Style II in a European context', *Acta Archaeologica* 69, 1–52.

Inker, P. 2006. *The Saxon Relief Style* (British Archaeological Reports British Series, 410), Oxford.

Jørgensen, L., Storgaard, B., and Thomsen, L.G. 2003. *The Spoils of Victory – the North in the Shadow of the Roman Empire*, Copenhagen.

Salin, B. 1904. *Die Altgermanische Thierornamentik*, Stockholm. Still a valuable study of the subject, with many useful illustrations.

Schön, M. 1999. *Feddersen Wierde, Fallward, Flögeln*, Bremerhaven.

Speake, G. 1980. *Anglo-Saxon Animal Art and its Germanic Background*, Oxford.

Suzuki, S. 2000. *The Quoit Brooch Style and Anglo-Saxon Settlement: a Casting and Re-casting of Cultural Identity Symbols*, Woodbridge.

Chapter 3: Rome Reinvented: the impact of Christianity

Bailey, R.N. 1996. *England's Earliest Sculptures* (Publications of the Dictionary of Old English, 5), Toronto.

Battiscombe, C.F. (ed.) 1956. *The Relics of St Cuthbert*, Oxford.

Blair, J. 2005. *The Church in Anglo-Saxon Society*, Oxford.

Brown, M.P. 2000. *In the Beginning was the Word: Books and Faith in the Age of Bede* (Jarrow Lecture 2000), Jarrow.

Brown, M.P. 2003. *The Lindisfarne Gospels: Society, Spirituality and the Scribe* (British Library Studies in Medieval Culture), London.

Brown, M.P. 2011. *The Lindisfarne Gospels and the Early Medieval World*, London.

Bruce-Mitford, R.L.S. 1969. 'The art of the Codex Amiatinus', *Journal of the British Archaeological Association* 32, 1–26.

Gannon, A. 2003. *The Iconography of early Anglo-Saxon Coinage, sixth to eighth centuries*, Oxford.

Hawkes, J. 2003. 'Sacraments in stone: the mysteries of Christ in Anglo-Saxon sculpture', in M. Carver, *The Cross goes North: processes of Conversion in Northern Europe AD 300–1300*, Woodbridge, 351–70.

Hawkes, J. 2009. 'The Church Triumphant: the figural columns of early ninth-century Anglo-Saxon England', in Crawford and Hamerow 2009, 45–64.

Ó Carragáin, E. 2005. *Ritual and the Rood: Liturgical Images and the Old English Poems of the Dream of the Rood Tradition*, London and Toronto.

Webster, L. 1999. 'The iconographic programme of the Franks Casket', in J. Hawkes and S. Mills (eds), *Northumbria's Golden Age*, Stroud, 227–46.

Webster, L. 2012. *The Franks Casket* (British Museum Objects in Focus), London.

Chapter 4: Celtic Connections, Eastern Influences

Bruce-Mitford, R.L.S. with Raven, S. 2005. *The Corpus of Late Celtic Hanging Bowls*, Oxford.

Gem, R. 2008. *Deerhurst and Rome: Aethelric's Pilgrimage c. 804 and the Oratory of St Mary Mediana* (The 2007 Deerhurst Lecture), Deerhurst.

Nordenfalk, C. 1977. *Celtic and Anglo-Saxon Painting*, London.

Youngs, S.M. (ed.) 1989. *The Work of Angels: Masterpieces of Celtic Metalwork 600–900 AD*, London.

Youngs, S. 2009a. 'From metalwork to manuscript: some observations on the use of Celtic art in Insular manuscripts', in Crawford and Hamerow 2009, 45–64.

Youngs, S. 2009b. 'Anglo-Saxon, Irish and British relations: hanging bowls reconsidered', in J. Graham-Campbell and M. Ryan (eds), *Anglo-Saxon/Irish Relations before the Vikings* (Proceedings of the British Academy 157), Oxford, 205–30.

Chapter 5: Art and Power, from Sutton Hoo to Alfred

Bailey, R.N. 2000. 'The Gandersheim Casket and Anglo-Saxon sculpture', in March 2000 (see below), 43–52.

Bailey, R.N. 2002. *Anglo-Saxon Sculptures at Deerhurst* (The 2002 Deerhurst Lecture), Deerhurst.

Bakka, E. 1963. *Some English decorated metal objects found in Norwegian Viking graves. Contribution to the art history of the 8th century A.D.* (Humanistik Serie, 1), Bergen, 4–66.

Brown, M.P. 2001. 'Mercian manuscripts?: the Tiberius group and its historical context', in Brown and Farr 2001 (see below), 278–93.

Brown, M.P., and Farr, C.A. (eds.) 2001. *Mercia, an Anglo-Saxon Kingdom in Europe*, Leicester.

Filmer-Sankey, W. 1996. 'The Roman Empire in the Sutton Hoo ship-burial', *Journal of the British Archaeological Association* 149, 1–9.

Ganz, D. 2011. 'The Text of the Inscription', Staffordshire Hoard Symposium: finds.org.uk/staffshoardsymposium.

Gem, R., Howe, E., and Bryant, R. 2008. 'The ninth-century polychrome decoration at St Mary's Church, Deerhurst', *Antiquaries Journal* 88, 109–64.

Henderson, G., and Henderson, I. 2011. 'The implications of the Staffordshire Hoard for the understanding of the origins and development of the Insular art style as it appears in manuscripts and sculpture', Staffordshire Hoard Symposium: finds.org.uk/staffshoardsymposium.

Hinton, D.A. 2008. *The Alfred Jewel and other Late Anglo-Saxon Decorated Metalwork*, Oxford.

Høilund Nielsen, K. 2011. 'Style II and all that: the potential of the hoard for statistical study of chronology and geographical distributions', Staffordshire Hoard Symposium: finds.org.uk/staffshoardsymposium.

Jewell, R.H.I. 1986. 'The Anglo-Saxon friezes at Breedon-on-the-Hill, Leicestershire', *Archaeologia* 108, 95–115.

Jewell, R.H.I. 2001. 'Classicism of Southumbrian Sculpture', in Brown and Farr 2001, 246–62.

Keynes, S.D., and Lapidge, M. (eds. and transl.) 1983. *Alfred the Great: Asser's Life of King Alfred and other contemporary Sources*, Harmondsworth.

Marth, R. (ed.) 2000. *Das Gandersheimer Runenkästchen. Internationales Kolloquium Braunschweig 24–26 Marz 1999*, Braunschweig.

Mitchell, J. 2010. 'England in the eighth century. State formation, secular piety and the visual arts in Mercia', in V. Pace (ed.), *L'VIII secolo: un secolo inquieto (Atti del Convegno internazionale di studi Cividale del Friuli 4–7 dicembre 2008)*, 262–70.

Okasha, E. 2011. 'The Staffordshire Hoard inscription', Staffordshire Hoard Symposium: finds.org.uk/staffshoardsymposium.

Plunkett, S. 1998. 'The Mercian perspective', in S. Foster (ed.), *The St Andrews Sarcophagus*, Dublin, 202–26.

Pratt, D. 2003. 'Persuasion and innovation at the court of Alfred the Great', in C. Cubitt (ed.), *Court Culture in the Early Middle Ages: the Proceedings of the First Alcuin Conference*, Turnhout, 189–221.

Rodwell, W., Hawkes, J., Howe, E., and Cramp, R.J. 2008. 'The Lichfield angel: a spectacular Anglo-Saxon painted sculpture', *Antiquaries Journal* 88, 48–108.

Tweddle, D. 1992. *The Anglian Helmet from Coppergate* (Archaeology of York, 17/8), London.

Webster, L. 1992. 'Death's diplomacy: Sutton Hoo in the light of other male princely burials', in R. Farrell and C. Neuman de Vegvar (eds), *Sutton Hoo: Fifty Years After* (American Early Medieval Studies 2), Oxford and Miami OH, 75–82.

Webster, L. 2001a. 'The Anglo-Saxon Hinterland: animal style in Southumbrian eighth-century England, with particular reference to metalwork', in M. Müller-Wille and L.O. Larsson (eds), *Tiere – Menschen – Götter. Wikingerzeitliche Kunststile und ihre neuzeitliche Rezeption*, Göttingen, 39–62.

Webster, L. 2001b. 'Metalwork of the Mercian supremacy', in Brown and Farr 2001, 263–77.

Webster, L. 2003b. 'Ædificia nova; treasures of Alfred's reign', in T. Reuter (ed.), *Alfred the Great*, Aldershot, 79–103.

Chapter 6: Mission and Reform

Cramp, R.J. 1986. 'The furnishing and sculptural decoration of Anglo-Saxon churches', in L.A.S. Butler and R.K. Morris (eds), *The Anglo-Saxon Church: Papers on History, Architecture*

and Archaeology in Honour of Dr H.M. Taylor (Council for British Archaeology Research Report 60), London, 101–4.

Deshman, R. 1995. *The Benedictional of Æthelwold*, Princeton.

Gameson, R. 1991. 'English manuscript art in the mid-eleventh century', *Antiquaries Journal* 71, 64–122.

Gameson, R. 1995. *The Role of Art in the late Anglo-Saxon Church*, Oxford.

Gameson, R. 1997. 'The origin, art and message of the Bayeux Tapestry', in Gameson 1997 (see under ch. 7), 157–211.

Gem, R., and Tudor-Craig, P. 1981. 'A "Winchester School" wall-painting at Nether Wallop, Hampshire', *Anglo-Saxon England* 9, 115–36.

Hinton, D.A. 1974. *A Catalogue of the Anglo-Saxon Ornamental Metalwork 700–1100 in the Department of Antiquities, Ashmolean Museum*, Oxford.

Keynes, S.D. 2008. 'An abbot, an archbishop, and the Viking raids of 1006–7 and 1009–12', *Anglo-Saxon England* 36, 151–220.

Webster, L. 2000. 'Style and function of the Gandersheim Casket', in Marth 2000 (see under ch. 5), 63–72.

Webster, L. 2008. 'Apocalypse Then: Anglo-Saxon ivory carving in the tenth and eleventh centuries', in C.E. Karkov and H. Damico (eds), *Ædificia Nova: Studies in Honor of Rosemary Cramp*, Kalamazoo, 226–53.

Williamson, P. 2010. *Medieval Ivory Carvings: Early Christian to Romanesque*, London.

Williamson, P., and Webster, L. 1990. 'The Coloured Decoration of Anglo-Saxon Ivory Carvings', in Cather, Parks and Williamson 1990 (see under General), 177–94.

Wilson, D.M. 1964. *Anglo-Saxon Ornamental Metalwork 700–1100 in the British Museum, Catalogue of Antiquities of the Later Saxon Period, volume 1*, London.

Wormald, F. 1945. 'Decorated initials in English manuscripts from AD 900 to 1100', *Archaeologia* 91, 107–35.

Wormald, F. 1952. *English Drawings of the Tenth and Eleventh Centuries*, London.

Wormald, F. 1971. 'The Winchester School before St Æthelwold', in P. Clemoes and K. Hughes (eds), *England before the Conquest: Studies in Primary Sources Presented to Dorothy Whitelock*, Cambridge, 305–14.

Chapter 7: The North Ascendant: The Viking Impact

Bailey, R.N. 1980. *Viking Age Sculpture in Northern England*, London.

Gameson, R. (ed.) 1997. *The Study of the Bayeux Tapestry*, Woodbridge.

Hall, R. 1984. *The Excavations at York: the Viking Dig*, London.

Kendrick, T.D. 1949. *Late Saxon and Viking Art*, London.

Roesdahl, E. 1998. *The Vikings*, London.

Williams, D. 1997. *Late Saxon Stirrup-Strap Mounts – A Classification and Catalogue* (CBA Research Report 111), Oxford.

Wilson, D.M. 1985. *The Bayeux Tapestry*, London.

Wilson, D.M., and Klindt-Jensen, O. 1966. *Viking Art*, London.

Afterword

Keynes, S.D. 2000. 'The Cult of Alfred the Great', *Anglo-Saxon England* 28, 225–356.

Pevsner, N. 1956. *The Englishness of English Art*, London.

Zarnecki, G., Holt, J., and Holland, T. (eds) 1983. *English Romanesque Art 1066–1200*, London.

Some useful websites

British Library Digitised Manuscripts: www.bl.uk/manuscripts

Corpus of Anglo-Saxon Stone Sculpture (CASSS): www.dur.ac.uk/corpus/casss/

Portable Antiquities website: finds.org.uk/database

Prosopography of Anglo-Saxon England (PASE): www.pase.ac.uk

Staffordshire Hoard Symposium: finds.org.uk/ staffshoardsymposium

Staffordshire Hoard official website: www.staffordshirehoard.org.uk

To find out more about objects in the collection of the British Museum, visit the website, britishmuseum.org. To explore the collection database of more than 1,800,000 objects, visit britishmuseum.org/research/search_the_collection_database.aspx

AUTHOR'S ACKNOWLEDGEMENTS

In recent years, many scholars have transformed our understanding of the distinctive and highly creative culture which this art embodies. Their work has greatly aided my attempt to take a longer view of Anglo-Saxon art and to understand it within its cultural background. I would like to express a particular debt to Noel Adams, Richard Bailey, Michelle Brown, Derek Craig, Rosemary Cramp, Tania Dickinson, Angela Evans, Carol Farr, Richard Gameson, Anna Gannon, Richard Gem, James Graham-Campbell, Jane Hawkes, Isabel and George Henderson, David Hinton, Karen Høilund Nielsen, Simon Keynes, David Leigh, Sonja Marzinzik, John Mitchell, Richard Morris, Laurence Nees, Éamonn Ó Carragáin, Jennifer O'Reilly, Steven Plunkett, George Speake, Alan Thacker, David Wilson, Ian Wood and Sue Youngs.

Many other individuals and institutions, too many to list here, have been extremely generous in responding to my requests for images for this book; I would particularly like to thank Martin Biddle, Christine E. Brennan, Richard Bryant, Derek Craig, Stephen Fliegel, Emily Howe, Bernard Meehan, Georgina Muskett, Tim Pestell, Alison Sheridan, David Symons, Stewart Tiley, Paolo Vian, Susan Walker, the Revd Pete Wilcox and Craig Williams.

Lastly, my thanks must go to Axelle Russo and Charlotte Cade at the British Museum Press, and especially to my editor there, Felicity Maunder, who has been extremely supportive at all times.

ILLUSTRATION CREDITS

All photographs of British Museum objects are © The Trustees of the British Museum, courtesy of the Department of Photography and Imaging. Their Museum registration numbers are listed below, with donor information in brackets. For other copyright holders see below. Every attempt has been made to trace accurate ownership of copyrighted images in this book. Errors and omissions will be corrected in subsequent editions provided notification is sent to the publisher.

Fig

Pages 12–13 BM, P&E 1949,0702.1
1 BM, P&E 1867,0729.5
2 BM, P&E 1939,1010.4 (Mrs E.M. Pretty)
3 © The Board of Trinity College Dublin
4, 5, 6 © The British Library Board
7 BM, P&E 1880,0214.1 (John Staunton)
8 BM, P&E 1970,0301.1
9 By permission of the Chapter of Lichfield Cathedral
10 Winchester Museums Service
11 BM, (*left*) P&E 1984,1101.1, (*centre*) P&E 1876,0521.1, (*right*) P&E 1995,0102.1 (Orbit Housing Association)
12 Ludlow Museum; photo Portable Antiquities Service
13 York Museums Trust (Yorkshire Museum)
14 Drawings by D. Leigh
15 Drawings by J. Farrant, BM
16 BM, replica: P&E SHR.2 (Made by the Royal Armouries); original helmet: P&E 1939,1010.93 (Mrs E.M. Pretty)
17 BM, P&E 1994,0407.1 (Purchased with the assistance of the Art Fund)
18 BM, P&E 1984,0104.1
19 © The Bodleian Library, University of Oxford
20 © Norwich Castle Museum and Art Gallery
21 BM, P&E 2001,0902.1 (Purchased through the Treasure Act with the assistance of the Art Fund and the British Museum Friends)
22 On loan from the Right Honourable Lord Northbourne to the Ashmolean Museum, University of Oxford
23 Museum Burg Bederkesa, Bad Bederkesa
24 Buckle: BM, P&E 1970,0406.26.a (Trustees of the Estate of F.W. Surridge); drawing by Judith Dobie, English Heritage
25 Drawing after Inker 2006
26 BM, (*top left*) P&E 1923,0507.1 (G.H. Hadfield); (*bottom left*) P&E 1882,0220.1 (Miss Stapleton); (*right*) P&E 1867,0204.6 (John Yonge Akerman)
27 Drawings by C. Williams, BM
28 BM, P&E 1893,0601.219
29 Drawing by S. Crummy, BM
30 Drawings by C. Williams, BM
31, 32 Drawings after Salin 1904
33 Drawing after Haseloff 1981
34 BM, P&E 1883,1214.19 (Revd Charles T.E. Whateley)
35 BM, P&E 1935,1029.1–3
36 BM, P&E 1883,0401.90 (Sir Augustus Wollaston Franks)
37 BM, (*left*) P&E 1918,0711.1 (Charles Wickenden), (*right*) P&E 1039'70 (Bequeathed by William Gibbs to the South Kensington Museum (later V&A), 1870; transferred to BM, 1895)
38 Drawings by C. Williams, BM
39 BM, P&E 1883,1214.19 (Revd Charles T.E. Whateley)
40 BM, P&E 1883,1214.2–3 (Revd Charles T.E. Whateley)
41 BM, P&E 1883,1214.1 (Revd Charles T.E. Whateley)
42 BM, P&E 1939,1010.1 (Mrs E.M. Pretty)
43 Courtesy of National Museums Liverpool (World Museum)
44 BM, P&E 1894,1103.1.a
45 © Biblioteca Medicea Laurenziana, Florence, reproduced by permission of the Ministero per i Beni e le Attività Culturali
46 Drawing after Bruce-Mitford 1969
47 © The Master and Fellows of Corpus Christi College, Cambridge
48 © The British Library Board
49 © The Board of Trinity College Dublin
50 By permission of the Chapter of Durham Cathedral
51 By permission of the Chapter of Lichfield Cathedral
52 Drawing after Bruce-Mitford 1969
53 Drawing after Battiscombe 1956
54 By permission of the Chapter of Durham Cathedral
55 © National Library of Russia
56 BM, P&E 1858,0814.1 (Revd Frederick George Lee)
57 © The British Library Board
58 © Kungliga Biblioteket, Stockholm
59 © Corpus of Anglo-Saxon Stone Sculpture, photographer T. Middlemass
60, 61 Photos, BM Anglo-Saxon Cross Index
62 V&A Images / Victoria and Albert Museum
63 BM, (*top*) P&E 1859,0512.1, (*bottom*) P&E 1145'70 (Bequeathed by William Gibbs)
64 After Gannon 2003
65 BM, (*top*) CM 1934,1013.1, (*centre*) CM 1903,1005.1, (*bottom*) CM 1862,0718.2
66 BM, P&E 1867,0120.1 (Sir Augustus Wollaston Franks)
67 BM, P&E 1973,0801.1
68 © Norwich Castle Museum and Art Gallery
69 © The Board of Trinity College Dublin
70 © The British Library Board
71 Dommuseum zu Salzburg / Josef Kral
72 Herzog Anton Ulrich-Museums Braunschweig, Kunstmuseum des Landes Niedersachsen, inv. MA 58; photo: Claus Cordes
73 © The British Library Board
74 © Biblioteca Apostolica Vaticana, all rights reserved
75 Photo Emily Howe
76 © Kungliga Biblioteket, Stockholm
77 BM, P&E 1939,1010.2.a–l (Mrs E.M. Pretty)
78 Birmingham Museums and Art Gallery/ Potteries Museum and Art Gallery, Stoke on Trent
79 Birmingham Museums and Art Gallery (2010.0138K0449)/Potteries Museum and Art Gallery, Stoke on Trent (2010. LH.10.K0449)
80 Birmingham Museums and Art Gallery (2010.0138K0655)/Potteries Museum and Art Gallery, Stoke on Trent (2010. LH.10.K0655)
81 Drawing by M.O. Miller, BM
82 Birmingham Museums and Art Gallery (2010.0138K0550) / Potteries Museum and Art Gallery, Stoke on Trent (2010. LH.10.K0550)
83 BM, (*top right*) CM 1913,1213.1, (*left*) CM 1896,0404.17, (*bottom right*) CM 2006,0204.1 (Purchased with the assistance of the Art Fund, the National Heritage Memorial Fund, the British Museum Friends, and a number of individual donations)
84 Derby Museum and Art Gallery; photo BM
85, 86, 87 Photos Emily Howe

88 Drawing after Plunkett 1998
89 © Biblioteca Apostolica Vaticana, all rights reserved
90 Reproduced by kind permission of the Syndics of Cambridge University Library
91 BM, P&E 1978,1101.1
92 © The British Library Board
93 York Museums Trust (Yorkshire Museum)
94 Sint-Catharinakerk Museum, Maaseik; photo M. Budny and D. Tweddle
95 BM, P&E 1858,1116.4 (Royal Archaeological Institute, London)
96 Suffolk Archaeological Unit
97 © North Lincolnshire Museums Services; photo, BM
98 © D. Baker / Bedfordshire County Council
99 Photo, BM Anglo-Saxon Cross Index
100 Herzog Anton Ulrich-Museums Braunschweig, Kunstmuseum des Landes Niedersachsen, inv. MA 58; photo: Claus Cordes
101 © National Library of Russia
102 Photo, BM
103 © The Friends of Deerhurst Church; photo Emily Howe
104 Berkeley Castle; photo L. Webster
105 © National Museums of Scotland
106 Photo Historic Scotland
107 BM, P&E 1893,0715.1 (Sir Augustus Wollaston Franks)
108 BM, P&E 1869,0610.1 (Thomas D.E. Gunstone)
109 © The British Library Board
110 BM, P&E 1880,0410.9 (John Jope Rogers)
111 Drawing, N. Griffiths
112 BM, P&E 1980,1008.1–6 (Purchased as Treasure Trove from H.M. Treasury)
113 BM, (above) P&E 1829,1114.1 (The Earl of Radnor), (bottom) P&E AF.458 (Bequeathed by Sir Augustus Wollaston Franks)
114 Ashmolean Museum, University of Oxford
115 BM, P&E 1952,0404.1 (Part-given by Capt. A.W.F. Fuller)
116 BM, P&E 1993,0102.1
117 BM, P&E 2009,8023.1 (Jointly purchased under the 1996 Treasure Act, with the assistance of the Art Fund, the National Heritage Memorial Fund, the British Museum Friends, the York Museums Trust and the Wolfson Foundation)
118 Drawing, N. Griffiths
119 Ashmolean Museum, University of Oxford

120 BM, P&E 1890,0209.1 (Sir Augustus Wollaston Franks)
121 © The Bodleian Library, University of Oxford
122 Corpus of Anglo-Saxon Stone Sculpture, photographer K. Jukes
123 Dommuseum zu Salzburg / Josef Kral
124–6 Photos BM
127 © KIK-IRPA, Brussels
128 © The Master and Fellows of Corpus Christi College, Cambridge
129 © The British Library Board
130 By permission of the Chapter of Durham Cathedral
131 © The British Library Board
132 © The Bodleian Library, University of Oxford
133 © The British Library Board
134 © The Bodleian Library, University of Oxford
135 By permission of the President and Fellows of St John's College, Oxford; photo © C. Phillips
136 By permission of the Master and Fellows of Trinity College, Cambridge
137–143 © The British Library Board
144 Herzog Anton Ulrich-Museums Braunschweig, Kunstmuseum des Landes Niedersachsen, inv. MA 59; photo: Claus Cordes
145, 146 © Bibliothèque municipale de Rouen. Photo Thierry Ascencio-Parvy
147–154 © The British Library Board
155 Photo, BM
156 Winchester Museums Service
157 Photo, BM
158 BM, P&E 1969,0401.1
159 © Corpus of Anglo-Saxon Stone Sculpture, photographer K.P. Saunders
160 Courtesy of National Museums Liverpool (World Museum)
161 Winchester Museums Service
162 BM, P&E 1974,1002.1 (Purchased with the assistance of the Art Fund)
163 V&A Images / Victoria and Albert Museum
164 Musée Sandelin, St Omer; photo, BM
165 © KIK-IRPA, Brussels
166 Musée de Cluny, Paris
167 BM, P&E 1960,0701.1 (Purchased with the assistance of the Art Fund and the Pilgrim Trust)
168 V&A Images / Victoria and Albert Museum
169 BM, P&E 1903,0323.1 (Given by the Friends of the British Museum, with the assistance of the Art Fund)

170 V&A Images / Victoria and Albert Museum
171 The Metropolitan Museum of Art, New York, Gift of J. Pierpont Morgan, 1917 (17.190.217). Image © The Metropolitan Museum of Art
172 V&A Images / Victoria and Albert Museum
173 © The Cleveland Museum of Art. Purchase from the J.H. Wade Fund 1953.362
174 BM, P&E 1870,0811.1
175 Winchester Museums Service
176 BM, P&E 1881,0404.1 (Sir Augustus Wollaston Franks)
177 BM, P&E 1999,1001.1 (Purchased with the assistance of the Art Fund)
178 BM, P&E 1997,0102.1
179 BM, P&E 1866,0224.1 (Sir Augustus Wollaston Franks)
180 Drawing after B. Kjølbye-Biddle
181 BM, P&E 1979,1101.1
182 © Corpus of Anglo-Saxon Stone Sculpture, photographer T. Middlemass
183 Drawing after Williams 1997
184, 185 © Corpus of Anglo-Saxon Stone Sculpture, photographer T. Middlemass
186 © Corpus of Anglo-Saxon Stone Sculpture, photographer J. Lang
187 York Museums Trust (Yorkshire Museum)
188 BM, P&E 1954,1201.1–2
189 Drawing after Hall 1984
190 Leeds City Museum; photo, BM
191 Drawing by Eva Wilson
192 BM, P&E 1904,0623.4
193 Reproduced by kind permission of the Syndics of Cambridge University Library
194 © The Bodleian Library, University of Oxford
195 © The British Library Board
196 BM, P&E 1951,1011.1
197 Photo, BM Anglo-Saxon Cross Index
198 Verulamium Museum, St Albans; photo BM
199 BM, P&E 1915,0205.1 (Revd F.G. Dutton)
200 Photo: akg-images
201 Winchester Museums Service
202 From Punch magazine, 3 March 1860
203 From L. Carroll, Through the Looking Glass, 1871
204 © The British Library Board
205 From Beowulf, Kelmscott Press, London, 1895
206 Photo, BM

INDEX

Page numbers in *italics* refer to illustrations